NEW YORK REVIEW BOOKS
CLASSICS

WHEN THE WORLD SPOKE FRENCH

MARC FUMAROLI is a scholar of French classical rhetoric and art. He is a member of the British Academy, the American Academy of Arts and Sciences, the Société d'histoire littéraire de la France, and the Académie française. Fumaroli received from the Académie française, before being elected a member, the Monseigneur Marcel Prize in 1982 and the Critique Prize in 1992, and he is president of the Société des Amis du Louvre.

RICHARD HOWARD received a National Book Award for his translation of *Les Fleurs du mal* and a Pulitzer Prize for *Untitled Subjects*, his third volume of poems. He is the translator of the NYRB Classics *Alien Hearts* and *The Unknown Masterpiece*.

WHEN THE WORLD
SPOKE FRENCH

MARC FUMAROLI

Translated from the French by
RICHARD HOWARD

NEW YORK REVIEW BOOKS

New York

THIS IS A NEW YORK REVIEW BOOK
PUBLISHED BY THE NEW YORK REVIEW OF BOOKS
435 Hudson Street, New York, NY 10014
www.nyrb.com

Originally published as *Quand l'Europe parlait français* by Éditions de Fallois, 2001

Fumaroli, Marc.
  [Quand l'Europe parlait francais. English]
  When the world spoke French / by Marc Fumaroli ; translated by Richard
Howard.
     p. cm. — (New York review books classics)
  Originally published in French: Quand l'Europe parlait francais.
  ISBN 978-1-59017-375-6 (alk. paper)
  1. French language—Europe—History—18th century. 2. Paris (France—
Intellectual life—18th century. 3. Europe—Civilization—French influences.
  I. Howard, Richard. II. Title.
  PC3680.E85F8613 2010
  440.9'409033—dc22

                         2010034847

ISBN 978-1-59017-375-6

Printed in the United States of America on acid-free paper.
10 9 8 7 6 5 4 3 2 1

To Liliane de Rothschild,
generous memory of
French Europe

CONTENTS

Gustav III, the Abbé Galiani, Grimm,
the Prince de Ligne, Admiral Caraccioli—
such persons of wit who discerned in France
a certain transitory perfection of society, have
never ceased adoring that country. Until we all
become angels, or men in pursuit of the same
object (as in England), our pleasure will best
be served by being French, as one was French
in the salon of Mme du Deffand.

—STENDHAL, *HISTOIRE DE LA PEINTURE EN ITALIE*

PREFACE

SOME BOOKS are premeditated, others not. This one has grown by itself and discovered by its own movement its form and its end, constantly baffling in the course of its growth the intentions that I naively strove, again and again mistaking a branch or a twig for a stem, to impose upon it. At first I thought it was going to be "a little anthology of French prose" written by foreigners in the eighteenth century. Then the brief headnotes I gave to these citations, in a sort of feuilleton that the review *Commentaire* kindly agreed to publish, assumed a certain amplitude: they became portraits. I then supposed that I was proceeding, without abandoning the anthology, in the direction of a gallery of portraits of foreigners—kings and queens, military leaders, ambassadors, great ladies, adventurers— whose declared Francophilia or irrepressible attraction to France had made into characteristic witnesses of "French Europe" in the Age of Enlightenment. Then the singular portraits became paired or interconnected, turned into brief biographies or slices of history. Indulging and even approving these developments, *Commentaire* continued publishing the feuilletons quarterly, unperturbed by the singular transformations they were undergoing. Some of these essays have emigrated into prefaces and little books, as was the case of the essay on Lord Chesterfield, transformed in the Rivages edition into a preface to his *Letters*, now translated into Italian and published by Adelphi. The one dedicated to the Comte de Caylus and the Abbé Conti is growing these days, almost against my will, into a full-fledged biography of the comte.

Frequently these essays overlapped my studies of "Conversation" and "The Genius of the French Language" that Pierre Nora had published in *Realms of Memory*, and that themselves expanded at times into prefaces to anthologies conceived by Jacqueline Hellegouarc'h and published by Classiques Garnier: *L'Art de la conversation* and *L'Esprit de société*. The little anthology of French prose written by foreigners in "French Europe," with which it all began, had gradually been transformed into an incessantly enlarged Grand Tour of Continental (Enlightenment) Europe in the company of its French-speaking and French-writing citizens.

Gradually, not only the stem but the foliage of the book that was being born appeared before my eyes, but it was only after the fact that its meaning and its title appeared as if of their own accord. The title was discovered during a telephone conversation with *Commentaire*'s director, Jean-Claude Casanova, whose readers had observed that the review's feuilleton no longer corresponded to the initial description. For that matter, neither the meaning nor the title that now appeared canceled out any of those, partial or intermediary, with which I had started, nor did they compel me to surrender any of them.

It was then that Bernard de Fallois, who had followed at some distance, with that floating attention that has nothing in common with the kind recommended to psychoanalysts but everything to do with the amused empathy of a great editor, decided that the plant had reached maturity, and that the time had come to pot it. I had to trim it here, restore equilibrium there, in order to respect the rib structure that had become evident in the course of time, and in spite of myself. Quite unfairly, and merely to take on myself alone any remaining weaknesses and mistakes, my name appears on the title page of a book of which I am something less than the author.

Indeed I could never account for all the inspirations, all the tributary springs and forms of sustenance that have allowed this book to spread and develop quite without my doing. The dedicatee of *When The World Spoke French*, Baroness Elie de Rothschild, unceasingly put at its service the inexhaustible resources of her collections, her library, her mind, and her generous heart. She has left us since but only to pursue *nostra conversatio in coelis*. Jacqueline Hellegouarc'h, Benedetta Craveri, Benoît d'Aboville, Benjamin Strorey, Marianne Roland-Michel, Pierre Rosenberg, and Françoise Waquet have all contributed. Éric de Lussy, of the Bibliothèque de l'Institut, and his colleagues of the Bibliothèque Mazarine have supplied it with photocopies. With patience extending over many years, Catherine Fabre, my assistant at the Collège de France, has given typographic body to a multitude of scattered fragments, all of which had something to do with the same idea. Pierre-E. Leroy, lecture chairman at the Collège de France, reread the first proofs; Bernard Minoret and the late Professor Bruno Neveu have graciously given their time and their celebrated *acribia* to reading the second ones.

———

Paris, August 2010, correcting the first proofs of the American translation—It is hard to find words for my gratitude toward my friend the poet Richard Howard, who loved the book and brought his exceptional linguistic skills and gifts to the translation. Thanks to my dear friend Robert Silvers, who endorsed Richard's project. Thanks to Rea Hederman, who was willing to publish the translation in the prestigious book series attached to *The New York Review of Books*. Thanks to Michael Shae, who took upon himself the task of surveying the proof-correcting process. Thanks to Grace Dudley, who followed with sympathy the different stages of this labor of love. I could not imagine such a happy transatlantic rebirth of this book, in many ways conceived on the two shores and achieved as a collective offspring of a group conversation, like so many plays, essays, and fictions in eighteenth-century Paris.

—*Marc Fumaroli*

INTRODUCTION

THIS BOOK is a promenade among various encounters between Frenchmen and foreigners during the eighteenth century, when the French were at home wherever they went, when Paris was every foreigner's second homeland, and when France became the object of Europe's collective curiosity.

The Age of Enlightenment begins in 1713–1714 with the signing of the treaties of Utrecht and Rastadt, which secured the essentials of France's position in Europe, and ends in 1814, with the Allies' entry into Paris and the fall of Napoleon's empire. As we proceed, we shall meet with that age's successive generations and the principal events that distinguish them. We shall journey as well through the Europe of the period and its various capitals: we shall start from Paris and Versailles, to which we shall often return, but we shall also find ourselves in London, Rome, Berlin, Dresden, Vienna, St. Petersburg, and Warsaw, from which cities we shall keep our eyes fixed on Paris and Versailles as if we were there.

AN AGE THAT BELIEVED IN EARTHLY FELICITY

Everywhere we shall encounter that disposition to happiness known as the Enlightenment, which makes this French century one of the most optimistic in the history of the world. By a remarkable (and seldom remarked) conservatism, the United States of America, that progeny of the eighteenth century and its enormous "realm of memory," still bears today the euphoric, naive, and "young" traces forever obliterated in Europe after the Terror of 1792–1794. The French Enlightenment? A thaw of the sacred, a poignant and profane religion of happiness and of the moment of grace that located its heavenly Jerusalem in Paris. Now militant, now quietist, with its high and low clergy, its believers, its libertines, its Tartuffes, it was persecuted in Paris itself by its own heresies whose fierce dogma was revealed by Chateaubriand:

> At the heart of these various systems abides one heroic remedy, avowed or assumed, and only its moment of application inspires any hesitation: this remedy is *murder*. It is simple, readily understood, and linked to that sublime Terror that, from one liberation to the next, has pursued us through the fortifications of Paris: the merciless slaughter of whatever impedes the progress of the human race.[1]

The wars of the eighteenth century were certainly not waged in kid gloves, but they were fought between professional armies, and their battles were merely diplomacy continued by other means. Nothing about them was comparable to either the War of the Spanish Succession (1701–1714), that long and terrible conflict Churchill called "the first world war," or the second, initiated during the French Revolution and ending only in 1815 at Waterloo, or a fortiori to the total wars of annihilation that began in 1914. Eighteenth-century Europe's seventy years of peace and prosperity, quite relative and unequal depending on the region, occasionally interrupted by local conflicts, are in every respect exceptional against the continuously grim and tragic background of European history. They encouraged every rational and irrational faculty of happiness and hope within the territories possessed by the Europeans, and with a singular *furia* by the French, to swell and sway in the clouds of an ever more promising future, like those hot-air balloons of the

---

1. *Mémoires d'outre-tombe*, edited by J.-C. Berchet (Paris: Garnier, 1998), vol. 2, pp. 583–584.

Montgolfier brothers that Louis XVI's subjects never tired of watching rise into the heavens and vanish downwind. Catholicism, despite Jansenist resistances, as well as Protestantism and Judaism, assumed the flattering colors of an imminent paradise still visible, by the light of their tall many-paned windows, in the ornamentation of rococo churches and synagogues.

Everywhere in this Europe convinced of a golden age or of its imminence, we encounter professional ambassadors, secret agents, or part-time intermediaries, citizens of the world and of the great world who find it only natural to operate in a magnetic field nourishing by its electricity the delicate and uninterrupted network of diplomatic negotiations, each of them controlling one of the filaments: such incessant negotiatory activity is the guiding principle of that relative, fragile, sensitive, but nonetheless real and beneficent activity that managed to secure Europe against major explosions. Versailles, the nerve center of this network, enjoyed the luxury of two diplomacies: one official, conducted by the minister of foreign affairs; the other clandestine and doubling the first: *le Secret du roi* (the King's Secret).

Men of letters, artists, musicians, virtuosi of the arts and antiquities market, frequently traveling from capital to capital, frequently corresponding with princes and sovereigns, invariably turn out to be, on closer inspection, either conscious collaborators in a tentative negotiation or else unconscious catalysts of the stabilized and/or reviving relations between one court and another. The Republic of Letters is one of the huge networks sustaining the general scheme. This cosmopolitan and quasi-clandestine club, born in Italy around 1400, spoke, wrote, and published in the catholic language of Renaissance Europe, Ciceronian Latin restored by the humanist linguists. Why, three centuries later, in the Enlightenment age, did this international community of the learned speak, write, and publish mostly in French? This then recent substitution was certainly a consequence of the successful war strategy and cultural politics led by Cardinal Richelieu in 1624–1642. The French monarchy since the treaties of Westphalia (1648) appeared as the modern and victorious model of statecraft, imitated and emulated in its own language on the Continent. Voltaire in the following century agreed with this explanation. But he added an important correction. He insisted rightly that hard power alone could not obtain such a linguistic success. The European public had above all endorsed the talent, wit, and clarity of expression in French of the realm's writers and thinkers. The worst political decision of Louis XIV, the revocation of the Edict de Nantes (1685), had turned in favor of the French language, if not of Versailles's image. In London, Leiden, Amsterdam, Berlin, Dresden, and Hamburg, colonies of French Protestant exiles created printing houses, weekly newspapers, and translation workshops, serving in French a European Republic of Letters but hardly the politics of Versailles or the religion of Paris and Rome. "King" Voltaire himself, when sojourning in Berlin and Potsdam, was not a simple intermediary between Versailles and the king of Prussia; his freedom of spirit made him dangerous for both courts and sympathetic to an entire European public.

The Republic of the Arts does not lag behind. The return to Paris of the Italian players, which the regent requested of the Duke of Modena in 1716, was a peace signal addressed to Europe. The sojourn of a French painter and sculptor in Stockholm became the pledge of a closer alliance between France and Sweden, ever threatened by St. Petersburg.

The clear-cut distinction we are tempted to make today between "culture" and "diplomacy" impedes the understanding of the eighteenth century in which diplomacy impregnates everything, because this century passionately sought a civilized peace it knew to be fragile; it realized that only an uninterrupted diplomacy, of the sort that in 1648 had put an end to the Thirty Years' War and achieved the treaties of Westphalia, could keep the pledge to respect an inevitable European diversity, even while constantly nudging it toward peace; it also realized that the masterpiece of the human mind, compromise between opposing passions and interests, is closely related to belles lettres and to fine arts, those fruits and ornaments of peace. It is this general conspiracy of minds, their various filaments so numerous as to defy description and analysis, that was utterly confounded and in large part dismantled by the extremism of the French Revolution, inconceivable and immobilizing for men accustomed to moderation and conciliation. The old diplomacy would nonetheless try, in the wake of Talleyrand and Metternich at the Congress of Vienna, to reconstitute itself as the nerve system of the European equilibrium. Whatever was fruitful in the nineteenth century was born of this prudential prejudice that even Bismarck adopted in seeking not to wound too gravely the conquered France of 1870, and that definitively collapsed in the nationalist hysteria of 1914.

CROWNED HEADS

Everywhere in this Europe enamored of happiness and peace that appears on the horizon of our promenade, we shall encounter what our democratic memory endeavors to forget: the grand figures of an aristocracy that, without forswearing its origins and its military vocation, had converted to the manners and the arts of peace, had assumed leadership, and had set an example. Several of these figures are crowned heads: representatives of ruling dynasties whose alliances cast another network over Europe, a reticulation of families whose unifying power cannot be overstated, despite the temptation, after the fact, to emphasize the seeds of conflict to be discerned in dynastic rivalries, quarrels of succession, failed marriages.

Enlightenment Europe a family affair? For us, family means Oedipus, Eteocles, and Polynices. But the eighteenth century does not hark back to Theban antiquity as readily as we do. Court manners, dulcified by so many Christian centuries, appear to have prevailed over the terror of Greek tragedy. No one wants to hear about the assassinations of tsars and tsarevitches in Moscow and St. Petersburg: European diplomacy, eyes fixed on the French, English, and Austrian royal families, relies on the humanly affective terrain of marriage and cousinage, exempt from any ideological or passional motive, to facilitate fruitful rapprochements or to cicatrize the wounds of conflicts that, without such family unguents, would remain open and purulent. In this sense, the Family Pact concluded by Choiseul in 1761 in order to unite the various branches of the Bourbon dynasty, and supplemented in 1770 by the dauphin's marriage to Marie-Antoinette of Austria, reconciling the two great broods of "hereditary foes," Bourbons and Hapsburgs, is the masterpiece of a diplomatic art that trusts to the happy endings of novels and fairy tales. In addition, the internal equilibrium of the (Germanic) Holy Roman Empire and its insertion into Europe depend on a Hercynian family tree whose branches extend to England, Scandinavia, and Russia, a filiation inadequate to forestall or restrain the Machiavellianism of Frederick II and the partition of that expiatory victim Poland, though affording diplomatic means to certain subtle and pacifying maneuvers that the ax of Napoleon, followed by that of Clemenceau, would make simpler, more rational, and more "transparent," but at the price of creating a concatenation of inexpiable hatreds.

PRINCES, MARSHALS, GENTRY

The aristocracy of crowned heads does not rule alone. It is inseparable from an aristocracy of court and city that we have managed to caricature retrospectively and without differentiation as a belated feudalism or a vampiric leisure class. It is nonetheless an aristocracy that does battle, retains its warlike demeanor, and pays a heavy tax of blood. From its ranks come great marshals and generals, and this will remain the case in the France of the Revolution and the Empire. Converted since the Renaissance to a peacetime savoir vivre, it was in the eighteenth century, of all the Enlightenment publics, the one most permeable to its principles and most generously won over to its practices. Rousseau, protected by Malesherbes and the Prince de Conti, the guest of the Maréchal de Luxembourg and the Marquis de Girardin, also found his most talented disciple in a young aristocrat, Chateaubriand. If the American Revolution encountered so much sympathy in Europe, if the French Revolution, during its first years, provoked a general enthusiasm that blocked the perception of the direction it was already taking, it is because the Enlightenment's enthusiasm for reform and progress, its crusading spirit in favor of the good against the evils of superstition and despotism, were shared by the greatest names of the French aristocracy, and spread by its example to the Continental aristocracies, educated by enlightened preceptors and fed on philosophical readings obtained from Paris. The remarks of the crown prince of Sweden to his elderly tutor Count Scheffer in 1767 suggest the "political correctness" that the future Gustav III was already beginning to mistrust:

> In Spain and Portugal the Jesuits are plotting to form a monarchy, not in honor of God but to further their own ambitions. They have been driven out of Spain and Portugal where the Inquisition is still active, and Father Malagrida condemned as a heretic, not a regicide. They are banished from France, yet in France Bélisaire and Jean Calais have both been burned at the stake. In France Rousseau is treated as a criminal and the *Encyclopédie* championed. The Jesuits may be eradicated, their establishment abolished, yet new errors will replace the old, and equivalent abominations, committed for other reasons, may cause us to regret the old ones. To hope to extinguish superstition and correct human wickedness is, I believe, to seek the philosopher's stone; as long as men live in society, as long as they have differing passions and interests, they will be wicked and cruel. It is a fine thing to try to correct them, it is nearly impossible to succeed in doing so.[2]

We shall understand neither the audacity nor the upshot of Voltaire's battle against *l'Infâme* (meaning what we call "religious

---

2. *Gustave III par ses lettres*, edited by Gunnar von Proschwitz (Stockholm: Norstedts/Paris: Touzot, 1986), p. 44.

fundamentalism") if we fail to see that the Seigneur of Ferney knew he could count on the sympathy of the French *noblesse d'épée*, by definition secular, *galante*, and rendered, by the Jansenist–Jesuit dispute, ever more disdainful of the clerical yoke and church morality. By its lifestyle and the form of open society it exemplified, the French aristocracy offered a sort of immediate and promising glimpse of the Enlightenment's faith in the propitious future it authorized and propagated. The very freedom of "living nobly" seemed to suggest that pleasure and happiness had appeared on the horizon of a humanity freed of its chains. Elegance, politesse, and a new sweetness of manners seemed to prefigure a world in which each man's freedom could accommodate the equality of all, and in which the vivacity of private passions would not disturb the joys of communal life. Furthermore, as artists of the private life of society, the urban aristocracy and their wealthy imitators managed to create in their mansions and their country houses veritable private academies in which the diverse plastic arts, the theater, music, the art of gardens and the table, the talents of the jeweler, the goldsmith, the tailor, and the dressmaker united to offer the art of conversation and gallantry a euphoric milieu in which the philosophes steeped their own enthusiasm and found a willing mirror for it.

Versailles and Paris

Diplomacy and freedom of manners, the Republic of Letters and of the Arts, royalty and aristocracy of court and city, "good company" mingling men of the world and men of letters, conformity of the arts and skilled crafts in the service of social pleasures, *Lumières* in every realm of the mind and their role as educators—on all these levels France was now mother and uncontested mistress. The Versailles of Louis XV has inherited from Louis XIV a tradition of diplomatic intelligence unrivaled in Europe, to the point where it is diplomats of French origin like the Comte de Mercy-Argenteau who are chosen to represent foreign courts, and this in France itself. The academies created or reformed under Louis XIV have shifted the center of the Republic of Letters to Paris, and Parisian high society, living in symbiosis with the royal academies, has become the audience and arbiter of the European reputation of books, as it has become, with the institution of the salon, the audience and arbiter of taste in painting and sculpture: its favor becomes the criterion of an artist's European reputation. The oldest monarchy in Europe, which had never had so much authority as under Louis XIV, continued under Louis XV and Louis XVI, with evident inflections but in the same magnificent ritual, to exercise its seniority and to impose its superior prestige on every European court. A numerous and brilliant aristocracy, bearing historic names that ever since the Crusades had spoken to the imagination of all Europe, constituted a crown around the king and the royal family in the most fabulous château and park ever built by any sovereign.

Along with this theater bequeathed by the Grand Siècle, there appeared after the Regency (1715–1723) a vast and manifold stage whose vitality, inventiveness, and influence outside France owed nothing to the court. Paris now became a laboratory of the charms of private life; urban aristocracy set the tone of its urbanity for all Europe. In order to serve a French and international clientele, the marketplace for the arts and luxury crafts was concentrated in Paris. It was here that rococo fashion and taste were crystallized: a decor appropriate to the leisures occupying social life, its conversation, its readings, its chamber theater in mansion and château, its amorous intrigues, its literary commerce, its commentary on all news and novelties. Only music escapes this Parisian hegemony. The French language in the eighteenth century is essentially a social charm, a marvelous rhetoric of dialogue. The arts with which it agrees best are the visual—the most social—ones. It lends itself less well than Italian or German to song, and its vocation for wit, but also for analysis, deflects it, at least in principle, from musical expression. Despite the genius of Rameau and the brilliance of the *concerts spirituels* given at the Tuileries, Italian music therefore prevails in the rest of Europe. This irritating oddity becomes the object, in France, of recurrent literary disputes throughout the century.

The Parisian press, relayed by the gazettes in French published in Amsterdam, London, and Germany, becomes the echo chamber of these flurries that divide the French capital into two camps. This European press is also, along with Parisian opinion, the ultimate judge of books and ideas. Parallel to the *Gazette de France*, which published the news of public and court life, many journals published in French in Paris, London, and Germany and an endless quantity of brochures and satires made known in Europe to the last detail the alliances and altercations that emerged from the Parisian *grande compagnie*. It was among this *grande compagnie*, a galaxy in which numerous planets revolved, that the fame of the philosophes prospered and extended beyond the frontiers, and this same company made their books fashionable and sought after even and especially when the Parlement, the Sorbonne, or the Archbishopric condemned them to public obloquy.

Until 1748, thanks to the tact of the minister of the royal household and of Paris, the Comte de Maurepas, who was charged with this responsibility among others, Versailles had retained a certain control, however invisible and discreet, over the Parisian "companies" and their men of letters. Versailles lost this command after the disgrace of this astute man. The disputatious independence of the city and the provocative audacity of the philosophes sure of the communication systems at their disposal escaped the prudence and the moderation of the ministers. This war of words and the numerous conflicts between the philosophes and their parlementary or ecclesiastical censors merely intensified the interest and the amusement of the courts and the foreign public, not always Francophile, in the polemical character of the literary, artistic, and worldly life of Paris. Each new *querelle* provoked a new wave of curiosity, and foreign sovereigns did not hesitate to intervene. No one at the time saw in this permanent agitation a threat to the ancient French monarchy. On the contrary, this was one more reason to befriend a realm capable at once of the glory of memory and of the most irresponsible and outrageous sarcastic impertinence.

It is evident that no one in Europe, not even the English, who had every reason to wish for the weakening of France, their chief rival on the Continent, foresaw that a revolution regarded initially as a new and particularly reckless manifestation of Parisian disputatiousness could overthrow in a matter of months every foundation of the realm, its dynasty legitimated by centuries, its aristocracy that had liberated America and overwhelmingly sided with the leading spirits of the Enlightenment, and even its church, naturally castigated by the philosophes, whose clergy nonetheless, according to Burke, was one of the most "enlightened" of the period. The stupor, the disillusion, the chaos created by the Terror measured up to the sympathy, the admiration, even the fascination exerted by the France of the Enlightenment. The Terror precipitated a crisis among even the most fervent "enlightened" adherents: the poets Chénier, Alfieri, and Schiller came to the defense of Louis XVI; Goethe and Wordsworth turned against the Revolution. Try as Mme de Staël did to isolate the *Lumières* from the Medusa that had arisen in their wake in 1792–1794, the nineteenth century would never cease meditating with the dark irony of Schopenhauer, Flaubert, and Dostoevsky upon this absolute evil that had revealed itself at the very heart of the passion for goodness.

The Universality of the French language

On every road taken, this book leads us to the encounter with an eighteenth century that converses and corresponds in French, even when it is not Francophile. Rivarol, in the years of disturbing euphoria that preceded the French Revolution, used to speak so pompously of the universality of our language, drawing an argument from the recent French victory over England, side by side with the American insurgents, and concluding that English had no future! The violence of Jacobin nationalism and the spirit of conquest of the Directory, the Consulate, and the Empire entirely stripped away the veil that had convinced the French and many Europeans that the language of the realm and the realm itself were to be identified with the humanitarian universalism of the Enlightenment. The Revolution had awakened the "genius" of nations, rousing in each the jealous love of its own language.

Until 1789 the quite relative universality of the French language, already contested in England, Italy, Germany, and Spain, benefited from the same powerful vectors that assured the preeminence of the French monarchy in Europe: the authority and intelligence of an excellent diplomatic network, the quality of the translations of every important European book published in French in Paris, Amsterdam, and London, the prestige of the etiquette of the premier court in the known world, the authority of the royal academies and of the Salon of the Academy of Painting and Sculpture; but also, in Paris, the attraction of the great sales of artworks and the quality of their experts, the magnetism exerted throughout the world by an urban aristocracy that had raised the leisures of private life to the rank of a fine art of living, served by artists from the first master of the hunt to the last kennel keeper, from the chef to the gardener, from the dressmaker to the jeweler, from the wigmaker to the perfumer, from the painter to the architect, from the poet of light verse to the philosopher—director of conscience and leader of thought—from the ballerina to the great actor, from the playwright to the novelist, from the tutor to the lady's companion, not to mention the gaiety of fairs, festivals, and the daily life of the streets of Paris, the charm and good manners of its actresses and its grisettes.

All these allures constituted the object of an indirect (and all the more penetrating) publicity by the typography, the engraving, the journals, the pamphlets, the French ambassadors at foreign courts, and the theater companies performing everywhere the French repertoire, classical or modern. Like today's America, without resorting to the voluntarism of a "cultural politics" or a "linguistic politics," eighteenth-century France and its language were quite simply contagious and irresistible because their image was that of the small amount of happiness and intelligence of which men are capable during their brief passage through this earthly vale of tears. It is as absurd to suppose that someone like Colbert ever imagined or foresaw or planned the long-standing seduction of such an image as to suppose today that an occult project of persuasion of the US Department of State seeks to imprint a pinup America upon the universal imagination.

Nothing is so mysterious in the history of Europe, and now of the world, as the vocation of certain languages to universality. The Latin of republican and imperial Rome, the Greek of the late Empire and then of Byzantium, the Italian and the Spanish of the Renaissance and the Counter-Reformation, the French of the seventeenth and eighteenth centuries, continuing on its own impetus to 1914, the English of the twentieth century, have experienced this vocation, but each time under conditions so different, so incompatible, and so incomparable that no common explanation can be proposed. Political and military power had long since abandoned Greece when the Greek language imposed itself as the koine of the Hellenistic Mediterranean that had come under Latin authority, and as the archaizing literary language preferred by the imperial Roman elite. French, having become hegemonic in Europe after the treaties of Westphalia in 1648, was a language in itself inconvenient, difficult, aristocratic, and literary, like Cicero's Latin or Lucian's Greek, inseparable like its ancient ancestors from a bon ton in manners, from a certain bearing in society, and from a quality of wit, nourished on literature, in conversation.

Yet it was this exigency of *style* that constituted its universal prestige, whereas the English that prevails today the world over is a vernacular and technological language dispensing with *style* altogether, and less comparable to the koine of the Roman Mediterranean than to the lingua franca of the Mediterranean after the Crusades: now it is just this summary, convenient, elementary, passive character, demanding of its speakers no commitment either in the manner or the matter of their utterance, that constitutes the essence of its power of attraction. The soft "transparency" of this global English is the contrary of the precise and lively *clarté* required by the French of the Enlightenment, even when it was spoken and written by Robespierre, whose bearing was impeccable, whose hair was always freshly powdered, whose diction and manners were those of a courtier. The question arises: What language in the twenty-first century will offer a civilized idiom to a "global" world?

Communication System or Feast of Minds?

This book makes no claim whatever to theorize or to defend any particular agenda. It has led me, nonetheless, as it has proceeded, to arrive at a clearer awareness of the obstacle preventing the French of today from understanding the real trump cards of their own language, which they still speak, however absently, and which they no longer dare to love.

On the one hand, politicians gladly listen to the linguists, who explain to them that, since French is a communication system, for this system to survive in a world "in constant mutation," it must free itself from the grammatical norms and semantic scruples inherited from another—aristocratic, reactionary, literary—world that would put it in a handicapped situation vis-à-vis "global" American, which is considered perfectly adapted to utilitarian information and amply sufficient for phony mediational "discussions." Adopt then a resolutely technological and yet voluntaristic attitude that will finally release an elementary neo-French from its old precision and facilitate succinct communication. Such is the discourse that imperiously dominates today. The pressure of mass education also proceeds, without acknowledging the fact, in the direction of a hexagonal idiolect refashioned to the measure of the global dialect. Yet try as it will to humiliate itself, to renounce its scruples over Franglais (as I write this in the summer of 2001, all film titles and several titles of novels are advertised in English in Paris), to renounce its grammar, to let the meaning of words drift, this Cinderella has not become that much more attractive or lively. It has lost its traditional friends abroad, more faithful to Molière, Saint-Simon, Balzac, Baudelaire, and Proust than drawn by the demagogic theories of our modern linguistic advisers. In France itself, the new French no longer claims to be the spinal column of a civilized education, and it has thereby lost the qualifications the old one still possessed in order to compete with a global American. Today it is in English, in English-language book reviews faithful to the tradition of the Republic of Letters but published in New York and London, that the last word on the worldwide value of books and ideas is printed and prevails.

On the other hand, we hear eloquent speeches in favor of a Francophone safeguard whose doctrine, a loose one to say the least, tends distinctly toward a gelatinous neo-French, the lowest common denominator between the members of this vast, vague, and multiple provincial community.

This promenade through the eighteenth century with foreigners speaking and writing French has proved to me the contrary of everything that passes today for politically correct evidence with regard to language. If French, at the moment when it exercised its liveliest attraction over an exigent and difficult world, answered the expectation of the Enlightenment, it was certainly not only as a communication system. Frederick II, who mistakenly regarded German as such a system, said that he reserved it for his horses and grooms, for which and whom, moreover, he cared deeply. If the Abbé Conti, Francesco Algarotti, and Vittorio Alfieri defended Italian, and Walpole English, against a too-exclusive hegemony of the Enlightenment French, it was because they judged that their own language was not a communication system but a way of being, thinking, and feeling different from that of the French, and because it mattered to them to inhabit their own first of all and by preference. They were polyglots, and it was in full awareness of the situation that they admitted or contested the preeminence of French. The greatest friends of our language, who were frequently the warmest partisans of the Enlightenment, did not separate it from the education of which it was the vector, from the literature on which it had been won, and from an entire art of living civilly—that is, happily—to which the local communication systems that sufficed for most of their compatriots did not lead. French grammar, the French lexicon, whose relative poverty Voltaire was not afraid to mock, French syntax, the demanding semantics of the French language, French versification, whose defects Walpole saw clearly a century before the *crise du vers* diagnosed by Mallarmé, the genres in which our language excelled, notably the intimate genres, the letter, the diary, the poetry of occasion, memoirs, and that oral literary genre that is conversation between friends—all this difficult apprenticeship had the meaning of an initiation to an exceptional fashion of being free and natural with others and with oneself. It was altogether different from communicating. It was entering "into company."

Willy-nilly, in the twenty-first century as in the eighteenth, anyone who wants to shake off the leaden cloak of conformism and mass communication, anyone who discovers that he wants before dying to participate in a civilized conversation, the image on this earth of *nostra conversatio quae est in coelis*, does so in French, and certainly not in the French that satisfies the consumers of the neo-French communication system for which its very champions have shown their disdain by preferring English to it. A publisher told me one day that the number of real readers in a country like France (by which he meant those who had amassed a real library) had not varied since the sixteenth century: between three thousand and five thousand. The demographic variations and the degrees of literacy had never altered anything. An optimist, I am led to believe by experience that the number of people in the present-day world capable of a real conversation in French (who are necessarily also real readers and owners of a library) has actually increased and that it has, since the eighteenth century, in fact diversified the world over.

The number of young candidates for this club has not diminished. Go anywhere in the world, to Japan, Argentina, the United

States, and you will doubtless find fewer menus in French, fewer hotels where French will be spoken to you, fewer ponderous colloquia in which the participants communicate in our language, but you will find today, as under Louis XV, artists of French conversation who do not issue from Francophone channels or the Berlitz academies of neo-French: they have followed untrodden ways in order to participate in the banquet of minds of which France was long the expert hostess, and whose memory will never be effaced. Everywhere these good people are already your friends, your confidants, your correspondents.

It is in this clandestine worldwide minority, and no longer in the visible minority, splendidly furnished but reduced to several capitals of the banquet of enlightened minds, that today resides, unknown to the statisticians, linguists, and programmers of the "novlangues," unknown to the majority of the French, the life and the future of their irreplaceable idiom, qualified as a literary language and the language of "good company." French, the modern language of the mind's clandestinity?

1. Paris at the Dawn of the Enlightenment: The Abbé Conti and the Comte de Caylus

THE SEVENTEENTH CENTURY dwindles and dies in the War of the Spanish Succession. From 1701 to 1714, the forces of the Hapsburg emperor, united with those of England and Holland, opposed Louis XIV's powerful war machine on several fronts, in Europe and overseas. The eighteenth century dawns once the rumors of secret peace negotiations between France and England, made possible by the new Tory government, begin to spread in Paris in 1712. A certain lassitude appears as a consequence of the terrible sacrifices and the permanent tension imposed on his realm for more than a decade by the Great King, who was himself failing, overcome by terrible winters, the defeats of his generals, and the deaths of his son and grandsons. The sole heir of the senior branch of the family is a delicate orphan born in 1710; this child, who in 1715 assumes the name Louis XV, is the eighteenth century.

PARIS AWAKES

An irresistible appetite for civil life, for relaxation and felicity, seizes the city of Paris; the energies awakened then will traverse every generation until 1789.

The French capital turns its back on Versailles and becomes a city of festivity once the Treaty of Utrecht is signed with London in 1713, soon followed in 1714 by the Treaty of Rastadt with Holland and the Hapsburg emperor. Old Louis XIV has saved the honor and the frontiers of the realm. His grandson Philippe d'Anjou is recognized by Europe as the king of Spain. France's trump cards in the game established by the treaties of Westphalia in 1648 remain intact. Paris, never seriously threatened, even at the war's worst moments, has long believed itself secure. The city's reactions in 1792 to the Duke of Brunswick's provocative threats were all the more hysterical in that Paris had regarded itself since the reign of Louis XIV as a sanctuary immune to any foe.

Private life made up for public anxieties and disasters. The Duchesse du Maine, escaping from the ceremonials of Versailles and Marly, collecting men of letters, poets, and grands seigneurs, gave the impetus and the example at the Château de Sceaux: around the capital, country residences suddenly multiplied. Even in the last wartime months, the pleasures of society hummed in the parks of great estates and in mansions whose tall windows opened onto gardens and pools: conversations, theatricals, and rustic diversions reinvented joie de vivre. An amazed Europe, eager to do likewise, observed the sudden transformation of the vale of tears into a sunny setting for *fêtes galantes*, the tone set by private persons and no longer by the court of the Great King.

The secret negotiations for the Peace of Utrecht between 1711 and 1713, necessarily conducted by indirect channels, in themselves afforded a special savor to Parisian parties, into which melted, incognito at first, such British emissaries as Matthew Prior and Henry St. John, officially unknown to Versailles, as Benjamin Franklin would be until Vergennes officially recognized his ambassadorial status. These were the first foreigners to be seen for a long while. Mme de Tencin's worldly career formally began in 1712, upon her liberation from the convent of the Cloistered Dominicans, in her sister Mme de Ferriol's mansion in the rue Neuve-Saint-Augustin. She entered society by becoming Matthew Prior's mistress and by imposing her wit upon the guests in the rue Neuve-Saint-Augustin: the Maréchal d'Uxelles, titular lover of the lady of the house; Vauban; Arthur Dillon, one of the handsomest men of his era; St. John; and especially the writer Fontenelle, who assiduously frequented the house, though he was the particular oracle of the company the

Marquise de Lambert gathered twice weekly in her house in the rue de Richelieu. In 1715 Mme de Tencin is at the Palais-Royal, the *maîtresse de maison* of the regent's former tutor, Guillaume Dubois, who will be made a cardinal in 1721 and appointed prime minister in 1722; she then took as her lover a man of letters, the Chevalier Destouches. The child he gave her, immediately abandoned on church steps, will become Jean Le Rond d'Alembert.

Gradually there emerge and take the stage the star performers of that comedy of the Enlightenment, Paris of the *Lumières*. In the rue Neuve-Saint-Augustin, the lovely Circassian Mlle Aïssé, brought from his embassy in Constantinople by the Comte de Ferriol and the eventual heroine of a love story over which all Europe shed tears, is in 1712–1715 still playing with the two sons of the house, the young Comte d'Argental and his brother, Pont-de-Veyle: both remain for the rest of their lives devoted friends and assiduous correspondents of Voltaire, their classmate at the Collège Louis-le-Grand.

Already as the new century begins, a more gracious manner than the grand style of Versailles is apparent at the banker Pierre Crozat's, whose brand-new mansion and vast gardens, completed in 1706, occupy the upper end of the rue de Richelieu, not far from Mme de Lambert's and the Palais-Royal. The concerts offered in his Montmorency country house by this financier so knowledgeable about works of art gather a crowd of men of fashion and lovely women, the painters Charles de La Fosse and Antoine Watteau, the arbiter of artistic elegance Roger de Piles, the young expert in drawings and prints Pierre-Jean Mariette, and certain learned and refined antiquaries from the new Academy of Inscriptions and Belles-Lettres, such as the Abbé Fraguier.

The Age of Enlightenment thus dawned well before the Sun King had vanished over the horizon in 1715. The regent, his nephew Philippe d'Orléans, for whom Crozat had assembled a collection of paintings and drawings, had long shared this Parisian aspiration to the pleasures of civil life and the arts of peace. One of the first gestures of this new master of France after the death of Louis XIV was to shift the seat of government to the Palais-Royal in the heart of

Paris, one of the two city residences, along with the Palais du Luxembourg, of the dynasty's junior branch.

Once the Treaty of Rastadt was signed, the young Colonel de Caylus, who had been given his rank at the age of fifteen and who had rapidly risen from it during several brilliant campaigns in Catalonia and Germany, informed his mother that, having more than adequately paid his share of the blood he owed his king, he was leaving the army. "My son informs me," the comtesse wrote to her aunt, the Marquise de Maintenon, "that he would rather leave his head on the scaffold than continue to serve." In the intervals between his campaigns he had frequented the Hôtel Crozat, formed friendships with its habitués, notably Watteau, and had studied with that painter the fabulous collection of paintings and drawings the banker had amassed along with those he was choosing for the regent. The young colonel's vocation as a "virtuoso," which he would combine with the frequentation of polite and frivolous society as well as the assiduous cultivation of arts and letters, had been determined.

His first impulse as a free gentleman returning to civilian life was to set off for Italy to complete his artistic education, remaining for almost a year; he would have remained even longer had not the news of Louis XIV's death recalled him to his mother's side in Paris. In 1717, the family situation having been stabilized, he set off again, this time intending to begin his education as an antiquary, for Greece and Turkey where he studied architecture, sculpture, inscriptions, and the topography of the Greco-Roman world. On his return in 1718, he encountered in his mother's house the Venetian Abbé Antonio Conti, philosopher, mathematician, poetaster, and essayist, a universal savant who corresponded with Newton and Leibniz but also frequented Luigi Riccoboni, director of the theatrical troupe that the regent had invited to Paris in 1716 to reopen the Théâtre des Italiens closed by Louis XIV in 1696, as well as such Venetian painters and virtuosi as Rosalba Carriera, Sebastiano Ricci, and Antonio-Maria Zanetti, all called to Paris under the Regency at the invitation of the wealthy conoisseur Pierre Crozat. After the English, it was the Italians who returned to the city. In a very few years, Paris quite naturally became the incontestable cosmopolitan capital of the Enlightenment.

Telemachus and Mentor

The Comtesse de Caylus, amazed and delighted by her new Venetian friend's conversation, sensibility, and total absence of bigotry, and eager to provide proper sustenance for her son's studious and inquiring mind, writes to the latter in 1718: "Make yourself the disciple of the Abbé Conti." And forthwith the Italian Mentor initiates the French Telemachus into the systems of Leibniz and Newton and so widens this neophyte's philosophical and scientific horizon that in 1724, armed with the abbé's letters of introduction, he makes a third journey that will consecrate him a citizen of the Republic of Letters and lead him to Amsterdam and London. And even as he visits, in the cities he passes through, the collections and cabinets of curiosities, he is welcomed by several European princes of intellect: in London by Dr. Robert Mead, in Amsterdam by the famous Calvinist refugees Basnage de Beauval and Jean Leclerc. Young Caylus henceforth becomes the Enlightenment Frenchman par excellence, preparing himself for the independent career that by midcentury will win him great fame.

In order to become not only an honnête homme in the seventeenth-century manner but an expert of international standing in several arts, an antiquary enjoying European authority, and a Maecenas and guide for many young artists, this sword-bearing nobleman of agreeable presence and lively conversation quietly engaged in a continuing process of ascesis; without ever aspiring to the notoriety of an author, he mastered several literary genres, from the most entertaining and fugitive to the most erudite and severe.

"To live nobly," that aristocratic mode whose superiority was established by the ancient Greeks and that in France remains, in peacetime, the only ideal comparable to a monk's contemplative life, would offer the Comte de Caylus the *vie de château* enjoyments of metropolitan company as well as the disinterested practice of intellectual disciplines borrowed from scholars and men of letters. Leisure, the *scholé* of the Greeks, the *otium* of the Romans, is the shared ideal of men of letters and gentlemen, studious for the former, nonchalant and *galant* for the latter.

The Comte de Caylus participated fully in both versions, which makes him an archetypal hero of the French Enlightenment. This man of the world will never be a worldling: he has an indubitable social spirit, attends the theater, is seen at pleasure parties, frequents several agreeable intellectual circles, and presides over Mme Geoffrin's Mondays; when in Paris he lives as a Parisian, but he also makes a fetish of friendship and never shrinks from the assiduous and active expenditure of his time in the service of beauty and truth. This descendant on the paternal side of a distinguished family from the Rouergue resembles Montaigne in his jealous consciousness of the meditative self and the requirements of intimacy. Invariably cheerful in society, he reserves the right to be a melancholic in his own company. Yielding to the "diversions" condemned by Pascal, he yet knows how to remain at peace in a small room.

Intercourse between this young officer released from armed service and the extremely learned Venetian abbé will extend, thanks to their correspondence, long after Antonio Conti's return to Venice in 1726, where Montesquieu will be his guest in 1728. Such companionship, and the easy manners and disinterested passion for things of the mind it supposes, are characteristic at once of the cosmopolitanism, the encyclopedism, and the sociability of the French eighteenth century. The Enlightenment had no need to wait for the generation of the encylopedists to spread in Paris and to radiate throughout Europe. Indeed the movement was never so felicitous and fecund as at its inception. On the threshold of this book, which gathers a portrait gallery of foreigners conquered by Enlightenment France, the portrait of this French Telemachus and his Mentor commands our attention.

Anne-Claude Philippe de Tubières, de Grimoard, de Pestel, de

Lévis, Comte de Caylus (1692–1765), of whom we have a portrait by Watteau painted in 1719, as well as a profile drawing engraved by Cochin much later, had nothing of the elegant leanness bestowed by his painter friend upon the male personages of his *conversations galantes*. Powerfully built, his face broad, his jaw heavy, an indefatigable walker, the comte might well have passed, at a distance, for a stevedore if, at closer range, the delicate contour of his nose and lips, his long sensitive fingers, and a gaze capable of authority as well as melancholy and ennui had not betrayed the grand seigneur. But this grand seigneur in early youth had shared the life of camps with his troops and was quite as much at ease with the people of the Paris streets and fairs as with the cheerful company of witty women and men. He still enjoyed exchanging his court garments for a twill jacket and duck trousers, mingling like the Saladin of the *Thousand and One Nights* with the swarming life of workaday Paris, engaging with his "characters"—the idler, the coachman, the milliner, the cobbler—savoring their easy ways, remarking their curious turns of speech, just as Montaigne took lessons from the patois of Gascon peasants.

Diderot's outspoken hatred of the comte (all the more murderous since the author of the *Salons* of the *Correspondance littéraire* owed a good deal to the Comte de Caylus's taste and ideas about art) has managed to erase from French memories this original figure who was in his way a prince of intellect: his mistake was to have been wellborn, to loathe the charlatanry of the philosophes, and to lead according to his own notions the apparently unconstrained and indefatigably fecund life of one of the Enlightenment's busiest bees.

A FÉNELONIAN TRINITY

The Abbé Antonio Conti—born in Padua in 1677, to an ancient family of the Venetian patriciate, and dying in the city of his birth in 1749—belonged to the preceding generation. In 1699 he had entered the Congregation of the Oratorio della Fava, where he completed his training as a humanist with intensive studies in philosophy and theology of a Platonist and Augustinian tinge. In 1709, without leaving the priesthood, he obtained leave from the congregation in order to gain a better acquaintance with novelties arriving from the north: Bacon and Descartes, Malebranche and Locke, Newton and Leibniz, innovations in mathematics, physics, and philosophy, all of which fascinated the best professors of the University of Padua. In 1713, the year of the Treaty of Utrecht, duly initiated in his homeland into the new science and the new doctrines, he made his way to Paris where he sufficiently impressed Malebranche for the latter to agree to discuss his metaphysical system with him, and where he frequented several eminent members of the Academy of Sciences. Far from being a dazzled innocent, Conti espoused no specific school of thought or new scientific theory, though he was careful to familiarize himself with all of them. To gain a better idea of the British counterpart of the Cartesianism dominant in France, he visited London where he met the astronomer Halley and the mathematician Newton. His mastery of the new science won him election to the Royal Society. He extended his peregrinations to Holland and Germany, where he met Newton's great rival Leibniz, with whom he remained in correspondence. His curiosity, his powers of assimilation and comparison, and his irenicism made this enlightened ecclesiastic an ideal audience and interlocutor for the greatest contemporary minds of the Republic of Letters.

On his return to Paris, Conti took the measure of the expansion of the *Querelle des Anciens et des Modernes* into the *Querelle d'Homère*: he then drew up for his friends, in French, an impartial balance sheet of the contending positions without concealing the fact that he tended to side with the ancients. The French and particularly the English moderns were all too ready, in his view as in that of the Neapolitan Vico (whose genius Conti was among the few to recognize), to discard the remote for the immediate, the divine for the instrumental.

It was at the beginning of his second Parisian stay, in 1718, that

Conti became acquainted with the Comtesse de Caylus and translated Racine's *Athalie* into Italian for her. An autumnal attachment, including a good share of love, united them. Mme de Caylus had been one of the Versailles beauties, more graceful and delicious than truly beautiful, and already more suited to Watteau's becoming gowns than to the ornamental carapaces in which ladies were corseted by royal etiquette.

In the absence of any surviving iconography for the abbé, it is difficult to imagine his physical appearance. In 1718 he was in his mid-forties, six years younger than the comtesse. One might be tempted to believe that this wellborn, well-mannered ecclesiastic, who lived for his mind alone, somehow reminded Mme de Caylus of the spiritual beauty of Fénelon, whom she had known well thirty years before at Versailles and at Saint-Cyr, and whose inner light she had found positively daunting. Both Mme de Caylus and the Abbé Conti conceived an enormous sympathy for the Chevalier Ramsay, Fénelon's most famous disciple, and they read in manuscript the chief work of this singular personage, *Les Voyages de Cyrus*, inspired, appropriately enough, by the *Aventures de Télémaque*.

On this point too they both inaugurated the Age of Enlightenment, which virtually worshipped Fénelon. Conti was too much a Platonist and an Augustinian not to savor the literary refinements and the negative theology that placed the archbishop of Cambrai above and beyond the doctrinal contradictions quite as familiar to him at this "crisis of European consciousness" as the disputes between Molinists and Jansenists. Mme de Caylus had herself suffered too much from the extremes of Jansenism, and then sampled the terrible Bossuet, not to relish in contrast Fénelon's exigent but heart-warming religion. Could this second swan from Padua whom she had discovered and to whom she had entrusted her son's tutelage lead the latter from agnosticism to faith? The abbé took care not to preach to this young ex-colonel whose character and tastes were already formed. He concentrated on encouraging his charge's passion for knowledge and his taste for meditation and literary composition. Recondite studies, for a soul closed to religion, might take the place of spiritual exercises. Until 1750 the leading principle of the Enlightenment in France is to be sought in this stage of piety for the Muses and the Graces.

Inviting the comte to collaborate with him in a critical examination of Newton's chronology, Conti also attracted into the comtesse's circle certain academicians of the sciences or great literary lights who made the maternal hearth even more appealing to the youth and who completed, by their conversation, the higher education of a military man converted to the life of the mind. If there is one distinctive characteristic of the eighteenth century, it is the faith it places in education, and the generosity with which it has reflected on its methods. This characteristic is intensely present in Antonio Conti and in Mme de Caylus; indeed the comte, who profited by it in their presence, would in turn paternally supervise the formation of numerous young artists.

In exchange for this tutelage, the abbé himself received and learned a great deal as the comtesse's intimate. He realized all that might be added to the life of the mind by the singular alliance of moral intelligence and all the heartfelt discernment such a woman might reveal she possessed: exclusively masculine dealings with the Republic of Letters had not granted him a glimpse of such responsiveness and, back in Padua, the Abbé Conti would find no compensation for the separation from his friend and the circle she attracted around her except in the letters he exchanged with the comtesse and in the brilliant Venetian musical life whose activities he faithfully reported to her, accompanied by many manuscript scores.[1]

During the years 1718–1726, and by a two-way Paris–Venice correspondence that remained assiduous until the comtesse's death in 1729, this mother, her son, and the Italian abbé who was the former's tender friend and the latter's mentor constituted a fond and

---

1. See Sylvie Mamy, *La Musique française et l'imaginaire français des Lumières* (Paris: B.N.F., 1996). Mamy has since published an edition of the Abbé Conti's letters to Mme de Caylus: *Lettere da Venezia a Madame la Comtesse de Caylus* (Florence: Olschki, 2003).

harmonious trinity sharing readings, ideas, friendships, interests, and tastes. It was probably to diminish her sadness at the abbé's departure for Venice in 1726 that Mme de Caylus dictated to her son her *Souvenirs de la cour de Louis XIV*, recollections that Voltaire was to make permanently famous by publishing them, with his own notes, in 1771. This trio was not to be daunted by the pursuit of pleasures and the folly of amusements that intoxicated the Paris of the Regency. Mme de Caylus managed to instruct her two young gentlemen that there is also a knowledge to be derived from mourning. She was familiar with the meaning of separation, grief, and the sentiment of age, glimpses of past youth and the past itself. She was unscathed by the naive—and increasingly abstract—euphoria that threatened so many Enlightenment figures.

The French language was the medium by which these three exceptional beings understood one another. Though the Abbé Conti shared, up to a point, his compatriots' impatience with the French exaltation of their language above all other modern tongues, and notably the Italian literary idiolect, and try as he would to familiarize his French friend and her son with the glories of Italian music and poetry (since both were singularly sympathetic to Italian cultural manifestations), he came to realize that the vindication the French made for their language had a certain basis of truth, and he had learned that language with the spirit of perfection he invested in all his endeavors. His essays and his correspondence in French are of great distinction and an impeccable correctness: all the same they reveal a certain *patavinitas*, the accent of Padua, as the ancient Romans would say of provincials incapable by definition of mastering the *urbanitas* of the Latin spoken and written by the natives of the *Urbs*. A modest man, Conti knew this all too well. For him, Paris was the modern and Christian Rome. It was in Paris that he had known a Diotima, a Monica. And she spoke the French of Louis XIV and Racine. In Paris, as in Livy's Rome, the literary language and the language of conversation, unlike those of contemporary Italy, were one and the same. This language had internalized, so to speak, the rhetorical demands of Latin *urbanitas*: clarity, precision, music, naturalness. It was the vocation of the French language to be the living Latin of the moderns. Into it the mind and the heart could enter with ease and make themselves heard, a kind of uninterrupted musical improvisation. No Venetian or Neapolitan voice, not even that of the prodigious castrato Farinelli, could make the abbé forget the French speech of Mme de Caylus.

The comtesse's son, who remained a bachelor all his life, was never so happy as in the company of his mother and this ecclesiastical elder she had bestowed upon him as a mentor. His life would begin to darken after Antonio Conti departed from them, and to an even greater degree when the comtesse's death left him alone. No matter how busily he engaged in his extensive and fruitful activities, he was never to fill the void left by his mother and his mentor. Theirs was a threefold emotive configuration that he had already known in his childhood, though in a more strident key.

The Quasi Queen and Her Niece

Two virtually inseparable women had kept vigil over his childhood. One is a legend who has reached our own times. The other is virtually forgotten. The less visible was his mother, young at the time and without resources: Marthe-Marguerite Le Valois, Marquise de Villette-Mursay, better known by the name she assumed at her marriage in 1686, Comtesse de Caylus. The other, a monumental matron, was his great-aunt Françoise d'Aubigné, better known by the name Marquise de Maintenon, which she owes to Louis XIV, her lover and then her clandestine husband.

Both great ladies had blossomed on the ancestral tree of a vigorous family that quite suddenly entered the *noblesse d'épée* in the sixteenth century. The grandfather of one (the great-grandfather of the other) was the formidable Agrippa d'Aubigné, the first nobleman of the family stock, hero of the Calvinist faction, great warrior, great lover, great humanist as well, and one of the most splendid French poets, author of *Les Tragiques* and the *Hécatombe à Diane*.

Mme de Maintenon was one of the children of Agrippa's only son, Constant d'Aubigné, who had received a humanist education but who preferred to be a redoubtable warrior, several times a betrayer of his father, and the murderer of his first wife. This bluebeard was passionately loved by his second wife, Jeanne de Cardailhac, daughter of the governor of the prison of Bordeaux where he had been incarcerated. Their daughter, Françoise d'Aubigné, endured a vagrant and miserable childhood in their wake.

One of Agrippa's daughters, Louise-Artémise, married Benjamin Le Valois, Sieur de Villette. Their son Philippe Le Valois, Marquis de Villette, fathered in his first marriage the future Mme de Caylus, who was originally known as Mlle de Mursay, born in 1671. Philippe de Villette had a brilliant career in the royal navy, as did his four sons, three of whom died in Louis XIV's wars. In 1695, this sea wolf was still hearty enough to marry a companion of his daughter in the educational establishment of Saint-Cyr, Mlle de Marsilly, who gave him several children, and who was later to become Lady Bolingbroke. It was then that Françoise d'Aubigné shed over her entire family something of her luster and her influence. She who, since 1685, had been the morganatic wife of Louis XIV, the "quasi queen," sustained, for example, her old trooper of a brother, worthy son of their father Constant d'Aubigné, despite his compromising escapades; she married off this brother's daughter, Françoise-Charlotte, to the Maréchal de Noailles, who would join the Council of Ministers under the Regency.

Nor did Mme de Maintenon lose sight of her niece Mlle de Villette-Mursay. She had taken the girl from her parents in 1680, when she was nine years old, to keep in her household in Versailles and converted her to Catholicism. She then married her off, at just under sixteen years of age, to the Comte de Caylus.

This was anything but a misalliance. The Caylus were a family of very old and illustrious military nobility, deeply rooted in the Rouergue but long since members of the nobility of both court and church. The comte's brother, the Abbé de Caylus, called to Versailles as *aumônier du roi*, cherished by Bossuet and Mme de Maintenon, became bishop of Auxerre in 1704. One of their ancestors had become a part of French legend: Jacques de Lévis, Comte de Quélus, one of Henri III's favorites, who was killed, to the king's despair, in a famous duel with d'Entraigues. He figures in d'Aubigne's vengeful poem *Les Tragiques*. But the husband whom Mme de Maintenon had given to the adolescent Mlle de Villette-Mursay enjoyed no such glamour, and had been chosen only on condition that he immediately decamp, leaving the aunt the exclusive enjoyment of her niece. The exceptionally endowed Mlle de Mursay was indeed the masterpiece of whom Mme de Maintenon, as an *éducatrice*, was extremely proud. Throughout her adolescence the girl enchanted the court of Versailles.

"Sport and mirth," wrote the Abbé de Choisy, "sparkled around her; her mind was even more lovable than her countenance; there was no time to breathe or be bored when she was with one ... and if her natural gaiety had permitted her to leave off performing certain rather flirtatious songs that all her innocence could scarcely justify, she would have been a totally accomplished being."

Even Saint-Simon, scarcely likely to show indulgence for anyone related to Mme de Maintenon, confessed to marveling at his old enemy's niece. "Never," he writes, "was there a countenance so witty and so touching, so eloquent, never such freshness, never so much grace or so much wit, never such gaiety and amusement, never a more seductive creature."

Racine, amazed by her diction and her talents as an actress, composed for her the prologue to the *Piété* in *Esther*, which he had written at Mme de Maintenon's request for the theater of Saint-Cyr. She performed not only this prologue but several other roles in the play, replacing young actresses who had taken ill, to the general delight of the poet, the king, and the court. She even triumphed in the main female role of *Athalie*, exceeding the memory of the famous Mlle Champmeslé by the grace of her diction and the sincerity of her emotion.

But the bewitching Mme de Caylus was constrained by the devout pomp commanded by an aging monarch. Saint-Simon writes that Louis XIV was intimidated by her gay and pointed sallies and imagined that he found in them a certain mockery of his person. "Entertaining as she was," he adds, "the king was not quite comfortable with her, and she, who was aware of being distanced by the king, was also ill at ease in his presence. He never enjoyed her and was always reserved, frequently severe with her. This distressed Mme de Maintenon."

She was indeed dismissed from Versailles, first in 1691; her liaison with the Duc de Villeroy brought her a second exile in 1694. She had to take refuge with her mother-in-law in Paris. It was then that for the first time she was obliged to share her husband's life, and they had two children. The older son was born in 1692, the future Caylus of the Enlightenment.

It is impossible to know how he was brought up. Most likely his uncle, Monseigneur de Caylus, leader of the Jansenist episcopate, frequently invited him to Auxerre. It is also certain that despite her animated life, Mme de Caylus took charge of his education as much as she could. Yet precisely between 1694 and 1707, when she was barred from Versailles, she flung herself into the most austere of devout activities, under the direction of the general of the Oratory, Père de La Tour, himself notorious for his Jansenism, which further aggravated the young woman's disgrace in the king's eyes. One may suppose that throughout this period, she zealously concerned herself with her two children, and notably with the intellectual formation of her eldest son. The argumentative and punitive Jansenism that Anne-Philippe initially encountered on all sides had permanently distanced the young man from religious faith. Such desiccation, though it did not make a libertine of him, left him a free mind typical of the Enlightenment.

In 1704 his father, whom Saint-Simon describes as "mortally blasé, stupefied for years by wine and brandy," and tucked away with his regiment on the northern frontier, died. Mme de Caylus changed her spiritual director and was cured of Jansenism. She was restored to favor and in 1707 returned to Versailles, enlivening her aunt and even the old king in the interstices of the dreary life at court, in the darkest hours of the "great war." Her eldest son was now fifteen years old, and she presented him to Louis XIV. He was sent off to the army, a sacrificial victim. He fought heroically at Malplaquet, a victory dearly won by the Maréchal de Villars and received with great relief at Versailles amid so many disasters. Upon the youth's return, the king seated him in his lap and exclaimed to the whole court: "Look at young Caylus here, he's already killed one of my enemies!"

If the rest of his life is to be understood, it must always be remembered that Caylus had been introduced into the holy of holies of the monarchy at a very early age, and that he had seen the Great King at Versailles eye to eye and close at hand. Even as a young man, mainly in disagreement as he was with certain aspects of Regency Paris, he remained deeply attached to this vanished "Great Age," the legend of which only grew apace under Louis XV and of which Voltaire, who knew intimately and greatly esteemed the comte and his mother, became the chief chorister in *Le Siècle de Louis XIV*, published in 1751. Mme de Caylus is cited and celebrated in this work. In 1770, after the comte's death, Voltaire published the manuscript of memoirs left by the comtesse, under the title *Souvenirs de la cour de Louis XIV*.

The death of Louis XIV in September 1715 might be thought to have scuttled the "Maintenon party" of which Mme de Caylus was the chief ornament, and to assure the triumph of its adversaries, the Duc d'Orléans, regent of France, and his partisans. Mme de Maintenon, in the heavy veils of widowhood, withdrew to definitive retirement at Saint-Cyr, becoming the mother abbess of her teaching convent. Mme de Caylus, whose income was threatened, was obliged to return to Paris where, foresightedly, she had arranged in 1714 to be lodged in a small house belonging to the Royal Buildings and situated on the grounds of the Palais du Luxembourg. By this virtually rural retreat she participated in the general centrifugal movement that afforded the eighteenth century its best opportunities for a private life. It was here that her eldest son joined her in 1715. The correspondence between the comtesse and her aunt abounds in praises of her son's character and of the sweetness of their shared existence. She writes to Mme de Maintenon:

My habitation is convenient, attractive, solitary.... Early each morning I hear the crowing of several cocks and the bells of several little convents that invite me to prayer.... My little garden is about twice the size of our little bedroom at Saint-Cyr, nevertheless nothing is lacking: two pavilions entirely covered by grapevines, many pots of flowers, and a stable that I shall take my time to fill with my carriages.... I am very comfortable here, I never miss a sunbeam or a word of vespers from the seminary where no woman is welcome: this is how life is constituted, on one side the Luxembourg [where the regent's daughter engaged in her orgies], on the other, praises sung to God.... I grant my son the freedom to be alone as much as he likes: I am quite content, evenings, when my company has left, to have him to myself once again. All the moral virtues are to be found in this young man, with the exception of piety, which we must hope will adorn his future; meanwhile, it is a splendid companionship that I enjoy with him.... His behavior is so correct and his intentions so fine. So much truth and remoteness from evil of any kind convince me that God will touch him eventually.... I dine, I sup alone or with my son. As a general rule my son and I play at trictrac together; I gossip with him, I work, he reads to me; at four or five in the afternoon, I receive company, sometimes to excess; by eight o'clock, everyone leaves. I remain alone in my solitude. Once I kept Mme de Barneval and M. d'Auxerre—more for my son than for myself; he is assiduous about keeping me company, and I believe it is good for him to get in this habit, so I am very careful to keep him from being too bored. I am very content with my eldest son, he is an honest man and a lovable friend.[2]

---

2. Extracts from several letters of 1715; see Mme de Maintenon, Mme de Caylus, and Mme de Dangeau, *L'Estime et la tendresse*, private letters collected and presented by Pierre-E. Leroy and Marcel Loyau (Paris: Albin Michel, 1998).

She writes to her son: "Be a father to your brother, and a friend to your mother. Comfort me in my distress, which is greater than you can imagine.... I hope some day to show how much I love and esteem you.... You have courage, wit, and all the resources of intellect: never forget it. You are my entire consolation, as you are everything that moves me here in Paris; continue so that nothing happens to me that might disturb my peace."[3]

If we are to judge by the sort of *journal intime* the Comte de Caylus kept between 1717 and 1747, of which all that remains are the fragments of *Maximes et réflexions* published in the nineteenth century, his mother had nothing to fear from a son whom she had formed, except for piety, in her own image, at once sociable and contemplative. It is with his mother that he assumed the regular habits that suited the life of studious leisure he had chosen. But this bachelor, whom his mother calls "my philosopher" or "my melancholic" and who left military life without regret, was above all enamored of personal liberty. He permanently avoided the Versailles of Louis XV and sought only the society of friends, on private terrain. In his *Maximes et réflexions* we find this fragment on travel, which gives the measure of his love of independence and his horror of oppression, especially worldly oppression:

> Traveling, one has not the faintest notion of duty. In any sojourn, even if one enjoys such society as is afforded, try as one will to take comfort in it, there is always some appearance to be kept up in the day's activity. In one's own country, one is encountered, on every occasion, by someone who knows one and whom one neither can nor may "drop." In a foreign city, on the contrary, one may propose as oneself whatever one chooses to be; one pursues one's every taste without question, one is properly responsive to the kindnesses one receives; in

3. Comtesse de Caylus, *Souvenirs et correspondance* (privately published by E. Raunié, 1881), pp. 303–304, letters 84 and 86.

one's own country, one is overwhelmed by a thousand preferences quite alien to one's own.

The "cottage" and its little garden where he resided with his mother were nonetheless hardly a Thebaid "in the desert." They were the discreet theater of hivelike commotion. A perpetual flow of visitors, gatherings, and dinners in the highest society of Paris combined a continuous and determined political and diplomatic activity with conversations and correspondences bearing on all the burning questions of the perod's literary, artistic, and musical life.

The letters of the Comtesse de Caylus to Mme de Maintenon between 1715 and 1719, though extremely discreet, reveal all sorts of confabulations and intrigues. These superior women, apparently overwhelmed by the death of the Great King, were far from having entirely renounced the world. In a biography of the Abbé Conti, published after his death in 1749, we discover an aspect of the life of Mme de Caylus and her son in their little house adjacent to the Luxembourg that hardly corresponds to the somewhat rustic appearance of the modest residence. The author of this biography, the Venetian astronomer Toaldo, who was very close to the abbé during his lifetime, writes:

> Conti entered Mme de Caylus's circle at this time, upon his return from England. He was her neighbor (living in the outbuildings of the Luxembourg). In her residence he had the pleasure of meeting the fine flower of Parisian society. Her own qualities had sustained all the friendships she had established at the late king's court. The Bishop of Fréjus, subsequently to be Cardinal de Fleury, was among her most intimate friends and frequently sought her company. Among the habitués of the household figured M. Boudin, the dauphine's physician, and M. Nicolas, the geometrician and collaborator of the mathematician Rémond de Montmor, of the Academy of Sciences. Quite regularly one might find seated

in the circle of her salon "her" marshals: de Villars, de Tallard, de Tessé, de Boufflers, and de Villeroy, as well as the Duc
de Villeroy, the Duc de La Feuillade, and the Maréchal-Duc
de Brissac. All these great noblemen were fond friends of the
Abbé Conti, for in him they found those things beloved in all
climes and regions. But Mme de Caylus enjoyed this privilege
more than anyone else. As soon as they knew each other,
there was born between them a reciprocal and particular esteem. Even after his return to Italy, they corresponded by
each return post, and indeed at great length. This was, it appears, the most perfect lady he had encountered in all his
journeys. He was profuse in his praises of her, and when he
was near death, of all the texts left on his desk he considered
only the letters he had received from Mme de Caylus as worthy to be read. These letters indeed awaken admiration for
her intelligence: they are full of literary and political news,
items of current interest retailed with the lightest conversa-
tional touches, all written with a natural grace that is altogether captivating. She had two sons, one who had left
military service to devote himself to travel and the fine arts,
the other who was in the king's service as a Knight of Malta.
The comte dined almost every evening with his mother, and
even after her death, in 1729, he continued corresponding
with the Abbé Conti, and was indeed the last and most faithful of his friends in France.

The gatherings of the "Maintenon party" and of the remains of
the late king's court around Mme de Caylus, secretly linked to the
august widow of Saint-Cyr, pursued interests quite opposed to the
financial excitations and orgies of the Regency. Yet the comtesse had
suffered from Versailles, and was never so happy as after leaving the
château and resuming her private life. For his part, her son the comte
frequented the Hôtel Crozat, which was virtually an extension of
the Palais-Royal: there he would see the Duc d'Orléans, and could
not be unaware of the atmosphere of the Regency. Neither mother

nor son was "of" the seventeenth century of Louis XIV and Mme de Maintenon, though they were not, having belonged to the late king's inner circle, "of" this new frivolous and pleasure-seeking age whose Prince Charming the regent sought to incarnate. Mme de Caylus and her son, as well as, in his way, the Abbé de Conti, were of their time, with all the intimate detachment of those who remember.

From Louis XIV to Louis XV

The nineteenth century will dwindle and disappear even more radically in the Great War of 1914 than the seventeenth did in the War of the Spanish Succession. The century of Victor Hugo obeyed the precedent of the century of Voltaire, engulfed by the cataclysm of the Terror and the revolutionary wars. The Dada years that followed November 11 afforded a worthy equivalent of the *Incroyables* and the *Merveilleuses* who appeared after the Ninth of Thermidor. In 1715, the French monarchy had received from Louis XIV such a quasi-pharaonic analogy with cosmic order that the transition to the next reign, despite the regent's taste for novelty, managed to produce a triumph of continuity. The Sun King died, but his widow took care that the young planet that succeeded him did not lose sight of his example and his tradition.

Mme de Maintenon, between 1715 and 1719, the year of her death, though "in retirement" in her apartment at Saint-Cyr, was not content to make her house of education for daughters of the nobility into a sanctuary of the cult of Louis le Grand. Buried, to all appearances, in widowhood and the exercises of piety, she remained no less an invisible power seeking, at a distance, to control the destinies of the realm at the dawn of the new century. She possessed in her niece, who corresponded with her regularly and paid her frequent visits at Saint-Cyr, a precious link to Paris and to all those loyal to the late king. And then there remained one further weapon in the armory of the king's widow: her genius as an educator, inseparable from her political genius.

As Michel Antoine has shown in his admirable biography of Louis XV, the illustrious widow, exiled from the court, retained a firm hand on the education of the boy Louis XV, which is to say, on the future. The Abbé Pérot, tutor of the child-king, was a disciple of Monseigneur Godet des Marais, the spiritual director of Mme de Maintenon and the superior of the house at Saint-Cyr. The governess of the dauphin, then of the young king, was the Duchesse de Ventadour, whose conduct and principles were constantly dictated by Mme de Maintenon, who actually directed the prince's education from the start. When the Maréchal de Villeroy succeeded the Duchesse de Ventadour as the king's personal adviser, he too was a member of the "Maintenon party" that directed the prince's intellectual formation. The maréchal would moreover become a faithful presence in Mme de Caylus's well-attended retreat at the Luxembourg, as would of course his son the Duc de Villeroy, captain of the king's guards, formerly Mme de Caylus's *amant en titre* and now her friend and assiduous guest. As for the maréchal, he had been the lover of the Duchesse de Ventadour, and this couple, eternally loyal to Mme de Maintenan, shared the responsibility for the young king's education during the Regency.

The confidential correspondence between Mme de Ventadour and Mme de Maintenon also continued as vigorously as ever after 1715. The king was thus raised in the cult of his great-grandfather and tutored according to the views of the latter's morganatic spouse, still served by the faithful Abbé Pérot. On February 15, 1717, Louis XV was seven years old. He was put in the care, still under the authority of Maréchal de Villeroy, of his new tutor, the former bishop of Fréjus, M. de Fleury. Mme de Ventadour would retire, to the loud protestations of her young pupil, but the "Maintenon party" lost nothing by the change. The Maréchal de Villeroy, loyal courtier of Louis XIV and of Mme de Maintenon, tolerated out of courtesy by the regent, educated the king according to the grand official manners indefatigably practiced at Versailles by his great-grandfather: the child-king must appear in certain ballets before the court and be initiated into the royal sport of venery. But Mme de Maintenon's major trump was the bishop of Fréjus, whom the king had taken care to name in his will, with his spouse's approval, as the future king's tutor. This was one of the secondary articles of Louis XIV's will, which the regent neglected to have abolished by the Parlement in 1715. The Abbé Pérot, the young king's first tutor and loyal to Mme de Maintenon, remained in place in the team of royal educators. François Chevalier, professor at the Collège de France, a mathematician and engineer of fortifications, was added to their company, and he had belonged, like other eminent members of the team, to the little academy recruited by Fénelon, with the endorsement of Mme de Maintenon, with whom he was very close at the time, for the education of the Duc de Bourgogne, Louis XV's father.

The continuity with the old court was consequently very strong around the young king, compensating for the influence and example of the regent and his coterie now in power. Mme de Maintenon supervised matters at a distance. On August 21, 1721, the Maréchal de Villeroy lost favor with the regent and was exiled from his governorship of Lyon. M. de Fleury was also dismissed from court. But the king himself requested his return, and obtained it. At this time the bishop had more influence than ever over the young king and encountered no real obstacle from the new preceptor, the Duc de Charost.

One of the first effects of the education Louis XV received was his declared will to return to Versailles, theater of the solar monarchy, where he took up residence again, after a Parisian sojourn of seven years, on June 15, 1722. The death of Philippe d'Orléans, prime minister after having been regent, occurred shortly after, on December 2, 1723. After a rather pathetic interval with the Duc de Bourbon, exiled to Normandy on June 10, 1726, along with his mistress Mme de Prie, an intimate friend of Mme du Deffand, Louis XV, even as he declared himself capable of taking matters into his own hands, entrusted the exercise of power to his beloved M. de Fleury, who would soon receive the cardinal's hat in 1726.

What a triumph for the "Maintenon party"! Mme de Caylus had not remained inactive in this turnaround in political fortunes.

We possess a letter from her written during the Regency to the Duc du Maine, Mme de Montespan's legitimate son, a cherished pupil of Mme de Maintenon and a great victim of the Regency, in which we find her very well informed about the conspiracy brewed by the duc with the Spanish ambassador, the Prince de Cellamare, to remove the regent. Gradually, under the Regency, the coterie of Mme de Maintenon, even after the latter's death in 1719, expanded to become a veritable conservative party, its program being to save the principles of Louis XIV's European policy. And this party had a candidate: M. de Fleury, Louis XV's tutor, installed in that position by Mme de Maintenon whose intimate friend he had been. He was seventy-three years old when the young king made him his prime minister. Like many habitués of Mme de Caylus's circle at the Luxembourg, he was a contemporary of the Great King. He was also a man of high culture, initiated by his erudition into the history and the age-old tradition of a monarchy whose longevity in Europe had no rival except the pontifical triple tiara. No one could better inspire in Louis XV a passion not to depart from Louis XIV's example. In one of the letters from Mme de Caylus to her aunt in retirement at Saint-Cyr, we find this observation heavy with insinuations and complicities: "I'm sending you a letter from M. de Fréjus: he comes to see me from time to time, and it seems to me that he is *one of ours.*"

The links between Mme de Maintenon and the bishop of Fréjus were of long standing. The Comte de Caylus had been involved in them; from 1711 to 1713, in command of his regiment, the young colonel had sojourned in Provence on his return from Spain and before marching to the Rhine frontier. Mme de Caylus writes to her son:

> I am delighted, my dear son, that you should be with M. de Fréjus; he is the most agreeable man in the world, and I should consider you only too happy were you to please him; nothing would be more likely to give me a good opinion of you. He has done a good turn to one of his best friends, which has

caused me infinite pleasure.... A thousand compliments to M. de Fréjus; we missed him greatly at a little country gathering we had yesterday at M. de Valincour's.

The warmth of this letter helps us understand the choice Louis XIV and Mme de Maintenon had made of M. de Fleury as the dauphin's tutor, a choice that ultimately determined his elevation to the rank of prime minister under Louis XV. Fleury's European policy took the opposite course to that of the regent and Cardinal Dubois. Versailles once again became the center of power. But from the depths of her tomb Mme de Maintenon would have been vexed to observe that another power had irresistibly appeared, contrary to all her expectations: the power of Paris.

THE ENLIGHTEMENT STILL UNDER THE AUTHORITY OF VERSAILLES

We may measure the at least apparent and provisional triumph of the old court over the Duc d'Orléans's Regency in the correspondence between Mme de Caylus and her friend the Abbé Antonio Conti after Cardinal de Fleury's triumph. Conti was not only a Christian philosopher, a poet, a theoretician of the beautiful; like many great men of letters of the time—Roger de Piles, Abbé Du Bos, Voltaire—at ease in the most various milieux, he was also a diplomat. And as a Venetian, he was so twice over. During his peregrinations as a savant, he also considered himself on a mission of observation. From 1722 to 1726, the Serenissima's new ambassador to Louis XV, Baron Morosini, was one of his intimate friends. Abbé Conti found himself beside Morosini in the best seats in the house from which to observe the transition from the Regency to the personal reign of Louis XV, from the ministries of Dubois and Bourbon to that of Cardinal de Fleury. From 1718 on he was associated with the invisible conspiracy striving to carry out plans bequeathed from beyond the grave by Mme de Maintenon. The abbé, the comtesse, and her son were somewhat deficient in political savvy in that they placed an extreme value on intimacy, inwardness, leisure, and contemplation, and felt themselves threatened or deflected in a new age in which the spiritual combat between Protestantism and Catholicism had taken on a new, subtler, and less discernible dimension, though one all the more ruthless. Upon his return to Venice, Conti composed a memorandum on the general political situation in France and in Europe. Long believed lost, this private manuscript has been published recently in its original French text.[4]

In the abbé's letters to Mme de Caylus, we may gain some notion of the mind that dictated that memorandum. The Venetian congratulated himself and his correspondent on Cardinal de Fleury's policy, which reversed the alliances contracted by Cardinal Dubois and returned to the policies of Louis XIV. Conti writes, for example: "I want to see France resume her earlier position in Europe" or again "to see France recover her earlier dignity and that original vigor which will always put her in the position of determining Europe's destiny, even when she does not choose to extend her actual conquests."

Fleury was capable of showing, he writes, "that it is not Great Britain's role, but that of France to rule Europe, and thereby deprive the English of that imperious notion that the wickedness of one of your ministers [Dubois] and the weakness of the other [the Duc de Bourbon] had only too fondly encouraged." The principle of the "Maintenon party," of which Mme de Caylus was the Egeria, is formulated in another letter Conti writes to her: "After the death of Louis XIV, there has been nothing great in Europe. English gold, spread by the court, triumphs everywhere and corrupts everyone."

He hopes once again that "France will take action entirely according to the system of Louis XIV." Cardinal de Fleury's conduct,

---

4. From a manuscript kept in the Biblioteca Joppi in Udine, Sylvie Mamy has published Conti's essay (very enthusiastic for Louis XIV's enlightened role in Europe) in her book *Lettere da Venezia a Madame la Comtesse de Caylus*, pp. 79-208.

in reviving this system, "has put France in a position to dictate laws to the Hapsburg emperor and to assure peace to Europe for the happiness of her peoples and the progress of the arts and sciences."

This last formula is capital. For the Venetian Conti, who is also a citizen of the Republic of Letters, France's authority as arbiter of Europe is inseparable from its role as the central source and focus of the arts and sciences. Here again is one of the principles that the "Versailles party" seeks to transmit intact from the century of Louis XIV to that of Louis XV. But from one reign to the other, from Torcy to Fleury, the application of such principles cannot be unaware of the difference in the times.

It was not, indeed, the great "King of War," the old Mars who had led France, at the cost of enormous sacrifices, to the successful conclusion of the War of the Spanish Succession, who was to be resuscitated from his tomb. France no longer needed to conquer its hegemony, merely to exercise it. Neither the situation in Europe nor the change in mood, manners, and taste that had brought France to pleasure and peace required the state of exception that the Great King had impressed upon the realm during the years of confrontation and peril. War is not excluded, but can no longer be anything but diplomacy continued by other means. The great question for Conti was the counterweight that only a Catholic, aristocratic, and royal France can and must oppose, on the Continent, to the divisive and rapacious egoism of England, now observing its own political model, an original utilitarist philosophy and a science applicable to industry. On the Abbé Conti's horizon of French geopolitics appears, in the 1720s, the Family Pact among the Bourbons of France, Spain, and Naples, which Choiseul concluded on August 15, 1761, and the reversal of alliances, symbolized by the marriage of the dauphin and Marie-Antoinette, that finally united Bourbons and Hapsburgs on May 16, 1770. The institutions of Catholic Europe, perturbed by a Lutheran Prussia, were thus allied against a Protestant future whose principles had found their secular arm in the English navy and the City's gold. The American war, apparently a victory over England, would in reality be the involuntary contribution of Louis XVI and Vergennes to the short- *and* long-term triumph of the philosophy of Locke, Adam Smith, and Bentham.

In the deadliest of his wars, the Great King had nonetheless been able to present another countenance: as chief of his army's general staff, he imperturbably remained a Maecenas king, a Catholic Apollo favoring the arts of peace and the nine Muses. The French Enlightenment of the new century was only as brilliant as it was because Louis XIV never sacrificed the arts of peace and the science of leisure to the weapons of war. The stake of a French hegemony in Europe was not merely a question of power: it involved the ultimate meaning of the new century's Enlightenment. The Abbé Conti, a Platonist and Augustinian Catholic, though one extremely well informed about all scientific and philosophical innovations, went to the heart of the matter: Would the Enlightenment incline to the empiricism of rapacious England, or would it remain under the prevailing influence of the France of Descartes and Malebranche, of Racine and the Abbé Du Bos, attached to the classical, Christian, and aristocratic presuppositions of the nobility of the mind—beauty and truth loved for themselves? Everything that in France tended to this solution reinforced the Catholic continuity of Europe.

The mentor of the Comte de Caylus thus oriented his disciple on a path from which he was not to stray. In his correspondence, Anne-Philippe declares himself a "tory" when he speaks of French affairs. He borrows the term from Henry St. John, now Lord Bolingbroke, chief of the Tory Party who sought refuge in France after 1714, since as the signatory of the Treaty of Utrecht he was accused of high treason and threatened with a death sentence by a Whig Parliament. Bolingbroke entered Mme de Maintenon's family by marrying Mme de Villette, the comtesse's young mother-in-law. In the ardent *Querelle d'Homère*, Caylus sides with Conti against the amnesia of antiquity recommended by Fontenelle and his disciple Houdart de La Motte.

Sharing the views of the enlightened conservative party and informed at first hand of the court intrigues that might weaken or deflect the monarchy's general policies, the friend and seasoned protégé of Cardinal de Fleury is careful not to adopt any administrative position whatsoever, devoting himself chiefly to the Muses, in close cooperation with the organs of the realm's spiritual primacy in Europe, the academies, the mechanism connecting royal power to the life of the mind.

His studious leisure, his works, and the passion he would invest, having witnessed at its source the birth of the Regency's rococo style, in reorienting the royal buildings, the French school of painting and sculpture, and the public taste toward a higher Louis XV style made him one of the most vital figures of French and European neoclassicism. With the support of his two immensely learned friends Pierre-Jean Mariette and Jean-Jacques Barthélemy, he succeeded in transferring to Paris the European movement toward the *retour à l'antique* in the arts, a privilege of Rome and London until 1750. He died in 1765, spared from seeing the reform of French taste, intended by him and his friends as an improvement of the Crown's image, preempted as the symbol of a radical political revolution.

TEXTS IN HOMAGE TO MME DE CAYLUS BY THE ABBÉ CONTI, THE COMTE DE CAYLUS, AND RÉMOND DE SAINT-MARD

The Abbé Conti to the Comte de Caylus

Monsieur,
For fifteen days I have not dared write to you, fearing the fatal blow whereof M. Blart's letter had forewarned me. In vain I flattered myself that your silence might have another cause than this great misfortune. Ambassador Canal had informed his friends, yet no one had dared speak of the matter to me. I had suspected something, upon hearing from the lady nun who is the ambassador's cousin; her words caused me great anxiety. One always deludes oneself in these last extremities, and I had the strength to withhold my tears for some moments, but at

the sight of the black seal on your letter, I was struck dumb and lost the courage to open it. Finally I was obliged to do so, and as great grief overwhelms the mind, I lost all awareness of what I was reading, until having read your letter two or three times to my sister, to my mother, to my cousin, and to all those who take an interest in the health of Mme your mother, I began to weep, and I am weeping still as I write to you. I cannot find consolation, nor can I hope to console you. The mind is indeed weak, as you say, in the presence of the heart's sentiments. A pinprick causes an outbreak of cries despite all the efforts of philosophy. It is unthinkable to suppose we can keep from grieving and from weeping when we lose everything. I can assure you without the slightest exaggeration that I would not be so desolate as I am had I lost my entire family. I might possibly imagine that these would be losses I might compensate upon reflection. But in the present case, all reflection has abandoned me, or rather all reflection merely increases the desolation of having lost all that is most lovable in the world. Try as I may to distract myself, I constantly see her either sitting with such calm grace in her garden or reading and studying in her apartment, and pondering with so much taste and good sense whatever subjects have won her attention.

What intelligence, what firmness of thought and feeling, but also what truth in everything that proceeds from the heart! I have no happiness save not seeing her suffer during her last illness, not hearing her last words nor receiving her last glances. Yet in spite of myself, my imagination shows her to me in this sad state. Spare me from shedding further tears as I write—I confess I scarcely know what I am saying, for instead of seeking to console you, I merely cause your tears by my own.

You offer me a communication for which I cannot sufficiently thank you; I am sorry not to have forestalled you, at the very risk of not being heeded, but you are too kind, and the memory of Mme your mother is too dear to you not to take some pity on her sad friends. Though we are separated by great distances, you are no less present to me, and I have always lived with you by my letters. I followed you everywhere, and it was a real pleasure to be informed of all your activi-

ties. How could I help loving you for your own merits, and for the deep tenderness Mme your mother has always had for you: a tenderness of which she gave you so many signs during your spells of illness? I have not forgotten the prostration and despair into which I have seen her cast for an entire month when she feared she might lose you.

The phrase of religious attachment you employ to indicate to me how much you love all that she loved touches me deeply and makes me realize the great kindness of your heart; it is to that heart alone I would speak, and to that heart that I submit all the interests of my own. On this basis I shall continue to write to you with the same esteem and the same tenderness with which I used to write to Mme your mother. How I pity all her friends . . . I beg you to tell them that I share their tears, though I am so far away. I hear their sighs, and with them I bear an irreparable loss for which nothing can console us.[5]

Here is the Comte de Caylus's reply:

Knowing your sentiments as I do, my dear abbé, I was not surprised by the moved and moving letter you have written to me concerning the greatest misfortune of my life. I felt, as I read it, a grief as unreasonable (in a sense) as that of the first moment; and I assure you that in the moment at which I write, I am filled and overwhelmed by my misfortune. With each day that I survive her, I feel more deeply the loss I have suffered. The merest details of this privation constitute a dreadful condition, and I yield to the mournful pleasure of sharing my affliction with you. I have no idea how to go on living. Yet you know that I possess sufficient mental resources to do so. I find myself utterly isolated. My country disgusts me. The affairs that always follow such misfortunes will probably cause me to leave my country. Philosophy is of no help, and I feel nothing but the mechanical operations of the least-enlightened creature. All that is most alluring in the most lovable

5. Luigi Ferrari, "L'Abate Conti e Madame de Caylus," *Reale Istituto Veneto di scienze, lettere, ed arti* 34/35, t. 94 (Venice, 1934): pp. 8–10.

relationship, all the pleasure and the exhaustion that it afterward entails is succeeded by a dreadful solitude.... [6]

Ten years later, in 1740, the memory of Mme de Caylus remained as vivid to her son and to the Abbé Conti, who died in 1749. It must have been on the anniversary of the countess's death that Rémond de Saint-Mard, a loyal member of her circle between 1714 and 1729, wrote for the comte, and perhaps for Conti, an admirable eulogy, which inspired Sainte-Beuve to create one of his finest female portraits, "Mme de Caylus, or Of Urbanity."

I have read that it was once said of the poet Aristophanes that the Graces, seeking a mutual temple, had selected his spirit in which to receive the worship of mortals. Such a panegyric a thousand times better suited the late Mme de Caylus. Knowing her, one abandoned without a thought one's mistresses, for they ceased to please, and it was difficult to live in her society without becoming her friend and her lover. What other divinities can produce such extraordinary phenomena?

The old poets had imagined another creature altogether as lovable; they called her Persuasion, and to give us an adequate idea of the eloquence of Pericles, they said that she lived on his lips. Did not everyone see her in every action and every word of Mme de Caylus?

The word "charm" is extravagently lavished, and the combined gifts of Venus and Minerva strike me as insufficient to deserve it; in brief, what cannot disgust us with the rest of the world is not worthy of such a word. Now I ask all those who have known the felicity of living with her, if in her presence they have not forgotten the whole of the natural world and only desired not to be elsewhere?

She was born with great wit, and had the advantage of being raised by a woman who had the greatest knowledge of what constitutes true amenities; hence no one had a nobler, readier manner, nor a greater exactitude for all the proprieties than Mme de Caylus.

---

6. Quoted by Samuel Rocheblanc in *Essai sur le Comte de Caylus* (Hachette, 1889), pp. 39–40.

Her own curiosity and the society of men of repute had made her learned in spite of herself, though such masters had always been, I believe, more concerned to please than to instruct her. Moreover her separation from what is called the company of clever minds corresponded to the natural beauty of her own and to the delicacy of her taste. . . .

After admiring the rectitude of her good sense in serious conversations, if one sat down to table with her, she immediately became the goddess of the occasion; it was then that she reminded me of Homer's Helen, for that poet, in order to represent the effects of his heroine's beauty and wit, pretends that she dissolved into the wine a rare plant she had brought with her from Egypt, whose virtue made the company forget all the disagreeable experiences they had ever suffered. Mme de Caylus exceeded Helen, for she spread about her a joy that was so gentle and so vivid, a taste for pleasure so noble and so elegant, that all characters seemed lovable and happy, so surprising is the power or rather the magic of a woman who possesses true charm. . . . [7]

7. Rémond de Saint-Mard, quoted by the Abbé Gédoyn, *Oeuvres diverses* (1745), p. 229.

2. A French Alcibiades and His English Plato: Anthony Hamilton and the Comte de Gramont

THE *GRANDE AFFAIRE* of Louis XIV's reign had been the English Revolution of 1688. Since Charles Stuart's return to the throne in 1660, the Great King had been able to keep England within the domain of his European policy. Restored in large part thanks to French support, pensioned by the king of France, and provided with mistresses selected and suborned by the French ambassadors, Charles II generally managed to circumnavigate his country's violent Francophobia and to avoid excessive interference with the plans of the king of France.

In many aspects, Charles Stuart was French. Son of Henriette of France, the sister of Louis XIII, and the brother of Henriette of England, wife of Louis XIV's brother the Duc d'Orléans, Charles II belonged to the French royal family; having grown up and engaged in his first military actions in France during Cromwell's "usurpation," his mind and manners were those of a French prince.

Of course he was nominally Anglican, like his father Charles I, but he had been raised by an extremely devout Catholic mother whose dream, as long as she reigned over England at her husband's side, had been to restore her new kingdom to the bosom of the Church of Rome. Charles II's younger brother and only male heir, the Duke of York, took the step that his elder prudently avoided: he converted overtly to Catholicism in 1673 and took as his second wife a Catholic princess, Mary of Modena. Such avowed papistry made him odious in England and largely provoked the revolution of 1688, which brought to the throne a Protestant prince, William of Orange, husband of Mary, the very daughter of the deposed sovereign, and principal justification for her husband to become king of England under the name William III.

FRANCO-ENGLISH AFFINITIES AND INCOMPATIBILITIES

For the majority of Englishmen—those attached to the Anglican Church or to various Protestant sects—their difficulty with the Stuart dynasty was at once political and religious. Political because traditionally this royal family of Scottish origin tended to absolute monarchy of the French type, a propensity that in 1649 had cost Charles I his life. And religious because such an inclination also favored Catholicism, a partiality that in 1587 had cost their great-grandmother Mary Stuart, widow of the Valois king of France, hers. This politico-religious difficulty was intrinsically linked to the dynasty's deep affinities with France, odious to the English in general not only for its Catholicism, which Louis XIV had brutally re-affirmed as the sole religion of his realm by the revocation of the Edict of Nantes, and for its absolutism, which collided head-on with English parliamentary tradition, but especially for its maritime power, both colonial and commercial, which hampered the interests of an island whose whole fortune, like that of Holland, derived from its seagoing commerce.[1] Between 1660 and 1688, only Charles II's ruses and the extraordinary virtuosity of Louis XIV's diplomacy and gold were able to contain the irresistible efforts impelling England to play all her trump cards in order to oppose France on the Continent as well as on the high seas.

After 1688, the Stuart brake now released, England became the principal enemy of Louis XIV, who imagined that he had caught the island kingdom in his snares and who even encouraged the Duke of York, who became James II upon his brother's death in 1685, to declare Catholicism the realm's official religion, as Mary Tudor had

---

1. See the brilliant recording of this epoch-making political drama in Steve Pincus, *1688: The First Modern Revolution* (Yale University Press, 2009).

done to her cost in the sixteenth century. Opposing the France of the aging Great King, whose manners were dictated by the ancient, noble, anti-mercenary ethic of generosity and whose mentality was dominated by a Catholic metaphysic Platonic in essence, the England of the Glorious Revolution adopted an intellectual master suited to its true *forma mentis*; in 1688 the philosopher John Locke, bitterly opposed to the Stuarts, published *An Essay Concerning Human Understanding*, which, contrary to an uninterrupted tradition renewed by no less a figure than Descartes, based human consciousness exclusively on sense experience and social morality on the properly understood adjustment of passions and interests. In 1690 Locke exhibited the political theory resulting from such an anthropology in *Two Treatises of Government*. As the new regime's commissioner of commerce and of the colonies, Locke did not of course gain a unanimous adherence of English minds: Oxford University (traditionally loyal to the Stuarts) had its own Platonists, and the British party of the ancients—usually recruited from the Tory ranks generally favoring the Stuarts and drawing inspiration from the ancients of Paris—defended tradition against the British moderns.

But on the whole, Locke's anthropology and theory of knowledge impregnated eighteenth-century English thought and meshed harmoniously with science as conceived by the Royal Society, heir of Bacon's inductive empiricism and committed to technological applications for navigation, commerce, industry, and agriculture, all sources of wealth for an aristocracy that did not believe, like its French counterpart, that such activities were derogatory to noble birth. The remarkable French translation of Locke's *Essai sur l'entendement humain*, the work of a Calvinist refugee, Pierre Costes, and published in Amsterdam, inaugurated English utilitarianism's Continental offensive, supported by Voltaire's encomium in his *Lettres anglaises* of 1727; along with Newton's cosmology, which Mme du Châtelet and (again) Voltaire popularized in Europe, Locke's *Essay* became the spearhead of an English philosophical and even scientific hegemony over the *Lumières* of the Enlightenment.

But it must be understood that the Franco-English conflict,

which assumed a metaphysical dimension after 1688, was not a clear-cut antithesis. If Anglomania progressed in Paris throughout the eighteenth century in the wake of the regent's (and Dubois's) Anglophile policy and was encouraged by Voltaire's *Lettres anglaises*, which made the "English model" the last word in France, on the other hand the English fascination with an aristocratic France *à l'ancienne*, with its manners, fashions, and "art of living" (rivaled only by the attraction exerted by the visual arts of Italy when discovered on the Grand Tour), powerfully influenced a British aristocracy that, however attached to economic foundations unknown to its French counterpart, was only the more disposed to employ its riches in the enjoyment of a noble leisure housed in Palladian castles, embellished with Italian paintings, refreshed by parks inspired by the landscapes of Nicolas Poussin and Claude Lorrain, and entertained by gallant manners that, without too openly competing with the elegant libertinage whose secret belonged to Catholic France, were ardently practiced intra muros; and there was no destination more favored by English aristocracy in the eighteenth century, in the intervals of peace between the two realms, than Paris or the fair provinces of France, to which this nobility escaped for long sojourns whenever possible. In the Stuart dynasty, under Charles I and Charles II, it was the relative symbiosis between the English nobility and its French counterpart (regarded since the Crusades, as is too often forgotten in retrospect, as the archetype of European aristocracies) that had facilitated the close alliance between Paris and London. Hence this reverence for the modern Mother Country of "living nobly" was far from having vanished in England after the revolution of 1688.

Lord Bolingbroke, whose second marriage was to the Marquise de Villette, an exquisite Frenchwoman brought up at Saint-Cyr, had adapted very well to a long exile in France. Lord Chesterfield, in the letters addressed to his son during the young man's Grand Tour, did not conceal the admiration that the French civilization of manners inspired in him, and flattered himself that it was Paris that virtually refined him from English barbarity. Horace Walpole, though the son

of the Whig prime minister who had been the mortal enemy of Bolingbroke and France, lingered from 1739 to 1741 in the French capital where he engaged in a long Platonic liaison with the Marquise
du Deffand, an old lady who in many respects was the quintessence
of aristocratic France and its aestheticizing attitude toward life.

Lord Bolingbroke experienced certain Jacobite temptations at
the beginning of his French exile. In other words, he kept company
for a time with James II's son, the "Pretender" to the crown who
held court at Saint-Germain after his father's death in 1701 and who
as long as he was supported by Louis XIV seemed to promise an
ambitious statesman some sort of future. English or Scottish, it was
these Jacobite noblemen in exile who went furthest in the adoption
of French manners and in the identification of the French aristocracy's frame of mind *à l'ancienne*. The Restoration of Charles II had
exported to London, and reproduced on the English stage, favored
by several years of peace, the *galant* manners and gynaeceum intrigues that had constituted the charm of the French court since the
end of the Fronde—a young king and his brother setting, for Paris
as for London, the example and the impetus for their court. Samuel
Pepys's *Diary* bears witness to the extraordinary mixture, in the
London of Charles II, of a puritanical repugnance in principle for
the debauchery of French and Catholic origin and a greedy appetite
for whatever crumbs could be snatched from the revels.

After 1688, it is true, it required a touch of folly or, what comes
down to the same thing, a rare sense of sacrifice to remain Jacobite
and Catholic in England; otherwise one had to seek by this noble
means an alibi to emigrate to France and live resolutely *à la française*, either as a hero like the Duke of Berwick, the illegitimate son
of James II and Louis XIV's brilliant general during the War of the
Spanish Succession, or else as a parasite of the operetta court of
Saint-Germain, supported by subsidies from Versailles. At the end
of Louis XIV's reign and throughout the eighteenth century, Jaco-
bitism, at the extreme right of the immense rainbow of English nobility, though rich in extravagant characters, represented the
ultraviolet of eccentricity, a color that did not quite blend, though

striving to harmonize, with the subtler nuances of pale blue, yellow, and pink of the butterfly wings and peacock tails flaunted under Louis XV by Parisian polite society, so frivolous and so endearing.

THE FRENCH ARCHETYPE OF THE YOUNG GENTLEMAN

Of all the Franglais Catholic Jacobites who followed James II into exile, there was at least one who showed himself to be more French than any Frenchman, both by the purity of the language he wrote and spoke and by the naturalness (untouched by provincialism) with which he entered into the French form of "living nobly." Anthony Hamilton, born in an ancient Scottish family, would have the honor of being received by Sainte-Beuve in the sanctum sanctorum of writers who have known the supreme beauties of the best French style:

> Antoine Hamilton, one of the most Attic writers of our language, was neither more nor less than an Englishman of Scottish descent. Other foreigners—Horace Walpole, the Abbé Galiani, Baron Besenval, the Prince de Ligne—have been said to possess or to play wondrously with *l'esprit français*; but for Hamilton, the performance is at a level which no longer permits us to distinguish anything else in it: he is that esprit itself.[2]

Hamilton's masterpiece, the *Mémoires du Comte de Gramont*, published anonymously in 1713, offers a special case that shows how well the author knew he had transcended the language and even the mentality of his own nation. Breaking the first rule of the very French and very aristocratic genre of *mémoires*, which demands that such "narratives in the service of History" be written in the first person, Hamilton secedes from his narration to become the third-person interpreter of the hero whose exploits he is recounting—this hero, a

2. Sainte-Beuve, *Causeries du lundi*, Vol. 10 (1855), pp. 95–97.

Frenchman, being his own brother-in-law, the Comte de Gramont. This nobleman had died in 1707, though his twilight may have been somewhat brightened by reading the story of his young life, at the beginning of the reign of Charles II nearly half a century earlier. English nationality could not have been abdicated with more elegance and forbearance than was shown by Anthony Hamilton, in order to inhabit and animate more completely the style and personality of a French aristocrat, whom he successfully designates as the ideal type of the gentleman in that season of life when he is most himself: his youth. For Hamilton, the French character, or as Sainte-Beuve says, with a touch of intentional contumely, *l'esprit français*, is summarized and concentrated in this hero of "fine birth," the modern heir of the Athenian *kalos kagathos*, but regarded here as superior to his ancient predecessor. He is proposed as an incomparable example to the young noblemen of Europe: "I am writing a life," proclaims the anonymous and invisible narrator, "more extraordinary than all those that [Plutarch] has bequeathed us."[3] His intention had been realized: the *Mémoires du Comte de Gramont* was an immediate success, and remained one until the Revolution. Chamfort testifies that for the generation that undertook to liberate America and the one that greeted 1789 with enthusiasm, this book "was the breviary of the young nobility."

This is the second singularity of these *Mémoires*: violating another rule of the genre, which deems that there be no great attention paid to youth, and that the narrative should deal, essentially, with the role of the adult memoirist in public affairs, Hamilton concentrates his account on his hero's happy youth from adolescence to the threshold of adulthood, when he still bears the mere title of chevalier. He shows the French gentleman "in bloom," as the Japanese say of their young stars of Kabuki and Noh. Gravity and grandeur do not suit the fine flower of youth; the shadows of retirement and the progress toward death that characterize all seventeenth-century *mémoires* disappear completely from this Life concentrated on its

---

3. Anthony Hamilton, *Mémoires du Comte de Gramont* (Seuil, 1994), chapter 1.

prime. In the image of Hamilton's Gramont, the noble heroes of the Enlightenment, Richelieu and the Prince de Ligne, remain eternally young and *galant*, forswearing age and darkness.

Yet the *Mémoires du Comte de Gramont* is quite the contrary of the Spanish picaresque narratives (of which Lesage's *Gil Blas* is the modern version done in French). Several episodes of Gramont's life (his successes, but also his gambling misadventures, the rather grotesque situations into which his pursuit of the most redoubtable feminine prey involves him, the burle he and his friends delight in playing on fools and bumpkins, or that their own Leporellos play on them) might be literally transposed into the world of Charles Sorel's *Francion*, the great success of the Regency days of Marie de Médicis, when a young gentleman, libertine by definition, descends directly from the picaro. But though he could not have read Retz's *Mémoires*, published after 1715, Hamilton knows, like the brilliant cardinal, how to sustain vigorous comedy, broad drollery, and even downright parody that the Chevalier de Gramont ceaselessly skirts in the noble if not heroic register, and he is abetted here by the lively but supremely elegant language in which he writes and in which his young nobleman "in bloom" speaks and writes too, as well as his clan of young men as mad as he is to live joyously. It is this very delicate balance between "the inexhaustible fund of good humor and vivacity" that Gramont expends and the grace by which his historian and he himself avoid any collapse into the ridiculous, between the scabrous situations into which the young nobleman unhesitatingly flings himself and the imperceptibly ironic though complicitous reserve maintained by the narrator, that is responsible for the quasi-Mozartian charm (the Mozart of *Così fan tutte*) of these *Mémoires* of which Voltaire—more like Maintenon than one might suppose—could write: "Of all the books of this age, this is the one in which the slenderest matter is embellished with the gayest, the liveliest, and the most agreeable style."[4]

---

4. Voltaire, *Le Siècle de Louis XIV*, "List of the various writers who were published..." (article on Hamilton).

Certainly there were many other "characters" in France besides the one Anthony Hamilton chose to describe with such lively features: the young nobleman in the *furia* of his natural splendor and his pursuit of peacetime pleasures, in the intervals of a military career that is already heroic and glorious, and that the narrator assures us will be still more so. In his insistence on showing only one of his hero's two faces, the one turned toward his loves, Hamilton, in 1713, sounds the keynote of the age of *Don Giovanni*: "Glory in arms," he writes with little trace of Cornelian tonality, "is *at most* only half the brilliance that distinguishes a hero. Love must put the finishing touch on the contour of his character, by the temper and temerity of his enterprises and the glory of their successes. Of this we have examples not only in novels but in the true history of the most famous warriors and the most celebrated conquerors."[5]

But there was no other character, in the ancient realm of France, from *Petit Jehan de Saintré* to Sorel's *Francion*, who incarnated more faithfully the tour de force of a young freedom and audacity functioning, without ever violating them, among the severe and recent rules of court life and the conventions of an extremely old aristocracy, a military caste that had also become a leisure class. To such a degree that it is this type of modern Alcibiades, the Lauzun of the court of Louis XIV, the Maréchal de Richelieu of the court of Louis XV, and their Austro-Walloon rival the Prince de Ligne, all modeled on the Chevalier de Gramont, who best represented *l'esprit français* to a Europe of the eighteenth century snobbishly enamoured of this type of young stylish rakes. In order that no one overlook the fact that he is describing the fine flower of a nation, Hamilton infallibly reminds us in passing that his hero is the grandson of Diane d'Andoins, Comtesse de Gramont, one of the mistresses of young Henri de Navarre. Though not legitimated, he still can claim direct descent from Henri IV, the most French of all French kings, and revives under Louis XIV the fashion of being valiantly young that was set by *le Vert galant*, Henri IV's favorite (le-

---

5. Hamilton, *Mémoires du Comte de Gramont,* chapter 4.

gitimate) son, Gaston d'Orléans, and by his other but illegitimate son by Gabrielle d'Estrées, César de Vendôme. To the audacious and gracious freedom of any French gentleman of the old nobility, Gramont added the pride and audacity of a descendant of royal blood. His gaiety, his disdain for economy, his passion for gambling, his sumptuous expenditures, his appetite for *galant* intrigues, his charm and his gifts as a lover, his wit, his valor, and even his impalpable touch of cynicism are so many characteristics of nobility that his youth makes all the more evident and that sum up in a springtime renewed from generation to generation the ancient genius of the aristocracies of which France is the modern homeland, and of which the French court, at the beginning of each new reign, is the most consummate theater.

Even when Gramont is obliged to sojourn at the court of Turin, ruled by Madame Royale, Louis XIII's sister, or (in disgrace with Louis XIV, with whom he had not hesitated to dispute the favors of a court beauty) to seek exile in London, he revives, transposed to lesser planets, a terrain of cruder adventures, though rich in exotic and aristocratic beauties, in which his training as a young Parisian affords him obvious advantages. Yet it is at the court *à la française* of Charles II and the Duke of York, in the dense network of his many strategies of conquest, among so many lovely young English girls well armed to defend themselves and in addition frequently well guarded by vigilant husbands, that the Frenchman, setting an example for his young English peers, enchanting the king himself—a real cockerel in this poultry yard of young dukes and duchesses disconcerted by his grace—encounters the young lady who is his only true equal, with whom this bold and practiced libertine will fall in love, and who will become the Comtesse de Gramont: Elizabeth Hamilton, one of Anthony's sisters. The wedding, as in fairy tales, will take place only after the last moment of the season of amours, at a date later than that of the *Mémoires*. This vocation for true love, this perception of a partner worthy of his hand and responsive to his expectations, this marriage of reciprocal inclination between equals, even if it in no way commits either member to vulgar fidelity, illustrates

Gramont's typically heroic and French quality, the one husband among all the Englishmen of his rank and his generation spared by matrimonial failure.

The *Mémoires*, a portrait in motion of Gramont, contains a host of miniature likenesses. The only full-length portrait that figures in the book, as it will later be inscribed in its hero's heart, is that of his future wife, with whom he is from the very first passionately in love, though unrelenting, even so, in his incidental erotic pursuits:

> She had the loveliest waist, the loveliest bosom, and the loveliest arms in the world. She was tall, and graceful in her every gesture. She was the original everywoman copied in the choice of her wardrobe and the fashion of dressing her hair. Her smooth white forehead was always prominent, surrounded by abundant locks obedient to that natural arrangement so difficult to achieve. Her complexion boasted a certain freshness that borrowed colors could never imitate. Her eyes were not large, but they were exceptionally bright, and her glance signified whatever she desired. Her mouth was all that is agreeable, and the contour of her face quite perfect. A delicate and retroussé nose was not the least ornament of an altogether lovable countenance. All in all, by her attitude, by her bearing, by all the graces of her entire person, the Chevalier de Gramont had no doubt that there was every reason to form certain prejudices to the advantage of all the others that remained. Her mind was virtually the mirror of her face. It was not by those vivacities whose sallies are merely importunate that she sought a distinction in her conversation. Yet she avoided even more sedulously that affected deliberation in her words always so tiresome in its languor; yet without giving the impression of speaking rapidly, she said all that was to be said, and no more. She made every imaginable distinction between genuine brilliance and the false variety; and without constantly seeking to embellish her every remark with gems of wit, she was reserved yet remarkably accurate in her choice

of what to say. Her sentiments were noticeably noble, and when need be, exceptionally proud. Yet she was less conscious of her worth than is usual when one possesses so much. Constituted as just described, she could not fail to be loved: but far from seeking that circumstance, she was exceptionally particular about the merits of those who might pretend to any such action.[6]

Such was the Frenchwoman of choice who was predestined to become the Comtesse de Gramont and whom the chevalier made sure to single out and privilege. Anthony Hamilton spared none of the young London debutantes who swarmed around Charles II and the Duke of York, offering themselves as fashionably winsome models to the court painter Sir Peter Lely and as frequently consenting victims to their young gallants. For of all these English girls at court, Elizabeth Hamilton was the only beauty possessing *de l'esprit*: "That lady, Mme Warrenhall [a friend of Miss Hamilton] was what is rightly known as an English beauty, molded of lilies and roses, of milk and snow as to color; apparently the purest waxworks in arms and hands, bosom and feet, yet all of this without soul and without expression."[7]

When we stand under the dome of the marvelous Louis XVI–style museum dedicated in 1918 to the ruined town of Saint-Quentin by Michel David-Weill's grandfather, surrounded by the contents of the studio of the portrait painter Quentin de La Tour, we feel we have been transported to an eighteenth-century salon, surrounded by young, animated, smiling, lovable faces, a host of men and women lacking only the power of speech and all looking alike though each different, each singular, each as unique in life as Fayum portraits are in death. It is a little as if the archetypes of the Comte and the Comtesse de Gramont, having definitively posed in 1713 in Anthony Hamilton's *Mémoires*, had multiplied over three

---

6. Hamilton, *Mémoires du Comte de Gramont,* pp. 118–119.
7. Hamilton, *Mémoires du Comte de Gramont,* p. 281.

generations, spreading that spark that makes the men and women of esprit instantly recognizable among them. If we then turn our minds to that admirable series of portraits David painted between 1787 and 1792, including the sublime picture of the Lavoisier couple that today reigns at the top of the monumental staircase of New York's Metropolitan Museum of Art, the last garland of that French charm that had extended through the eighteenth century well beyond the nobility of court and town, we experience a shudder of horror: there is virtually not one of these handsome young people, so witty and so obviously created for happiness, who escaped beheading on the guillotine between 1792 and 1794.

A Jacobite Transformed into a Frenchman

Who was Anthony Hamilton? The author of the *Mémoires du Comte de Gramont* was born in 1646, into the large family of Sir George Hamilton, of ancient Scottish Catholic stock, and Mary Thurles, herself born to a great Irish Catholic family, the Ormonds. His eldest brother James, one of the English friends of the Chevalier de Gramont at the court of Charles II, was a gentleman of the bedchamber and colonel of a regiment of foot soldiers. He was killed during a battle with the Dutch in 1679, and his uncle the Duke of Ormond erected a monument to him in Westminster Abbey. His second brother, an even closer friend of Gramont's, had been a page to Charles II during his exile in France. Officer of the Horse Guards in London until 1667, he then entered the corps of "English *gendarmes*" insuring Louis XIV's personal safety, which raised him to the rank of field marshal and gave him the title of count. He was killed in the French ranks during the Battle of Saverne.

The young man had accompanied his second brother to France, and the latter frequently sent him to Ireland as a recruiting agent for their elite regiment. In 1681 he played the part of Zephyr in Philippe Quinault's ballet *Le Triomphe de l'amour*, performed before the king at the Château de Saint-Germain. Such, at the time, was the symbiosis between the French and English courts that this officer in the service of Louis XIV could be appointed governor of Limerick in Ireland by King James II in 1685. One of the new governor's first gestures was to attend mass publicly and officially.

He fought in the fierce military battle James II led against the swift rebellion of a large part of his realm, a struggle that continued for two years after William III was legitimated by Parliament. Hamilton was wounded at the siege of Ennenskilden and barely escaped massacre at the Battle of the Boyne on July 1, 1690, which definitively ended the reign of the last Stuart king, if not his hopes and his attempts to regain the throne.

After returning to France, Hamilton was attached, until his death in 1720, to the Stuart court in exile, to which Louis XIV had assigned as its residence one of his finest châteaux, that of Saint-Germain. Hamilton would be invited to the Duchesse du Maine's festivities in her own château that have remained famous under the name *Grandes nuits de Sceaux.* He was befriended by the Abbé de Chaulieu and the Marquis de La Fare, both Epicurean poets in the circle of the Duc de Vendôme, all of whom also frequented Sceaux where they could meet the very young Arouet, the future Voltaire.

Retiring from service, he devoted himself to the pleasures of poetry and the brilliant literature of improvisation in prose—tales, dialogues, humorous essays, maxims, and moral reflections—the only genre that the French aristocracy judged worthy of its leisure, its nonchalance, and the pleasures of society. The Comte de Caylus was already practicing this sort of language games at the same period with as much facility as would be shown at the century's end by the Prince de Ligne.

Hamilton's major literary enterprise, encouraged by Boileau in 1705, would be the apocryphal *Mémoires du Comte de Gramont*, which, frequently republished in France and in English translation, enjoyed a luxurious edition supervised by Horace Walpole at the press of his Strawberry Hill estate, gallantly dedicated to Mme du Deffand. Between 1749 and 1776, Hamilton's unpublished and posthumous works appeared in seven volumes in both Paris and London.

At Saint-Germain, Hamilton preferred to the impotent intrigues of this little court in exile the intimacy of the circle of the Duke of Berwick. He formed with the latter's sister-in-law Henrietta Bulkely, *la belle* Henriette, an affectionate and platonic liaison that cheered his final years and that he sustained by an assiduous commerce of letters and literary offerings. It was for her that he composed four contes, samples of a court genre fashionable at the time, which enjoyed a great public success when they were published in 1730, after circulating in manuscript among a company ravished by the author's talents. The court of Louis XIV held Hamilton's French style in high esteem. Even his trivial letters were read and discussed as if they had been those of Mme de Sévigné, and Dangeau had occasion to inform him, apropos of the encomia he had addressed to the Duke of Berwick and that the duke had shown to the king: "They cheered the very taste of every honest man in Marly."

Of grave temperament, anything but brilliant in conversation, reluctantly worldly, as different as possible from his brother-in-law Gramont whom he had made his hero, this bachelor became a very pious man in his later years, as was frequently the case with French and Catholic aristocracy. But nothing affords a clearer notion of his Atticism in the French language and the Epicureanism of his manners than the dialogue *On Pleasure* that follows.

The text is an elegant pastiche both of Plato (chronicler of the Athenian jeunesse dorée attracted to Socrates, such as Agathon, Phaedrus, and Alcibiades) and of Xenophon (memorialist of the young Cyrus). The theme of this dialogue is very closely related to that of the "Hussars" represented in the *Mémoires du Comte de Gramont* and of their adventurous pursuit of pleasure. At first sight we may be surprised that such a theme should be preferred by a Jacobite writer who had several times risked his life in battle for the cause of English Catholicism and his king.

Since the beginning of the sixteenth century, unanimous Protestant opinion—of Lutherans, Anglicans, and Calvinists—had associated the Roman Catholic religion and paganism, papist faith and

libertine conduct in a sort of Black Legend. Today, Catholicism itself, rigorist once again, is retrospectively outraged that such an un-
natural alliance of the Roman faith and the pleasures of society and
the arts should once have been possible. In the seventeenth and
eighteenth centuries, it seemed natural enough that there should be
several mansions in the house of the pope, of his Very Christian
Majesty, and of the Catholic Stuart kings.

If we can trace the Catholic Epicureanism of a literary figure such
as Hamilton back to a conciliating tradition of the High Renaissance,
one that originated with the Catholic humanist Lorenzo Valla, author of *De Voluptate* (1435), and that flourished in France in the
writings of Rabelais, Montaigne, and Gassendi, we must also take
into account, in order to understand the freedom of manners of the
Chevalier de Gramont and of his young English Catholic friends,
that the Roman Church of the period had the sense of both deco-
rum and suitability that took care not to demand too soon and too
suddenly of young officers on leave, and especially of those belonging
to a nobility of birth, the behavior of monks or graybeards. One of the
decisive moments in the *Mémoires du Comte de Gramont* is the chevalier's choice of a military life instead of the ecclesiastical one preferred by his mother. Such a choice once made (and approved by the
pious lady), the young man could and was entitled to behave with
the *furia francese* on the battlefield and as a thoroughbred on the
loose in civilian life. Evidently there was room in the Catholic society of the time, if not within the ranks of the Roman Church long
since open to younger sons of the hereditary nobility, for a youthful
form of *la vie noble* that ancient poetry and philosophy had once exalted to almost the same level as the life of a sage. Hamilton knew this
so well that he caused his hero to refuse the councils of wisdom and
prudence offered him in London by a "lay philosopher," the exiled
Frenchman Saint-Évremond: "to live nobly" for a young man would
be to live dangerously, joyously, generously, assuming all the risks of
such a choice. To be wise or devout would be no concern of his, at
least for the time being. Adulthood and old age deserve another
lifestyle.

Anthony Hamilton: *A Dialogue on Pleasure*

Yesterday the young men made their traditional sacrifice to Mercury; and truth to tell, it would be difficult to find anything more appealing than Athenian youth. The ceremony completed and the day being fine, most of them emerged from the city to take advantage of the leisure afforded by the festival and to divert themselves with country pleasures. They were still wearing the garlands that they kept on their heads the whole day, as they engaged in various sports and exercises on the banks of the Ilissus. The older youths had brought horses with them, to ride across the plain and display their skill to their juniors; these observed them at such equitation or played games of their own appropriate to their age. Of course there were lovers among them, for you must know what our laws permit; and I, though not a lover, happened to be there as well, I know not why. Agathon arrived, more glorious than the day itself, and so well made as to impel even the most indifferent to love him. He was followed by a great troop, all of whom, it seemed to me, were touched by his beauty, as could be easily seen from their behavior. Some did not move, but remained as if frozen where they stood, yet with glances so passionate that it was not difficult to see that they were more sensible of feelings than the rest who were excessive in their gestures and in their every action. I had occasion to notice the presence there of Corybants, and also of some priests of Bacchus; but what a difference in their frenzy from that which love inspires! Those infected with the latter passion reveal indeed wild eyes, terrible voices, and streaming locks in great disorder; yet the god of love causes them to seem only all the more appealing; he bestows upon eyes, as upon hearts, tenderness as well as vivacity; the sound of the human voice, when ruled by him, becomes extremely touching, and the soul's sentiments overlay each action with a sweetness and a grace no other divinity can inspire. All eyes were fixed upon this youth, and I cannot escape comparing him to Homer's Helen, whose charms overcame Priam himself. I followed him like the others, among whom there were many older than I. When I was close enough to this youth to hear what he was saying, I discovered that several young men of the troop, who seemed more

serious than the rest, implored him to repeat the words of his conversa-
tion with Aspasia on the subject of pleasure, a colloquy to which he had
many times referred. He awhile demurred, claiming some other occa-
sion to be more appropriate, and added with a smile that he had not
supposed them to be concerned with such important matters. Yet ulti-
mately he yielded, and the whole company having gathered around
him, he spoke these words with that felicity so natural to him:

"I am more than willing, my friends, to satisfy your curiosity, but I
fear I may do so only imperfectly, for it would require some time to
summon up Aspasia's very words; and you catch me unprepared. But
so you would have it, and I charge you to remember that I am yielding
to your desire. You know the role Aspasia plays in our government, by
the love she has inspired in Pericles; and you know as well that the
reputation of her merit and her mind has drawn to her some of the
greatest philosophers, including among others Anaxagoras; and So-
crates, who never speaks seriously, nevertheless admits that she has
instructed him in rhetoric. Hence you will not be surprised that her
words correspond to her learning, and that they far exceed the lan-
guage ordinarily heard on women's lips. One day, then, when I was
alone with her and had broached the subject of pleasure, because she
could not help awakening ideas on the subject, and because I have
learned from Socrates that one must speak to each individual of the
subjects in which that individual excels: 'Most men,' she said to me,
'know debauch rather than pleasure.'

'Indeed!' I replied, 'is pleasure then so different from what is found
in debauchery?'

'As white from black,' she said, 'and I believe you are a true volup-
tuary rather than a debauchee.'

'I beg of you, teach me to know myself, and to know what pleasure
is, as opposed to debauchery, so that when Socrates comes with his
questions, to prove to me that I do not know myself, I shall have weap-
ons with which to defend myself and shall be able to make him realize
that you have had more than one disciple.'

Aspasia could not keep from smiling, and taking up the conversa-
tion at this point, this is what she said: 'Nature has instilled in all

living things a certain desire to be happy; and it is this inclination that causes each creature to seek the pleasure appropriate to its being. Man, who participates in the divine essence and for whom, it is said, Prometheus stole fire from heaven—man alone knows how to enjoy pleasure by means of his mind and upon reflection; and it is this inclination of the mind, this reflection, that distinguishes pleasure from debauchery. The perfect man knows pleasure, but the man who, indulging his preferences, is no different from the beasts except by his figure, knows only debauchery, which is nothing but a transport derived entirely from impressions of the senses: reason, which has been bestowed upon us to distinguish us from all other animals, has no part in it; for reason has a flexibility of its own and can conform itself to the things that suit the nature of a wellborn soul, which is joined to the body only by fragile and delicate links. To speak precisely, it is only such characters who are lovable; all others are hardened and reveal no inclination for virtue or courtesy; hence they can never be said to experience true pleasure. But dare I, Agathon, speak of yet higher things, and dare I speak of them to you? I fear I forget myself, yet I may be pardoned if I forget myself with Agathon. You know Anaxagoras. On a certain occasion he was with me as you are with me now; most of the young men were serving in the army, and my room was filled with no society but that of philosophers. The conversation turned to serious subjects, and Anaxagoras began to speak, dogmatizing thus (perhaps contrary to his conviction): "Before the world began," he was taking a long view, "the elements were mingled, and matter formed what the ancient poets used to call chaos; then pleasure or love contributed to this chaos a certain warmth that is never without movement; and from movement," said he, "derive the order and the arrangement of the universe; each part of matter uniting with that which suited it and remaining in equilibrium with the neighboring bodies, according to the greatness of its volume," these are the terms I remember his using, "and man, as the most accomplished being of all, possesses the greater part of this universal fire, which in each particular body, as in the whole mass of matter, is the principle of life and of movement. This being who possessed the most was also the more nearly perfect, receiving more of that fire that generates the incli-

nation to pleasure." I interrupted his discourse as if I were qualified to do so. "Truly," said I, "I am glad you have acknowledged fire as the first principle of all things; for I have never understood those who claim that such a principle might be water, which is why I have never liked the beginning of one of Pindar's odes. And truly," I added, "not to mention the arts alone, but fine manners, vivacity, and all such things would be remote from us indeed if there were nothing but water in the composition of the world." 'And I am quite certain,' Aspasia said to me, 'that water would never have inspired you to write the fine tragedy that you read here recently and that ever since that occasion has invariably been referred to as the Flower of Agathon.'

I was so delighted, so absorbed by her discourse that, without being distracted by her flattery, I interrupted her: 'But Aspasia, have I not heard Socrates himself say that pleasure was the inception of every evil, because men let themselves be ensnared by it like fish by a baited hook?'

'It is quite true,' she replied, 'that the very inclination that tends all of us to pleasure has need of philosophy in order to be properly ordered; and that is the quality by which one recognizes an honest man, who by precise attention controls every action of his life, and always knows what he is doing. The others, on the contrary, wandering at random and with no other guide than the impressions of their preference, are constantly under the tyranny of one brutal passion or another. It is the manner of using pleasures that distinguishes the voluptuary from the debauchee.'

I broke in: 'Then it is the voluptuary who knows the art of using pleasures with delicacy and enjoying them with feeling? Give me some examples, Aspasia, of such a case, so that, no longer doubting the principle of the thing, I might know how to determine its consequences.'

'Most willingly,' said Aspasia, 'and where else shall we find such an example than in love, the one pleasure most capable of delicacy and grossness alike? He who indulges in love by an inclination that does not rely on discerning taste and refined sentiment is no true voluptuary but a debauchee. But he who loves the qualities of the soul more than those of the body; who strives to unite them, as much as it is

possible to do so, by a virtuous intercourse of wit and sentiment; who, following a tested program of gallantry, seeks only to enjoy a lovely body with a soul equally perfect—such an individual may be regarded as possessing a true taste for pleasure. Such a taste sweetens reason rather than weakening it, and preserves the dignity of human nature.'

'I see clearly now,' I told her, 'that we must pay no heed to our wise men who condemn all pleasures alike.' 'I daresay,' she answered, 'that such wise men lack a sufficiently distinct notion of pleasure, which they confuse with debauchery; for is not truth somehow the very pleasure of understanding? Poetry, music, painting, eloquence, sculpture—do not all these constitute the pleasures of the imagination? The same is true of exquisite wines, of delicious dishes, of all that can delight the taste without spoiling the temperament. Provided reason can maintain its empire, all is permitted, and provided a man does not cease to be man, each action is just and praiseworthy, since vice exists only in disorder....One can be a philosopher and yet sacrifice to the Graces; and cannot these goddesses, without whose intervention love itself fails to please, come to terms with wisdom? I have always found that an inclination for lovable things refines conduct, makes for good manners and honesty, and prepares the way for virtue, which, like love, can exist only in a sensitive and tender nature.'

And that, my friends, was Aspasia's discourse, by which I am entirely convinced. Since that day, I have no longer been of the same opinion as those philosophers who maintain that pleasure and debauchery are merely two names for the same thing. But such men are only too fond of us, and abandon their sanctuaries for us only too frequently. And whatever they may say, their actions convince me, ultimately, that they are not far from sharing Aspasia's sentiments."[8]

8. *Oeuvres diverses d'Antoine Hamilton, en vers et en prose* (A. A. Renouard, 1813), pp. 1–8.

3. An English Cicero in the France of Louis XIV: Henry St John, Viscount Bolingbroke

A RECENT BOOK by Bernard Cottret, *Bolingbroke: Exil et écriture au siècle des Lumières* (Bolingbroke: Exile and Writing in the Century of the Enlightenment),[1] is the first in a long while, in the French language, to draw attention to this singular eighteenth-century figure, detested by English bigotry, forgotten by French frivolity, misunderstood or caricatured by the historical or ideological conventions that manacle the Age of Enlightenment. Manifestly it will take further efforts to interest French readers in the one English statesman and political philosopher who enjoyed, in his lifetime, a greater prestige in France than in his own country. The enormous French bibliography devoted to the "origins" of the revolution of 1789 and to the movement of ideas that prepared its advent has no entry for Bolingbroke. It is true that he was the leader of the Tory Party. It is also true that he enjoyed himself greatly in the country of Louis XV. This is unpardonable in the France of our times, but has not kept American historians, on the heels of English historiography, from studying what drew the attention of the Founding Fathers, notably Jefferson, to the thought and action of this "enlightened" conservative.

Bolingbroke managed to transform his political failure into an enduring message. This message (and the key words he introduced into the political vocabulary, notably "patriot" and "patriotism") is, to say the least, ambiguous: British and American historians still fiercely dispute its meaning. One would like to know how it was

---

1. Paris: Klincksieck, 1992.

understood in eighteenth-century France. Cottret's book is not enlightening on this point. This Tory statesman, who briefly supported the Stuart restoration, nonetheless (the better to oppose his Whig adversaries) played his part in the revolution of 1688 and espoused certain aspects of Locke's thought. Furthermore, his system of "patriotism," outside England, could accommodate itself to a radical and even Jacobin interpretation.

And yet, Jacobite or Hanoverian, under the sinuosities of a political ideology making tactical concessions to the philosophes on the other side of the Channel, Bolingbroke still remains a conservative viscerally attached to his idea of England: for him this was an obvious fact dictated by his own nature and by the jurisprudence of the ages. Burke, who fiercely opposed the viscount's posthumous influence over George III and the new Tory generation, was in many respects inspired by his views on historical jurisprudence, a stage of natural law, when he wrote in high passion his *Reflections on the Revolution in France* in 1790.

In her novel *Orlando*, Virginia Woolf describes the transition from Elizabethan England to Puritan and Cromwellian England as a sudden change of climate. We shift (a little as, in Gibbon, we shift from the Roman Empire to a Christian and barbarian Europe) from sun-drenched seasons to a perpetual foggy and rainy November, from a "Merry England"—young, ardent, violent, generous, bright-colored—to a severe Albion old before its time, wearing mourning, hypocritical, calculating, moralizing, already Victorian. With every fiber of his being, Henry St John belonged to the England of Henry V, of Falstaff, and to the reign of Elizabeth that he regarded as exemplary. This magnificent, heroically built descendant of an aristocratic landed family, highly endowed for the sports of his caste (love, venery, stag hunting), and even more highly endowed, if possible, for speech, friendship, and wit, never concealed his desire to combat the "corruption" of his nation's "genius" and to restore its "liberty."

Like Shakespeare's Henry V, he was in his youth a great debauchee, a great drinker and smoker. All his English biographers call him a "rake"; none fails to refer to Congreve's naughty comedies in order to avoid specifying his turpitudes in detail. He made his Grand Tour on the Continent in 1698–1699, remaining a long while in Paris, where he made the French language his own to an astonishing degree. In 1700 he made a marriage of convenience with a rich heiress of his own circle who adored him, bored him, and endured with dignity the perpetual public scandal of his debauchery. That same year he entered the House of Commons, occupying the seat that had already been his father's and grandfather's, that of the family district of Wooton-Basset, in Wiltshire. His improvisational genius as a political orator was immediately recognized in his crushing responses to the still-faltering speeches of the man who was already his sworn enemy and who would become, under the first two Hanover Georges, the master of England for twenty years: Robert Walpole. In 1700 St John was the rising star of the Tories, Walpole that of the Whigs.

At the age of twenty-three in 1704, Bolingbroke became secretary of war in Robert Harley's Tory government under Queen Anne, the last Stuart monarch to rule England. The War of the Spanish Succession was raging on all fronts. Marlborough, commander in chief of the English and Allied troops on the Continent, formed a close friendship with his young minister. In 1707, the Harley cabinet was forced to give way to a Whig government led by Walpole. St John retired from the Commons to his meditations and studies, obeying an alternation between philosophical retreat (pleasures included) and political combat that henceforth governed his life. Exile would allow him to plumb the depths of his opposition to Walpole.

In 1710 Queen Anne recalled Harley, who this time made St John his secretary of state, thereby restoring his seat in the House of Commons: his brief lightninglike career had begun.

English opinion (notably the landed electorate, which saw in war and its cost its own eventual ruin as well as the immediate fortune of the City) inclined toward peace, even a separate peace with France. St John and his friends acted unhesitatingly in this direction. They launched a journal, *The Examiner*, to accompany their action, and the formidable talent of Jonathan Swift (an early ally of St John) supported them with his pamphlets. In November, the Duchess of Marlborough was dismissed from the queen's entourage. Though an increasingly violent jealousy divided Harley and St John, peace negotiations with France—represented by the chaplain of the Catholic embassies in London, the Abbé Gaultier—were secretly commenced by the Tory minister, with the consent of the queen and of her favorite, the Jacobite Lady Masham. Louis XIV and Torcy also strongly favored a separate peace, and offered proposals of compromise through Gaultier. Marlborough, dismissed from command, was replaced by the Duke of Ormond, also a Jacobite. An English negotiator was appointed and left for Paris: the poet Matthew Prior, one of the brilliant men of letters St John always attracted to himself. On September 27, a preliminary peace treaty was signed, its commercial clauses favoring England concealed from the Dutch and Austrian allies. The latter, after a fit of indignation, were obliged to join the peace conference held at Utrecht beginning in January 1711. At the same moment the Tory-majority Parliament chose to stand in judgment on the previous government, and Robert Walpole, convicted of corruption, was stripped of his seat and imprisoned in the Tower of London: Bolingbroke would never cease hammering the word "corruption" against Walpole and his regime.

By now the revelation of the link between the extension of the war and the enrichment of the Whigs, highlighted by the virulent pamphlets of St John's friends Swift and Arbuthnot, succeeded in inflaming public opinion in favor of peace. The last difficulties (raised by the dauphin's death in 1711 and the Duc de Bourgogne's in 1712, which left no obstacle other than a sickly child to the accession of Philip V of Spain to the throne of France) were resolved by an agreement between St John and Torcy. Ormond received secret orders to restrict military operations, and the Allied troops ceased receiving payment from the English treasury. Denain's French victory on July 27 saved face for Louis XIV and intimidated England's allies.

At the beginning of August the queen created St John Viscount Bolingbroke. He had hoped for a less modest title and suspected Harley (named Earl of Oxford in 1711) of having intrigued against him. "My promotion," he let it be known, "is a mortification." That same month he reached Paris, accompanied by Matthew Prior and the Abbé Gaultier. He was received as head of state by Louis XIV and the French court at Fontainebleau. Entertained later in Paris, he sampled, after Matthew Prior, the charms of Mme de Tencin and her sister, Mme de Ferriol, who was to remain his faithful friend and correspondent for the rest of his life. At the Opéra he found himself sitting not far from James III, the Stuart Pretender (with whom he was suspected of already engaging in negotiations).

This enthusiastic French reception was no help to him in London. Harley temporarily confined the remaining arrangements to Lord Darmouth, another Tory minister. But it was up to Bolingbroke to complete the edifice he had so skillfully begun. Despite new difficulties between London and Paris, the treaty was at last officially signed on April 1, 1713. The emperor abstained. Louis XIV and Torcy had every reason to congratulate themselves on this relatively favorable conclusion to the war, which could have turned into a total disaster for the realm if the Allies, remaining united, had pressed their advantages.

The Whigs never forgave Bolingbroke for his policy of appeasement with France or for the precautions he took, in the tormented months that saw Robert Harley's disgrace and preceded the death of Queen Anne on August 1, 1714, to attempt to assure, with Louis XIV's support, a Stuart succession. Having reached London in time, the elector of Hanover, heir to the throne according to the rules of the "Protestant succession" established in 1688, took the name of George I, was crowned at Westminster, and immediately afterward saw to the election of a Whig Parliament. Having become George I's private counselor in 1714, Robert Walpole was named prime minister in 1721. The hour of Whig vengeance and of Walpole's long reign had arrived. The authors of the Treaty of Utrecht were immediately arraigned before the House of Commons. Bolingbroke chose to escape to France, while Parliament stripped him, as well as the Duke of Ormond, of all his citizen's rights and his rank as a peer of the realm. By going into exile he believed, perhaps correctly, that he had just escaped the scaffold.

Warmly received in Paris, Bolingbroke reassured Lord Stair, ambassador of the Hanoverian regime, but Louis XIV was still alive, and the chances of a Stuart restoration, supported by Torcy and the king of France, were not negligible. The negotiator of the Treaty of Utrecht met the Pretender at Commercy and agreed to become his secretary of state. He received the title of earl, which Queen Anne had denied him. But on September 1 Louis XIV died. The regent was determined not to disturb Franco-English relations. Under these worse than unfavorable conditions, and unknown to his "ministers," the Pretender decided to provoke an uprising in Scotland, which failed lamentably, and Bolingbroke was blamed. This brought to an end his Jacobite phase, which moreover, like Chateaubriand's legitimism subsequently, was an attachment to a principle without the faintest illusion as to its incarnation. The son of James II, even more than his father and yet less than his own heirs, was a political cripple. The little court with which he had surrounded himself was grotesque. The consequent blundering left Bolingbroke out in the cold, and the label of conspirator stuck. Walpole would never cease to use it against him.

France smiled at the shipwreck and came to the rescue, which assumed the features of an adorable widow, Marie-Claire Deschamps de Marcilly, Marquise de Villette. A companion of the Comtesse de Caylus at Saint-Cyr, she and her friend had triumphed (the king was in the audience) performing roles in Racine's *Esther*. Having married a graybeard uncle of Mme de Caylus—the Marquis de Villette, a first cousin of Mme de Maintenon—Marie-Claire had been a widow for nine years. Was it at Mme de Caylus's or at Mme de Ferriol's that Bolingbroke first met Mme de Villette? In any case, it was love at first sight for both parties. This highborn, lovely, good-humored, and vivacious Frenchwoman, endowed with all the intellectual graces so often lacking in Englishwomen of her caste, became permanently attached to the former "rake," devoting to him a tender and admiring affection that his fits of ill-humor, drunkenness, and subsequent sensual relapses never managed to alter. With the marquise, whom he married in 1719 (his first wife, abandoned in England, had died a few months earlier), Bolingbroke recovered his rank in society as well as a home life and was able to resume with peace of mind and heart the reflections and readings he had initiated in the years 1707–1709.

After 1720, the couple took up residence in the Château de La Source near Orléans, overlooking an immense landscape of which the ornament and the name was that generous spring, the source of the Loiret. Bolingbroke often visited Ablon, where he owned a small residence, and from here he could easily reach Paris to participate as an honored guest in the meetings of the Club de l'Entresol founded by the Abbé Alary, his friend and his initiator into French internal affairs; this private academy of political sciences was frequented by Montesquieu. Robert Shackleton, biographer of the great Bordelais magistrate, has carefully measured the debt that the future author of *L'Esprit des lois* owed the English statesman, whose profound experience of the affairs of his own country and of Europe was increasingly illuminated by historical intelligence, the achievements of modern philosophy, and his literary talent and taste.

At La Source, Bolingbroke regularly received Lévêque de Pouilly, who published a monthly journal, *L'Europe savante*, and who along with the Abbé Alary contributed to the theoretical development of the viscount's political experience, to which the exile assiduously applied himself. The prestige of the "English Cicero," as eloquent and elegant as he was erudite, now became universal in France, increasing still further after the resumption of Bolingbroke's combat with Walpole on English soil. In 1752, the *Journal britannique* would publish in translation this judgment of Lord Orrery's, which corresponded to the general sentiments of the French elite: "His passions calmed with age and with certain reversals of fortune; whereupon more serious studies and reflections further refined his faculties; in his retreat he brilliantly distinguished himself with a special luster that escaped vulgar attention. The libertine politician became a philosopher equal to those of antiquity. The wisdom of Socrates, the dignity and the grace of Pliny, the wit and finesse of Horace, all were equally legible in his writings and his conversation." Indeed Bolingbroke incarnated, like Alexander Pope, England's Augustan Age, that temperate preface to a neoclassical France that, in its case, turned to blood.

The young Voltaire, who had excellent antennae, visited La Source in December 1722, and read *La Henriade* to Lord and Lady Bolingbroke. He was dazzled by the master of the house: "I must give you some notion," he wrote from Blois to Thiériot,

> how delighted I was with my journey to La Source, and with Milord Bolingbroke and Mme de Villette. In this illustrious Englishman I found all the erudition of his country, and all the politesse of our own. I have never heard our language spoken with more energy and *justesse*. This man, who all his life has plunged so deeply into pleasures as well as politics, has nonetheless found the means to learn everything and, what is more, to remember everything. He knows the history of the ancient Egyptians like that of England, possesses Virgil as well as Milton, loves English, French, and Italian poetry, but loves them differently, for he perfectly discerns the different genius of each.

Voltaire saw Bolingbroke again at Ablon, from which he wrote to Mme de Bernières in May 1723: "I believe I am already a hundred leagues from Paris. Milord Bolingbroke has made me forget both Henri IV and *Mariamne* [title of the tragedy he is writing] and actors and booksellers into the bargain." As late as 1754 he wrote to d'Argental apropos of Bolingbroke's recently published *Works*: "The English seem created to teach us how to think." Indeed, the master-to-disciple tone Bolingbroke adopted at the beginning of his correspondence with the young poet reveals the extent (but also the limits) of his influence over the young philosophe:

Your imagination [he wrote to Voltaire] is an inexhaustible source of the finest and most various ideas. Everyone grants you this, indulge it to your heart's content. But restrain yourself when it comes to correcting your works or determining your conduct. Do not permit your imagination to enter the realm of judgment. The two make poor yoke-fellows; as Montaigne might have put it: they do not walk apace. Indeed there is something more to be said. Imagination is bestowed by Nature, which does not include the power to acquire Judgment. The former requires only Nature, the latter needs to be formed. And that is what is difficult to do, if you do not begin early on. Each year it becomes more difficult, and after a certain number of years it becomes impossible to raise judgment to a certain degree of strength and to a certain point of precision. It is true that you have more than enough such years ahead of you. But do not be fooled into thinking you have time to lose. Nature has given you a great gift. Make haste to make it function properly for you.

In 1726, Voltaire met Bolingbroke again, that time in England: somewhat rehabilitated, the leader of the Tory Party had taken up arms once more against Walpole, though he could not regain his seat in the House of Lords. Relations between the French writer and the English statesman cooled. Voltaire's *Lettres anglaises*, which extensively mythologized England, do not reflect the reality of the struggle in which Bolingbroke and Walpole were opposing champions. In 1731, however, Voltaire paid homage to Bolingbroke's political heroism by dedicating his tragedy *Brutus* to the viscount.

Installed with his French wife at Dawley, near Uxbridge, in 1725, Bolingbroke, having remained in constant correspondence with Swift and become the friend as well as the mentor of Pope (he would provide the philosophical canvas for the latter's *Essay on Man*), was now in a position to be the soul of opposition to Walpole. He figured as the educator of a new generation of Tories. He founded a periodical, *The Craftsman*, of which he was the editor in chief and in which he criticized with biting irony the domestic and foreign policies of George II's government. In 1737, a French translation of these "editorials" on English policy was published in Amsterdam. The leaders of French diplomacy and politics, Chavigny, Bussy, and Silhouette, read these analyses carefully. In 1749, the work Bolingbroke had written in 1738 for the opposition to George II and Walpole was also translated and published in France (*Lettres sur l'esprit du patriotisme, sur l'idée d'un roi patriote, et sur l'état des parties qui divisaient l'Angleterre lors de l'avènement de George Ier*).

In 1736, exasperated at not having been restored to the House of Lords and weary of conducting a fruitless battle, Bolingbroke returned to France. The couple took up residence at Chanteloup, in Touraine (the future retreat of Choiseul in his disgrace), then at the Château d'Argeville, on the banks of the Seine, between Montereau and Fontainebleau. Here Bolingbroke continued his meditations and indirectly, by correspondence, his action within the Tory Party, still in the minority despite Walpole's disgrace. In 1743 he moved with his wife to the family castle of Battersea, on the Thames: his father's death, the year before, had finally made him its possessor. Once again the young talents of the opposition gathered around him.

It was here, and not at Chanteloup, that Marie-Claire de Marcilly, Lady Bolingbroke, died in March 1750, leaving her husband overcome. He shortly followed her into the family tomb in December 1751.

Very much the grand seigneur, Bolingbrook had always disdained to publish his writings. His *Craftsman* articles appeared pseudonymously. His treatise on *le roi patriote* (destined for Crown Prince Frederick) was initially published in a limited and confidential edition, without being avowed as his, and in a version "revised" by Pope. It is the only one of his texts that, under constraint, Bolingbroke was obliged to publish himself in order to refute piratical interpolations. Yet he did not abandon Pope in his last illness but mourned him in tears. He angrily discovered the "treasonous translation" by his friend only after Pope's death in 1744.

Published by his secretary David Mallet, Bolingbroke's *Works*, in five volumes, appeared posthumously in 1754. The deism and anticlericalism of his views with regard to history and religious philosophy revolted the Anglican clergy and alienated official criticism in France. These views and his analyses of European history (Tory classics, later celebrated by Disraeli) remained misunderstood in France; it was generally concluded that Bolingbroke's prestige had depended only on his magnetic personality, his eloquence, and his conversation.

Henry Mansfield's fine book *Statesmanship and Party Government: Bolingbroke and Burke*,[2] Isaac Cramnick's studies, H. T. Dickinson's biography,[3] and a subtle article by Quentin Skinner (among a rich secondary literature) afford a better understanding of how Bolingbroke's philosophy, adjusted to the English embattled forum, could be misinterpreted in absolutist France.

As a great reader of Montaigne and the ancients, Bolingbroke rejected the modern notion, shared by Hobbes and Locke, of the contractual basis of society and civil laws, which saves men from a state of nature incompatible with their survival and contrary to their individual interests. For Bolingbroke, civil society had emerged without a break from the first natural society: the family. Natural law (an expression of divine Providence) and their own natural tendency incline men to sociability. War within families and between nations (aggregates of families) appears only with a strictly political society. If it consolidates such a society, it is something of an afterthought. Such is the basis of Bolingbroke's Tory conservatism, the "patriotism" he recommended to his king, along with confessional tolerance (natural religion has no knowledge of the conflicts nourished by arbitrary theological constructions). The natural condition, the "genius" of the English nation, the "free" political form it has assumed since the Middle Ages (here again Bolingbroke separates

---

2. University of Chicago Press, 1965.

3. London, Constable, 1970.

himself from the moderns who situate that political origin in 1688), and the long historical jurisprudence of the British people required a royal prerogative based on, and organizing, a broad consent.

The fact remains that in order to erase his Jacobite taint and the better to confound with their own principles the Whigs, who claimed to be the sole legitimate heirs of 1688, this "enlightened" conservative retained much from the moderns (Machiavelli, Hobbes, and especially Locke); thereby he contributed to favoring a radical interpretation of the English model in the France of Louis XIV. Detached from its British context, stripped of its semantic iridescences, the paradox of Bolingbroke, who attacked bipartisan regimes, who advised a "patriot king" to entrust government only to "virtuous" statesmen, and who at the same time was the first to elaborate the theory (and practice) of a systematic opposition aimed at purging the country of the "corruption" of power, readily lent itself in France to justifying an initially revolutionary, subsequently totalitarian Jacobinism.

Bolingbroke's works and the essentials of his correspondence were written in splendid English prose. But the English statesman also left a number of letters in French that attest to a no less splendid ease in our language. These were published in 1808 by General de Grimoard, from whose edition I here reproduce three.

To Mme de Ferriol

London, December 17–26, 1725
We have returned from our exertions in Bath. My own health is adequate for a man who has few desires: that of the marquise is not, it seems to me, entirely satisfactory, yet she is incomparably better than she was last year.

You are right: I take a very warm interest in the young Breton; and regardless of what my housekeeper [Mlle Aïssé, a pretty Circassian girl ransomed by the brother-in-law of Mme de Ferriol and brought up by her] will say, I beg you to regard him as a child of whose mother and father I am very fond.

What you report of Voltaire and his projects is entirely within his character, and altogether probable: what he himself tells me is quite the contrary. I shall answer him shortly, affording him his inveterate satisfaction of supposing me his dupe because of a handful of rhetoric.

I have no interest whatever in hiring the cook who applied to M. le Chevalier de Rochepierre: he is not a bad cook, though far from being half as good as he imagines, and besides he is mad. What I want is a fellow who has some taste, the first principles of his trade, and a certain docility; I shall do the rest, and make his fortune into the bargain if he will put himself in my hands.

The paragraph about wine in your letter pleases me the more, since this year it will be surprisingly scarce, and I fear that most of our gentlemen will be reduced to punch. God preserve us from the wicked influences of such a decoction.

The failure of M. de Fontenelle's speech[4] is hardly a surprise to me. I have often thought he is quite a lot like Law in some respects: they are both intelligent men, in their different ways; they are not geniuses. Yet pride and self-satisfaction have made them propound quite shamelessly what an authentic genius would attempt only with trepidation. Instead of respectfully following in the footsteps of their great predecessors, they have ventured to present themselves as originals. The project has not succeeded: the tinsel of the one has had no more currency than the other's paper: others have shown themselves to be impertinent frauds, the dupes of their own systems. Kindly permit me, my dear Madame, humbly to kiss your hands and to use what paper remains to send a note to my friend d'Argental.

To M. d'Argental (Mme de Ferriol's son)

Let us speak first of all, my respectable magistrate, of the object of our loves, from whom I have just received a letter whereof you provided the

---

4. See, in *Recueil des harangues de l'Académie française*, vol. IV, p. 402, Fontenelle's speech on the Provençal poets, in response to La Visclède's speech in honor of the adoption of the Marseille Académie by the Académie Française, November 12, 1725.

occasion, and I thank you for that. Seeing you, she remembers me; and I am terribly afraid that seeing me, she does not remember you. Alas! seeing the Sarmatian [nickname for Mlle Aïssé's lover, the Chevalier d'Aydie, because he had been in Poland, known to the ancients as Sarmatia], she remembers neither of us. Can you imagine any good reason for such a thing? Do give her my tenderest compliments. I shall have the honor of answering her at the very first opportunity.

Continue, if you please, to concern yourself with the matter of La Source, and let me know the situation there. Farewell, my dear councillor, I care for you with all my heart.

A thousand compliments to M. your brother [Pont de Veyle, Mme de Ferriol's younger son]. I adore my charming housekeeper [Mlle Aïssé]: send me the news of her heart; in your presence it overflows.

To the Abbé Alary

June 25, 1723

I have no liking for apologies, nor any need for them. I have preferred a long exile to an equivocal return; but everything is equivocal for the ignorant, ill-informed as to the facts, and for the weak-minded, who cannot judge even when informed. If there were any question of going into detail about what has occurred the last few years, I should write a book: a letter would not suffice; but here, my dear friend, is an answer to close the mouth of any man who has not renounced reason and a certain natural impartiality: I served the late queen until her death, nor do I believe I can be reproached for having been remiss in anything I owed her. Since that time, I have served the interests of the Knight of St. George [the designation by which the pretender to the English throne, James III, was known], and on any occasion chosen by those who accuse me of having failed to honor such interests, I am prepared to account for the manner in which I assumed them and the manner in which I discharged them. For the time being, I request you to say in my behalf, to those who utter the slander you have mentioned to me, that if they can advance a single proven fact to justify any of such accusations, I shall confess myself guilty of all that the iniquity of some and the imbecility of others have spread abroad. After which declaration, those who can offer no such facts accompanied by proofs must hold their tongues or be scorned as calumniators.

4. The French Achilles of the Hapsburgs: Eugène, Prince of Savoy-Carignan

NAPOLEON held Prince Eugène to be one of history's seven greatest military leaders; the other six were Alexander, Hannibal, Julius Caesar, Gustav Adolph, Turenne, and Frederick the Great. The emperor still believed in a Homeric world kept alive in the European imagination by the eighteenth century's great literary dispute, the quarrel between the ancients and the moderns, which focused on the *Iliad*. Prince Eugène and Bonaparte claimed the same mythic ancestor from that epic: Achilles. Just as Alexander conquered Persia with the *Iliad* under his pillow, Bonaparte brought with him to Egypt a copy of Ossian, the Celtic *Iliad*. What did General Colin Powell read on the frontiers of Iraq and Kuwait, at the head of his electronic and atomic arsenal?

Frederick the Great considered Prince Eugène his model and his master, referring to him as the Atlas of the Hapsburg monarchy and the true Germanic emperor. Voltaire, in *Le Siècle de Louis XIV*, which he completed in Potsdam, credited Eugène with having rivaled the greatness of his own hero in bringing the Ottoman power to its knees. Today the prince's equestrian statue stands in the heart of Vienna, his palaces are among the most admired and frequently visited in the Austrian capital, and his collections of drawings and prints constitute the glory of the Albertina.

THE SON OF A WITCH

Born in Paris on October 18, 1663, son of Eugène-Maurice de Savoie-

Carignan, Comte de Soissons, and the flamboyant Olympia Mancini, one of Cardinal Mazarin's nieces, the prince was raised in the Hôtel de Soissons built for Catherine de Médicis. His mother was considered one of the brightest planets in Louis XIV's Parisian galaxy (Saint-Simon went so far as to call her "the center of all the court's gallantry, intrigue, and ambition"). From all appearances, this child ought to have enjoyed a great career in the Sun King's France. How was it, then, that he became, by the beginning of the eighteenth century, the most redoubtable adversary of the Great King, who narrowly escaped the same disaster that Eugène's victories inflicted on the Great Turk?

The Comtesse de Soisson's brilliant position at court had dimmed after her husband's death in 1673. In January 1680, she was compromised in the Affair of the Poisons and suspected of shortening her husband's life and attempting to do the same to her king's. Louis XIV granted her a choice: voluntary exile or the Bastille followed by an ignominious trial. The comtesse left France for Brussels and never returned, abandoning her children, the sixteen-year-old Eugène among them, in a stripped mansion in the care of their grandmother Marie de Bourbon, Princesse de Carignan.

The young prince, negligently brought up, had been extremely attached to his mother. The debauchery in which the comtesse had lived had been passed on to her son as well as to several of her daughters. To spare Achilles the death awaiting him at Troy, Thetis had hidden her son in drag among the daughters of Lycomedes, on the island of Skyros; the future Atlas of the Hapsburg dynasty, adopted under his mother's eyes by a wild troop of playboys including the famous Abbé de Choisy, who, in perpetual drag, played the part, painted and bejeweled, of "Madame l'Ancienne" among these gay blades. Eugène suffered only the more deeply from his mother's departure, aggravated as it was by the woefully scandalous and humiliating circumstances of her disgrace. Louvois, in order to encourage the sorceress to decamp more promptly, had organized a hue and cry of insults that went on for three days in front of the Hôtel de Soissons. And all the way to the Belgian frontier the comtesse's carriage was assailed by an infuriated populace. In Brussels, as she was leaving her first Sunday mass, she was greeted by a chorus of screeching cats tied together by their tails. To emerge from such an abyss, the young prince would require a will of iron. Misfortune forged that instrument.

Louis XIV occasionally took notice of this stocky adolescent whose enormous nose, buck teeth, and stiff shock of dirty hair made him quite hideous. The king decided to make an ecclesiastic out of him, had him tonsured and put into a soutane, and never referred to him except as "the little abbé."

And no Ulysses came to rescue this young Achilles from Skyros; he left of his own accord. Determined to embrace a military career, he imposed a harsh discipline on himself to strengthen his body, studied mathematics under an excellent master, Joseph Sauveur, and plunged into military literature. His pillow book became Quintus Curtius's *Life of Alexander the Great*. After three years of secret training, in February 1683 he persuaded his cousin Armand de Conti, nephew of the Grand Condé and Louis XIV's son-in-law, to present him to the king in order to enter his armed services. The king received him and faced the insolent little abbé with a scornful rejection that admitted of no further consideration. In his eyes, this dwarf was "a man incapable of anything" but being a priest. From that day a new Hannibal, Eugène of Savoy swore vengeance on Rome: he would leave France and never return unless armed for the kill. At least that was the resolve quite plausibly attributed to him by the Prince de Ligne in the apocryphal *Mémoires du Prince Eugène écrits par lui-même*, which he published in Paris in 1810.

VIENNA PRESERVED: THE SECOND BATTLE OF POITIERS

At the news that one of his brothers, an officer in the Austrian army, had been killed in battle against the Turks, Eugène convinced his friend Armand de Conti to head for the eastern frontier, both of them in drag. They set out the night of July 26, 1683. Despite a general mobilization on the French frontiers and the alert given to all French diplomats, the two young men managed to escape discovery and arrest until they reached Frankfurt. Subjected to the severest pressure, the Grand Condé's nephew returned to Paris, leaving his friend some money and a valuable ring that would enable him to continue on his way. Presented to Emperor Leopold, who had taken refuge at Passau, Eugène was immediately allowed to take the oath and enter the service of the imperial army, by definition multiethnic and multiconfessional. French by tongue, training, and tastes, Eugène had no less Hapsburg blood in his veins; by his great-grandmother the Infanta Catherine, daughter of Philip II of Spain, he was a descendant of Charles V. Louis XIV had left him a glorious future in this direction alone.

It was a tragic hour. Under the eyes of an anguished Europe, Vienna, already besieged in the previous century by Suleiman the Magnificent, was once again in the talons of the Great Turk, of whom Louis XIV—in order to weaken the rival Hapsburg dynasty, and despite Christendom's higher interests—was the loyal ally. More than a hundred thousand men, under the orders of the grand vizier enthroned among his sumptuous *smalah*, encircled the capital of the Holy Roman Empire where morale was at its lowest ebb. The emperor and the court had taken flight. The grand vizier temporized, waiting for a surrender that would avert the sack of the city and leave all the booty in his own hands. Profiting by this unhoped-for delay, the king of Poland, John Sobieski, had had time to form a European army that advanced toward Vienna and on September 12, 1683, after attending an open-air high mass at Leopoldsberg, victoriously attacked the Turkish camp. Vienna was saved, and Europe breathed again. Louis XIV concealed his chagrin. French amnesia, even in republican guise, has remained loyal to that chagrin ever since.

Eugène's conduct during the battle, the first in which he took part, had been so brilliant that the emperor promised him a command, which he obtained the following winter. It was with the rank of colonel that he participated in the successful offensives of the imperial armies in the direction of Budapest, which was liberated in 1686. A crusading enthusiasm and the brotherhood of European arms attracted to the Austro-Turkish frontier two Lorraine princes, Commercy and Vaudémont, the young Turenne, Eugène's cousin and Armand de Conti's brother, as well as the Marquis de Fitzjames, illegitimate son of James II and the future Duke of Berwick. The Neapolitan Marquis Antonio Carafa received command of the imperial armies in Hungary. Commercy became Eugène's inseparable comrade and perished at his side, a modern Patroclus, at the Battle of Luzzara in 1702. Their cousin and mutual friend the Duc de Vendôme commanded the French army they were fighting against.

Since 1685 the little prince had been promoted to the rank of major general. In February 1687, during the army's winter recess, Venice offered the ostentation of its carnival and the charms of its women to the conquering heroes' repose. Eugène was present at the rendezvous, but the Venetian ladies were disappointed. Austria soon nicknamed him "Mars without Venus."

That spring he set off on a campaign on the Turkish front. During the battle that concluded with the capture of Belgrade, on September 6, 1685, Eugène was seriously wounded, but recovered many months later, in 1689.

First Arms Against Louis XIV and Victory over the Turk

The time had come for him to bring his quarrel with the king of France to a closer encounter. During the autumn of 1688, in order to weaken Emperor Leopold, victorious in the east on a different front, Louis XIV had ordered the invasion of the Palatinate without a declaration of war. The England of the Glorious Revolution, the Low Countries, and the Empire were obliged to form a Grand Alliance to contain him. Prince Eugène, in agreement with the leader of the coalition, William III of England, vainly attempted to convince the emperor to make peace with the sultan in order to turn all his forces against France. However, he succeeded in bringing the Duke of Savoy into the Grand Alliance, which Spain had also joined. Hence all Europe was in league against the rogue state, but in this instance that state was the Kingdom of France, in possession of a magnificent army, a considerable navy, and human and financial resources regarded as inexhaustible.

The multiplicity and the frequent incompetence of the various armies' leadership and strategic routines, and the poor discipline of ill-paid or unpaid troops, incited Eugène to propose a general reform. Despite opposition from the Austrian general staff and the imperial court, he eventually managed to reach the emperor, who, impressed by his zeal and intelligence, named him field marshal, one of the highest ranks in the army. He was not yet thirty. Yet it was by the efforts of William III and his diplomacy of unity that the Allies were able to obtain a peace somewhat unfavorable to France, signed at Ryswick in September 1697.

The year after Ryswick, in order to respond to a new Turkish offensive supported by French subsidies, Eugène was named supreme commander of the imperial army. Some weeks later, in mid-September, he defeated the Ottomans in a crushing victory at Zenta, which inaugurated the definitive decline of Turkish power in Europe and incited Louis XIV to sue for peace. Crossing the Croatian mountains, Eugène then laid siege to the Turkish city of Sarajevo; when one of his emissaries to the city was killed, he ordered it to be assaulted, sacked, and burned to the ground. He returned to Vienna as a conqueror during the winter. Two years later, on January 26, 1699, the Sublime Porte signed at Carlowitz a humiliating treaty with the Christian powers: Austria, Venice, Poland, and Russia. The Achilles of the Hapsburgs could now build in Vienna his Winter Palace, designed by the great architect Fischer von Erlach, and on a hill southwest of the city, designed by Johann von Hildebrandt, the two palaces and gardens of the Belvedere. A collector's passion filled what appeared to be the void of his affective life.

EUGÈNE AND MARLBOROUGH, CONQUERORS OF BLENHEIM

The War of the Spanish Succession began as soon as Louis XIV accepted Charles II's will declaring Philippe d'Anjou, his grandson by the late Queen Maria Theresa, heir to the crown of the Spanish Hapsburgs. The Emperor had his own candidate, the Archduke Charles.

This "first world war" finally offered Prince Eugène his opportunity to get the best of the king of France. Named president of the war council in 1703, Eugène, as supreme commander of the imperial armies, could now impose his reforms and conceive a global strategy capable of defeating Louis XIV's attempt to make the other Hapsburg empire—that of Spain, including the Milanese lands, the Catholic Low Countries, and the American colonies—a client of the Kingdom of France and his auxiliary in the subjection of the Holy Roman Empire.

During the winter of 1701–1702, a second Grand Alliance among England, Holland, Austria, and most of the principalities of the Empire (except Cologne and Bavaria, allies of France) united its forces on several fronts to frustrate the Great King's intentions. On the Italian front, Eugène had successively defeated the marshals successively dispatched by Versailles: Catinat, Villars, and even Vendôme, his own cousin and a childhood friend. But the condition of his troops did not allow him to achieve a decisive victory. Once he was given supreme authority by Vienna, he had simultaneously to correct the troops' financing and morale and also to combat a serious Hungarian rebellion that was weakening the Empire from within, at the moment when Franco-Bavarian troops were threatening to invade Austria.

On the English side, another great figure of political and military history, the Duke of Marlborough, had vigorously taken in hand the operations against Louis XIV. It was clear that Austria risked collapse if the England of Queen Anne, successor of her brother-in-law William III, did not powerfully intervene in Central Europe. That intervention implied a close cooperation between London and Vienna. Wratislaw, the emperor's ambassador in London, managed to achieve it; Eugène supported him without reservations. In May 1704, Marlborough, by means of forced marches, his English troops strengthened by Danish, Dutch, and German reinforcements, crossed Holland and Germany, leaving doubts as to his eventual direction, and at last suddenly headed for the Danube.

Eugène arrived ahead of his English colleague at Mandelsheim on the Neckar, where they congratulated each other and concerted their aims: a "brotherhood of arms," of which Churchill has written that it had no equivalent in military history, was lastingly established between the two commanders. Yet the contrast between the two men was remarkable. Marlborough was imposing, serene, distant, but extremely civil. Eugène astonished everyone by his diminutive stature and his ugliness, yet a repressed rage, an austere uniform and lifestyle, and a cold and frequently cutting determination, in action giving way to a veritable heroic frenzy, made him beloved of the military.

The tactic this pair devised to prevent the concentration of the Franco-Bavarian troops and to create the conditions of a decisive battle to free Austria from their threat functioned to perfection. On August 13, 1704, the Allied army (52,000 men) found itself face-to-face at Blenheim, on the left bank of the Danube, with the troops (56,000 men) of the Maréchaux Tallard and Marsin. The great French army was defeated and Tallard taken prisoner. Eugène and Marlborough personally participated in the fighting.

Blenheim, like the raising of the siege of Vienna, has nothing to say to French memory. For English and German historians, it is one of the greatest dates in European history, the Waterloo of the eighteenth century. In both cases, Europe made France realize it could not claim to be both the arbiter and the arbitrary tyrant of Europe. English policy has made the most of this obstinate error, shared by Louis XIV and Napoleon I.

From the Battle of Blenheim, Winston Churchill, Marlborough's descendant and biographer, dates the hegemony of England and of the English model in Europe and above all, by a supreme irony, in France. A grateful English government granted Marlborough, on land near Woodstock, the gigantic castle and park of Blenheim, of which the plan and the grounds recall the battle order of August 13, 1704.

Indeed Eugène of Savoy, at the head of the imperial and Dutch troops fighting side by side with Marlborough's English soldiers, shared equally in the victory's merits. That was how the matter was judged by continental Europe. As Marlborough's biographer, Churchill adopted this point of view, which prepared him to engage the double-headed Anglo-American alliance in time of war.

Conclusion of the "First World War"

Sir Winston, wherever he happened to be between 1939 and 1945, religiously celebrated the anniversary of the Battle of Blenheim as he did in peacetime, *en famille* and *au château*. Throughout World War II he was ceaselessly sustained by the precedents of the War of the Spanish Succession, by its vicissitudes, the psychology of its strategies, its diplomacy, and the popularity of the two heroes of whom he had become the Homeric celebrant, before himself imitating one of the pair.

In 1704 a humiliated Louis XIV was far from considering himself defeated. Eugène, after Blenheim, proposed marching with Marlborough on Versailles itself. Rákóczi's rebellion in Hungary and the military promenade of the Duc de Vendôme, the Duc d'Orléans, and the Maréchaux Marsin and La Feuillade in Italy, two cruel thorns in Austria's flanks, kept him from doing so. Forced to command the imperial counteroffensive in Lombardy and Piedmont, he benefited from a financial transfer arranged by Marlborough and the City, an indispensable injection of cash to reaffirm the morale and the firepower of his troops, which were unpaid, underequipped, and numerically inferior to the French army. His name alone made Versailles tremble and his strategy continually surprised the French military leaders. All of this led him to a crushing victory before Turin on September 7, 1706, after which the emperor appointed him governor of Milan. He negotiated with the French for their evacuation of Italy on March 6, 1707, instead of crushing them: a grave chivalrous error, according to Sir Winston.

Nonetheless everything seemed to favor the invasion of France from the south, though it was delayed by the appearance from the north of an unexpected and redoubtable adversary: the king of Sweden, Charles XII, conqueror of both Peter the Great and Augustus of Saxony, king of Poland, who seemed determined to cross swords with the new Holy Roman Emperor, Joseph I. Again it fell to Marlborough, as skillful a diplomat as he was a great strategist, to disengage Austria by persuading Charles XII to turn against the tsar. Eugène managed to march on Toulon, then under the supposed protection of an English fleet. The city was a fortress à la Vauban, defended by a garrison of 30,000 men under the command of Maréchal de Tessé. The assault was begun, gains were made, but the city remained impregnable, and Eugène, enraged by the English admiral's incompetence, was obliged to sound the retreat. He took his revenge by seizing Susa on his return to Italy.

His happy cooperation with Marlborough was resumed when the emperor sent him to the Flemish front. In Brussels he once again visited his mother, who died a few weeks later, unregretted by her son, according to Saint-Simon. Never, since his initial flight from France, had he been closer to Versailles. The army he had reunited with that of Sir Winston's ancestor blocked the invasion of the Duc de Vendôme's French forces at Oudenarde and thoroughly routed them on July 11, 1708. A landing in the Somme was envisaged by Marlborough, strongly approved in retrospect by his modern Homer. Eugène preferred to seize Lille and proceed to Paris from there. The town of Lille surrendered, then its citadel on December 9, 1708; Ghent and Bruges had been wrested from the French before winter, but Paris and Versailles remained out of reach. During the most terrible winter in French history, Louis XIV resigned himself to negotiating. The Allies' conditions proved so draconian that he appealed publicly to the nation's pride and, confident of its solidarity, refused point-blank. The bloody Battle of Malplaquet on September 11, 1709, which gave the advantage to the French armies led by the Maréchaux de Villars and de Boufflers, proved his strategy to have been correct.

The surrender of Lille had nonetheless given rise to one of those chivalrous gestures between grands seigneurs that even in the eighteenth century compensated for the horrors of war. Boufflers, who was in command of the citadel and had negotiated its honorable surrender, invited his conquerors, Eugène and his general staff, to dinner. The prince requested the same menu that the besieged had been obliged to endure, and was therefore served roast horse.

In April 1710 serious peace negotiations began at Gertruydenburg, in Utrecht. The luck of the Great King would have it that the Whig "falcons" who supported Marlborough were obliged to hand the government over to Tory "doves," who immediately, supported by public opinion and the talent of Jonathan Swift, broached the (secret) conditions of a separate peace with the king of France. At that very moment, the death of Joseph I mobilized Eugène against an eventual Franco-Bavarian attempt on Vienna, and the Austrian candidate to the Spanish succession, Archduke Charles, was elected emperor. From the virtual Charles III of Spain he suddenly became the real Charles VI of the Holy Roman Empire. One of the chief war goals of the Grand Alliance disappeared.

The new emperor, in an attempt to save the coalition, sent Eugène to London. Publicly acclaimed a hero in January 1712, he found Marlborough in disgrace. Swift became the interpreter of Queen Anne's hostile sentiments, as well as those of the new government, in a thundering pamphlet: *The Conduct of the Allies*. The little prince was never to have his ultimate revenge upon Louis XIV.

His attempts to resume the assault on France, with Dutch support, were sabotaged by Marlborough's successor, the Duke of Ormond, and on the Rhine he found in Villars an adversary capable of scattering his own troops, deprived of the English war mettle. In the emperor's name, Eugène was obliged, in his turn, to enter into peace negotiations with the French marshal. The Treaty of Rastadt, signed on March 6, 1714, concluded a war already half-extinguished by the signing, the year before, of the Treaty of Utrecht between England, France, and the Protestant Low Countries. With considerable elegance Eugène took part in this compromise, which deprived him of a full revenge. With Villars as his intermediary, he informed Louis XIV that he "embraced his knees," that he sincerely regretted all he had been obliged to undertake against France, and that on this occasion of peace, a time of clemency, he took the liberty of begging the king to receive the assurance of his deep respect. By the same means, Louis informed the prince that he congratulated him, as one of the emperor's subjects, on having done his duty.

OTIUM CUM DIGNITATE

After a final campaign against the Sublime Porte in 1716–1718, concluded by a military triumph that definitively liberated Belgrade, Serbia, Bosnia, and Wallachia, Eugène, who was just over fifty, was virtually obliged to retire. In peacetime he would become a considerable encumbrance of the Viennese court. Since imperial Rome, this has been is the classic political fate of the hero who dares survive his victories and who puts the reigning prince in the shade. Corneille staged such a figure in his last masterpiece, *Suréna*. The old Viennese families powerful in the Hofburg, notably the Schönborns, hated Eugène. The emperor feared him. Intrigues to get rid of him multiplied.

He withstood them in his palaces, gathering a little court around himself, ornamented chiefly by Countess Batthiany. Lady Mary Wortley Montague, visiting Vienna in 1717, spoke enigmatically of Eugène as "Hercules in Omphale's lair" without clarifying her meaning.

As a matter of fact, this quite un-Viennese "court" had all the features of a Parisian *compagnie*. The philosopher Leibniz and the poet Jean-Baptiste Rousseau (banished from France in 1712) found hospitality there. Eugène tried in vain to profit by Leibniz's presence in Vienna to create an academy like the ones founded by Colbert in 1666 and later by Frederick II in Berlin. Pierre-Jean Mariette, incontestably the greatest connoisseur of prints and drawings of all time, spent two years at the Belvedere (1717–1718) classifying Eugène's collection, which had mostly been purchased in Paris, at the shop of the Mariettes, father and son, in the rue Saint-Jacques. Cardinal Alessandro Albani, an eighteenth-century version of Bernard Berenson, was also one of the prince's guests.

Eugène had thus become, in a rather philistine capital, the Mitteleuropa equivalent (all things considered) of what the banker Pierre Crozat had become in Paris: a generous Maecenas of the arts and a formidable collector. He employed the two greatest Austrian architects, one for each of his buildings. An enthusiast of botany, he personally cultivated his gardens (with the help of French masters of this art) and embellished them with many rare plants. In their midst he built a zoo that he filled with wild animals imported from remote countries.

In France, he had his correspondents and his merchants; in Holland and Italy, his painters. The Venetian Giuseppe Maria Crespi and the Neapolitan Francesco Solimena were the chief beneficiaries of his commissions and his favor. Of the four hundred paintings he collected, many were attributed to the greatest Italian old masters, including several masterpieces, though most were "school of." His connoisseurship was more acute with regard to Flemish and Dutch painting. Moreover, in 1717 he bought from the future Maréchal de Belle-Isle, through the intermediary of Mariette, the famous bronze statue by Lysippus, *A Child at Prayer*, which Foucquet had purchased in Rome on the advice of Le Brun to embellish the Château de Vaux.

His fabulous library of five thousand printed books bound by master craftsmen such as Étienne Boyer, brought from Paris for the purpose, and thirty-seven precious manuscripts was more fortunate than his collection of paintings; today it is treasured in the National

Library of Vienna, where a sumptuous baroque jewel case was constructed for it under Fischer von Erlach's dome. The son of Olympia Mancini was, after all, the grandnephew of Cardinal Mazarin, and he benefited from the friendly advice of another great ecclesiastical bibliophile and art connoisseur, the future Cardinal Domenico Passionei, papal nuncio at Vienna.

Eugène died at home at the age of seventy-two on April 21, 1736. The two previous years he had retained sufficient energy to serve the Hapsburgs well, during the War of the Polish Succession and, as usual, against French armies. It was said that at the hour of his death, at three in the morning, the lion in the Belvedere zoo, which the prince had enjoyed feeding with his own hands, gave signs of restlessness, wakened, and roared.

Eugène spoke and wrote only in French; he had mastered Italian but knew no English or even German, which obliged him to resort to secretaries and interpreters. By a paradox quite characteristic of French Europe, this fanatic enemy of Louis XIV's policies and military ambitions was the best ambassador of Parisian aristocratic civilization at the very heart of the baroque Holy Roman Empire. Lacking an edition of Eugène's French correspondence, I shall quote two fragments from volume II of Winston Churchill's *Marlborough: His Life and Times.*

To the Duke of Savoy, during the Bavarian campaign of 1703

To draw a true picture of Marlborough: here is a man of high quality, courageous, extremely well-disposed, and with a keen desire to achieve something, all the more as he would be ruined in England should he return empty-handed. With all these qualities he understands thoroughly that one cannot become a general in a day, and he is diffident about himself. General Goor, who was killed in the Donauwörth affair, was the kind of man on whom he leaned, and he is a grave loss at this juncture, being a man of courage and capacity, who by all accounts brought about the attack that evening, sure that to wait for the next morning, as most of them wanted, would have been to waste half the infantry without succeeding. I have been made conscious of the death of this man by seeing the duke, according to the news, more than a little hesitating in his decisions.

They have been counting on the Elector coming to terms. They claim of course that no time has been lost over that; nevertheless since the action nothing has been done, although the enemy so far has let them have all the time they wanted. They have amused themselves with the siege of Rain and burning a few villages instead of, according to my ideas, which I have put before them plainly enough, marching straight upon the enemy. If unable to attack him, take up a position, encamp half an hour away from him, and by their being so superior in cavalry in an open country, cut his communications with Augsburg and Bavaria and stop him from foraging; it being certain that he has no supplies in Augsburg and would have been obliged to quit that post. Then there would be the time to exploit the retreat and pursue the enemy so closely that he would not have been able to avoid a battle. It was even in their power to prevent his junction with Tallard, who is already near Villingen and has delayed there longer than I can explain.... But to put things plainly, Your Royal Highness, I don't like this slowness on our side, the enemy will have time to form magazines of food and forage, and all our operations will become the harder.

To the Duke of Marlborough, during the Danube campaign in 1704

Camp of Münster, two hours from Donauwörth,
August 10, 1704

Monsieur,
The enemy has advanced. Without a doubt the entire army will cross the Danube at Laüingen. They have driven a lieutenant colonel I sent to reconnoiter as far as Höchstetten. The Tillingen plain is full of soldiers. I have held fast here all day, but with eighteen battalions I dare not risk remaining tonight. Yet I leave with much regret, occupying a good position that, if captured by the enemy, we shall have great difficulty recovering. Tonight, therefore, I am sending the infantry, as well

as a portion of the cavalry to a camp I have marked on the map near Donavert. I shall remain here as long as I can with the cavalry that has arrived from the camp of V.E. and those dragoons I have here. As soon as the first portion of your infantry arrives, I shall order mine to advance again, if the enemy has not occupied the position. Everything depends, Milord, on the diligence with which you get your forces moving in order to join mine tomorrow; otherwise I fear it will be too late. Furthermore, the entire army is involved. The enemy has left at least twelve battalions at Augsburg with Lieutenant Chamarante. Even as I write, word has come that indeed the whole army has crossed. So there is not a moment to lose, and I believe we may risk an advance by crossing the Lek and the Danube—which shortens the maneuver a good deal, and there is a better road. I await an answer, Milord, to determine what I must do. Everything depends on our not allowing ourselves to be trapped between these mountains and the Danube.

5. Lelio and Marivaux

IN 1697, Louis XIV ordered his police lieutenant to close the Hôtel de Bourgogne in the rue Mauconseil, where the Italian theater
had flourished since 1680. In this gesture the Princesse Palatine saw
the effect of the ostentatious piety that Mme de Maintenon had
made the rule of the reign. It was claimed for the public that the
Italians had performed a play entitled *La Fausse Prude*, and that
this female Tartuffe had deeply offended the king's morganatic
spouse. This theater, which had constituted the court's joy and the
city's delight, was more likely the simultaneous victim of the terrible bishop Bossuet, who would have liked to close every theater, and
of the anti-Italian and anti-ultramontane nationalism that soured
Louis XIV's Gallican doctrine: the poor Italians put paid to all the
theaters of Paris because they were the most talented and the most
successful. Since Henri III, troupes of Italian comedians, almost
without interruption, had succeeded one another from generation
to generation in Paris and at court, infusing France with the irony,
fantasy, corporeal skills, and springs of human action proper to one
of the most original inventions of the Italian Renaissance: commedia dell'arte. Since the sixteenth century, the Italy of Shakespeare
and the Spain of Lope de Vega, as subsequently the France of the
young Corneille, had received the lay gospel of the boards from these
same missionaries of capers, lazzi, and irony. Molière had shared the
playhouse of the Palais-Royal with the troupe of Domenico Biancolelli (known for playing Arlecchino) and had retained many of
their *scenarii*, performance techniques, and poetic inventions. The
Comédie-Française, which claimed to follow the example of Moli-

ère, was to the latter what Le Brun's painting academy had been to Poussin, whose teachings it too claimed to perpetuate: severed from the Mediterranean *estro*, the *comédiens-français*, like the academician painters, gradually assumed the pomposity of all the official arts of the north. In 1697 "everyone" at court as in Paris was inconsolable at having lost that irreplaceable "remedy for the vapors" (said the Princesse Palatine). Claude Gillot and Claude Audran III made their careers and fortunes as artists with drawings and paintings that represented the vanished *illusion comique* of the Pulcinellas and the Zannis. Marketplace and fairground theaters drew crowds by plagiarizing their *scenarii* and imitating Arlecchino. It was in the Parisian wake of the Italian theater that the young Watteau's genius ripened as the portraitist of *comédiens* and the painter of *fêtes galantes*.

One of the regent's first gestures, after arranging for the Parlement to quash Louis XIV's testament, was to ask the Duke of Modena, traditional Maecenas of the best commedia dell'arte troupes, to send him the best he had. This was in the tradition of French kings since the Valois. The regent, a great reader of Rabelais and eager to restore to his countrymen the mirth and merriment of the "splendid sixteenth century," opportunely recalled their source. The duke sent him the troupe of Luigi Riccoboni (known as Lelio, a figure he was famous for playing onstage). By May 1716 the troupe was in Paris, performing for the regent, who reopened the theater in the Hôtel de Bourgogne, faithful to the liberal tastes of his mother, the Princesse Palatine. Lelio—brought up on the boards—was surrounded and supported by distinguished comedians: in this profession (which rigorists accused of public prostitution), one is tempted to say "in this tribe," endogamy was the rule, and sons succeeded fathers as daughters mothers, rather in the fashion of the Japanese Noh and Kabuki troupes. Lelio's second wife, Elena Baletti (known as Flaminia), competed onstage with her sister-in-law Zanetta Benozzi (known as Silvia), the wife of Antonio Balletti (known as Mario). The son of Domenico Biancolelli, Molière's friend, had inherited from his father the Bolognese tradition of Arlecchino. All these actors were well read and frequently poets as well as virtuosi of performances that always included singing and dancing. This was the secret of commedia dell'arte: each actor was a complete artist who invented for herself or himself the ever-growing text of the role she or he interpreted, in intimate cooperation with all the others during rehearsals as well as onstage *all'improviso*: as a sort of guyline, they had a summary scenario conceived by one member of the troupe. This was quite different from the French arrangement, a literary theater in which the performers interpreted a text composed in advance by a writer-dramaturge. In Paris, in order to overcome the language barrier, and despite the expressive vigor of their stage business, the Italian comedians had found themselves obliged since 1680 to appeal to professional French writers—Regnard, Dufresny—or to generous amateurs who enjoyed such a task and produced for them fully developed *scenarii* in French. These the comedians could learn by heart and perform with their strong Italian accents. Such *scenarii*, which we know from Gherardi's *Recueil*, published in Paris in 1700, were faithful to the commonplaces of the commedia dell'arte but already corrupted its vital principle: the actor as poet.

Lelio's troupe, when it arrived in Paris in 1716, already had an Italian history. Luigi Riccoboni, devout and much concerned with respectability, had sought the assistance of famous Italian men of letters who, daunted by French literary pride, were ashamed of their commedia dell'arte and wanted to prove that the Italian stage, too, had its Corneille and Racine.

So Lelio and Flaminia had exhumed certain dramatic texts from the Renaissance, such as Trissino's *Sophonisba* and Tasso's *Torrismonda*; they had also created onstage the tragedy *Merope*, composed by the famous Veronese scholar and antiquarian Scipione Maffei. The Italian public failed to respond, finding these academic representations tedious. Concurrently, Italian men of letters exchanged dissertations on Maffei's *Merope*, which Voltaire would shamelessly pillage for his tragedy of the same name, performed at the Comédie-Française.

Convinced nonetheless that the future and dignity of the Italian theater called for a literary reformation on the French model, Lelio was not at all interested in reviving the *all'improviso* tradition interrupted by Louis XIV in 1697. On the contrary, he sought to liberate himself from it. The French public, for its part, wished to recover its Italians. Lelio found it easy to ask certain French authors to compose texts to be performed by Italian speakers. But now these authors were writing comedies *à la française*, quite detached from the tradition of the *scenarii dell'arte*. However, a miracle occurred: the encounter of this Italian troupe in search of French authors with ... Marivaux.

Marivaux had no fondness for Molière and still less for the tradition of the Comédie-Française, which looked back to Molière. A friend of Fontenelle's (Corneille's nephew), his genius allied him to the emotional intelligence of the author of *La Place royale* and to the (profound) preciosity of La Fontaine's *Amours de Psyché*. Rather than in Lelio, who dreamed of finding a new Molière for Italians, Marivaux discovered among his troupe the poetic and interpretative talents that offered body and soul to what he had hitherto sought in vain: the coincidence of contraries, lyricism and irony, life and dream, the magic sweetness of love and the harshness of reality as calculated by vanity. Silvia (Zanetta Benozzi), born in 1700 to a family of comedians, became the feminine incarnation of Marivaux's poetic ideal. Casanova, who knew the actress well, gives us the portrait of a *femme d'esprit*:

> She had an elegant figure, a noble expression, delightful manners, being affable, cheerful, clever in conversation, and without any kind of pretension. Her countenance was an enigma, for it inspired a lively interest, pleasing everyone she met, yet despite this, upon examination, it did not possess a single good feature; no one could call her beautiful, yet no one could have confessed to finding her ugly.... There has never been an actress to take her place, for such a creature would have to unite in herself all the qualities Silvia possessed in the difficult art of the theater: action, voice, physiognomy, bearing,

and a great knowledge of the human heart. All her virtues were those of nature, and the art that perfected it was always hidden.

In the series of fixed types of which an Italian troupe consisted, she played what was then called the *seconde amoureuse*, frequently partnering her husband, Mario, the *second amoureux*. The *scenarii* of Italian comedy played off the idealism and aristocratic elegance of these lovers against the grimacing greed of the hypocrites, pedants, and doctors and the naiveté or cynicism of the servants. This last group was well represented in Lelio's troupe by the Arlecchino type, sometimes played by Domenico Biancolelli, sometimes by Tomasso-Antonio Vicentini, called Tomassino. According to the wisdom of commedia, reality mocks the naive youth of the ideal, and the ideal reveals the crude manipulations of superannuated reality. Silvia and Arlecchino are the two poles of this general irony. Marivaux grafted onto this poetics of the stage (which Corneille had already acclimated to French in his *Illusion comique*) all the resources of a language sharpened by the analyses of the French moralists and by his own explorations of the hide-and-seek of mind, heart, and body. The French tradition of the *Roman de la rose* finds new life in its alliance with the robust tradition of commedia dell'arte undergoing a century of French naturalization. Starting on October 17, 1720 —the date of the premiere of *Arlequin poli par l'amour*—Marivaux gave the Italians a series of masterpieces whose success was disturbed or retarded in vain by his enemies' cabal. After 1724 he alternated the production of his plays with the Comédie-Française, for which he wrote *La Seconde Surprise de l'amour* and *L'Île de la raison*.

Voltaire detested Marivaux. The author of the *Lettres anglaises* represents, much better than Molière, French common sense and its frequently low ceiling. Riccoboni never regarded Marivaux as anything more than one of his theater's occasional collaborators. He, like several of his comrades, wrote comedies and imperturbably pursued the scheme of wresting Molière away from the Comédie-

Française in order to turn him into the model of a reformed Italian theater. In 1730 he published in Paris his *Histoire du théâtre italien*, in which he attacks the shamelessness, vulgarity, and futility of the lazzi of his ancestors, as Goldoni would do subsequently. In 1736 he published his *Observations sur la comédie, et sur le genie de Molière*, in which he produces a theory of comedy *à la française*. It is from this essay (in which Riccoboni takes the occasion to remind the French, and notably the *comédiens-français*, of all that Molière the dramaturge owes to the—rarely published—*scenarii* of the Italian comedians) that I have selected the pages that follow.

Far from revealing in Molière (the performer) the métier of the commedia dell'arte, Riccoboni seeks to elevate the commedia to the level of Molière (the dramaturge). An increasingly vigorous current of contemporary research, chiefly in Italy, has had to exert an immense effort of archaeology and erudition to revise the insipid and humiliated vision of the commedia that Riccoboni bequeathed to us in his labors as historian and critic published in French and that therefore enjoyed, in the eighteenth and nineteenth centuries, a largely uncontested international authority. In the pages cited below, where he raises the characters of Molière's comedies to a dramaturgical norm, Riccoboni implicitly sees them as an advance over the types of Italian comedy. The latter differ from the characters *à la française* in that they are metamorphic, even while outwardly retaining the same features and sometimes the same mask. The character (in Molière, as in La Bruyère) is closed, *sibi constat*. The commedia dell'arte type is open. The former draws a social and moral stereotype inscribed within a plot logically constructed to set it in a certain relief; the latter postulates a poetic site, generator of a free fantasy that is as much verbal as it is gestural. The best twentieth-century theater, from Gordon Craig to Peter Brook, from Stanislavsky to Grotowski, is an effort of reminiscence, parallel to that of the best contemporary theater historians, to restore to the actor the poetic and inventive plenitude of the comedians of the old Italian theater, before the destructive "reforms" of Riccoboni in Paris and

Goldoni in Venice. For eighteenth-century Paris had become a laboratory where two stage traditions, the French and the Italian, pursued a fruitful creative dialogue, begun by Corneille and Molière in the preceding century. Marivaux, seconded by Silvia and by Arlecchino, invented the dialogue of mind and heart that Lelio, obsessed by Molière's great shadow, failed to recognize in his own theater as his century's most poetic invention.

CHARACTERS TO BE USED IN THE THEATER

Not all characters are suitable for use on the stage. Simple or leading characters must always be preferred, for they are more striking, and more capable of theatrical action, whereas accessory characters hardly ever furnish the substance necessary to a plot. I call a simple or leading character one who, without sharing qualities with any other and without borrowing qualities from any other, can sustain the action of a play by his own agency; and I call an accessory character one who emanates from another and who, in order to sustain his existence, requires assistance from some other character. The Miser *is a leading character, who furnishes abundant matter for a five-act play; but if we were to stage the* Householder, *a character accessory to the* Miser, *we should find that such matter would not be sufficient, nor even as theatrical, as that of the* Miser.*

Every passion has its degrees, and for this reason every character is either leading or accessory: sympathy *and* friendship *are characteristics accessory to* love, *as* suspicion *and* defiance *are accessory to* jealousy; *yet all these degrees of character, and others like them, cannot furnish matter suitable for comedy. Moreover some of those characteristics I have called accessory may sometimes be unsuitable to form a theatrical character because instead of being a passion or a vice in society, they are regarded as a virtue or a merit: such, for example are* economy *with regard to* avarice, *and* friendship *with regard to* love. *Hence what I have said should apply only to those* accessory *characteristics that are defects in society, such as* suspicion *and* defiance, *and not to* sympathy *or* friendship. *From which we may conclude that the passions and the vices are more suitable to the stage, since even as they afford the means of correcting manners, they still present us with the ridiculous extremes of those passions.*

It is not sufficient to have selected a suitable character, what is more important is to treat it appropriately. In order to succeed in this instance, I believe it is essential not to oppose such a character to any other character capable of sharing the audience's interest and attention. We had proof of this in a comedy lately put on at the Théâtre Français and composed by an author whose merit is generally acknowledged; one of the personages of this comedy, whose character is blunt and familiar, drew the audience's attention and deprived the leading character of the sympathy and applause that had been appropriately given at the beginning of the play. The dominant character in the plot was obliged to yield, and the crude jokes of the Tax Collector *almost entirely eclipsed the subtle and delicate features of the* Fop: *from that point on, the chief object of the play became, so to speak, a mere episode, and this character conceived solely to serve as a contrast to the* Fop *prevailed to such a degree, and was so well received by the public, that it was almost entirely due to the* Tax Collector *that the play scored its brilliant success.*

I make no claim, however, to exclude all characters of ordinary strength, and to condemn their connection with the leading character, but only to assert that the latter must so dominate and prevail over the other characters that the public is never beguiled by the effect or the action they might exert to the leading character's detriment.

From all I have just said, it must not be concluded that there cannot be comedies of mixed character; entertainments of this sort differ greatly from those called simply plays of character, *as we shall explain later on. Comedy of mixed character must be considered from two very different points of view. Firstly, the poet may sometimes make use of a leading character, and even make that character the principal object of his story and associate that character with other subaltern characters, without the action becoming overcharged and confusing. Secondly, he may join together several characters of the two kinds we have identified, without giving any of them such strength as to make them prevail and outshine the others.*

Molière, in The Misanthrope, *provides an example of the first way of considering the comedy of mixed character. This author makes the Misanthrope the leading object of his story, and at the same time links him with the characters of the Coquette, the Scandal-monger, and the Fops without the leading character joining in their part of the action and the plot; but it is also true that all the characters surrounding the Misanthrope, and everything that happens in the course of the action, connects with him. The Sonnet, the Trial, the Coquette's conversations, and the Fops' routines are added only to make him stand out more clearly, and they become, so to speak, so many beams of light that make him shine all the more brightly. It is an admirable art that we owe to Molière, and the only one to be employed in a play of this nature. If you do not want to go so far as to acknowledge the Misanthrope as a purely metaphysical character, you must at least confess that he is so in part, since we cannot put him on the level of those ordinary characters of which the human race affords us examples at every step of the way and whose marked features make their presentation all the easier and lessen the poet's labors. Molière has not dealt similarly with* avarice, love, jealousy, *and other characteristics of this sort: he makes them prevail absolutely over the accessory characters, over all parts of the plot, and over the very action they perform and are associated with as if chained to it: it is the dominant passion that gives movement to the action, and it is that passion that resolves the action in the form that the nature of the character requires.*

The second sort of comedy of mixed character is, as we have said, formed of several characters, each of whom does not shine so brightly as to be distinguished from the rest or to be regarded as the leading character. The best examples of this are, I believe, The School for Husbands, The School for Wives, The Countess d'Escarbagnas, *and several others; here we find a collection of characters who, by their equality, can do no harm to each other. Molière has sometimes made use of one of the characters of his plots to provide the principle of the action—such as Agnès or Isabelle—but although this character functions, so to speak, preferentially in the play, he or she does no damage to the others, who for their part do none to him or her; they are all of equal strength, and if we consider them closely, we shall see that none of them could serve as the leading character because none of them has sufficient strength to dominate the rest, and to make them subaltern or accessory characters: such is the character of* Isabelle *in* The School for Husbands, *who, though she represents the principle of action, does no damage to the characters of* Sganarelle, Ariste, *and* Léonore: *and if the characters of* Isabelle *and* Sganarelle *shine brighter than those of* Ariste *and* Léonore, *it is because they are more in play, for it is on them that the poet builds his plot; the same is true of the characters of* Arnolphe *and* Agnès *in* The School for Wives: *these two characters never do any harm to each other.*

Molière did not accord the same treatment to such plays as The Miser, Georges Dandin, The Imaginary Invalid, The Bourgeois Gentleman, *and several others he composed as comedies of leading or dominant characters, for actually that is what they are. If in the essay in which I spoke of the plot appropriate to a play of character, I gave as an example only two plays,* The School for Husbands *and* The School for Wives, *although these two plays are comedies of mixed character, it will easily be seen that in each of these plays I could have cited a leading and dominant character; but I chose to demonstrate, in the specific discussion of the comedy* The Miser, *the quality and strength of a dominant character; and that is how I justify my opinion concerning the plot suitable to plays of this kind, and concerning the distinction I make among the various characters....*

Let us concede, however, that such a reformation could not be the work of a single dramatic author, and that even Molière might not have managed to correct the theater, had he not enjoyed the protection and favor of the most enlightened and just Prince ever to grace the Monarchy, and whose rare and delicate taste sets the tone not only for his Realm but even for his century. For one dare not hope that there might be men zealous enough for the public good, and so entirely generous as to offer their work to the world, with the moral certitude of receiving disagreements and contradictions, of not enjoying the fruit of their labors, and of obtaining only when no longer alive the successes that ultimately follow the wise innovations they seek to establish despite custom or prejudice.

Luigi Riccoboni[1]

1. Texts taken from *Observations sur la comédie* (Paris, 1736), pp. 32–43 and 273–274.

6. Louis XV's Condottiere: Hermann-Maurice of Saxony, Marshal of France

THE EIGHTEENTH CENTURY of Montesquieu and Boulain-villiers was enraptured by the notion of those Germans described by Tacitus, ancestors of a feudalism that was supposed to have imported the notion of freedom to Western Europe from their natural forests; a whole aestheticizing pathos of the Enlightenment, particularly virulent in Diderot and Rousseau, pits the "cowardice" of civilized moderns, miniaturized by the conventions of an artificial society, against the great beasts and great crimes of antiquity, source of ulterior dreams and shudders. Before long, a great crime, dictated by Saturn-as-History, would suppress in France what few unarmed descendants still subsisted of those "free" feudal warriors, who, ever since the Renaissance, had been compared by scholarly fantasts to Plutarch's heroes or Homeric demigods.

In the Versailles of Louis XV and Mme de Pompadour, a condottiere from the depths of the Hercynian forest, Hermann-Maurice de Saxe—prefiguring in his fashion the fate of another condottiere, this one from Mediterranean antiquity: Napoleon Bonaparte—renewed the frisson of the Homeric hero or the Scythian sage, two fashionable myths of the civilized Paris of those days: strong, frank, direct, intelligent, and barbarous, he would be both idolized and detested by the complicated lilliputians he had fleetingly preserved from what he himself called their confusion—their *embrouillamini*.

The genealogy of Hermann-Maurice of Saxony is as old and shadowy as an ancient oak from the Brandenburg forest, the cradle of his maternal family, the lords of Königsmark. The glory of his great-grandfather, Johann Christoph von Königsmark, the first condottiere to leave this nest of gyrfalcons, had wrested the family from the mists of time: commanding the Swedish armies in the service of Gustav Adolph, he had ravaged Saxony and Bohemia and organized the cruel sack of Prague in 1648, the juiciest spoils of which he had shared with Queen Christina, who rewarded him with the title of marshal and the government of Bremen and Werden.

Heroes or just military ruffians, his sons lived adventurous lives, one in the Order of Malta, the other, under the Italianized name of Conismarco, in the service of the Venetian Republic. But one of his grandsons, Philipp Christoph, growing up in the Dresden of the future Augustus the Strong, became a courtier in a violent and daring style quite remote from Castiglione's *Cortegiano* but remarkably similar to Stendhal's *Chroniques italiennes.* His assassination put an end to his thwarted amours with Sophie Dorothea von Brunswick, married against her will to the future king of England George I, heir to the house of Hanover. Philipp Christoph's sister, the lovely, intelligent, and quite fearless Aurora von Königsmark, determined to obtain vengeance for her brother's death, came to Dresden to seek it from his best friend, the elector of Saxony (who had become the king of Poland as well), Augustus the Strong. She succeeded only in sharing his bed, and was soon replaced and discarded.

But she gave birth to a son: Hermann-Maurice, acknowledged subsequently by his father and given the title of Count of Saxony. Heir to a line of knights and the bastard descendant of a royal dynasty, Maurice de Saxe nursed an idée fixe, remotely shared by his mother: a Königsmark of royal blood must conquer a crown. Trained from childhood to the career of arms by General-Count von der Schulenberg, the young count received at the court of Dresden the veneer of a French education from his Calvinist tutor, M. d'Alençon. At the age of thirteen he participated at Stralsund in battles against Charles XII, then in Flanders, in the offensive of imperial forces led by Prince Eugène of Savoy against those of Louis XIV, engaged in the War of the Spanish Succession. With Schulenberg he studied on the ground the strategy and tactics of the two greatest military leaders of the early seventeenth century, Prince Eugène and Marlborough. In 1711, at the age of fifteen, he was promoted to the rank of colonel.

In 1714 he was married to a rich heiress, Johanna Maria von Loeben. Their union was dissolved in 1721. The previous year, Maurice de Saxe had discovered the Paris of the Regency. The superb young athlete from the east attracted the sympathy of the old Princesse Palatine, and received from the regent a field marshal's commission. He indulged in gambling and debauchery, but managed to study, between orgies, the sciences of modern warfare, mathematics, engineering, fortification, and strategy with the age's Clausewitz, the Chevalier de Folard. It was at this time that he encountered the one great passion of his life: Adrienne Lecouvreur.

This daughter of the people, a laundress noted for her beauty and her voice by her neighbors at the Comédie-Française, and adopted and trained by their doyen, M. Le Grand, an excellent professor of diction, had become the great tragedienne of her generation. Yet not to her should be applied the tortuous *Paradoxe sur le comédien* subsequently devised by Diderot (and inspired by introspection at least as much as by the study of Clairon's acting): Adrienne Lecouvreur performed according to the ancient precept that makes the actor a kind of pelican: "If you want to make the public shed tears, begin by being moved yourself." In order to interpret sublime roles, she risked revealing the depths of her own intimate capacities for emotion.

Her passion for Maurice de Saxe, who lost his heart to her at a performance of *Phèdre*, and to whom she was introduced at the residence of the Marquise de Lambert in 1721, was the supreme risk from which she never shied for a moment. Their happiness lasted three years, punctuated by absences filled by the admirable lamentations we hear in Adrienne's letters. She writes from Paris to the count, who remained at Fontainebleau with the court:

Better for me had I remained where I was. I was seeing you, nothing marred my happiness, and I believe myself, here, to have fallen from the clouds because you were not with me. Come back, dear count, console me, and by your presence afford me the sweet and sole consolation I desire. Myself, I can no longer do without you.

But in 1725 Maurice de Saxe returned to Dresden, lured by a proposition made to him by the local nobility that he become Grand Duke of Courland. This chimerical adventure was to occupy him for three years (1726–1728). It came to nothing, lacking Russian endorsement and the support of Augustus III. Once he returned to Paris, the "Sarmatian ogre" yielded to the allure of other victims. Having wasted away, Adrienne died in the arms of the man she loved, while Voltaire, in several of whose plays she had triumphed, nervously paced back and forth in the next room. Christian obsequies having been denied her by the rigorist curé of Saint-Sulpice, her corpse, abducted after dark by the police, was thrown into a ditch in the first empty field they could find and covered with quicklime. One of Voltaire's most famous odes would avenge the great artist for this detestable ecclesiastical machination:

> *The moment she is no more, she is a criminal!*
> *She charmed the world, for which you punish her…*

The War of the Austrian Succession, which began in 1740 with Frederick II's accession to the throne of Prussia and the quasi-simultaneous death of Emperor Charles VI, would afford Maurice de Saxe the occasion to give his military measure and to provide the French monarchy with a secular arm at just the right moment. In 1732, drawing the conclusions from his experience and from his studies with Folard, he had delineated, in *Mes Rêveries, ou mémoires sur l'art de la guerre*, his doctrine as a military technician (published in 1756, this work, as indeed the marshal's entire career, would be attentively pondered by Bonaparte).

The first military operations in Bohemia under the Maréchal de Belle-Isle and the capture of Prague in 1742 furnished sufficient proof to Louis XV, to his octogenarian prime minister, Cardinal de Fleury, and to their nation's public opinion that no French marshal possessed the prestige, the luck, and the military science of this German, indeed this Lutheran prince whom the regent had had the wit to name field marshal in 1721. He had already given his proofs of service to France in 1733–1734, under Marshal Berwick, when the army of the Rhine disputed Philippsbourg with the imperial troops. On that occasion, he had been named lieutenant general, but now his superiority had become strikingly apparent to all Europe.

In 1743, with the title of Marshal of France, he received the command of the army of the Rhine. In 1745, in the presence of Louis XV, he scored the notable victory of Fontenoy, followed by the brilliant siege operation that wrested the chief cities of Flanders from the imperial troops and made any further English landing impossible. The king bestowed on his marshal the principality of the Château de Chambord and its domain, named him governor of Alsace, and covered him with pensions and privileges.

D'Argenson, minister of foreign affairs, who intrigued in favor of the Prince de Conti, was not the only man at court to find Maurice de Saxe an encumbrance, not to say dangerous, for this giant acknowledged neither Parisian gamesmanship nor that of Versailles. Yet his popularity in France was prodigious, prefiguring that of the victor of Marengo. In Brussels, which he captured in February 1746, he surrounded his Oriental sultan's couch with a harem of ravishing actresses, recruited for the theater of the armies. Oblivious of envy, he encroached on the Marquis d'Argenson's domain by negotiating, that same year, the remarriage of the widowed dauphin with his own niece Marie-Josepha de Saxe, the daughter of his half brother Augustus III. This union between France and Saxony would facilitate the peace of Aix-la-Chapelle.

The condottiere had become the tutelary genius of the monarchy, and he knew it. He filled an empty compartment in the mind of the most powerful, the most gifted, but also the most feminine nation in Europe. In a secret letter to the Count von Brühl, Maurice de Saxe actually wrote, on October 10, 1746:

If they did not have me, they would not know what to do with themselves.... Furthermore, the troops and the State trust me, for I keep up their hopes, and that goes far to sustain the internal condition of the State and the tranquillity of the monarchy. As for myself, who have no other weapon but the shield of truth, I am feared, the king loves me, and the public believes in me.

One is reminded of Richelieu's comment on the lack of *esprit de suite* that prevents the political and moral nation of France from keeping abreast of the physical nation.

Between Conti (aspiring, in the wings, to the management of affairs) and the hero of Fontenoy had begun one of those fierce and muffled struggles that undermined the ancien régime. The marshal scored an important victory when he engineered, on January 10, 1747, the dismissal of d'Argenson, Conti's chief supporter. Conti continued nonetheless to benefit from the sympathy of his cousin Louis XV. The contest between the prince's pretensions and the marshal's good sense would end with the latter's death, but that availed his "rival" nothing, destined as he was to remain an eternal candidate.

Contrary to the advice of the marshal, who was in a better position than anyone else to know that the capture of Maastricht and Berg op Zoom would permit France to dictate conditions ("we concede little or nothing"), the peace of Aix-la-Chapelle, in 1748, stipulated the restitution of Flanders to Austria. The Conti coterie contrived to raise the specter of the lasting proconsulate of a "new Verrès" at Brussels.

Maurice de Saxe became only more popular on that account, and French public opinion was outraged by the terms of the treaty: "Stupid as the peace" became the unanimous outcry in Paris. Later, the pitiful conclusion of the Seven Years' War (1756–1763), the cession of Canada, and the reversal of traditional alliances would complete the nation's loss of confidence in the absolute monarchy's virtues and fortunes in war.

Undaunted, the marshal, before retiring in 1748 to his "principality" of Chambord, offered to Louis XV, to the queen, to Mme de Pompadour, to the court, and to fifteen thousand spectators a fabulous military parade on the Plain of Sablons. He presided, in the uniform of an uhlans colonel, at the procession of mounted mercenaries, Africans, Tartars, Wallachians, Poles, and Germans, all harnessed and helmeted in opera costumes, brandishing their lances, followed by marching dragoons and light artillery. Under the Empire, Parisian parades of the Grande Armée, in Napoleon's presence, revived memories of those swaggering hours that a torrential rainstorm had not managed to spoil.

The enervating peace and the royal splendor deployed at Chambord accelerated the rhythm of intrigues—in theater loges and alcoves—that animated the ogreish marshal's leisure time, only rivaled, in the eyes of ladies, by the farmers-general Epinay's and Dupin de Francueil's money or by the young playwright Marmontel's sex appeal. In 1749, returning from a trip to Dresden, Maurice de Saxe visited Sans, Souci[1] where Frederick II, then France's ally, received him as an elder, a master, and a king. To Voltaire, a friend of both men, the "Solomon of the North" wrote:

> Here we have seen the hero of France, this Turenne of the age of Louis XV. I am instructed by his discourse, not in the French language but in the art of war. This marshal could well be the professor of all the generals of Europe.

This was the eighteenth century's monarchic summit. Afterward begins the slope down which it rushes into the abyss. While Maurice de Saxe was the guest of Frederick II, Louis XV made the mistake of dispensing with the indispensable Maurepas, impelling Voltaire to leave Versailles for Potsdam.

The following year, the king's master trump on the European

---

1. Sans, Souci is a charade. It does not mean "Without Worry" but "Without such a place of solace, life for a king would be only worry."

checkerboard disappeared: the Maréchal de Saxe died on November 30 at Chambord, officially of pneumonia. He was fifty-four. Rumor, amplified by legend, maintained that he had fought a duel in the woods with the Prince de Conti, which had inflicted a mortal wound.

To the Spanish ambassador, ignorant of the news and deploring the king's "considerable loss of ships," Louis XV replied: "I have just incurred a much greater loss than that. Ships can be rebuilt, but not men like the Maréchal de Saxe." General mourning made d'Alembert himself something of a poet when he published this epitaph for the great man in the *Nouvelles littéraires*:

> *From his earliest youth, to reversals inured,*
> *Beloved by the army, the king, and Victory!*
> *By courtiers loathed, and by the English feared,*
> *No circumstance failed to minister to his glory.*

The body of this Lutheran, whom Cardinal de Tencin had vainly attempted to convert, was transported with great pomp to Strasbourg, to the Church of St. Thomas, where the sculptor Pigalle erected, twenty-seven years later, a magnificent tomb.

The greatest service the marshal rendered to French literature was to have engendered, with Marie Rinteau, whose stage name was Mlle de Verrières, an adulterine daughter called Aurore after Mme de Königsmark, her grandmother. Widowed and remarried to Dupin de Francueil, Aurore de Horn gave birth to Maurice Dupin, eventually the father of George Sand. The novelist had even more genealogical distinction than the proud Marguerite Yourcenar.

The former student of M. d'Alençon spoke the exquisite French of the period, but he could never master spelling. He invariably wrote phonetically. In 1746, the frenzies of fashion already being what they are today, a faction was formed within the Académie Française to elect the victor of Fontenoy one of the Immortals. Naturally the future academician was promised an *election de maréchal*. In his elegant biography of Maurice de Saxe published in 1963, the Duc de Castries reproduces without "correction" the exchange of letters on this subject between the eventual candidate and one of his most loyal supporters at court, the Maréchal de Noailles, Mme de Maintenon's nephew: "I am propozd," writes the "King of Chambord,"

> to membership in the Academie Française. To wich I anserd that I new nothing of orrthografy, to me it meens all a page meens to a cat. Wereupon I was told that the Maréchal de Vilar nose not how to write, and he is in there. It is a persecushion: you are not in there, which makes my defens the stronger. No one is witier than you, nor speeks and rites better, why are you not in there? It is an embarasment for me. I have no wish to show disrespect to anyone, all the more to a body wich includs men of merrit. On the other hand, I feer absurditty, wich seems to me more than likely. Be so kind as to anser what I shoud do.

Noailles answered him:

> I received only yesterday, at Saint-Germain where I had gone for some fresh air, my dear Marshal, the letter in which you consult me on the proposition made to you about becoming a member of the Académie Française. I am entirely of your mind that nothing would suit you less, and as for someone's citing the Maréchal de Villars's membership, that was a piece of foolishness he permitted himself, along with several others, despite his great and good qualities. I have always regarded this distinction as unsuitable for a man of war, and even for a man of serious accomplishments. If it were only the Academy of Sciences! Patience, there are certain dignities that may suit all professions. But to associate with persons who can only trifle with words and alter the old orthography—I confess that I should be sorry to see my dear Count

Maurice among them. He requests me to report my sentiments to him, and I do so with the frankness and sincerity I
shall always have with regard to what concerns him.

So the Maréchal de Saxe, like Molière, missed the glory of the
Académie. Yet he wrote a great deal all the same, as naturally and as
piquantly as he spoke. Among his very numerous letters that have
been published (though their orthography has been restored), I have
chosen two addressed to Adrienne Lecouvreur from Mittau, where
the Comte de Provence, the future Louis XVIII, was to spend long
years of emigration and where the Maréchal de Saxe struggled in
vain to assert his rights to the Grand Duchy of Courland.

LETTERS FROM THE COMTE DE SAXE TO MLLE ADRIENNE LECOUVREUR

1726[2]

Why[3] *should I not always love you? And indeed I cannot see why I
should ever fail you, at least I believe myself incapable of such a thing
at present. . . .*

As for poor d'Argental,[4] *he is probably the purest soul, the most fair-
minded and gentle spirit nature has ever produced. . . . O hundredfold
blessed climate, where wise and indulgent Nature forms such masterpieces!*

*Your days in France are threaded with silk and gold, and though
one sometimes complains, the pain one feels is not pain or is so only in
comparison to the delights among which our happy days are passed.
Such is not the case here, and I might say to travelers so unfortunate as*

---

2. *Adrienne Lecouvreur et Maurice de Saxe: Leurs lettres d'amour* (Paris: A. Mes-
sein , 1926), pp. 226–229.

3. The beginning of the letter is missing.

4. Charles-Augustin de Ferriol, Count d'Argental (1700–1788), counselor to the
Parlement of Paris, in love with Mlle Lecouvreur and a great patron of the theater,
as well as a faithful friend of Voltaire, who called him his "angel."

to approach these localities what Pharasmanes says to Rhadamistes,[5] during his first audience, I think it is. The customs of this country resemble the savagery of that discourse, though the rest is not quite so bad, and I miss my soldiers: otherwise, soon, upon "entering Iberia, I shall distract the Sarmatians from all concern with Armenia." Stop there! I can't manage the pompous style—back to the source, which is surely preferable.

It has not been easy for me, as you seem to think, to have no letters from you. But if I haven't reproached you, the reason is more likely to be lack of confidence than indifference, and I preferred to blame the irregularity of the post rather than you. But you—how could you think I enjoy such peace of mind, since you know perfectly well that your letters constitute my sole consolation, that I ardently long for the days, the moments when they arrive, indeed I would sacrifice all the days of my life for the sake of those when the post brings your letters, I mean that I would willingly give up the days that separate me from such happy moments. I know I've told you that when the post comes and brings me nothing how sad I am, and you wrong me to suppose I am or could be indifferent....

I hope that M. the Comte de Charolais[6] will manage to improve; he has the substance of which splendid princes are made, but there is still much trimming and paring to be done. Perhaps as he grows older he will become the sort of connoisseur who can love true beauty, yet this seems to be a problem, for he hates reading, and it seems unlikely he will ever change. I am deeply obliged to him for the many kindnesses he has shown me, I thank him for them, and shall try not to lose his good opinion of me.

Most things worsen with distance, but I can assure you that my situation would seem quite different it were seen close to, and I cannot

---

5. "It is the flaming torch one must carry in Iberia / Which distracts me from the burden of venturing into Armenia" (Crébillon, *Rhadamisthe et Zénobie*, Act II, scene ii).

6. Charles de Bourbon-Condé, Comte de Charolais, brother of the Duc de Bourbon, born on June 19, 1700, died July 23, 1760. Maurice de Saxe had encountered him among the troops of the Hungarian army.

believe it is comparable to anyone else's. The opening of the Diet[7] *will take place the day after tomorrow, we shall see how it all turns out. Daily I discover intrigues, and certain people whom I counted on have failed me for fear of losing a few sheep on the Polish frontier. Yet a good number are on my side, and I doubt that the most partisan supporters of the Republic can look me in the eye. I now have a real understanding of what irreproachable conduct can effect, the boldness it makes possible, and the impression it produces on the vilest souls, the respect it compels, and how heroic conduct annihilates whatever stands in its way.*

What a strange thing the favor of the multitude is, and its hatred as well, altered by a suspicion, a caprice! I have seen these Courlanders ready, in a first impulse, to sacrifice everything, and four days later altogether intimidated, then turning around to lament their weakness and calling for help, then no longer seeking any such thing, then reversing their attitude once again, and ultimately unable to know where they stand. I have seen these multitudes suddenly, when a single old woman has pronounced, with a mysterious expression: "There is something underneath"—I have seen these fervent folk suddenly drop all their convictions and return to their initial vacillation. So you see, I am facing the most difficult and delicate moment of all. If I emerge successfully from this ordeal, I shall no longer believe anything is impossible. The difficulty is, I have no support from anyone, and my mediocre eloquence is all I have to confront every situation. It is my sole weapon. One must say little, and yet not seem mysterious, and manage to persuade.... Bless me, my child, all this is very difficult indeed, and I am beginning not to care so much for these Courlanders anymore. Farewell, I embrace you very tenderly and with all my heart. Love me as well. Farewell....

---

7. This concerned the last formality for the consecration of the vote made in his favor on June 28. The charter that would establish reciprocal obligations of the electors and the new duke was signed on July 5, and the Diet was closed on July 6.

At Mittau, January 10, 1727[8]

I shall always tell you the same thing, you are quite adorable, and I love you very much. Nothing can equal my tenderness and the esteem for you that increases every day, all of which is what makes for a true passion. Your letter of the 15th of last month raises my soul to the third heaven. Where else in the world can I find someone who unites an agreeable countenance with rare talents, a lively and sincere tenderness, and the qualities of a charming mistress with the most indissoluble merits? Where can I find, I am saying, someone who knows how to love as you do, someone who is constant, loyal, faithful? For it comes down to the fact that I believe this to be the case, and indeed I should be quite mistaken to do otherwise, for which I am very happy. Yes indeed I am, and I shall be so, for as long as you love me. Yes, for heaven's sake, and it is with the sincerest and best impulses of my heart that I tell you so. My fortune will never frown on me so long as I can share it with you, and however dark it may seem, it will always be certain to render yours agreeable if I do not cease pleasing you....

---

8. *Adrienne Lecouvreur et Maurice de Saxe,* p. 232.

7. Frederick II and Voltaire

I made a fire,
Forsaken by the sky,
A fire to be my friend
A fire to be happy

PAUL ÉLUARD'S QUATRAIN might accurately summarize what Paris and the French court represented for eighteen-century Europe: life, gaiety, wit, conversation, social and profane happiness. Christianity's twilight and the aristocracy's Indian summer permitted the appearance—irresistible and ephemeral—of an astonishing, entirely terrestrial success, the French *art de vivre*. To Stockholm as to Dresden, to Madrid as to Moscow, to Naples as to Vienna, to Berlin as to Leipzig, precious brands of this fire were carried in order to dissolve the weight of habit and to animate the ordinary sadness of the days. Only London and its merchants resisted, despite rare traitors in the English aristocracy such as Lord Chesterfield or Horace Walpole. Against the Glorious Revolution, the French polity had adopted the Jacobite cause and in America had insignificantly hampered the expansion of British commerce. In order to escape the bourgeois utilitarianism that prevailed at home, the spleen of young English noblemen showed its superior breeding by dissipating itself in Italy rather than in France.

The biographies of Frederick, Crown Prince of Prussia, and of his sister Wilhelmina, the future miserable Margravine of Bayreuth and author of excellent *mémoires* in French, give a fair idea of the fascination worked upon the European imagination, regardless of differences of religion and national character, and beneath the close interplay of political and military rivalries, by this French *esprit de joie* that since 1715, like Greek fire, had danced more brilliantly than ever on the roof of the majestic and formidable edifice that Louis XIV had made of his realm in times past. This unique alliance of intelligent power and insolent joie de vivre had been the century's true enlightenment, and its attraction was registered far and wide, even in the cold regions ruled by Frederick and Wilhelmina's cruel and greedy father, King Frederick William I, who spat in the dinner plates of his children before they were served and beat them afterward with his own cane. The little crown prince, born in 1712, was, like his sister, permanently divided. His actual life, at least until his father's death in 1740, was one long physical and moral torture that doubtless forged a soul of steel, in the image of the blade that, before the boy's eyes and on his father's orders, decapitated his best friend, Hans Hermann von Katte, whose only crime had been to attach himself too closely to the heir to the Prussian throne and to comfort his torments. Thus Frederick was well prepared to imprint a carnivorous will upon a docile bureaucracy and upon the army of giants, recruited for their height, bequeathed him by his father. The other life of the crown prince, and then of King Frederick II—the life of the mind, of taste, of the senses, of inner release—was altogether elsewhere: in French, the only language he ever consented to speak and write. From childhood it attached him, as if by an umbilical cord, to that Parisian feast of the gods he never knew directly but in which he saturated himself at a distance by books, prints, pictures, and stories. He sought to reconstruct it as soon as he could, first in his castle at Rheinsberg, where, as Pierre Gaxotte describes it, "he attempted to transport a corner of France, a Trianon fragment with its festive decor, its painted ceilings, its marble figures, its aerial mythologies, its rings of chubby cupids," as well as his own Watteaus, his vintages of Champagne, Volnay, and Pommard; and later at Sans, Souci, near Potsdam, to which, now king of Prussia, he transported the Watteaus and definitively travestied the elegant Parisian *style rocaille* as the gaudiest possible rococo.

In Rheinsberg days, he had written Voltaire an adoring letter, painstakingly phrased: "I should consider myself richer by owning your works than I should be by possessing all of Fortune's fugitive and despicable endowments...." Thus began one of the strangest flirtations of politico-literary history, between the most famous French writer and the most ambitious monarch of the age, who quickly revealed himself to be too great a politician and strategist not to submit his own Francophile fascination to the interests of his propaganda and his double-dealing. Voltaire, flattered, enchanted, let himself be lured. The torrents of praise he poured over the head of his crowned admirer (Caesar, Julian, Alcibiades, Solomon), who for his part hailed the celebrated Frenchman as Cicero, Demosthenes, Plato, Virgil, Thucydides, and Sallust, did not keep him from feeling an initial disappointment when, as soon as Frederick was crowned, he was received at Cleves not as a prime minister, as he had hoped, but as a *vieux confrère*. He returned to France at once, but the comedy of this friendship served him too well for him to interrupt it on his own initiative. The correspondence between the philosopher and the philosopher-king sufficed to astonish Europe. Voltaire undertook to correct the style and then to publish the *Anti-Machiavelli* of this cynical Machiavelli! In 1750, finally, still reeking of his victory over Austria, from which he had wrested the riches of Silesia, Frederick II achieved his aim. Though covered with honors and pensions by the court of Versailles, Voltaire was not treated there on equal footing by Louis XV, as Virgil had been by Augustus. Moreover he had been contemptibly lodged in a mezzanine overhanging stinking latrines. Hence he departed for Berlin, seduced by a shower of gold. This time (July 26, 1750) he was received as a conqueror: "150,000 victorious soldiers, no proxies, opera, comedy, philosophy, poetry, a hero poet and philosopher, grandeur and grace, grenadiers and muses, trumpets and violins, Platonic banquets, society and liberty." After several months, the philosopher sang a different tune. By the time he made up his mind to leave Prussia, Frederick was already treating him in public as a low creature and pursued him on the return journey with one shabby persecution after the other. Voltaire took what revenge he could, yet common interests were too strong. He continued to pride himself on his royal "pupil," and the pupil to benefit from the legend, complacently spread by Voltaire and the French philosophical press, of the "enlightened legislator" setting an example to Europe, and notably to Louis XV, of the intransigent struggle against prejudices and superstitions. This combat in favor of humanity took the form, among others, of the savage partition of Catholic Poland with Russia and Austria. D'Alembert, no less cunning than Voltaire, also made the journey to Prussia and he too, pensioned by the king, served him with a militant zeal. In 1766 he wrote to Frederick: "Your Majesty will find in me the docility a philosopher owes to one whom he regards as his leader and his model."

At school and in conversation with Voltaire, Frederick had polished his French style not only in prose but also in verse. Gladly taking up his pen and flooding Europe with essays, pamphlets, and poems, he provided numerous heads of state an example of literary narcissism of a deftly promotional variety. All the same, Frederick's correspondence with Voltaire, in which the two peacocks spread their tails, exchanging the roles of cat and mouse under the shameless veil of flattery, remains the crown jewel in the abundant production of this king of Prussia, who believed only in himself and in the French language.

LETTERS FROM FREDERICK II TO VOLTAIRE

[Remusberg, March 6, 1737][1]

Monsieur,
I was agreeably surprised by the verses you were so good as to address to me; they are worthy of their author. The most sterile subject becomes fecund in your hands. You speak of me, and I no longer recognize myself; everything you touch turns to gold.

---

1. Voltaire, *Correspondance,* vol. 4, edited by Theodore Bestermann (Geneva: Institut et Musée Voltaire/University of Toronto Press, 1969), letter D1294.

My name will be known by your famous rhyme.
Defying the contumely of injurious time,
I shall be born ever anew, even as your pages,
Triumphant over envy, down through the ages
Reap the grateful suffrage of posterity
And charm men's minds to all eternity...
A foot of your deathless verse, nay a hemistich,
Where you place my name like a saint in his niche,
Grants me of that immortal life a share
Alone bestowed by the great name Voltaire.

Who would know that Alexander the Great ever existed, had not Quintus Curtius and several famous historians taken the trouble to transmit to us the story of his life? Valiant Achilles and sage Nestor would not have escaped oblivion had not Homer celebrated them. I am not, I assure you, either a representative or a candidate for the status of great man; I am merely a simple individual known on only a small part of this continent and whose name, to all appearances, will serve only to decorate some genealogical tree, afterward to fall into obscurity and oblivion. I am astonished by my own imprudence when I reflect that I have addressed you in verse. I disapprove of my temerity even as I commit the very fault. As Despréaux tells us,

An ass, at least, taught by Nature herself,
Readily obeys Instinct as his guide,
Nor fondly seeks, with his outlandish voice,
To challenge the sweet songs of woodland birds.

I beg you, monsieur, to consent to be my preceptor in poetry, as you might be in all things. You shall never find a more docile or ready disciple. Far from taking umbrage at your corrections, I shall regard them as the most certain marks of your friendship for me.

My leisurely way of life has afforded me time to occupy myself with the sciences I enjoy. I attempt to profit by this idleness and to render it useful by applying myself to the study of philosophy, of history, and by amusing myself with poetry and music. I live at present as an ordinary citizen and find this life infinitely preferable to the majestic gravity and the tyrannical constraint of court routine. I have no taste for any sort of life measured by appearances. Freedom alone appeals to me.

Certain perhaps biased individuals may have drawn for you an all too flattering portrait of me. Their friendship stands in place of any merit I might have. Remember, monsieur, I beg you, your own description of renown,

Whose lips, indiscreet in their frivolity,
Are prodigal of lies as well as truth.

When persons of a certain rank have covered half a career, one attributes to them the value that others receive only after completing it. What is the source of this strange differentiation? Either we are less capable than others of doing well what it is we do, or else base flatterers exaggerate and extol our slightest actions.

The late King Augustus of Poland calculated large numbers with some facility; everyone eagerly praised his profound knowledge of mathematics; he was ignorant of the merest elements of algebra.

Exempt me, I beg you, from citing several more examples that I could advance.

In our time, there has been but one truly learned great prince, Tsar Peter the First. He was not only his country's lawgiver but possessed a perfect knowledge of naval science. He was as well an architect, an anatomist, a (sometimes dangerous) surgeon, an expert soldier, and a consummate economist: indeed, for him to be a model for all princes, he needed only to have had a less barbarous, less savage education than the one he received in his country, where absolute authority was recognized only by its cruelty.

I have been informed that you were an amateur of the fine arts, which has persuaded me to send you a head of Socrates that I believe is quite finely worked.

I trust you will be satisfied with my intention.

It is with real impatience that I await that Philosophy and Poetry, which lead directly to the hemlock. I assure you that I shall maintain an absolute secrecy on this subject. No one shall ever learn that you have sent me these two works, nor shall they be espied here. This will be a matter of honor with me, and I cannot say more to you on the subject, feeling aware as I do of all the indignity of betraying, either by imprudence or by indiscretion, a friend whom I esteem and who has put me under obligation to him.

Foreign ministers are the privileged spies of courts. My confidence is not blind, nor lacking in foresight with regard to such officers. Where could you have heard the epigram I had made concerning M. La Croze? I had given it to him alone. This good and cheerful scholar occasioned such badinage: it was an imaginative gesture whose point consists in a rather trivial play on words, perhaps likely enough in the circumstances in which I composed it, but actually quite insipid. Father Tournemine's drama is to be found in the French library. M. La Croze has read it.

He hates the Jesuits as Christians hate the devil, and regards as true religious only the members of the congregation of Saint Maur, of which order he has been a member.

So you have now left Holland. I shall feel the weight of this double remoteness. Your letters will be rarer, and a thousand vexatious obstacles will converge to render your correspondence less frequent. I shall make use of the Sieur du Breuil's address that you have given me. I shall urge him to dispatch my letters and yours in return as speedily as he can.

I trust you will enjoy at Cirey all the pleasures life can afford! Your happiness will never equal the good wishes I have for you, nor what you deserve. Be sure to tell Mme the Marquise du Châtelet that it is only to her that I can bear to surrender M. de Voltaire, as it is only she who is worthy to possess him.

Even if Cirey were at the end of the earth, I would not renounce the satisfaction of visiting it some day. Kings have traveled for less reason, and I can assure you that my curiosity equals the esteem I have for you.

Is it surprising I should wish to see the man worthiest of immortality and who harbors it in himself? I am with all imaginable respect, monsieur, your very affectionate friend,

Frederick

I have just received letters from Berlin, by which I learn that the emperor's minister has received the printed text of La Pucelle. *Do not accuse me of indiscretion.*

Ruppin, April 19, 1738[2]

Monsieur, I lose in every imaginable way when you are ill, as much by the interest I take in everything that concerns you, as by the loss of an infinity of good thoughts I should have received if your health had permitted it.

For the love of humanity, do not further alarm me by your frequent indispositions, and do not suppose that such alarm is metaphorical; unhappily, it is all too real. I tremble to apply to you the two finest lines Rousseau may have ever written in all his life:

We shall not measure by years,
The hero's course on earth.

Caesarion has given me a precise account of the state of your health. I have consulted physicians on this matter; they have assured me, on a doctor's faith, that I have nothing serious to fear with regard to your life; but as for your comfort, or lack of it, they report that your condition cannot be radically cured, the damage being too inveterate. They have decided that you must be suffering from a visceral obstruction, that several areas of elasticity have given way, that a certain amount of phlegm and flatus or some sort of renal colic are the causes of your discomfort. That is the diagnosis of the faculty of medicine at a hundred leagues' distance from their patient. Despite the dearth of faith I have in the judgment of these gentlemen, frequently more inept than

---

2. Voltaire, *Correspondance*, letter D1482.

*even that of metaphysicians, I nonetheless implore you in all serious-
ness to have an account drawn up of the* statum morbi *of your infirmities, in order to determine if perhaps some skillful physician might be
able to afford you some relief. What would be my joy to contribute in
some fashion to the restoration of your health! Therefore send me, I beg
of you, the enumeration of your infirmities and your miseries, in their
barbarous terms and baroque language, and with all possible exactitude into the bargain! You will truly oblige me by doing so; this will be
a little sacrifice that you shall be obliged to make to my friendship.*

*You say you have received several works of mine, yet you do not add
any criticism. Do not suppose I have neglected the critical comments you
consented to make on my earlier pieces. I include here the new corrections to the* Ode on the Love of God, *added to a little item addressed
to Caesarion. The mania of versification plagues me unceasingly, and I
fear that this may be one of those diseases for which there is no remedy.*

*Since the Apollo of Cirey consents to enlighten the little atoms of
Remusberg, all the arts and sciences here are being cultivated.*

*I enclose a letter from a young man, who lives in my establishment,
to one of his friends; a word from you in his regard would infinitely
encourage him; his genius will assuredly be brought to light by culture,
yet he has ceased to produce, for fear of doing so inadequately.*

I wish that you had had some use for my Ode on Patience *to console
you for the rigors of a mistress, not in order to support your infirmities.
It is easy to give consultations on what one does not suffer from oneself,
but it is the effort of a superior genius to triumph over the sharpest
pains and to write with complete freedom of mind from the very depth
of his sufferings.*

Your Epistle on Envy *is inimitable. I almost prefer it to its twin
sisters. You speak of envy like a man who has known the harm it can
do, and of generous sentiments as your patrimony. I always recognize
you by the expression of great sentiments: you feel them so deeply that
it is easy for you to express them.*

*How to speak of my writings after mentioning yours? What you
consent to say of them is touched by a certain irony. My verses are the
fruit of a wild tree; yours are from a higher stock. In a word:*

The noble eagle mounts the skies,
The swallow skims the earth.
My verse's sign is Philomel;
And whose the thunder-bearing bird?
It is Voltaire's alone.

How utterly I agree with your sentiments about plays! Love, that charming passion, should be employed in them only as spices in a stew, but not as a main ingredient, for fear a uniform taste will blur the palate's discernment. Your Merope *will surely correct the corrupt taste of the public, and liberate Melpomene from the scorn that the tinsel of her ornaments has attracted. I have utter confidence in the corrections you will have made in the two last acts of this tragedy. A touch here and there will render it quite perfect: it is assuredly so, even now.*

Corneille, and after him Racine, followed by La Grange, have exhausted all the standard locutions of tenderness and gallantry. And Crébillon, one might say, has brought the furies into the theater; all his plays inspire horror, everything in them is dreadful, everything is terrible. It was absolutely necessary, after these plays, to leave the beaten path, in order to follow a fresher, more brilliant one.

The passions you bring to the stage are quite as capable as love might be to move, to interest, and to please. All that is required is to treat them as you have in Merope *and in* The Death of Caesar.

Heaven chose you to enlighten France, and when
You turned triumphant from the grand career
The Epic offered to your fierce desires,
How gloriously—a new Thucydides—
You wore the laurels due to History!
Soon after, by a higher flight, your hand
Revealed what Newton had from Nature won,
And languishing Melponene at last
Awaits the guerdon of your sumptuous gifts.

I leave the lights of poetry to sink with you into the abyss of metaphysics: I abandon the language of the gods, in which I can only stammer, to speak that of divinity itself, which is unknown to me. It is a question, now, of raising a flag whose colors are entirely uncertain. Here is a spider's web open to air on every side, and whose structure is sustained by the subtlest of threads.

No one can be less likely to speak in favor of his own opinion than I am of mine. I have discussed the subject of absolute fatality with all possible application, and I have found in it virtually invincible difficulties. I have read any number of systems, and I have found none that is not bristling with absurdities, which has cast me into a dreadful Pyrrhonism. Moreover, I have no particular reason to favor absolute fatality rather than freedom. Whether such a thing exists or not, things will always proceed in the same way. I argue out such matters as well as I can, in order to see how far one might conduct such reasoning, and on which side may be found the greatest quantity of absurdities.

It is not quite the same in the case of sufficient reason. Any man who seeks to be a philosopher, a mathematician, a statesman—in a word, any man who wishes not to have limited views, must acknowledge sufficient reason.

And what is this sufficient reason? It is the cause of events. Now every philosopher seeks this cause, this principle; hence every philosopher acknowledges sufficient reason. It is based on the most obvious truth of our actions. Nothing can produce a being, hence nothing exists. It must of necessity be that beings or events have a cause of their being in that which has preceded them, and that cause is called the sufficient reason of their existence or of their birth. It is only the vulgar mind that, not knowing anything of sufficient reason, attributes to chance the effects whose causes are unknown to him. Chance, *in this sense, is a synonym for nothing. It is a being emerging from the empty brain of poets, and that, like those soap bubbles children play with, has no body.*

Now you are going to drink the lees of my nectar on the subject of absolute fatality. I am very much afraid that you will not understand, upon the application of my hypothesis, what happened to me the other day. I had read in some anatomical text about the cephalopharyngeal muscle. So I consulted Furetière in order to be enlightened. He says that the cephalopharyngeal muscle is the orifice of the esophagus, called pharynx. Ah! finally, I say, now I've become a clever man. Explanations are often more obscure than the text itself. Let's get to mine.

First of all, I assert that men have a sentiment of freedom; they have what they call the power to determine their will, to perform movements, etc.

If you call the act to perform movements, the act of making a resolution, of committing some action—if you call these actions human freedom, I agree with you that man is free. But if you call freedom the reasons that determine man's resolutions, the causes of the movements that they perform, in a word, that can influence these human actions, I can prove that man is not free.

My proofs will be derived from experience; they will be derived from observations I have made on the motives of my actions and on those of others.

First of all I assert that all men are determined by reasons (either good or bad), which has nothing to do with my hypothesis; and these reasons have as their basis a certain idea of happiness or of well-being. How does it happen that, when a librarian brings me Voltaire's La Henriade *and Rousseau's filthy epigrams, how does it happen that I choose* La Henriade? *It is because* La Henriade *is a perfect work, of which my mind and heart can make excellent use, and because the filthy epigrams befoul the imagination. It is therefore the idea of my advantage, of my well-being, that leads my reason to determine in favor of one of these works in preference to the other. Hence it is the idea of my happiness that determines all my actions. Hence that is the mainspring, the incentive I depend upon, and this incentive is linked to another, which is my temperament. This is precisely the wheel with which the Creator operates the springs of the will; and man has the same freedom as a clock. He has certain vibrations, in a word, he can take certain actions, etc., but all subdued to his temperament, and to his more or less limited way of thinking. . . .*

I prefer to speak to you on some other occasion about your excellent essay on anatomy. This work certainly deserves to have another letter devoted to this subject alone. I shall also fulfill my promises concerning Le Siècle de Louis XIV; *and to this letter I shall add certain considerations on the condition of Europe's body politic, which I shall nevertheless request you to share with no one. My intention was to have these considerations printed in England as the work of an anonymous author. Certain reasons have obliged me to postpone their completion.*

I await the Epistle on Friendship *as a piece that will be the crowning glory of all the others. I am as hungry for your works as you are diligent in composing them.*

I was quite surprised, in truth, when I understood that the Marquise du Châtelet found me so admirable. I have sought the reason in Leibniz, and I am tempted to suppose that this great admiration on her part derives from no more than a tiny grain of laziness. She is not so generous as you with her time. I declare myself forthwith to be Newton's rival, and according to the Parisian fashion, I shall compose a lampoon against him. It will be up to the marquise alone to make peace between us. I gladly yield to Newton the preference that the priority of knowledge and his superior merit have gained for him, and I ask for no more than a few words written in some trivial moments; in exchange for which I shall hold the marquise released from any admiration.

I have sounded the tocsin intemperately in the last letter I wrote you. You desire to continue your correspondence by means of M. Thiériot. My suspicion, upon reflection, was ill founded. I am quite comfortable about that, since it will bring me your answers all the sooner.

You can have no notion of how much I esteem your thoughts, and how fond I am of your heart. I am deeply vexed to be the Saturn of the planetary heaven in which you are the sun. What is to be done? My sentiments bring me close to you, and the affection I feel for you is no less fervent. I am ever, monsieur, your perfect and very faithful friend.

Frederick

Potsdam, September 26, 1770[3]

I've not been at all vexed that my sentiments, expressed on the subject of your statue in a letter to M. d'Alembert, should have been divulged. These are truths of which I've always been intimately convinced, and which neither Maupertuis nor anyone else has erased from my mind. It was quite correct that you enjoy public recognition in your lifetime, and that I should play some part in the demonstration made by your contemporaries, given the pleasure your works have given me.

The trifles I write are not of this order; they are an amusement for myself. I educate myself by thinking in a philosophical manner, at which moments I occasionally scribble my thoughts somewhat too boldly. That text on the System of Nature *is indeed too bold for the present-day readers into whose hands it may fall. I have no desire to scandalize anyone; I have spoken only to myself in writing the thing. But when it is a question of public expression, my constant maxim is to bear in mind the delicacy of superstitious ears, to shock no one, and to wait till the age is sufficiently enlightened for one to think aloud with impunity.*

Therefore I beg you to leave this inept work in the obscurity to which the author has condemned it, and give to the public, in its place, what you have written on the same subject, which will be so preferable to my chatter.

I have no further intention of speaking of the modern Greeks. If the sciences ever flourish again among them, they will be jealous that a Gaul, by his Henriade, *should have outstripped their Homer, and that this same Gaul has surpassed their Sophocles, drawn abreast of their Thucydides, and left far behind their Plato, their Aristotle, and their entire Stoic school.*

For myself, I suppose that the barbarians who now possess these lovely countries will be obliged to beg their conquerors for clemency, and that they will find in the soul of Catherine as much moderation in concluding peace as energy in conducting war. And as for that fatality

---

3. Voltaire, *Correspondance*, letter D16667.

that presides over events, according to the claims of the author of the System of Nature, I do not know when it will bring upon us those revolutions that might revive the sciences buried so long in those enslaved countries so degraded from their ancient splendor.

My chief occupation is to combat ignorance and the prejudices in the countries that by the accident of birth I govern, to enlighten minds, to cultivate manners, and to make men as happy as human nature allows, and as the means I can employ to do so will permit.

At present, I have only just returned from a long journey; I have been in Moravia, and I have seen again that emperor who is preparing to play a great role in Europe. Born in a bigoted court, he has shaken off its superstitions; raised in luxury, he has adopted manners of the greatest simplicity; gorged on incense, he is modesty itself; inflamed with the desire for glory, he sacrifices his ambition to filial duty, scrupulously performed; and having had none but pedantic instructors, he yet has sufficient taste to read Voltaire and esteem the merit thereof.

If you are not content with the accurate portrait of this prince, I should say that you are hard to please. Besides these advantages, he has a very competent possession of Italian literature; he quoted to me almost an entire act of Il Pastor Fido *and a number of Tasso's verses. Which is where one must always begin. After belles lettres, during the age of reflection, comes philosophy; and when we have studied it deeply, are we not obliged to say with Montaigne:* Que sais-je?

What I do know is that I shall have a copy of that bust Pigalle is working on, and being unable to possess the original, I shall at least have the copy. This is to be satisfied with little enough, when one recalls that in the past one possessed this divine genius himself. Well, youth is the age of splendid adventures; when one becomes old and decrepit, one must renounce fine minds as well as lovely mistresses.

Continue to take care of yourself, so that you may further enlighten, in elder years, the end of a century that boasts of possessing you and that can recognize what a treasure it possesses.

Frederick

8. Frederica Sophia Wilhelmina, Margravine of Bayreuth, Sister of Frederick II

THE ONLY WOMAN for whom Frederick II felt an enduring tenderness was his sister Frederica Sophia Wilhelmina von Hohenzollern, who was two years his senior. The crown prince of Prussia and his sister learned the meaning of their kinship in childhood, at the cruelest school the heart knows, that of shared persecution.

Power, according to the wisdom of nations, drives men mad. Hence it is no exaggeration to invoke what today we should so readily call "culture" (nothing less, in its original meaning, than the ensemble of preventive medicines against *la folie du pouvoir*) to ward off this major menace, beside which the furies of nature seem slight indeed. But culture, in this higher political sense, failed to shed much luster on the barracks court of the drill-sergeant king, father of Frederica Sophia Wilhelmina, Frederick, and nine subsequent children. Even the Christian religion, in Europe so felicitously allied with culture in modulating the natural savagery of minor chiefs and great princes, failed to exert upon the Prussian government that antiviolence therapy we today wrongly suppose to have been dispensed by the clergy to subjects of monarchies in particular. Lutheranism was, in Prussia, the national religion: a subaltern function of the state. Luther had abolished the Catholic polarity between spiritual and temporal powers and had permitted lay princes every latitude to exert ad libitum the absolute power they had received from God upon the sinners gathered in political society.

Neither the mitigations of culture (alluded to by Talleyrand when he said of Napoleon: "What a pity so great a man should be so ill-bred") nor the merest vestige of religious spirituality had managed to influence the conduct of this potentate drunk on beer and ambition, politically straining at his leash in his dealings with the Hapsburg emperor and his own nobles, but venting his frustrations only the more furiously upon his own subjects and his children, all treated as slaves, with the exception of those exceptionally tall uhlans he had collected throughout Germany to constitute his personal guard. At times, however, he had fits of sentimentality, when his prodigious egotism, as possessive as it was calculating, considered itself sufficiently assuaged to judge its victim anemic. He even experienced seizures of pietist bigotry, when his melancholy humor compelled him to submerge his entourage in moralizing sermons.

The wife of Frederick William I, Sophia Dorothea of Hanover, though she too was exposed to the brutalities and insults of her lord and master, was nevertheless the proud sister of George II of England. Like him she was descended from a German prince regarded with contempt by the Hohenzollerns but whom the consequences of the English revolution of 1688 had set upon the throne. Sophia Dorothea found in her brother's exaltation a guarantee against her husband's worst excesses, and a raison d'être that consoled her for everything. The least that could be said of this haughty and conniving princess is that there was nothing about her of the loving mother. Mortally jealous of his brother-in-law (and neighbor), now the king of England, Frederick William raged at the double alliance that Sophia Dorothea had made it her life's sole ambition to arrange: the marriage of her eldest daughter to her nephew, son and heir of George II, and that of her eldest son, the future king of Prussia, to her niece, the sister of the future king of England. This was now the grand affair of state and set the king and queen of Prussia at each other's throats, along with all their respective confidants, favorites, and spies. The two factions were unable to eliminate each other, but their children, stakes of the conflict, served as their battlefield.

The sole comfort of the two victims was their mutual tenderness, comparable to the sort that consoles prisoners in their jail or hostages in their dungeon. If the education of Sophia Wilhelmina was neglected more than that of Frederick, who was after all heir to the throne, the young prince was very soon the target of redoubled violence on his father's part. The drill-sergeant king was devoured by a veritable Oedipus complex in reverse that compelled him to regard his heir, as he grew older, as a redoubtable rival to be broken and overwhelmed with humiliations. Naturally Sophia Wilhelmina became the confidante of the disappointments and smothered rebellions that racked her brother.

Though this royal couple of Prussian miscreants inspires a certain quite appropriate horror, we must avoid constructing a melodrama à la Victor Hugo. The two royal children were hardly helpless victims violated by executioners. Pride and the calculations of ambition, imbibed with their mother's milk, sustained their young stoicism from an early age, and the cruel snubs that their affectionate impulses received steeled them to assume their ultimate rank without hesitation. We are in the cave and tutored by wild beasts.

Once married, by her father's will and to her mother's despair, to the eldest son of the Margrave of Bayreuth (descended from a cadet branch of the house of Hohenzollern), Sophia Wilhelmina, herself bitterly disappointed and humiliated by her own barbaric and shabby little court, would subsist by proxy on the increasing glory of her brother, king at last. They exchanged a correspondence in French that was to be much praised by Sainte-Beuve. To distract herself from her melancholy, the margravine sponsored tasteful architectural projects and wrote (in French) her memoirs, of which only the first portion was discovered and published in 1810. These disappointed Sainte-Beuve, shocked by their frequently derisive realism.

In their childhood and wretched youth, brother and sister had found in the French language the code of their confidences and of their shared hope for better days to come. Consolation and even gaiety was to be had from the French Huguenots, whom Louis XIV's revocation of the Edict of Nantes in 1685 had obliged to accept exile in Berlin but who had brought with them their language, their taste for belles lettres, and that "spirit of joy" which the Calvinists of the realm, heirs of the Renaissance like Henri IV, had shared since the Edict of Nantes in 1598 with their Catholic compatriots. The governess of the royal children, old Mme de Rocoules, had never learned German: she wrote verse like all readers of the *Mercure galant*, and her conversation remained lively and humorous. Frederick invariably referred to her as his "dear good Maman." Their tutor, Duhan, son of Turenne's Champenois secretary who had become a state counselor in Prussia, was a well-read officer who not only imparted a taste for books and French manners to both brother and sister but made of his spoken French, colorful and racy as it was, their quasi–mother tongue.

Even in Bayreuth, Sophia Wilhelmina would find a respite in the "relaxed and easy conversations" and the broad and florid mind of the Huguenot physician Superville. For Frederick (who could make brief journeys to France) as for Sophia Wilhelmina (who could never leave Bayreuth), the nation of Scarron and Voltaire, glimpsed at a distance as through an air vent, was (especially for the sister, her position a more contemplative one) a second fatherland, that of civil manners and the awareness of what counted in life. This did not keep them from remaining Hohenzollern princes attached beak and claws to the interests of their house. For them France was not the French state but a state of mind.

Comparisons have been made between the Margravine of Bayreuth's *Mémoires* and those of the Duc de Saint-Simon. What is surprising in both texts, indeed, is the language and the style, which stand out against the French prose of professional writers of the eighteenth century, even the most original ones. The margravine and the duc give the effect of speaking a colloquial language that has never passed through the filter of Latin themes and that owes its syntax and vocabulary to a juicy dialect of which one finds no trace in the carefully pruned prose of Fontenelle or Voltaire. Saint-Simon writes in an idiosyncratic dialect turned into a language of art, entirely personal and original. If he had invented his fearless style, he did not invent the oral dialect to which he gave such a superior form. This dialect, native for him, was spoken in the everyday conversation of Versailles and in his milieu of great aristocratic families. It was an oral language, unheard by grammarians and academicians, protective of archaisms, and permeable to crude words and expressions usual among a numerous domesticity well representative of the provinces and the common people. Proust, a good reader of Saint-Simon, borrowed for his own *Recherche* the two Muses of the *Mémoires*: the court type of the Duchesse de Guermantes and the provincal type of the servant Françoise. However frequently the Margravine of Bayreuth, a grande dame to her fingertips, read Boileau and Voltaire, she wrote with unself-consciousness and talent in a language she inherited orally from the nobility of the French provinces, which included Mme de Rocoules and those court officers from whom the tutor Duhan was descended. The aristocratic disdain of pedantry, in the Prussian margravine as in the French duc, gave each a very fine ear and a very sure discernment preferring to the French of academy or administration the succulent French of the old school, purged of any trace of abstraction.

But it must be acknowledged, even if the pitiless liberty of Saint-Simon, the "little duke," bequeathed nothing to Louis XIV, his ministers, or the court of Versailles, that the "etchings" of the French Tacitus can match their realism with a sentiment of the true grandeur of the reign and a sense of the prodigious spiritual resources of a nation that this reign might well have smothered: such resources crop up in abundance even in the gilded cage of Versailles. Neither Tacitus nor Suetonius had encountered a Racine or a Fénelon or a Duc de Beauvilliers in the sinister imperial courts of Rome; Procopius did not find either any solace or motive to admire in the Byzantine court of Theodora. Nor did the margravine know anything of the hidden mirror that makes the terrible light of Saint-Simon's *Mémoires* able to aureole instead of assail. The daughter of the drill-sergeant king is doomed to a continuous satirical virulence whose grotesque verve can be traced back to Scarron's *Roman comique* of 1651, which seems to have been the first literary source, common to the margravine and her brother, of their resistance by laughter and caricature to the adults who so abused them. Scarron's language was the very same that the French servants of the Berlin court had taught them, the seventeenth-century language of the

Place Maubert and the provinces. Voltaire taught Frederick II to correct his style and to write a proper academic French. The margavine, for our good fortune, remained, in her *Mémoires*, loyal to her childhood, to the language and the devastating drollery that had permitted her in those days, along with her brother, to stand fast—to survive.

Despite the honors he reserved for her when she came to Berlin and the affectionate letters he wrote her, Frederick—now Frederick II—dropped the old solidary tenderness that had so attached him to his sister. The margravine, in Berlin for his coronation in 1740, made no mistake about that: "One is clear-sighted when one loves; friendship has that much in common with love; I was not fooled by his futile demonstrations, and I realized he no longer cared for me." When she died, on October 14, 1758, Frederick II, though doubtless very affected, did not permit himself to be disheartened: he immediately commissioned Voltaire, who admired Sophia Wilhelmina's talents and had corresponded with her, to create a poetic monument worthy of a great Hohenzollern princess. Voltaire immediately saluted her with an elegy that begins with this verse:

Illustrious shade, dear shade, heroic soul and pure . . .

For several months Frederick remained silent, then reiterated his request as if he had received no more than a trifle: "Europe must mourn with me a virtue all too rare: the world must know that she is worthy of that immortality it is your responsibility to bestow upon her." To this already Napoleonic command Voltaire acceded by composing, this time in the grand genre, his *Ode on the Death of the Margravine of Bareith:*

O Bareith! O Virtue, O beloved graces . . .

I have chosen for this selection two characteristic passages from the margravine's *Mémoires*. The first describes Tsar Peter's visit to Berlin in 1722 and the second the new bride's first impressions upon her arrival in Bayreuth in 1732. The Prussian princess's eye is that of a Parisienne exiled to Quimper-Corentin or Le Mans, but who knows how to rank the various degrees of provincial barbarism: she drily concludes that Berlin, seen from St. Petersburg or from Bayreuth, is in spite of everything a stage above them. Paris remains *hors concours.*

EXTRACTS FROM THE *MÉMOIRES* OF THE MARGRAVINE OF BAYREUTH

The Tsar Visits the King of Prussia (1722)[1]

I forgot to mention in the preceding year the arrival of Tsar Peter the Great in Berlin. This anecdote is sufficiently curious to merit a place in these memoirs. This prince, who delighted in travel, arrived from Holland. He had been obliged to stop near Cleves, the tsarina having suffered a miscarriage there. Since he had no interest in either the local people or the ceremonies, he requested that the king lodge him in one of the queen's country houses, in the outskirts of Berlin: this princess was quite vexed by such an obligation: she had built a small palace there, which she had taken great care to decorate magnificently. The porcelain gallery alone was a splendor, as well as the many rooms adorned with mirrors, and since this house was a true gem, it was so called: Mon-Bijou. The gardens too were delightful, bordered as they were by the river, which added greatly to their charm.

The queen, in order to forestall the disorders the Russian gentlemen had produced in all the other houses in which they had resided, had the entire house stripped, removing all the most fragile articles. The tsar, his wife, and their entire court arrived at Mon-Bijou by water some days later. The king and queen received them at the riverside. The king gave his hand to the tsarina to help her onto the landing; once the tsar had disembarked, he gave the king his hand and said: I am

1. Margravine of Bayreuth, *Mémoires,* preface by P. Gaxotte (Mercure de France, 1967), pp. 43–45.

very pleased to see you, brother Frederick. He then turned to the queen whom he attempted to embrace, but she repulsed him. The tsarina began by kissing the queen's hand, which she repeated several times. She then presented to her the Duke and Duchess von Mecklenburg, who had accompanied them, along with four hundred so-called ladies who composed her suite. These were mostly German servants who performed the function of court ladies, companions of the bedchamber, as well as cooks and laundresses. Almost every one of these creatures was carrying a richly swaddled infant in her arms, and when asked if these were their own children, they replied, bowing and scraping in the Russian fashion: "The tsar has honored me by fathering this child." The queen did not wish to greet these creatures. The tsarina, on the other hand, treated the royal princesses with tremendous hauteur, and it was only with great difficulty that the king persuaded her to greet them. I observed this entire court the next day, during the visit the tsar and his wife paid to the queen. This princess received them in the grand apartments of the castle, and preceded them as far as the guard room. The queen gave her hand to the tsarina, leaving her right hand free, and led her into the audience chamber.

The king and the tsar followed them. Once this prince saw me, he recognized me, having seen me five years previously. He took me in his arms and scraped my entire face as he kissed me. I slapped him several times and struggled as hard as I could, saying that I wanted none of these familiarities and that he was dishonoring me. He laughed loudly at this idea and began a long conversation with me. I had learned my lesson; I spoke to him of his fleet and of his victories, which delighted him to such a degree that he observed to the tsarina that if he could have a daughter like me, he would gladly surrender one of his provinces. The tsarina too gave me many caresses. The queen and she were seated beneath a dais, each of them in an armchair. I stood beside the queen, and the royal princesses sat facing her.

The tsarina was short and squat, very dark-complexioned, and had neither grace nor bearing. One had only to look at her to perceive her low birth. She might have been taken, in the outfit she was wearing, for some sort of German actress. Her gown appeared to have been pur-

chased at some secondhand emporium; it was in the old style and covered with silver trinkets. The front of her skirt was embroidered with all kinds of semiprecious stones, in a strange design: a two-headed eagle, its feathers embellished with tiny pieces of gold and crystal. She was also wearing some dozen medals and as many portraits of saints and relics attached to the entire length of her cloak, so that, with each step she took, one seemed to be hearing a pack mule: all those medals rattled against one another, making a considerable racket.

The tsar on the other hand was extremely tall and quite well made; his countenance was handsome yet there was something so crude about his physiognomy that he looked rather frightening. He was dressed like a sailor in a one-piece uniform. The tsarina, who spoke almost no German at all and who failed to understand anything the queen said to her, summoned her lady jester and chattered with her in Russian. This poor creature was a Princess Galitzin and had been reduced to such a wretched profession in order to save her life: having been involved in a conspiracy against the tsar, she had been given the knout two times. I have no idea what she said to the tsarina, but this princess immediately burst into loud peals of laughter.

Finally we sat down to table where the tsar was placed beside the queen. It is well known that this prince had been poisoned in his youth, a subtle venom had affected his nerves, which caused him to fall into frequent convulsions he was quite unable to control. This misfortune came upon him at table, he performed several contortions, and since he was holding his knife at the time and gesticulating with it quite close to the queen, this princess was alarmed and several times attempted to leave the table. The tsar reassured her and begged her to calm herself, assuring her he would do her no harm: at the same time he seized her by the hand, which he squeezed with such violence between his own that the queen was obliged to cry for mercy, which made him laugh heartily, saying that she had more delicate bones than his Catherine. After the collation everything had been made ready for the court ball, but the tsar escaped as soon as he stood up from the table and returned to Mon-Bijou alone and on foot. The next day he was shown all the remarkable sights of Berlin, among others the cabinet of medals and ancient statues. There was one among the latter, I am told, that represented a pagan divinity in a very indecent posture: this figure was used in the time of the ancient Romans to embellish the nuptial chamber. The piece was regarded as a great rarity, and passed for one of the finest in the entire collection. The tsar admired it greatly and ordered the Tsarina to kiss it. She attempted to avoid doing so; the tsar grew angry and said to her in his faulty German: Kop ab, *by which he meant: I shall have you beheaded if you do not obey me. The tsarina was so frightened that she did just what he desired. He straightway asked the king for this statue and several others, which could not be refused him. He did the same with regard to a cabinet entirely inlaid with amber. This cabinet was unique of its kind and had cost King Frederick I an enormous sum. It suffered the sad fate to be taken away to Petersburg, to everyone's great regret.*

This barbarian court finally departed two days later. The queen immediately went to Mon-Bijou, where the desolation of Jerusalem prevailed; I have never seen anything like it, everything was so broken and soiled that the queen was obliged to reconstruct and refurnish amost the entire house.

The Margravine's Arrival at Bayreuth (1732)[2]

I arrived here on January 22 at six o'clock in the evening. Perhaps the circumstances will be of some interest: herewith. Within gunshot of the town, I was harangued on behalf of the Margrave by M. de Dobenek, chief magistrate of Bareith, a grand figure of a man greatly concerned with his appearance, affecting to speak a refined German and possessing the declamatory art of his country's stage folk, but nonetheless a kind and worthy man. Thus we entered the town to the sound of a triple discharge of cannon, whereupon the coach in which the gentlemen were riding began moving, followed by mine, which was harnessed to six post-nags; then my ladies; after them the people of the bedchamber; and lastly six or seven baggage carts closed the ranks. I was somewhat irritated by this reception, but allowed none of my dis-

---

2. Margravine of Bayreuth, *Mémoires,* pp. 220–224.

satifaction to appear. The margrave and the two princesses his daughters received me at the foot of the grand staircase with the whole court; he conducted me first to my apartment, which was so fine that it merits a brief description: I was led into it down a long corridor lined with spiderwebs and so filthy that it could turn one's stomach. I then emerged into a very large room whose principal ornament was its ancient ceiling; the antique tapestry on the wall had been, I suspect, quite lovely in its day, but was now so old and so dark that its subject could not be discerned without the help of a microscope; the figures represented were so huge and the faces so shabby and faded that they seemed to be ghosts. The adjoining boudoir was filled to bursting with a suite of dust-colored brocade pieces; next to this was another room of the same size, whose quilted green damask furniture made an admirable effect; I say quilted, for it was in tatters, the backcloth showing through everywhere. I went into my bedroom, entirely furnished in green damask with frayed golden eagles. My bed was so fine and new that in fifteen days' time there were no curtains left, for as soon as they were touched they fell to pieces. Such unaccustomed magnificence came as a great surprise. The Margrave offered an armchair; we sat down in order to conduct a proper conversation, in which Télémaque and Amelot [the French translator of Gracián's L'Homme de coeur*] were not forgotten. Then the gentlemen of the court and the foreigners were presented to me: here is their portrait, beginning with the margrave [the present ruler of the Bayreuth, her father-in law].*

This prince, forty-three years old at the time, was handsomer than he was ugly; his false physiognomy did not portend difficulty or ease, it might be counted among those that promise nothing; he was extremely slender, and his legs were knock-kneed; he was neither expressive nor graceful, though he strove to give an impression of those qualities; his doddering body contained an extremely limited spirit, and he was so little aware of his faiblesse *that he presumed himself quite witty; he was very polite, without possessing that ease of manner that must season politesse; infatuated with conceit, he spoke of nothing but his administration of justice and his grand art of ruling; he sought to pass as having great firmness of will, on which he indeed prided himself, but instead he possessed a great deal of timidity and weakness; he was false, jealous, and suspicious; this last defect was to some degree forgivable, this prince having contracted it by dint of having been duped by those in whom he had confided; he had no talent for affairs, reading Télémaque and Amelot had clouded his mind; from them he drew maxims of morality that suited his character and his passions; his conduct was a mixture of the lofty and the low; sometimes he played the emperor and introduced ridiculous rules entirely inappropriate to his position, and at others he demeaned himself to the point of forgetting his dignity; he was neither avaricious nor generous, and never gave anything without reminding you of it; his greatest defect was his fondness for wine: he drank from morning to night, which greatly contributed to weakening his mind. I believe that his heart was inwardly good. His popularity had brought him the love of his subjects; despite his lack of any sort of genius, he was endowed with a good deal of penetration and knew well those who composed his ministry and his court. This prince prided himself on being a physiognomist, and by this art his ability to identify the character of those around him. Several rogues, whom he made use of as spies, led him to commit injustices by their false reports; I have frequently suffered from their calumnies.*

The Princess Charlotte, his eldest daughter, might pass for a true beauty, yet this creature was merely a lovely statue, being altogether simple, her mind occasionally deranged....

Baron Stein, his prime minister, belongs to a great and illustrious family; he has good manners and a worldly talent; he is a very respectable person, though he never sins in the direction of wit; he is one of those persons who say yes to everything, and who never think an inch beyond their own nose.

M. de Voit, my majordomo, of quite as illustrious a family as the latter, is the second minister. He is a man of quality who has traveled widely and frequented the great world; he is quite agreeable in society and a man of repute withal; his hauteur and his decisive tone often render him odious; his desire to dominate compels him to commit egregious errors; his indecisiveness and his panic fears have won him the nickname Father of Difficulties. And indeed he constantly takes umbrage and perpetually worries about everything with no rhyme or reason.

M. von Fischer, another minister, though commonplace, has pushed himself forward by degrees until he has reached his present eminence. He possesses the merit of men of his sort, who rise commonly with good fortune and forget the lowness of their extraction; he gives himself the airs of a grand seigneur; his muddle-headed, conspiratorial, and ambitious character makes him a man of little worth, though he possesses the Margrave's confidence; vexed at having had no part in arranging my marriage, of which M. de Voit, his sworn enemy, was the architect, he transferred all his fury to the prince and to myself, causing us many cruel afflictions.

M. de Corff, master of the horses, might reasonably pass for the greatest dullard of the age; he has no common sense at all and supposes himself a great wit, being what is usually called a nasty beast, for he is an intriguer and a talebearer.

The master of the hunt von Gleichen is a fine upstanding fellow who minds his own affairs; his Ostrogothic countenance bears the imprint of his fate; the horns of Actaeon suit his métier; he wears them patiently enough, having consented to a separation from his wife, who had bestowed them upon him, in order to marry her lover. I have often enough seen this lady in the company of her two husbands; the former is still alive, the latter, who was M. de Berghove, is now deceased.

Colonel de Reitzensein is an extremely unpleasant man, crawling with vices and exempt from virtues; he is no longer in service. M. von Wittinghoff was the replica of the aforementioned. I pass over the rest in silence, having mentioned these two only because they play a part in these memoirs.

I was anything but edified by this court, and still less so by the wretched dinner we were served that first evening: sodden stews seasoned with vinegar, tired raisins, and enormous onions. I was quite ill by the meal's end and obliged to withdraw. No one had gone to any trouble in my behalf, my apartments had not been heated, the windows were in fragments, producing an unbearable chill. I was sick to death all night long, which I spent in grave distress and absorbed in melancholy reflections upon my situation. I found myself in a new world surrounded by people resembling villagers rather than courtiers; poverty prevailed everywhere; try as I might to find the riches that had been promised me, I saw not the slightest appearance of any such thing. The prince [her husband, the margrave's eldest son] made some effort to console me; I cared for him deeply; conformity of humor and character binds hearts together; this was the case with us, and it was the sole comfort I found for all my pains.

I kept to my apartment the following day. I found my ladies as disagreeable as the gentlemen the day before. Baroness Stein would not yield precedence to my housekeeper. I asked the Margrave to put these affairs in order; he promised to honor my request, but did nothing of the kind. . . .

9. Francesco Algarotti and Frederick II

AS A BOARDING STUDENT at the Collège Louis-le-Grand from 1704 to 1711, François-Marie Arouet had the luck to be born to intellectual life in an institution remaining open to the wide world, despite a war in which France opposed the rest of Europe. He heard talk of China, New France, and South America from the Jesuit missionaries who returned from these places, and he found in Father de Tournemine, director since 1701 of the *Journal de Trévoux*, one of those most attentive to the "crisis of European consciousness" of which the chief centers were then in London and Amsterdam.

Even so Voltaire suffered from claustrophobia, or to put it another way, from French exception, in his early years. We know today that even if he had not been subjected to exile after the affair of the Chevalier de Rohan and imprisonment in the Bastille in 1726, he would have left for England, for he had long since prepared himself to discover this island that was already so powerful, but for many reasons still so mysterious for Continental Europeans. Boileau had never ventured beyond Auteuil, and Racine no farther than Uzès; La Fontaine's longest journey had taken him to the Limousin. This French literary sedentarianism ceased with the end of Louis XIV's reign. Voltaire took up where peregrine Erasmus left off, though like Erasmus he had no great love of travel for travel's sake. He had no rest until he found, after Cirey, after Sans, Souci, after Les Délices, a little realm of his own where he could feel safe, write in peace, and let the world come to him, as it did in the days of the

Collège Louis-le-Grand. This Parisian, after 1726, lived for the most part far from Paris, and when he settled at last, it was to take up residence at Ferney, on the French-Genevan border. France made him anxious.

The traveler king of the European Republic of Letters never saw Italy. But he corresponded with any number of Italians: Marquis Albergati Capacelli, Severio Bettinelli, the Abbé Galiani, and even Pope Benedict XIV Lambertini, to whom he dedicated his tragedy *Mahomet*. Later, by his campaigns in favor of Calas and Sirven, he made the European fortune of Cesare Beccaria, author of *Dei delitti e delle pene* (*On Crimes and Punishments*, 1764), a work that inspired Voltaire's action as a reformer of French penal procedures.

Gallant Popularization

The Italian who amused him most was incontestably Francesco Algarotti. In 1735 the sage of Cirey addressed him in a friendly *épître en vers*. And later Algarotti was the consolation of his sojourn with Frederick II in Prussia, where for Voltaire *la vie de château* was not always a bed of roses. And in Ferney, while in uninterrupted correspondence with this Italian star of the Republic of Letters, whom he was fond of calling, in the fashion of Frederick, "the swan of Padua," he welcomed a host of Italians announced and recommended by his favorite peninsular acolyte.

Born in 1712 to a family of wealthy Venetian merchants, Algarotti distinguished himself by his studies with the leading teachers of Italy, in Bologna where he explored medicine and experimental physics, but also in Padua and Florence where he completed his literary training. He settled in Paris in 1734, and it was here that he wrote the book that won him an international reputation: *Il Newtonianismo per le dame* (Newtonianism for Ladies), published in Milan in 1737. This work, revised several times by its author, was intended to do for Newton's glory and his optics what Fontenelle had done in his *Entretiens sur la pluralité des mondes* for the glory of Descartes, his physics and his astronomy: an amalgamation of fan and compass, such scientific vulgarizations were effected by the pleasant gallantry of a conversation in a boudoir or a park, in the company of a pretty woman.

Voltaire had been alerted to this new talent's arrival in Paris by his usual informant, Nicolas-Claude Thiériot, who wrote to him in 1735: "We have here the Marquis Algarotti, a young man familiar with the language and manners of every country, who writes verses like Ariosto, and who knows his Locke and his Newton." Voltaire, in petto, was rather severe about this impure mixture of mundanity and science concocted by Fontenelle's imitator in his first book: "The smell of the copy," he wrote to Thiériot, "is too strong. I believe there is more truth in ten pages of my *Éléments* [*de la philosophie de Newton,* also published in 1737] than in his whole book." Nonetheless he had, with his usual flair, immediately incorprated Algarotti into his network of European correspondents, addressing him in a first *épître en vers*. He invited him to Cirey, where the young Italian made the most favorable impression on Mme du Châtelet and on her lover as well.

Elegant, gifted, a brilliant encyclopedic jack-of-all-trades, this Venetian would have been another Alcibiades of the Enlightenment had his plebeian origin not kept him from uniting the pen to the sword. For lack of military glamour, he trifled with diplomacy. With regard to amours, Algarotti manifested every inclination: his *bel indifferent* androgyny abetted his worldly successes in several courts and several capitals. Italy in the early eighteenth century had in the erudite grand seigneur Scipione Maffei, a friend of the Abbé Conti, its own literary prince, greatly respected in Paris, where he first encountered the handsome Francesco in 1734 and declared him to be a charlatan, adorned with the false title of marquis. It was only when Algarotti had been dubbed a count by Frederick II, and his European authority as a "virtuoso" affirmed, that Maffei offered his friendship and entered into a continuing correspondence.

A Latin Lover in London

After France and Voltaire, Francesco made the conquest of learned England, which elected him a member of the Royal Society. All doors, even those of the court, were immediately open to him thanks to letters of recommendation from the sage of Cirey. A portrait by Liotard, dating from this period, reveals other assets: the melting eyes and the well-outlined lips of a Rudolph Valentino in powdered hair. He acquired the simultaneous adoration of two "lions" of London society: Lord Hervey, the young political star of the Whigs, who made no secret of his erotic preferences, and Hervey's great friend Lady Mary Wortley Montagu, a grande dame of English letters and an ardent, even militant feminist. She was twice Algarotti's age, her heart was fallow, and she conceived a violent passion for the Italian, while introducing him to the literary figures she "sponsored," the most celebrated of the day, Pope and Gray.

The two jealous admirers paid their court to Algarotti in French, both written and oral. He would have preferred making progress in English, but at the time the language of Voltaire and Marivaux passed for the parlance of gallantry. To speak and write in French added a romantic salt to the fine expression of desire and *chagrins d'amour*. In a note from Lord Hervey to Algarotti, who on the eve of his departure for Italy had dined at Lady Mary's unbeknownst to her friend, we read:

> In truth, it does excessive honor to the place where you supped to make a mystery of it—if it was to spare *her* reputation; and if it was to spare *yours*, I forgive you. But the ungrateful creature has boasted of the occasion, and not content with her victory and her pillage, she has sought a public triumph.... She roams London boasting of her conquest, and after making you serve the lowest of turns, she insults your memory by declaring them to the public: *veni, vidi, vici* is her choice motto.[1]

---

1. Robert Halsband, *The Life of Lady Mary Wortley Montague* (Oxford University Press, 1956), p. 157.

Lady Mary's letters to Algarotti are no less impassioned:

> How timid one is when one loves! I fear to offend by sending this note, though my intention is to give pleasure. As it is I am so mad in all things regarding you that I am not sure what I think. My reason whispers the follies of my heart without possessing the strength to destroy them. I am torn in a thousand directions that are of no interest to you whatever, and I know not why I make you my confidant. What is certain is that I shall love you the rest of my life, despite your caprices and my reason.[2]

After his departure, Algarotti no longer answered Lady Mary's letters, in which she compared herself to Dido abandoned by Aeneas; at least Lord Hervey could boast of remaining in regular correspondence with the faithless one. Even so the great lady did not cast off her "sylph" and continued to send him her cris de coeur, following him at a distance as he circulated abroad from city to city. In 1739 he returned to London, but to take up residence with Lord Hervey. This failed to discourage his *amoureuse*, more inflamed than ever by his disdain. She decided to move to Italy in order to be certain of seeing him again and perhaps of recovering his attentions. A rendezvous was stipulated in Venice. She arrived. He never appeared, but the correspondence between them resumed.

RUSSIAN REPORTAGE

In 1739, Lord Baltimore, the English ambassador to Tsarina Anna Ivanovna, invited Algarotti to join him on the *Augusta*, which would take them from Amsterdam to Copenhagen, from Stockholm to St. Petersburg. Algarotti embarked. From this expedition to the empire of the tsars he would produce *Viaggi di Russia*, essay-letters

---

2. Halsband, *The Life of Lady Mary Wortley Montague*, p. 157.

addressed to Lord Hervey, collected and published in 1764. After the example of Voltaire's *Lettres anglaises*, Algarotti attempted the genre of a special envoy's reportage from a country long mysterious and now important.[3]

Though he hardly left St. Petersburg, where he had been invited to attend the extravagant entertainments at the court of Anna Ivanovna, he described in these fictive "letters," as if he had been an "ocular witness," the Russo-Turkish War of 1736–1739. With the same fervor and partiality as Voltaire, he retrospectively paid homage to the "new Prometheus," the "Genius of Russia," Peter the Great, and to the "window" the despot had opened onto Europe by "creating" the city and port of St. Petersburg. In a footnote to his unpublished correspondence, this Venetian more truthfully described Russia's new capital as "an Asiatic encampment of cabins lined up at attention," to be admired at a distance. He describes at first hand (though scrupulously softened) the spectacle of Anna Ivanovna's court, and at second hand the manners, economy, and geography of the "White Bear," an object of growing curiosity in London as in Paris. The work was judged "worthy of a minister's desk" and his tableau of the barbaric and savage manners that prevailed in the empire of the tsars represented for the eighteenth century what Astolphe de Custine's *La Russie en 1839* would eventually mean for the early nineteenth.

THE CYTHEREA OF FREDERICK II

The great encounter of Algarotti's life, as moreover of his friend Voltaire's, was Frederick II, who was his own age and whose tastes he shared, though with an exclusivity somewhat less severe. Algarotti first met him on the return journey from St. Petersburg, at Rheinsberg where Frederick, still crown prince, was eager to assume the privileges as well as the responsibilities of rule. Apparently

3. See the edition of *Viaggi di Russia* edited by William Spaggiari (Parma: Fondazione Pietro Bembo, Ugo Guanda Editore, 1991).

their *coup de foudre* was reciprocal. For his part, in 1739 Algarotti described the occasion to Voltaire: "I have seen, *O me beato*, this adorable prince. . . . I cannot recount the quantity of pleasures I have had!" The following year the new king invited him to the court of Berlin; he was seated beside Frederick II as a royal mistress might have been in the coronation carriage. He remained at the Prussian court in 1740–1741, being assigned various diplomatic missions. He then went on to the court of Saxony, bearing the rather singular title of counselor of war.

On this occasion, Voltaire, definitively won over by Algarotti, addressed to him a second *épître en vers* (February 1744):

> *Son of Pindus and Cytherea,*
> *Sapient Algarotti upon whom*
> *Heaven has bestowed the Arts*
> *To Love, to Write, and to Please,*
> *And whom, supreme privilege,*
> *One of the best kings of the earth*
> *Has made his Counselor of War,*
> *Now that he seeks to live in Peace:*
> *There, in your palace of porcelain*
> *Receive these frivolous phrases*
> *So easily, so artlessly strung together*
> *In the charming land of pompoms.*
> *O Saxony to whom we owe our love!*
> *O Saxony to whom we further owe*
> *Beyond our love, our ardent gratitude!*

Was it inspired by this epistle that Algarotti decided to become the Ovid of the Age of Rococo, welcomed this time by Augustus-Frederick? In 1745 he published in Naples a brief allegorical work, *Il congresso di Citera*. Here again, as in "Newtonianism for Ladies," summing up in the Italian language those "questions of the heart" of which the *Mercure galant* (Fontenelle had been the French monthly's assiduous collaborator, and the dramatist Charles Dufresny had become its director in 1711) had made a specialty among the feminine public and readers of the world of fashion. The French translation, *Le congrès de Cythère*, appeared in 1768, in a tiny pocket format embellished with an attractive frontispiece engraved in rococo style, and was constantly republished until 1789.

Writing in Italian, for a European public who spoke and read that language as well as French, Algarotti nevertheless insisted on emerging from "the French exception." Comparison of the amorous behaviors of the three civilized nations of Europe—England, France, and Italy—allowed him to exalt a fourth model, which benefited from the lessons of the other three: that of the court of Frederick II.

It all begins with a melancholy scene of the first years of the century, ravaged by war, when Amor has everywhere been sacrificed to Mars. When peace returns, and with it pleasure, division has nevertheless persisted, for in the three civilized countries, love has been practiced in a fashion so different and imperfect that Venus has determined to summon a congress to put an end to such rivalries. Three ladies—one English, one French, and one Italian—are selected to set forth the varying points of view. They are brought together, arrayed in all their finery, to the Temple of Love on the island of Cytherea. The Englishwoman, Lady Gravely, nostalgic for the reign of Charles II, complains of the sour moralism that has succeeded those gay times: it separates the sexes, each to its own, and men have forgotten how to excel "in the most important affair of all."

The Frenchwoman, Madame de Jazy, does not beat about the bush: "One might say that it is only in Paris, the true theater of Love, that living may bear the name, everywhere else one merely vegetates." And she describes the pleasant and easy amorous behaviors, purified of jealousy and dispute, that in Paris guarantee, along with the amenities of wit, "a continual reproduction of desires and pleasures" between the two sexes, all the more exquisite in that it knows itself to be ephemeral, and prefers that state of affairs. France has wrought to its modern perfection Ovid's *Ars amoris*.

The Italian representative, Signora Beatrice, protests: the Temple of Love has been profaned. Unfortunately Italy has submitted herself to the modern school of the French, whose amorous motto is: Pleasure without Pain. Yet voluptuous pleasure does not proceed without trials and suffering. There must be a return to the masters of the true art of loving: Dante, Petrarch, Bembo.

Voluptuous pleasure then speaks and pronounces sentence, which occupies a middle ground between the fashionable Frenchwoman and the Italian lady nostalgic for Plato. True pleasure is accompanied by the imagination. It cannot be ignorant of jealousy but protects itself against the rational madness of suspicion. Among the true Sybarites, Venus's myrtle is interlaced with the laurel of Apollo, physician of souls and patron of the arts. If each nation has its manners, each must temper them by taking inspiration from what is best in those of its neighbors. The French sacrifice to an excess of secrecy and mystery that, if they do not degenerate into duplicity, are the condiments of voluptuous pleasure. The Italian Platonists are represented by excessively ideal loves. Ovid, better understood than by the French, is the superior teacher. Rome, in the person of Julius Caesar, has lost nothing of its heroism by learning the arts of love and by tasting, like the gods themselves, the nectar poured by Ganymede as well as by Hebe.

At the end of this extremely allusive harangue, which leaves all three ladies bemused, the representatives of Europe attend a carefully victualed banquet under a Persian tent in a grove surrounded by flowering gardens and strewn with inviting upholstery. Everything suggests that this delicious Cytherea is to be identified with Potsdam's Sans, Souci: "What makes these gardens still more charming," Algarotti concludes, "are the Nymphs and Sylvans who populate them, to whom the God of love grants the gift of intelligence, Venus the gift of pleasure: all their pastimes are voluptuously spiced." London, Paris, and even Italy have no further allure, Algarotti insinuates, once one has known his paradise of true sybaritism. This was also the opinion of Frederick II, who, already in possession of a *Departure for Cytherea* by Lancret, made a further acquisition, between 1752 and 1765, of the second version of Watteau's *Embarcation for Cytherea*. Potsdam had no further reason to envy Paris.

Algarotti, Art Lover and Journalist of Art

Augustus III, prince elector of Saxony and king of Poland, did not keep his new counselor of war at his court but sent him to Italy on a "diplomatic mission," the pretext for buying works of art for the Dresden art galleries (unless we are to understand the reverse). The prince's father, Augustus II, "the Strong," had already made his picture gallery into one of the finest in northern Europe, and the purchase at Modena in 1746 of a hundred masterpieces dispersed by Duke Francesco III of Este would bring it the very first rank. In 1742 Algarotti, precursor of museography, had presented the king with a *Progetto per ridurre a compimento il Regio Museo di Dresda.* On his mission in Italy, he would consequently buy only at the highest level. He began in Venice, taking advice from Giambattista Tiepolo: he admired the "fecund fantasy" of that painter, who made Veronese live again. Algarotti gave literary advice to the great fresco painter for the subjects of his huge compositions and commissioned from him, for his personal collection, a voluptuous *Diana Bathing.* He also passed on more important commissions, of a nobler taste, for Augustus the Strong and for his prime minister, Count de Bruhl.

In 1751 Algarotti sent his Parisian friend Pierre-Jean Mariette, the supreme authority on the matter in Europe, a balance sheet of his official purchases: Sebastiano Ricci, Il Borgognone, Palma Vecchio, Piazzetta, Tiepolo, and the great pastellist Jean-François Liotard (who executed his portrait, which today is in Amsterdam) figure prominently in this brilliant catalog. From the study of Newton's optics, Algarotti had moved on to art connoisseurship, in which he succeeded in making a name for himself.

He did not possess an infallible "eye," any more than his friend the lordly expert Mariette. He took for a Holbein masterpiece a picture he had noticed in the Palazzo Dolfin in Venice, *The "Burgomaster Mayer" Madonna,* which was soon discovered to be a seventeenth-century copy made for Marie de Médicis. Neverthless his amateur's taste and his literary virtuosity permit him to figure honorably in the long Italian tradition—and since the reign of

Louis XIV, French as well—of art writers. In 1744 he had sketched a *Discorso sulla pittura*, published in Dresden in 1746. But it was in Venice that he published, after rewriting it several times, his *Saggio sopra la pittura*, with a dedication dated 1755, the year Winckelmann, then conservator of antiquities in Dresden, published the enlarged edition of his initial investigations of Greek art, postdated 1756. That same year appeared Piranesi's *Antiquities of Rome* and Burke's essay *On the Sublime and Beautiful*.[4]

This was the moment of the great aesthetic turn of the Enlightenment: the beginning of the shift toward neoclassicism. From many points of view, Algarotti's two essays on art do not take this turn; they extend the views and the taste of which the Frenchman Roger de Piles, oracle of Pierre Crozat's circle, had been the "colorist" theoretician at the beginning of the eighteenth century. Algarotti remained faithful to post-Regency French preferences and to those of Frederick II. He borrowed from Piles the "painters' scale," which granted each great master his share of strength and weaknesses, and the model of the "bunch of grapes" attributed to Titian: variously illuminated, it sets the tone for the painter's gaze, in order to judge the lights and shadows, the reliefs and recessions that make any historical composition vital and harmonious.

Yet he also abided by the principles of Gian Pietro Bellori, the late-seventeenth-century Roman theoretician; he renounced neither Raphael nor Poussin, but saw no contradiction between this "academic" and Roman conception of art and the inventive enthusiasm of the Venetian colorists. The Bolognese of the school of the Carracci, the Venetians from Titian to Tiepolo, and especially the Emilian Correggio, idol of the early eighteenth century, were the masters of his "Idea of the Beautiful" in painting, exemplifying a Franco-Italian rococo eclecticism.

Hence Algarotti was an excellent late witness of the refined and liberal taste ripening in the Europe of the great amateurs until the

---

4. See William Spaggiari's edition of the *Saggio sopra la pittura* (Rome: Archivio Guido Izzi, 2000).

1750s, a taste that Caylus, Piranesi, and Winckelmann then inflected toward the "return to the antique."

In 1746 Algarotti returned to Frederick's court, his Cytherea. The king of Prussia named him chamberlain and a knight of the Order of Merit and awarded him the title of hereditary count, with a considerable pension. He remained in Berlin and Potsdam until 1753. During this interval he had ample opportunity to observe the squalls in relations between the king and Voltaire, without losing the friendship of either one. In Berlin he wrote numerous essays, sometimes in a genre analogous to the one Voltaire devised for the articles of his *Dictionnaire philosophique*, or more happily in the genre of the discourses of the pan-Italian Academy of Arcadians (of which he was a member, as was Voltaire) or of the memoranda of the French Academy of Inscriptions.

DEFENSE OF LITERARY ITALIAN IN FRENCH EUROPE

Algarotti's 1750 *Saggio sopra la lingua francese* and his other *Saggio sopra la necessità di scrivere nella propria lingua* were actually arguments in favor of Italian. Far from contesting the supremacy of the French phenomenon, Algarotti complemented it with the duty of Italian literary men to illustrate and pursue their great literary tradition in their own language,[5] which enjoyed certain virtues that French lacked. We are still a hundred leagues from Herder and Hamann and their Romantic theories on various peoples' linguistic roots; hence Algarotti's moderation would be accused of antipatriotism by Foscolo and Tommaseo in the nineteenth century. His works were scorned as those of an *afrancesado*.

Returning to Italy, he remained a prince of the peninsula's liter-

---

5. On the Franco-Italian linguistic quarrel that begins under Louis XIV, see *Discussioni linguistiche del Settecento*, edited by M. Puppo (Turin: UTET, 1956 and 1966), as well as Corrado Viola, *Tradizioni leterarie a confronto: Italia e Francia nella polemica Orsi-Bouhours* (Verona: Fiorini, 2001).

ary life. He died in 1764. On his tomb, in the Campo Santo of Pisa, Frederick ordered the following inscription to be engraved: *Ovidii aemulo, Newtonii discipulo, Fredericus Rex.*

In conformity with the principles declared in his *saggi*, Algarotti wrote most of his works in Italian, a language that remained, from the sixteenth century on, familiar to all of cultivated Europe. French Europe was by and large polyglot. Voltaire himself wrote in Italian to the "Swan of Padua." The world of music, theater, and the arts, from London to Dresden, from Paris to St. Petersburg, spoke Italian. And even in France, there was no question, for anyone with the least pretension to letters, of being unable to read *Orlando furioso* and *Gerusalemme liberata* in the original. The relative hegemony of French, which in the theory of its Parisian apologists could assume a scornful and polemical character, had nothing threatening or corrosive about it with regard to the other languages of Europe.

Of course the cosmopolite Algarotti could speak and write a good French. Popularizer of Newton and an honorary Londoner, he was also quite comfortable in English. To Frederick II, on whose partiality for French we have remarked, he wrote in the language of Voltaire. Here are some examples of the correspondence between the king of Prussia and his confidant.

CORRESPONDENCE BETWEEN FREDERICK II AND COUNT ALGAROTTI

From Crown Prince Frederick to Francesco Algarotti

Remusberg, September 1, 1739

Pupil of Horace and Euclid,
Fair and engaging citizen
Of Reason's native realm,
Where the Void must recognize
The rule of Number & Name;

Naturalized by Ovid within
The empire of all diversion,
Where Imagination herself
(Vivacious charmer) prefers
To naked Truth such brilliant
Heroes as Fiction and Gaiety;
O new creator of Light,
Phoebus of your natal earth,
It is that shining career of yours,
And your effulgent knowledge
That already lights our way:
The pliancy of your genius
Wakens your response to talents:
A Newton in philosophy,
A Bernini in architecture,
In poetry another Homer
Who by his verse made gods
As saints are made in Rome,
Where a man is often placed
Unworthily in the heavens.
Yes, already Virgil and Tasso,
Surprised by your high deeds,
Politely cede you pedestals
Supposedly theirs forever.

I have received it all, my dear Algarotti, from the divine poetry of the Swan of Padua to the estimable works of the sublime Candide. Happy those mortals who can enjoy the company of men of wit! Happier still the princes who can actually possess them! A prince possessing only such subjects would be reduced to no populous empire; yet I should prefer such indigence to others' wealth, and gladly find myself principally flattered if I could hope that

You would embellish these regions
With your lyre and your compass;

Exceeding Virgil, by your genius
You could see your life run its course
With those who walk in the wake
Of Augustus and of Maecenas.

Indulge me this comparison, and remember that something must be conceded to the poetic tyranny of form.

I hope my first letter has reached you. I will soon have done with my refutation of Machiavelli; I am now merely reviewing the text and correcting some few negligences of style, and certain errors committed against the purity of the language that may have escaped me in the heat of composition. I shall send the work to you once it is completed, so that you may undertake responsibility for seeing it through the press. I am doing all I can to be worthy of such an enterprise.

I shall never forget the eight days you have spent with me. Many travelers have succeeded you, but none compares with you, nor do I expect any to do so. I shall not soon leave my retreat where I live in repose, as they say, dividing my hours between study and the fine arts. I hope you will let nothing erase from your memory the citizens of Remusberg: take them for what you will, but never do them any injustice as to the friendship and the esteem in which they hold you. I am, my dear Algarotti,

Your faithfully affectionate
Frederick

From Francesco Algarotti to Frederick II

Dresden, May 2, 1742

Sire,

All the letters with which Your Majesty honors me are assuredly worthy of cedar; but I should wish, Sire, that the latest was written on incombustible linen; so that down through the ages, victorious even over fire, it might forever be a monument to the kindnesses with which Your Majesty deigns to honor me. Posterity would see therein the treasures of Y.M.'s mind more clearly than ever in the fine verses with which the missive is enriched; would admire the great projects that fill your soul; would envy me the badinage and affectionate expressions on the part of a King, all of which would constitute its admiration and delight: expressions one is accustomed to find only upon the lips of those by whom one is most dearly loved. What commentaries and what research would not be made concerning me! I should be perpetually on men's lips: my name would live beside that of Y.M. and in speaking of Achilles one would sometimes remember Patroclus. In what way, Sire, have I deserved these new favors on Y.M.'s part? Is it because I love and admire Y.M.? But, Sire, if fear must increase in proportion to the number of one's rivals, in what anxieties must I not be living now? I surely have, at the very least, as many as those who have the honor of seeing Y.M. or who read the Court Gazette, were it only the one from Vienna. But, Sire, not content with so many marks of kindness, not content with making me live in poetic scenes that the French Correggio would call his own, Your Majesty further honors me with his orders. This would be, Sire, my crowning happiness, did I not find in myself certain insurmountable obstacles to their execution: and I must indeed, Sire, bewail my fate, that of so many commissions with which Y.M. might honor me, there is precisely one that falls to my lot that I cannot credit to my glory and for which I feel myself altogether inept. All that can console me, Sire, is that if I do not obtain by success the pleasure of obeying Y.M., I could certainly not lose, by the admission of my incapacity, the inestimable treasure of his esteem that I shall ever regard as my most precious possession in all the world. Moreover, Sire, if Y.M. permits me to add two more words to the above, I believe that the surest means of having what Y.M. desires is to request, or to insinuate Y.M.'s intentions to the Court. They can only be grateful to Y.M. for affording them a means of strengthening the bonds of a friendship with Y.M. that to them must be at once so pleasant and so useful. For myself, Sire, I am preparing my admiration for whatever Y.M. will permit us to see within a month. I am sure that Y.M. will cull a splendid result from the Austrians and from Fame.

Everyone is convinced, Sire, that the fate of the Empire and of Europe is in your hands. Hurl the lightning, Sire, even as Jupiter, but like

him establish peace on earth, and serenity in heaven once Y.M.'s jus-
tice is satisfied.

Algarotti

From Count Algarotti to Frederick II

Berlin, September 2, 1749

Sire,
Far from one evil never coming without another, Y.M. has indeed
proved the contrary to me by the letter with which Y.M. deigns to
honor me. I see, Sire, that Jupiter has not poured his benefits upon me
from that cask he keeps on his left, without ever seeking to open the one
on his right. The consultation that Y.M. is so good as to send me (for
Apollo is also a physician) is a divine emanation from that beneficent
cask, and will probably be a balm to my troubles. Despite my parlous
state, the confidence a patient must have in his physician will certainly
not fail me, for I entrust myself almost as much to Frederick *signed at*
the bottom of a consultation as I would trust myself to Frederick *at the*
head of sixty thousand men. I have already begun, Sire, following
Y.M.'s prescriptions. My diet is very severe, and from it I have abso-
lutely removed supper. The publication of my book is a pleasant dis-
traction, unless the slowness of the printers disturbs the secretion of
that juice so necessary to the equilibrium of our animal economy. I offer
Y.M. the humblest thanks for the permission granted concerning
M. de la Métrie, and much more for the fact that Y.M. expresses the
desire that I complete my cure under his very eyes. That is a powerful
reason to encourage my printer, in order to bring myself into the pres-
ence of the august physician of whom I have the honor to be the patient.
Algarotti

From Frederick II to Count Algarotti

Potsdam, September 6, 1749
Here is a much-abridged canvas of the opera of Coriolanus. *I have*
submitted myself to the voices of our singers, to the whim of the

decorators, and to the rules of music. The most touching scene is that of Paulino with his father; but since recitative is not his strong point, what is most touching must be put in Astrua's mouth, which might provide a recitative with accompaniment. You shall see that I had no desire to create a long opera; if it lasts three and a quarter hours with the ballets, that is long enough. I beg you to have Filati read through it with you; but please note that there are long recitatives only in the fifth scene of the third act. Astrua's first-act recitative has no need to be long. Senator Benedetto's narrative at the opera's end must be touching without accompaniment, because this senator performs it without passion; yet it is essential that the poet touches all the points I have indicated.

As for ideas, I look forward to yours, for with your help this piece will have some relation to French tragedy. As for the poet, he is permitted to pillage all the fine sources applicable to the subject; and when the poet has no further need of my rough draft, you must see that it is put in Graven's hands, for there are all sorts of things for the tunes that, with regard to certain details, concern him. Be the Prometheus of our poet. Inspire him with that divine fire you have stolen from the heavens; and may your inspection suffice to produce as many fine things as your great talents can bring to light. The public and I will be obliged to you for making our spectacle illustrious and for having furnished us with reasonable pleasures.

Frederick

From Count Algarotti to Frederick II

Berlin, September 11, 1749

Sire,

I beg Y.M. to permit me to congratulate him on his opera Coriolanus, *the effect of which he will see much better than Y.M. could do by reading. I have heard two rehearsals; all the interest is there despite the brevity of the recitatives; and Y.M. had given his orders for the music so that in the midst of the most agreeable variety, this same interest is increased to the point where* Coriolanus *will draw almost as many tears from the lovely eyes of Berlin as* Iphigenia *extracted during the last carnival. Y.M. has found the surest method of having the finest operas in the world, which is to make them himself:*

> . . . totamque infusa per artus
> Mens agitat molem.

If after Coriolanus, *Sire, it is permissible to speak of myself, I should say to Y.M. that M. Lieberkühn has quite insisted that I take the waters at Egra for a few days. He regards this remedy, quite as Y.M. does, as the fundamental basis of my recovery: indeed it seems to me that I am beginning to feel the good effects already. Y.M. will have doubtless seen the* specificum universale, *so to speak, in a letter from M. Cataneo that Count Podewils mentioned to me: though I am as incredulous about such remedies as I am with regard to perpetual movement and the quadratures of the circle we are shown daily, I shall nonetheless write to Venice to try to obtain certain details concerning this matter. But at the same time, Sire, I regard this sort of faith I now find in myself as a symptom of my disease.*

My publication does not proceed so rapidly as I should like, but as fast as it is possible for me to manage. It seems that my printer has taken for his motto festina lente.

Dare I ask Y.M., whose moments are worth others' years, what epistle, what ode, what poem is now in his hands? We consume our life turning a few phrases, arranging words: Y.M. in his spare moments can create the finest things, which will forever constitute the delight of those who will know what it is to wed the most useful philosophy to the truest poetry.

Algarotti

From Frederick II to Count Algarotti

Potsdam, September 12, 1749

I am greatly relieved to know that you are taking the waters at Egra. I am certain that after the cure you will feel greatly relieved. You are proceeding much more wisely than I with your works; you polish them and after that you have them printed; myself I print, I repent, and then I correct. You ask me what I am doing. I am erasing a lot. I am up to my eighth epistle, and to keep from reviewing my text so often, I give it a certain time to rest; I shall look at it again soon enough, after which I shall proceed with the printing. We shall have the rehearsal of Coriolanus *after dinner. I shall be able to give you the news once I've heard the opera.*

Voltaire has just played a trick that is unworthy of him. He deserves to be branded on Parnassus. What a shame such a splendid genius should be united with such a cowardly soul. He has all the graces and all the naughty tricks of a monkey. I'll tell you what happened when I see you next; but I shall give no sign that I know a thing about it here, for I need him for my study of French elocution. One can learn fine things from a rascal. I want to know all I can of his French; what do I care about his morality? The creature has found a way to unite contraries. One admires his mind and at the same time despises his character. The du Châtelet has given birth to a book, and we're still waiting for the child; perhaps in a moment of absentmindedness she will forget to give birth, or if the embryo ever appears, it will be a Collected Works.

I urge you to make no use of the panacea Cataneo is going on about. I don't believe a word of the news he's spreading, even if it's all true; I don't want to make use of any medicine he praises, even if he's tried it on himself, and worst of all, a panacea! Chemists invent such things. Everyone believes in them when they first appear, but soon enough the truth is out. I recommend good humor, diet, dissipation, and taking good care of that machine that gives you such good ideas.

Farewell.

Frederick

10. Charlotte-Sophie d'Aldenburg, Countess of Bentinck: "The Sévigné of Germany"

OF MODERN DEMOCRACY it might be said, to paraphrase the famous gibe "How beautiful was the Republic under the Empire," that it was never so beautiful as at its birth under the ancien régime in France, when still-powerful hierarchies and still-decisive characters bent without breaking under an aspiration of wealth to equality (by talents) and to liberty (by self-affirmation). This double aspiration had not yet discovered its own self-destructive power, as Chateaubriand so clearly understood; he writes, in his *Life of Rancé*: "Here, under the protection of women, began society's commixture and here was formed, by the fusion of ranks, that intellectual equality, those inimitable manners of our ancient nation. The politesse of intellect joined the politesse of manners; one could equally live well and speak well." This same Frenchman of the Age of Enlightenment, inconsolable for its wreck, could declare himself at once a "democrat by nature" yet an "aristocrat of manners."

In the Catholic and monarchic France of Louis XV and Marivaux, the collision of old religious, moral, and social principles and of modern appetites for independence had been much attenuated. To the great scandal of soured Jansenists, women were the first to create this diplomatic climate and to benefit from it. Eighteenth-century Protestant Europe—the Denmark of Königsmark, the Geneva of Julie d'Étange, the Germany of Werther, the Scotland of Corinne and Lord Nevil—was much harsher than France for women. It would take a very high-minded soul and much confidence in the solidarity of French Europe to permit oneself, in such regions, openly to contest the biblical and patriarchal conventions.

Charlotte-Sophie d'Aldenburg, Countess of Bentinck (1715–1800), never went to Paris. She was nonetheless French, which did not signify merely Francophone. To choose to be and to feel oneself French came down to sharing an aristocratic way of being above the conventions. It was also, for a woman, a way of being free, not by law but by merit and courage.

Until lately this grande dame, so celebrated in eighteenth-century Europe, had received only English and Dutch biographies. Since the relatively recent discovery, in her family archives, of numerous notes and letters from Voltaire (the great man did not as conscientiously preserve his correspondent's replies), she has now been adopted by French research under the double patronage of the Voltaire Foundation at Oxford and feminist studies.[1]

Charlotte-Sophie was born the only daughter and a princess of royal blood to the cadet branch of the Danish royal family. From her tutor Monsieur de Launay and her grandmother Charlotte-Amélie, born Princesse de La Trémoille (a Calvinist seeking voluntary exile with her Danish cousins and in 1680 marrying Count Antoine d'Aldenburg), she received an entirely French education. At the age of twelve in the Château de Varel, on the shores of the North Sea, inspired by the self-portrait of her great-grandmother the Princess of Tarento, which the Grande Mademoiselle had published in 1659 in her famous *Galerie des portraits,* Charlotte-Sophie described herself thus:

I am quite often told that I have an invincible sense of humor,

---

1. In 1997 these two authorities collaborated on the first book in French devoted to the countess, entitled *Une femme des Lumières: Écrits et lettres de la Comtesse de Bentinck, 1715–1800* (Éditions du CNRS), an excellent biography and anthology by Anne Soprani (author of *La Révolution et les femmes,* 1988) and André Magnan (first editor, in 1976 and 1982, of Voltaire's letters to the countess). In 1996, Charlotte de Bentinck's life was filmed as a historical drama by Dutch director Ben Verborg. The same year the novelized biography by the famous Dutch author Hella S. Hasse appeared in a French translation by Anne Kroon under the title *Madame Bentinck l'Indiscrète* (Paris: Seuil).

and I must accept the charge. I have a contrary spirit, which makes me a disagreeable conversationalist. When I want something, nothing but authority is capable of driving it out of my head. I am told this, and if one must speak frankly, I believe that what I am told is true. I am tired of speaking ill of myself. May God correct me and make me the worthy daughter of the most honorable father and the most virtuous mother who ever lived. May God make me his child.

This precocious aristocratic "self-consciousness," the art of thinking, speaking, and writing in the most elegant French, certain numismatic, artistic, and musical talents, and a love of beauty and a passion for happiness constituted the best of the dowry, entailed by huge debts, left her by her father at the time of his death in 1738. Meanwhile he had encouraged her to marry a rich, noble, and powerful neighbor, Willem von Bentinck, a Dutchman connected through his family's senior branch to the House of Orange and the English court, as well as having become a count of the Empire by purchasing the title at the Viennese court. The fiancé was in a position to cover the outstanding debts of the Aldenburgs, receiving in exchange certain rights to their lands. Yet at the age of eighteen, Charlotte-Sophie was already the mistress of her cousin, Count Albrecht-Wolfgang of Schaumberg-Lippe, who gallantly offered to break his own marriage to elope with her:

Madame, you have loved me since childhood, I have had the happiness to make the first impression upon your heart it ever received, and I esteem and know you sufficiently to be certain that you will never change, that you will preserve those affectionate feelings for me that are my particular glory.... You must avoid a marriage that will in essence be no more than a crime.

Charlotte-Sophie chose to do violence to herself in order not to disobey her father. Yet she did not long abide by this cruel choice.

Incapable of yielding to an imposed marriage, she soon returned to her great love, Albrecht-Wolfgang. She waited, however, until her father died, in 1738, to abandon publicly a union that had already made her the mother of two sons. She was obliged to sign a disastrous deed of separation that deprived her of the revenue of her Dutch, German, and Danish lands and forbade her to see her children again.

She was the object of universal scorn in the courts of northern Europe. Though attempting to conceal the birth of a third son (fathered by her lover) at the Château de Varel, where she had spent her childhood, she knew she was being hunted down. "The very foundations of my soul have been so shaken that the dreadful shocks it has received have nearly overwhelmed my reason, my memory, my health, and my repose," she would write in a sketch of apologetic *mémoires* she never completed or published.

But she stood fast. With her mother, who sided with her, and her young adulterine son, soon followed by two others, she took up residence in the Château de Bückeburg, the capital of tiny Lippe, of which her lover was the count. She reigned there herself, as at once the Marquise de Montespan and the Marquise du Châtelet, overshadowing the count's pious legitimate wife and setting the clocks of this little northern haven by the books, the conversations, the music, and all the arts and festivities of Paris.

When Frederick II, in 1740, the year of his coronation, made a brief sojourn with his suite at Bückeburg, Charlotte-Sophie befriended Maupertuis, who accompanied the young king of Prussia. She was to remain in correspondence with the illustrious French savant, and enjoyed manipulating microscope and telescope according to her new master's instructions.

The same year, en route to Berlin, Voltaire made a stop at Bückeburg. The lovely and brilliant countess who, like Frederick II, had read everything by the French philosophe (even his study of Newton's *Elements of Physics*), gave the great man the delicious impression of rediscovering the Marquise du Châtelet far from home. For Charlotte-Sophie and her circle he gave a reading of his tragedy *Mahomet*. Another correspondence began for the Countess of Bentinck.

In 1743 the ruling princes of Anhalt came to receive the homage of the Princess d'Aldenburg and the Countess of Bentinck at the Château de Varel, of whose lands these princes were suzerains. Their daughter, the future Catherine II, then fourteen years old, was fascinated by the countess's talents and by her freedom. The girl recorded in her *Mémoires*: "I had never seen a woman riding a horse; I was enchanted at the sight; she rode like a cavalryman.... She danced whenever she chose, sang, laughed, capered about like a child, though she must have been well over thirty." Her parents were shocked at the bad example set by such French behavior. It was too late. The lovely Sophie von Anhalt-Zerbst, the future tsarina Catherine the Great, was already French in mind and manner.

In 1748 the Count von Schaumburg-Lippe died. Charlotte-Sophie was obliged to plead against her ex-husband (now a powerful minister of the Dutch states) in order to save something of her wealth, alienated by an unconscionable divorce contract. The affair was dreadfully complicated, being determined by the jurisdiction of the chancelleries of both Denmark and the Holy Roman Empire. In order to obtain Prussia's support for her case, the countess moved to Berlin in 1750, where she found her two French correspondents, Maupertuis (now president of the Prussian Academy founded by Frederick II) and Voltaire, gentleman of the king's bedchamber. The life of the courtier-philosopher at the side of this young "Solomon" was not always an easy one. Voltaire became even more attached to the Danish countess, whom he nicknamed "the Queen of Sheba." When his service at Potsdam kept him away from her, and even when he resided with the king in Berlin, an uninterrupted epistolary conversation brought them together, and the philosopher became an effective advocate, close to Frederick's ear, of the countess's tangled affairs. In one of his notes, dated from Potsdam, he writes to her:

> M. de Maupertuis has let himself be robbed at supper of a letter from you. I protested with the gentlest possible violence. We are jealous of each other only in order to serve you more

effectively. I read your letter aloud to the king, and we have named you the Sévigné of Germany. You have long since been a subject of our conversations. You make your way wonderfully, Madame: one always succeeds when one knows how to please.

Before leaving Berlin, Charlotte-Sophie was forced to sign in 1754 a humiliating agreement with her eldest son's representatives, paired with a modest income guaranteed by Prussia and Denmark. She had no further recourse except an appeal before the aulic council of the Holy Roman Empire in Vienna. She proceeded there, making a stop in Leipzig, where she formed a close friendship with the greatest figure of German letters of the period, the Francophile Johann Christoph Gottsched, with whom she afterward maintained an assiduous correspondence. In Vienna she cut a much more impressive figure than in Berlin, where Frederick II could not bring himself to pardon her liaison with his younger brother Prince Heinrich. Maria Theresa now occupied the imperial throne, and still another woman, governess of the older archduchesses (one of whom was Marie-Antoinette), Princess von Trautson, dominated the court: Charlotte-Sophie received a warm welcome from the first and became the intimate friend of the second. At the Hofburg, Chancellor von Kaunitz offered no more resistance to her charms than had Prince Heinrich in Berlin.

When she left Vienna on May 17, 1758, for a brief Grand Tour in Italy, she took care to make a long visit to her great friend Voltaire at Les Délices. She wrote to Gottsched:

M. de Voltaire is at present a divinity worshiped by the entire world. I have never seen an idolatry more highly developed than this one, which seems to be universally shared. However, he understands perfectly how to deserve it by his behavior: he is charming, affable, gracious, sociable. Indeed, Monsieur, you would certainly not recognize him. First of all, he is coquettish, carefully powdered, and dressed to the nines. He insinuates himself quite regularly into the company here, addresses everyone familiarly, deigns to communicate with all and sundry; he sups, he gambles, he strolls, he lives like everyone else and speaks as no one has ever spoken. His house is furnished like a prince's residence, and he is the only person in this entire country who lives in such opulence.[2]

On the other hand, nothing pleased this good Lutheran in Calvin's city. In 1791, she wrote to her granddaughter, Charlotte Milnes, in Greece at the time:

M. de Voltaire himself has vainly tried to make me find the place agreeable. In this town everything strikes me as of an insolent mercantilism I find repellent. One arrives on foot in a great crush, and one envies rank to the most absurd degree. Even in the streets, one vies for the right-hand lane in the mud! The atmosphere is pedantic, preachy, harsh, and caustic. Courts are mocked and vices exaggerated; people are false and envious of distinctions courtiers are accused of vying for, and that oneself courted greedily though it led to nothing.... And Lake Leman is the most boring lake on earth.

This is a condensed version, only a little earlier, of Chateaubriand's impressions of Philadelphia and Tocqueville's of Boston.

Back in Vienna, the countess gradually became persona non grata. The development of the Seven Years' War constrained Maria Theresa to support, with France, the Danish interests, and to abandon the Aldenburgs' cause. Charlotte-Sophie's great worldly and gallant career ended with her departure from the Austrian capital in 1761. Initially she withdrew to her old château at Jever, then in 1768 she moved to the rich Hanseatic city of Hamburg, which she never left until her death in 1800. Her correspondence with her mother and her friends throughout Europe, and the bright interlude represented

2. *Une Femme des Lumières,* p. 106.

by the all too brief embassy of the young Noailles couple ("the marquis is the most lovable Frenchman I recall having known at that period of my life"), compensated somewhat for her difficult material circumstances and her lack of enthusiasm for this bourgeois city. But having been to a remarkable extent a loving daughter, a star of the great world, a woman of affairs and intrigues, she then fulfilled her vocation as a mother and grandmother; two of her adulterine sons (notably the younger, Weisbrod, who became a first-class engraver in Paris and who printed for her the catalog of her splendid collection of ancient coins and medals) kept her company to the end. The children of the younger of her legitimate sons, defying Willem von Bentinck's ban on visits, frequently came to gladden the countess by their youth and their affection.

When the Revolution began in France, she had already taken sides. Her house in Hamburg became a refuge and an information center for the princes' faction. Her letters to her friends Baron de Johnn, a distinguished Danish diplomat, and General Nicolaï, in the service of the Duke of Wurtemberg, showed with what passion and political lucidity she followed the events in Paris day by day.

This woman of the Enlightenment had every reason to approve or to desire the emancipation of her sex. She had even written certain *Lettres*, which she neither finished nor published, setting forth her ideas on the exclusive and excessive masculine "empire," and on the better education that women merited in order to reestablish the natural balance. Yet neither Condorcet's abstract views nor those of Olympe de Gouges on the rights of man reconciled her to the French Revolution. On the contrary, she saw in this cataclysm the conclusion of an evolving movement in which she had participated from within, and indeed a brutal reaction of the "masculine usurpation": "The Revolution," she wrote, "has completely done away with amenity and good manners, for which it has substituted violence." David's *Oath of the Horatii*, his *Rape of the Sabine Women*, and the hatred of which the unfortunate Marie-Antoinette was the object all the way to the scaffold did not contradict this resolutely feminist interpretation of events; in December 1789, the countess wrote to Baron de Johnn:

I feel twice over the painful scorn that masculine principles and arrangements have long since inspired in me. Forgive me, Monsieur, for this notion. M. de Voltaire, or his hero, says in his *Henriade*:

> *In this sex, after all, you [Queen Elizabeth I] are not included:*
> *Of it, the illustrious Elizabeth has only the seductive appearance.*

I am telling you something of the kind, Monsieur. You too possess, of that despotic and irresponsible sex, only the degree of enlightenment and intellectual strength that education grants you more than us; and if all men were like you, I believe that everything would go much better, to the degree that things would go well by reversing everything as men have done by the abuse of force according to Nature's clear law whose universal basis is the perfect equality of rights between the two sexes: an abuse that has consequently resulted in disorder and vice everywhere. Laugh as you will at this idea! It will one day take effect, I am convinced. It will be conjectured, ultimately, as was the case with liberty. And it is only after this natural and necessary order will have been established that it will become possible to imagine and to achieve good government and good laws, an arrangement yet to be achieved as long as we treat inhumanely and render cowardly and passive a good half of human creation.[3]

The countess wanted free women to be natural, not just masculine citizens in the feminine case. She still had time to witness, from a distance, the rise of Napoleon Bonaparte, who did not make her change her mind about the regression of the cause so dear to her. The hypocritical Victorian morality of the nineteenth century, which she

---

3. *Une Femme des Lumières*, p. 141.

was chagrined to see dawning in her English grandsons, and what has replaced it since have retrospectively shown how right she was.

I reproduce here three characteristic letters by the Sévigné of Germany from the Soprani-Magnan edition. The first shows her, in all her admiration for Voltaire, delighting in his Parisian triumph in 1778, as if she had been in the first row of the audience of *Irène* at the Comédie-Française. The second, quoted in part, establishes with what political lucidity this Voltairean adept, in despair that her great man is no longer alive to interpose his views, comments at a distance, in July 1789, on the beginnings of the Revolution, without the slightest indulgence for the Genevan Necker. The third, addressed to her English granddaughter Sophie Hawkins-Witsched in 1794 (the countess is an eighty-year-old grandmother), reports her conversations with Voltaire at Les Délices, a country house near Geneva, about the person and the works of Rousseau.

LETTERS FROM THE COUNTESS DE BENTINCK[4]

To Voltaire

Hamburg, April 17, 1778

I feel I should be claiming a miracle has occurred, Monsieur! What? Men have become just? What? Truth has triumphed and reduced prejudice to silence? Yet this is what I see, heaven be thanked, almost without daring to believe it. The revolution in England seems incomprehensible; the one you have just wrought is a hundred times more surprising. We have seen nations fall from the pinnacle of power, but when did we ever find entire peoples deaf to the voice of fanaticism, who failed to punish the sage for having dared to enlighten them and labored to make them happy?

It is not you, Monsieur, it is France I congratulate upon complete victory over her proud rival. Hence it is not only the precarious empire of the sea, it is that of common sense and sound philosophy that our

---

4. *Une Femme des Lumières*, pp. 122–123, 131–133, 165–167.

nation has just won from England. You have just performed in moral-
ity the task of brave Washington. The two of you are hailed, blessed,
admired. In what age are we living, Monsieur?—could it be that the
comet your friend Euler fired off for us was on the point of turning us
upside down? You make me apprehend such a thing more than all our
calculations of the Apocalypse. Need I tell you after that, Monsieur,
with what a transport of joy I savored your pleasure, and that glory so
sweet (since so deserved) that has caused so many worthy folk to shed
tears of satisfaction? I confess that there is some presumption on my part
in seeking to flatter myself that in the midst of so many transports of
acclamation, my faint voice could be heard over that of the public. But
it is my heart's voice that I listen to and that is my guide. It tells me
that the seniority of my rights, the constancy of my attachment, will not
escape the equity of yours. I have not waited for such brilliant homage
in order to consecrate my own to you; and France, indeed all Europe,
merely confirms what I have dared to say and to think for forty years.

Amid so many felicities, I am nonetheless not without a moment's
anxiety. How will your precious health resist such violent movements;
and after the pure air of the countryside, how will your lungs with-
stand the unhealthy fogs of a city, and of a river too slow to carry off
these fatal exhalations of which our more considerable Elbe shows me
the daily drawbacks? I put all my hopes in Mme Denis and M. Tron-
chin. I pray to God and to them to compel you to journey to Ferney. I
am quite aware of the pleasures of being adored, but I recognize that it
is even more agreeable to live in good health. All Paris is quite winded,
Monsieur, have mercy! Permit love and admiration to breathe! With-
draw to your labors for us in your agreeable retreat, and return in a
season less dangerous for an urban sojourn to harvest new laurels. It is
veneration and friendship that wrest from me the liberties that feeling
alone can justify.

If only I might see you again for even a single day before I die! I
confess it is with redoubled joy that I should see at your side your friend
the illustrious Franklin. The brightest jewel in your crown has been
your mutual presence, in those memorable moments that have deter-
mined America's fate and the thinking of the universe.

Farewell, Monsieur, live well and remember that you have nothing finer to do than just that, after having said and done all the rest.

To Baron de Johnn

Hamburg, July 21, 1789

What have you to say, Monsieur, about the unforeseen and incomprehensible events that yesterday's post from France has brought us? I presume you already have these astonishing details, which so furiously affect and intrigue us here. Since, however, it may be that you have not yet been informed of such things, and that today's post from Holland was not yet supplied with them (the Leiden gazette being always a dilatory post), I shall include our German gazette, which must come today at noon and will surely contain them all. We have had in the gazette of the court of France a violent action from the Comte de Mirabeau. This detestable firebrand, who creates as much trouble by action in Paris as by writing in Berlin, has occasioned a deputation and representation to the king, on the part of the States General, in order to make to him, in an extremely insolent and shocking fashion, the extravagant proposition of dismissing the foreign regiments, which are described as barbarians, and the troops in general, which he had ordered to approach both Paris and Versailles in order to put down the popular restiveness, which has caused great anxiety to those insubordinate gentlemen who feel the spirit of rebellion sprouting under the splendid name of patriotism.

The king, apparently soured by this bitter and impertinent address, and feeling the danger he is in when anyone dares speak to him in this tone, egged on by the Comte d'Artois [his younger brother] and his clique, which is opposed to Necker's (Necker being absent), has latterly reacted very strongly, out of weakness (at least it is thus that by putting together the facts I attempt to explain the situation to myself, without anyone's hitherto having explained matters to me). Louis XVI has doubtless been made to feel that if he yielded to this demand of the States General, his authority would be lost without recourse, and that his person itself and the States General would remain exposed to the caprice and the fury of the people governed by the Third Estate, which is the strongest at present; the court, the clergy, and the nobility being now obliged to accept everything Mirabeau and his consorts choose to impose upon them. From which it necessarily follows that M. Necker, who had high-handedly sought the favor of the people of whom he remains the idol, would never yield to such false and dangerous undertakings. So that he is the first figure who must be dismissed. That is how I believe this poor prince has been persuaded, ever inclined to follow the advice of the last to have had his ear.

The banishment of the Genevan minister thus pronounced, the remainder of his colleagues, seeing the turn affairs would naturally take and the absolute necessity for the monarch to remain firm as a rock after the strong gesture he had been forced to make, perhaps judging the good Louis XVI incapable of sustaining any such role and foreseeing in consequence the storm that in this case would fall upon the ministers who were present, requested a general resignation, meaning "Sauve qui peut!" *Notably that poor Montmorin, a close friend of Necker's as well as a friend and favorite of the king though he may be,* sieht ihn doch, ohne zweifel, nicht vor vol an *(doubtless has no confidence in him even so).*

It is thus, Monsieur, that I have managed to put together and to interpret for the moment this entire sideshow, which may decide the fate of France and that of her kings, until some better-informed person will kindly explain the matter to me a little more clearly. Meanwhile, what will be the outcome of all this? For either I am mistaken or we are in the midst of the strangest events, whose meaning God alone can foresee and calculate. If the king had the courage and the firmness of the great Frederick, or of that masterful woman who lays down the law in Russia and in half the world, I should say that everything might still be put to rights: the monarch suddenly recalling that he is a man and a sovereign, realizing that for him all is lost if he cannot seize the reins of government that have slipped from his weak hand; wakened by these powerful shocks from his lethargic sleep and putting himself at the head of the fifty thousand men whom he must summon to his service, the king of France could lay down the law to the States

General and, sword in hand, dictate the constitution as he would have it to his people.

But when I think that for this to happen the troops in question must stand with him, and he himself must then maintain a decisive resolve despite every obstacle, and overcome imminent difficulties and the most eminent dangers, I realize that the hope of such a success is an impossibility, a chimera. And when I see what actions have nonetheless been undertaken, however reluctantly, my hair stands on end with regard to the consequences that, as I see them, can only be dreadful and disastrous. Please God I may be mistaken and see things too darkly. But I confess to you that there are no horrors I do not anticipate and brace myself to confront. How happy I should be to be mistaken! But alas, I have already been too good a prophet, when I saw M. Necker return to the ministry, to deliver his king to the Third Estate and obtain for himself the love of the people at the expense of his master's authority and glory. I then was first to prognosticate that a foreigner, a self-made man of the people, professing a banned religion and puffed up by an eminent position, surrounded by envious enemies, to whom he offered an aspect so weak and a conduct so readily denigrated, could scarcely survive beyond a moment of effervescence, barring a miracle. It is true that I gave him another five or six weeks' reign, and did not expect to see him already on the very edge of the abyss. Despite all this, I should not swear that in the course of some new convulsion that may seize this poor realm, he might be recalled once again and, spurred on by his frenzied ambition, he might be mad enough to accept the responsibility and, seeking to revel in the brief pleasure of returning to Paris in triumph, would perhaps ultimately conclude even more tragically.

To Sophie Hawkins-Witsched

December 2, 1794

You are the rarest and most lovable little creature in the world, my darling kitten, but your charming prattle of last November 11 alarmed me at first (a miscarriage!) and then amused and cheered me up all over again, by the naiveté of your pretty notions and all your extrava-

gance about J.-J.Rousseau. I would have preferred your choice of the Grand Mogul as your godfather than this apostle of the French Revolution. You ask me questions that I shall answer as frankly as my extremely limited knowledge permits (I who cannot have opinions on philosophy, being merely a poor old woman who can say that she knows this or that fact, but cannot judge principles beyond her knowledge and her capacity). The subject has been so widely discussed by enlightened persons that each of us may now draw arguments for and against the ideas of this extraordinary man who has played such a great role since his death. I never knew him personally, but I read each of his works as it appeared in print. I often heard Voltaire discuss with the king of Prussia (at supper, in the home of the king's sister Mme the Margravine of Bayreuth) this celebrated original, his character, and his works, and we have further spoken of him together more than fifty times. I shall tell you about all that, and then you may conclude as to the results.

The first person who was infatuated with Jean-Jacques's style and ideas was the late Princess von Anhalt-Zerbst [mother of Catherine the Great], who from our earliest youth honored me with her friendship. This lady joined to many talents and capacities a considerable intellect and an often bold speculation that tended to the sublime and sometimes to the singular. She was a walking library who, owing only to herself and to her studies the knowledge with which she had embellished her superior mind, had received it without method and without that order that scientific method has put at our disposition and that is so necessary to its perfection. Her native genius frequently sufficed, but just as frequently it was carried away. J.-J.'s first work had the latter effect. She was infatuated, to the point where she told me that "this young author, if he continues in this fashion, will one day be the Haller of France, which is to say he would surpass Voltaire, Montesquieu, and your own illustrious Pope." At that time she had read only Rousseau's text on the danger of knowledge among men. She told me to throw away or to burn all my books of morality and logic, and to make room on my shelves and in my head for this philosopher who alone would develop everything of which humanity was capable, which is to say that we know nothing.

I saw at first that she was intoxicated and that the powerful course of her own imagination had carried her away; I did not greatly fear that an intellect as thoughtful and just as hers would wander long in that wilderness, and I was convinced she would soon recover from this minor aberration. But I realized then and there the danger of that enchanting style, since it left such profound impressions on so fine a mind, and I took care to guard my own (it being much easier to seduce) against an overwhelming influence. Jean-Jacques himself helped me find weapons against his philosophy. His Social Contract, *a work that has done so much harm in France, seemed to me to deserve the attention of the most skillful among our nation's teachers, but to be quite above my own understanding. I had heard discussed these higher matters by persons likely to judge them on good grounds. I realized that theirs shared the fate of almost all humanity's judgments, which is to say: they differ among themselves, and are never in agreement— rarely in mathematics, never in morality, and solely in arithmetic.*

Rousseau, consequently, remained the creator of a code admired by some and censured by others, its merit being undetermined.

His Héloïse *created a sort of revolution that his* Émile *made complete [1761–1762].*

The same difference in judgments was evident in the case of the former work, and this novel is still the apple of discord among people of taste and moralists of any severity. It is a controversy that I believe will never be resolved and that, very fortunately in my opinion, has been set aside in favor of a work even more dangerous to judge, being such a mixture of good and bad, pernicious and excellent, that Solomon himself, were he to be resuscitated in order to decide the matter, would be furiously embarrassed. I am speaking of Émile, *that sketch of education that Rousseau's temerity dared to present to the frivolity of France and to that of its neighbors, who have yielded to the same epidemic.*

This memorable work, which created a revolution in our minds (before its code produced one in the rest of Europe), attracted for a time the attention of all those who read and very promptly occasioned surprising and precipitous changes, without perhaps sufficient reflection, in the important realm of private and even, in some places, of public education.

All I can add, my dear Sophie, is that these two works, Héloïse *and* Émile, *though inspiring us in several respects with admiration and pleasure, nonetheless cured us* radically—*the Princess von Zerbst of enthusiasm and I of the uncertainty I had continued to feel about the author's true character. The disastrous effects this wretched code has occasioned, the distraction of men's minds, the loss of manners, the destruction of religion, of order, and of laws, the total oblivescence of humanity itself, the horrible anarchy that has been its consequence in France (and may soon be the same in the rest of Christendom), will perhaps determine the merit and the danger of these works, whose intention at least seems to have been pure, and whose author cannot be directly censured as guilty of the abuses so frequently made of his ideas, which have been so misunderstood, so falsified, so exaggerated, being perhaps susceptible of generating fine ideas in wise minds, but turning poisonous in the perfidious hands that have abused them in order to destroy order, religion, morality, and happiness.*

I have told you, or at least I have tried to tell you, my dear Sophie, what I think of your celebrated godfather. I am not telling you that this is how you must think, for in truth the subject tends to dissolve my mind. But what I have said to you is the result of my reflections and of what I have managed to digest mentally for some thirty years, though I have not reconsidered these matters for three or four: and my age and my infirmities, and a thousand more intimate matters, having weakened my memory and all my faculties, I am no longer left with very consecutive ideas; I have retained little more than the results that I have offered you here, and that lead me to the judgment that this famous Jean-Jacques has uttered and published good and excellent things, but also foolhardy and dangerous ones. And the event proves, unfortunately, that even if he had the best intentions in the world, Jean-Jacques has yet done much more harm than good, and his imprudent torch has set the world on fire instead of enlightening it.

As for M. de Voltaire, I believe I have remarked that he neither loved nor hated him. He sometimes held against him the little jealousies current in the profession, but I have always known him to render justice to his mind, to his style, without the slightest fear of being thereby eclipsed. I once heard him, in Geneva, actively defend him, but without passion as he had [done] against La Beaumelle and Fréron. He told me one day, which I remember very distinctly, that "the chapters in Héloïse *on dueling and suicide were masterpieces of truth and common sense, which left nothing more to be said." But he derided the whole notion of the novel as a novel, and I believe he was not mistaken, for which reason I should be quite annoyed if your father's desire that you grow up to resemble its heroine Héloïse (I pass over that superficial Sophie) were to be granted, for that Héloïse was, saving your respect, nothing but a cocotte, and Sophie gave every promise to become the same. I have no concern whatever that your godfather should have formed your manners, and I praise God that it is to your worthy mother, and your own good sense, to which this moral task is assigned, which thanks be to heaven has been performed very nicely as it appears, by which conditions I hope that you will abide, without making your own daughters either Héloïses or Sophies à la Rousseau, but with a pure mind and a pure heart, without searching for difficulties where there are none, and trying, like that sublime Rousseau, to be always more judicious or at least always* different *from the rest of the world, a perspective that, given the national English taste, would be even more dangerous than in France.*

His principles, embellished by the grace of his intellect and his style, lead to unsuspected excesses, and it is quite likely that the execrable morality that he has retailed concerning the most dangerous vice of all, without exception, by its effects, has already taken excessive effect in England. The vice I refer to is inebriation; this dreadful passion is at the moment, dearest kitten, on the verge of making England lose all her national preponderance in realms of inspiration, of principles, of mind and manners. Jean-Jacques has been its reprehensible apostle [in the Letter to d'Alembert*], and were it only in regard to this error alone, there would be much to reproach him for.*

But I am rambling. Farewell.

11. The Parisian Model Seen from London: Lord Chesterfield, His Son's Tutor

GREAT LORDS, notably those of the eighteenth century, pass for execrable *pères de famille*. Philip Dormer Stanhope, fourth Earl of Chesterfield (1694–1773), is the very type of the Enlightenment version. The libertinage of his manners as well as the wit that made him feared in London and esteemed by Swift and Voltaire seems hardly propitious to paternal love and tutorial perseverance. And yet it is the father and the tutor who, in Lord Chesterfield's posthumous renown, have prevailed over the scandalous wit and the ironic man of the world. In 1774, a year after his death, appeared the work that has made him, perhaps against his will, a classic of English literature: the letters he addressed to his son from 1737 (Philip was then a child of five) to 1768 (the year Philip died, five years before his father). Never has a father shown himself to be so affectionate and farsighted as this lord who passed for dry and blasé. Never has a son been guided, followed, accompanied, indoctrinated, counseled, instructed, and lectured with more patience and vigilance than this lord's son. Only Rousseau's Émile—a creature of fiction—was educated with such love and intelligence, although along opposite principles.

Even brief fragments, in a nineteenth-century French translation, can give readers some notion of this prodigious Pygmalionism by correspondence: 430 letters, all in English, are still extant. But the European education Lord Chesterfield intended for his son was essentially in the French style, and the counsels he addressed to him were never so deeply felt as during the two years from 1750 to 1752, when Philip, at the end of his Continental Grand Tour, resided in Paris, a city where this English grand seigneur was quite at home.

At least so he flattered himself. The lamentable failure of his precep-torate may have been due to the fact that from the behavioral fluid-ity of the extremely good society of the Paris of his day, he attempted to derive a system that he believed himself to incarnate, but of which no adolescent boy riddled by an illegitimate birth was at all likely to fit the mold.

THE ENLIGHTENMENT, AN EDUCATIONAL CONFLICT

Several times in these letters, there is some mention of M. and Mme Dupin, whom Rousseau served as secretary and of whom Lord Ches-terfield was a frequent guest: Could he, in their home or elsewhere, have encountered Rousseau? It is unlikely that he did so. It is diffi-cult to imagine two men as incompatible as these contemporaries. We speak so easily of the Age of Enlightenment as if everything converged, for our happy modernity, in a single well-lighted salon. Chesterfield himself does not believe the myth: as a good Whig, hos-tile by family tradition to the French political regime, he was de-lighted to learn, while reading Duclos's *Considérations* (dedicated to Louis XV), that "there is a germ of reason that is beginning to de-velop in France." From this he deduced that the Very Christian mon-archy, its divine right, and its papistry would not survive the century.

But for Lord Chesterfield, father and tutor, the two of whom work together, there are conventions much more traditional than merely political ones. Lord Chesterfield raised his son as he would have wished to be raised; he fashioned the boy after a pattern he was proud to have received and illustrated. Rousseau, who far exceeds anyone in the eighteenth century in his rejection of all historical tradition, had clearly felt the conservative force of such a paternal instinct. In *Émile*, the tutor had suppressed the father, who would have hampered him; he had even suppressed the mother. These two inaugural deaths, in a work that is a sort of myth, are already an entire program. Émile is an orphan. The field is thus left entirely free to the philosopher-tutor, who exerts an absolute empire over the child and who is therefore in a position to form him according to his views of natural law. Lord Chesterfield, who had tutors at his command, sought the freedom to perpetuate himself, with all he represents, in his son. Rousseau raises Émile far from Paris, against Paris. For him the capital of the ancien régime is that of the deepest corruption of the natural man. Lord Chesterfield, who sees in Paris the "sojourn of the graces," asks the city to complete and perfect his work.

The Whig grand seigneur might very well desire a reform of the French political system. Yet he, like Edmund Burke, also a Whig, had no desire to dispute the moral success of royal France, eldest daughter of a European civilization several centuries old. Much more than the differences of political constitution between England and France, it was this European civilization that mattered to Lord Chesterfield, and it was to this civilization that he wished to attune his son, as he himself had been attuned. He may well have supported the English policy directed against the arbitrating hegemony in the Europe of Louis XIV's and Louis XV's France. Nonetheless, he saw in France the matrix of civil manners that controlled the entire European operation. For Rousseau, Paris was for that very reason the quintessence of evil, the new Babylon. His tutor intentionally formed Émile as alien to and even as a conqueror of his false civilization. The pedagogic myth of *Émile ou de l'education* was as radically revolutionary as the political philosophy of *Le Contrat social*, published the same year.

The century, and not only the century but the history of Europe, turns on the hinges of these two books. Lord Chesterfield wrote not a book and still less a myth. For twenty-five years he had made use of a style of education that had been elaborated since the Renaissance and that, with numerous variations, had become that of all civilized Europe. His was merely the merit of making that style explicit with a luxury of details entirely his own, by means of a correspondence he alone was capable of sustaining with such abundance, such goodwill, and such naturalness—a naturalness that Rousseau, eager to develop in his Émile as the child of nature, would have regarded as the supreme art of civilized corruption.

The debate that did not occur between Lord Chesterfield and Rousseau carries us retrospectively into the heart of the Enlightenment's latent tragedy. Émile is raised as a "noble savage," capable of passing through the world of cities without letting his native integrity be breached. *Le Contrat social* provides, in the same year, political means to regenerate the corrupted cities. These are two books of radical rupture, inspired by a veritable religious prophetism, as evident in the "Profession of Faith of a Savoyard Vicar" in *Émile* as in the chapter on civil religion in *Le Contrat social*. The *Letters of Lord Chesterfield to His Son* could have been written, with variations, by any father of his rank and of his period, if any other father than he could have taken it upon himself to play at being tutor, when there were excellent and numerous servants to perform this office. One of these was Pangloss, created by Voltaire, who in 1759, in his masterpiece *Candide*, had already put Chesterfield (of whom he was fond) back to back with Rousseau (whom he did not yet detest). The only education that counts is the most unforeseen one, that of life itself.

Chesterfield had nonetheless had certain modest models, for instance, the Marquise de Lambert's *Avis d'une mère à son fils*, which he cites, or better yet *Advice to a Daughter*, addressed by Lord Halifax, his grandfather, to Elizabeth Stanhope, his own mother. The *Letters* figure in a long tradition of aristocratic pedagogy. In 1762 Rousseau could easily reject it from beginning to end as a mountain of "habits that stifle nature": this tradition had age-old origins; it dated back to Quintilian's *Institutio Oratoria* and found a new departure in the great educators of princes of the Renaissance; it was developed, transmitted, and then modified from nation to nation, from generation to generation: in the eighteenth century it enjoyed a "natural" authority and prestige that only time and experience could confer. But for Rousseau this traditional "nature" was merely a delusion: it had the false evidence of historical concretions that seize us from the cradle and rob us of the free use of our energy and our true nature. Rousseau had been preceded, in a quite ecclesiastical mode, by Fénelon; the education of the Duc de Bourgogne, secretly directed against the model of his grandfather Louis XIV, had sought to form, at the heart of a corrupt court, a truly Christian prince, a crowned philanthropist. This profound reform of the realm by a prince's pedagogy, even if it did not have an immediate political effect, anticipated Rousseau's revolution. *Les Aventures de Télémaque* (1699) had prepared the way for *Émile*. But the tradition still had a spell of fair weather in its future.

L'Avis d'une mère à son fils had been published against Mme de Lambert's will. *Advice to a Daughter* had appeared after Lord Halifax's death. These were actually quasi-esoteric texts for private use, inseparable from a social, familial, aulic context within which they assumed their meaning. This context itself was, by definition, the principal educator. The written orientations were limited to facilitating or accelerating the lessons of a tradition carried by the child's society. Nothing in common here with the founding myth that Rousseau created in *Émile* and that separates the child from his familial and historical society as radically as did Plato's *Republic*. Like Mme de Lambert or his grandfather Halifax, Lord Chesterfield had not written his letters with a view to publication. He would very likely have regarded with indifference their eventual appearance. But the second edition of the *Letters* in 1775 (the first, published the preceding year, had quickly sold out) bears a title that would all the same have mortified their author, laden as it was with sermonical and promotional pedantry: *Lord Chesterfield's Advice to his son on men and manners, or a New system of education in which the principles of politeness, the Art of acquiring a Knowledge of the world, with every Instruction Necessary to form a Man of honour, virtue, taste and fashion, is laid down in a plain, easy, familiar manner. This edition to which was then added the Marchioness of Lambert's Advice to her son* (1775). What a revenge for the "undistinguished" woman and heiress of the letters Philip had married unbeknownst to his father, whereas the latter had so urgently recommended that he take amusing and charming mistresses while awaiting the brilliant marriage he himself would have arranged! Thus were the secrets of the tradition proper to an aristocratic education merchandized, *embourgeoisé* like any other consumer product. It was a sign of the times.

The *Letters*, if they are in fact a literary masterpiece, are not a literary work, anymore than the *Mémoires*, the *Correspondences*, the *Testaments of a father to his son*, and other manuscripts for the internal use of ancien régime aristocracy. Improvised in the course of writing by one of the most florid wits of eighteenth-century England, they were attuned to the growth of the child to whom they were addressed and gradually spread before our eyes the resources of memory and experience accumulated by their author. By successive touches they create his complete portrait, lifelike and animated, and it is first of all this self-portrait that, by imitation and contagion, is intended to act on the child's soul and impart to it the desired shape.

But it is a portrait at a distance. Lord Chesterfield was almost constantly separated from his son. He could not exert upon him the mimetic effect of a direct and familiar example. It is therefore a portrait that writes or, rather, that speaks in writing and that gradually reveals the entire inner edifice erected by the father that is to be reconstructed in his son's mind. A prodigious decanting, as fascinating to observe as certain great natural phenomena! Rousseau sought to oppose culture and nature in a radical fashion. Thanks to these letters, which attempt to compensate for an absence, we can see that a second nature, by the force of traditions and the talent of their representatives, can animate the phenomena of culture and confer upon them a sort of generative energy.

An exceptional, impassioned, and constant inspiration produced this regular epistolary flow. An intimate accident, as we shall see, was at the origin of this educative ardor. But the memory into which the noble lord generously delved in order to feed this abundant correspondence had nothing subjective about it. The passion to educate his son drew from Lord Chesterfield's pen a summa of knowledge and civil wisdom accumulated since the Renaissance, its elements creating by successive layers the ideal form of the perfect gentleman, a synthesis of the ancient Orator according to Quintilian and Cicero, of Castiglione's *Cortegiano*, and of the honnête homme *à la française* according to La Rochefoucauld and the Chevalier de Méré. This ideal form, elaborated and enriched by the experience of successive generations, was already, for just that reason, "natural." Lord Chesterfield could rightly consider that it was his, that it was "natural" to him. He incarnated this moral habitus according to his own invention and his singular and personal vocation. It had become his own nature. It was himself.

A FRANCOPHILE WHIG GRAND SEIGNEUR

Lord Chesterfield's education had been less willed and organized than the one he so methodically directed by long distance in his son's interest. It had been for that reason much more ordinary. His father, the third Earl of Chesterfield, who died in 1726, had very little interest in him; he was in fact raised by his maternal grandmother, who inculcated in him an admiration for her husband, George Savile, Marquis of Halifax (1633–1695), who had died a year too soon for his grandson to know him. This highly literary grand seigneur, who made Montaigne his pillow book, had played a decisive and moderating role in the delicate transition from the Stuart monarchy of James II to that of William III of Orange in 1688. One of the founding fathers of the new regime, he had nonetheless been one of the closest friends and collaborators of Charles II, the most intelligent and political of all the Stuarts. An orator, a polemicist, and a moralist, Halifax offered his grandson, retrospectively, the perfect type of the liberal statesmen who wielded power over four centuries of British politics. This example had been transmitted to him directly by oral and familial tradition. In 1714, already instructed at his grandmother's residence by a tutor of French and Huguenot origin, M. Jonneau, who had taught him a perfect French, Philip Stanhope entered Trinity Hall, Cambridge, at the age of eighteen. As a member of the Witty Club, one of those literary associations characteristic of English university life, he studied the classical poets and orators closely and learned Horace by heart.

But the young man who resolutely undertook such exercises did so all the more willingly, knowing how indispensable they were to his already formed purpose. From childhood in his grandmother's house, he had encountered statesmen whose conversation, practical wisdom, and decades of experience had given him, with the still-living memory of Lord Halifax, the notion of what he sought to become. He recorded the words of Lord Galway, who had told him one day, when he was still only a youth: "If you have any intention of becoming a statesman, you must get up early. In the eminent offices which your talents, your rank, and your fortune will lead you to occupy, you must be in a position to receive visitors at any hour of the day, and unless you constantly rise very early, you will have no leisure for yourself."

All his life, therefore, he never rose later than eight o'clock, even when a party or some debauchery had kept him up until four in the morning. His near contemporary, the Duc d'Orléans, abided by the same discipline, and his orgiastic nights obtruded on neither his leisure nor the affairs of his regency. The education of the future Lord Chesterfield was thus largely of his own making, and a living example counted even more for him than books. Hence he remained just over a year at Cambridge, long enough to accumulate the solid classical literary baggage that a man of his caste and ambition owed it to himself to possess. He would write one day to his son:

> I recall, when I left Cambridge, that I had contracted, in the commerce of the pedants of this dreary seminary, a certain literary effrontery, a satirical and scornful turn of mind, and a particular taste for argument and contradiction; but once I had made my entrance into the world, I observed that this was not the proper tone, and I adopted a very different character; I concealed my knowledge, I frequently applauded without approving, and I generally capitulated without being convinced. *Suaviter in modo* [gentle in manner] was my law and my prophets, and if I happened to please (between you and me),

it was much more for that reason than for my knowledge and my actual merit.

Paris, where he settled in 1714–1715 after Antwerp and Brussels on a preliminary Grand Tour, was the decisive experience for him. Here he shed his timidity and his aggressivity, and it was a French-woman of good society who enabled him to make, in an order capital in his eyes, the most rapid progress. He repeated, in a letter to his son, the first observations she made to him, and he did so in French:

"Do you know, when I took this young man on, he had to be reassured? For myself, I believe I made his conquest, for he emancipated himself at that moment, to the point of telling me, trembling, that it was a very warm day. You must help me polish him. What he needs is a passion, and if I do not find myself worthy of being such a thing, we must look about for someone else who is. Furthermore, my novice, do not spoil yourself on opera rats and actresses who may spare you the expenses of sentiment and politesse, but will cost you much more in every other respect. I repeat, if you sink to that level, my friend, you are lost. Those wretched girls will ruin both your fortune and your health, will corrupt your manners, and you will never attain a presence worthy of company."

Everyone laughed at this sermon, and I was simply thunderstruck. I didn't know if she was serious or if she was joking. One moment I was pleased, and the next I was ashamed, now encouraged, now dejected. But I was later to discover that the lady, as well as the company to which she had presented me, was guiding and supporting me in society—gradually I gained assurance and began to have no further shame in my efforts to become civilized. I imitated the best masters, at first with servility, then more freely, and ultimately managed to harmonize the habits I had imitated and those I myself had invented.

The Cantabrigian chrysalis had opened: the butterfly took wing. But this miracle of art and nature could take place only in Paris. Lord Chesterfield was such a success there that he rapidly was taken, throughout Europe, for one of the masters of "wit." He did honor to this reputation with all the more resolution because it had cost him so dear: his independent and redoubtable spirit, which made him an heir of Anthony Hamilton and the Comte de Gramont, a rival of Swift and Voltaire, isolated him in his own party, the Whigs, and almost continually compromised his career as a statesman. The head of the party, Sir Robert Walpole, whom Chesterfield, since their simultaneous studies at Cambridge, had ranked among the bores, was thereby even better attuned to the provincial pedantry of the Hanovers and their mediocre London court. Walpole, irremovable prime minister of George I and then of George II, would have nothing to do with Chesterfield in his successive cabinets. The most he granted him, upon George II's request, was to be ambassador to The Hague from 1728 to 1732.

This did not keep Chesterfield from shining, by his eloquence and his irony, in the House of Commons, and then, after his father's death in 1726, in the House of Lords, frequently opposing bills proposed by his own political friends. He became a journalist and a polemicist of the first order, in the tradition of his friend Swift. His position on the English scene was thus one of singular independence. This Whig was the intimate of the liberal Catholic Alexander Pope and of Dr. Arbuthnot, a moderate suspected of Jacobite sympathies. He even went so far as to make a sort of political rapprochement with Lord Bolingbroke, head of the Tory Party, who had been forced into long periods of exile in France. By his affinities, by his tastes and his wit, by his form, then, Lord Chesterfield was in certain respects a Tory, even a Jacobite, whereas his political convictions, from which he never varied, made him a faithful servant of the regime resulting from the Glorious Revolution of 1688. His "French" or, rather, his "Parisian" side nuanced his loyalism in principle to the Hanover dynasty, for he privately despised its low manners, priggishness, and vulgar mistresses.

France: "Sojourn of the Graces"

Hence it would be difficult to maintain that Chesterfield's attachment to the form of the perfect gentleman, in precisely the version that monarchic France had consummated and given as a model to all Europe, was the semi-treason of an entire life. France, for Chesterfield, was still Montaigne and his *Essais*, as it was for Lord Halifax or indeed for Montesquieu. But it was also the "Graces" that would have seemed servile to Montaigne, and that Montesqueiu had nonetheless honored in his first work, *Le Temple de Gnide.* Their tradition, since Mme de Rambouillet and Vincent Voiture, had prevailed in Paris: it was better suited than the *Essais'* philosophy of "leaps and bounds" to serve the court's purposes and methods. This form was of Italian origin: born at the court of the Renaissance popes, whose European prestige and diplomacy it had served, it had ripened at Urbino, at Ferrara, at Venice; it had been tinged in its usage by ministers and ambassadors of the Spanish monarchy, whose cautious intrigues had for a century sustained Castilian military power; but since the treaties of Westphalia (1648) and the Peace of the Pyrenees (1659), of whose founding character Lord Chesterfield frequently reminded his son, it had been the French court's turn to arbitrate Europe's military and diplomatic operations. The Italo-Spanish form of the aulic civil servant had become French. Relieving the *noblesse d'épée* of what Montaigne called the sage's philosophical liberty, this French version had become Louis XIV's political instrument, the indispensable complement of his army and navy. A magnificent livery of his representatives, it was imitated by his adversaries.

But for an English grand seigneur to adopt the bedizenment of this livery, which had set the style for the courts of Europe, was to declare an allegiance to a French Europe and not to the court of Versailles. It was to recognize and respect the rules of a game, and not to identify oneself, in all servility, with the best player. Lord Chesterfield had assumed the French style, the French language, but he was an Englishman, he was a Whig, he was himself. He belonged to a generation for whom the French form was the European uniform, and he could consider it indispensable for English statesmen and diplomats to show themselves on a level with their French rivals and Continental counterparts. And it was quite true that to be a gentleman *à la française* in London, under the Hanoverian George I and George II, had a signification of pride and freedom à la Montaigne quite different from what it would be for a French nobleman to function as a courtier at Versailles and an *homme de salon* in Paris. Chesterfield was at the time the friend and correspondent of Voltaire and of Montesquieu, and although his three Parisian sojourns were relatively brief, he knew the worldly geography of Paris as well as the machinery of the court of Versailles. He lived in Paris by his wits. When during his third stay in France, in 1741, he made friends with Bolingbroke, who had been the negotiator in 1713 of the Treaty of Utrecht, which rescued Louis XIV (a treaty young Stanhope, making his debut in the House of Commons in 1714, had described as "treasonous," calling for Bolingbroke to be hanged), he took another step toward the France that fascinated him: in such a case it is easy to see to what degree a choice of style can determine at least a political oscillation. In Chesterfield's mind the European and French ideal of civilization, which he shared with the Tory leader in exile, had ended by counterbalancing a Whig alliance that was indeed intransigent, though anything but doctrinaire. Ultimately his reputation as a gentleman hero in the French style, acknowledged by his Parisian peers, always compensated, in his eyes, for the remoteness from political power to which Walpole had reduced him.

There was always, in Chesterfield, a certain degree of aesthetic display, the London reflection of a French *gentilhomme's* accelerated formalism, of which Horace Walpole, son of his old enemy Sir Robert, would in the next generation become the most polished mirror. But only to a certain degree. In Chesterfield's brief term as viceroy of Ireland (January 1745–April 1746), he had performed this impossible task with an admirable combination of political intelligence and humanity. We may glimpse here one of the sources of the exceptional but sumptuous energy he expended for twenty-five years in order to "reproduce" in his own son Philip a form of mind and manners, more European than French, that in London had rapidly become for him, by the very fact of his relative political quarantine, his singular raison d'être.

He was thus the London Garrick in a role burnished by centuries of experience, nuanced by each of the three great Latin nations, but inhabited by a vigorous quality of entirely English independence and entirely his own. He sought to transmit its professional secrets to his son. What director of actors, from Molière to Copeau, from Stanislavsky to Decroux, could be compared to this eighteenth-century grand seigneur? What actor's training period, outside of Japan, had lasted twenty-five years? When Chesterfield came to the point—after fifteen years spent stocking his son's memory and forming his character—of guiding his first steps on the world stage, in Italy, then in France, with what detail and meticulous precision of a true maestro he proceeded! Facial expression, placement and modulation of the voice, bearing, attitudes, hand gestures, style of entrance and approach, care of the body, clothes—nothing was left to chance.

This comparison with the art of the theater could be extended to other arts. Like his eighteenth-century Parisian and European peers, Lord Chesterfield was in fact a universal artist. For him, the art of society summarized and contained all the others. The mirrors that Rousseau's iconoclastic prophecy sought to shatter—not just the stage but the plastic arts as well—Chesterfield cherished and cultivated because in them he recognized himself. The noble lord was an amateur antiquarian and a collector of ancient statuary: in August 1755 he was elected a foreign member of the Académie Royale des Inscriptions et Belles-Lettres, becoming the colleague of the Comte de Caylus. The form of the perfect European gentleman that Chesterfield chose to incarnate and reincarnate was first of all an idea, an ideal statue. Chesterfield had contrived to be, for himself, the Pygmalion of this statue. By imitation he had interiorized and vivified the marble hero that the legendary Marquis of Halifax, his grandfather, had been for him since childhood. He had singularized the statue by lending it his own life, his idiosyncrasies, and now he sought to produce a copy of it. A paternal Pygmalion, he had chosen to lend the ideal statue the life, the features, and even the defects of his own son.

After sculpture, painting: an art that is often in question, meta-phorically speaking, in the *Letters*, which draw, then paint, feature after feature, touch after touch, posing session after posing session, on a "canvas" that gradually assumes life and likeness, the full-length portrait of that ideal form that Lord Chesterfield strove, with a Balzacian passion, to perpetuate. This portrait, even if it re-sembled Lord Chesterfield, was in many respects the moral testa-ment of French Europe as it stood in 1750, though it betrayed at its very heart signs of wear and frivolity. Might the passion Chester-field expended to keep it intact be a symptom of the nascent diffi-culty of transmitting, from his own generation (contemporary with Louis XIV) to that of his son, a model of humanity that, from the Rome of Leo X and the Escorial of Philip II, had matured at the court of Versailles, whence it had spread throughout all Europe? This model had developed, had been altered and handed down, as though naturally, by the contagion of aulic experience, by family example, legend, the arts. What great efforts, how much time it would take now to put such a masterpiece consecrated by the ages into another frame! Rousseau, from 1750 to 1755, invoking an origi-nary Nature in the thunder of his two *Discours*, had shaken Eu-rope's faith in the most artistic secretions of its own history.

To draw this ideal portrait, to paint it, to patinate it on the living canvas of his own son, Lord Chesterfield experienced the joys and anxieties of the ancien régime artist in his studio, pursuing the tra-dition of the masters, scrutinizing the progress of his oeuvre, and trembling to see it completed. As well as statues, bas-reliefs, busts, and ancient medals, Lord Chesterfield had indeed collected, in his Palladian mansion in Grosvenor Square and in his castle at Black-heath, paintings by Italian masters. He was a connoisseur and he had not failed to form his son as a virtuoso capable in his turn of artistic discernment.

In these *Letters* we see him utilizing his son's skills to negotiate, at an important sale in Paris, the possible purchase of two portraits by Titian. He had authorized Philip to buy a cartoon by Thomas Blanchard after Domenichino. Expertise in works of art was one of the talents of the perfect European gentleman; it entered, as did the theater, that mirror of human life, into his education. At this period the arts and education shared, in fact, the same generating principle: mimesis, imitation. This was not a simple mechanical tracing; it was an act of regenerating the model, like paternity itself, like the springtime rebirth of vegetation. At the origins of the Renaissance, Petrarch, in a famous letter to his disciple Boccaccio, had framed for several centuries the natural law of same and other that made mimesis a vital function common to biological generation, to invention in the arts, and to human education. The poet wrote to his disciple:

> The resemblance of a literary work to its model must be analogous to that of a son to his father, which frequently acknowledges a great physical difference, and which consists of a mere nothing, of an "air," as the painters nowadays call it: as soon as one sees the son, the father recurs to memory, when the comparison between the two shows them to be quite different, and yet a mysterious je ne sais quoi sustains the similarity. Into everything we write after a model we must introduce many differences, and leave veiled what subsists of resemblance, so that it cannot be remarked, except upon reflection, and rather as a suspicion than as a certainty. We must then take our inspiration from a natural fecundity and from the virtues of its style, but not repeat its own terms: in the former case resemblance remains hidden, in the latter, it emerges crudely: in the former, we are dealing with a poet; in the latter, with a monkey.

Chesterfield, impregnated with this tao of humanism, sought to be a poet, regenerator of a tradition, mediator of revitalized forms;

he rejected a monkey-son who would merely repeat an emptied form, without animating it by his own will. And he was not unaware that the painting of the Renaissance, notably that of Rome and Venice, had played an essential role in the flowering and vitality of the models of courtly civilization. Raphael's portrait of Balthazar Castiglione, as much as and even more than this papal ambassador's treatise *Il Cortegiano*, had been conceived as a living example for the monarchies' diplomats and high dignitaries to imitate and to reinvent. Titian's portraits of young men were so many variants of the same universal type: the gentleman prepared for political affairs and international negotiation as much as for warfare on land and sea. They pause, before leaping onto the world stage. The gods and allegories of the "history paintings" of the artist of Charles V, Philip II, and Pope Paul III Farnese—*Venus and Mars*, *Venus and Adonis*, *Jupiter and Antiope*—populate the memory and orient the élan vital of these young heroes about to depart for the conquest not of the Holy Land but of the Golden Fleece of European courts. In one of his finest portraits, the *Man with a Glove*, which like Raphael's *Castiglione* is one of the glories of the Louvre, Titian unites the meditative gentleness of an adolescent's face and gaze with the assured breadth of an adult bust. The Roman sculptors, admirable portraitists of the Empire's elite, were already capable of bestowing plastic power on these paradoxes of age and soul. But the Venetian painter completes this oxymoron of head and bust by that of the arms and especially the hands, instruments of prehension and action within time, in the world of the senses. Of the two vigorous but delectable hands of Titian's handsome anonymous model, one is bare, its forefinger pointing down, the other, in repose, is elegantly gloved. This is the emblem of a conduct, a project of ardent and subtle life, in only apparent contradiction with the almost feminine softness of the gaze and its passional reserves. Such a portrait is suffused with the magical power of creating imitators, ancien régime Rastignacs and De Marsays.

Peter Paul Rubens, the humanist painter and diplomat rehabilitated in France, under Louis XIV, by Roger de Piles, had understood better than anyone, at the beginning of the seventeenth century, before Velázquez, before Van Dyck, this elevated function of educating a European political elite that the great painters of the Renaissance had contrived to impart to their mimesis. Naturally enough, these masters had become the fiercely disputed prizes of the princely collections of Europe. They were also the silent professors of an Institute of Advanced International Studies.

And quite as naturally, born and trained for the upper echelons of politics, Lord Chesterfield was a virtuoso amateur of Italian pictures. To make his son understand that the time had come to put the finishing touch to his education as a gentleman–civil servant, he had recourse to the vocabulary of the connoisseur and the art critic. He wrote to Philip, still in Naples and preparing to journey to Paris: "In a virtuoso's terms, your canvas is, I think, a good one, and Raphael Harte [his son's learned tutor] has admirably drawn the outlines: nothing is now wanting but the coloring and the graces of Titian and the *morbidezza* of Guido; but that is no small thing."

Lord Chesterfield had his Roger de Piles at his fingertips. During the reign of Louis XIV, this critic and historian of art (1635–1709) had become the oracle of connoisseurs and amateurs of painting. He had first made himself known, in his *Conversations sur la connaissance de la peinture* (1677), by his apology for Rubens and more generally for the colorist painters he sought to redeem from the disdain in which they were held by the Académie Royale de la Peinture. Under Charles Le Brun's ferule, this institution had imposed a severe classical taste worthy of the Great King; its models were Poussin and the masters of the Romano-Florentine school: draftsmen, as opposed to the Venetian-Emilian colorists.

Roger de Piles's hour had come in the last years of Louis XIV's reign, with the success of his *Cours de peinture par principes* (1708) and his *Abrégé de la vie des peintres* (posthumous, 1715). Now Watteau's genius became apparent to Parisian connoisseurs. "Drawing" was no doubt linked, in this poetics of painting, to the Platonic idea and to its transcendence, triumphing over the sensuous. "Color," on the other hand, suggested the mind's regression to the sensuous and its shifting illusions, and to the art of promptly clearing a path through them, of choosing the right touch. "Drawing" referred to the contemplation of untrammeled essences, "color" to fleeting and flattering appearances. The former was philosophical and religious, the latter sophistical. But in the final analysis, the debate had a political stake. In France, "drawing" referred to the grand official genre of history painting, a direct mirror of royal grandeur and the monarchy's august foundations. "Color" shunned the grand genre with which Louis XIV had identified himself for eternity: it enveloped the art of command in the undulating veils of aesthetic, even erotic seduction. It demanded of government the same sense of nuance and the same fine discernment of social artifice that the moralists and novelists of the age of Louis XV required of the new heroes of court and town, a Maréchal de Richelieu or a Prince de Conti. The transition from classical "drawing" to rococo "color" signifies the evolution of a monarchy that sought less and less to intimidate, more and more to seduce and harmonize.

FRANCE: ACADEMY OF COURTIERS, SCHOOL FOR DIPLOMATS

At the origin of this powdering and of this "rococo" scintillation of language in society, we can already discern, in the margins of Louis XIV's reign, the Epicurean and libertine luxury of La Fontaine's *Amours de Psyché*; but we must also see that this very luxury was about to become the method of French diplomacy, the ingenious strategy of royal power and of its representatives. Power corrupts and corrupts itself. La Fontaine, whose links with London are well known, was a friend of Louis XIV's ambassador to the court of Charles II, Paul Barillon, whose personal charm managed to support itself on French louis d'or and the attractions of Louise de Keroualle, Duchess of Portsmouth, mistress of Charles II and a spy for Louis.

Roger de Piles was an art critic, but he was above all the preceptor and secretary of Michel Amelot du Fournay, ambassador of the French king to Venice. This minor diplomatic agent of Louis XIV had convergent preoccupations with another Amelot, of lesser station, the translator in 1684 of a Spanish best seller, under the French title *L'Homme de cour*. Roger de Piles celebrated in his art criticism the colors of Rubens, the painter-diplomat and student of Justius Lipsius, as well as an admirer of Seneca and Tacitus. Amelot for his part published—besides *L'Homme de cour*—an essay on Tacitus (1680) as well as a translation of the Roman historian's *Annals*. He also translated Machiavelli's *The Prince*. He even edited the Cardinal d'Ossat's *Lettres* (1692), a classic of diplomatic correspondence. In 1682 he put in print the first edition of the Duc de La Rochefoucauld's *Mémoires*. After his death appeared his own edition of the same author's *Maximes*. If Roger de Piles was seeking among the Italian and Flemish colorist painters a mirror of the refined seductions of which the men of the French court had become capable, Amelot sought among the Spanish and Latin moralists and in La Rochefoucauld the secret of combining the art of pleasing with the strength to conquer, *ad majorem regis gloriam*. A fascinating superposition of contraries: inner implacability and external shimmer of the Graces. Lord Chesterfield summed up for his son this aristocratic oxymoron or conjunction of contraries in this Italian motto: *volto sciolto, e pensieri stretti*, that is to say *countenance cool, and thoughts concise*.

The moral question raised by this courtly conduct is that of dissimulation, and more precisely the delicate difference of degree separating this art of secrecy from simulation and lies. Dissimulation is a political and social necessity that can and must remain invisible; simulation and lying are conspicuous vices of the heart. Dissimulation is the general index of social relations: it is inseparable from propriety, which is a penetrating attention to another person and to his singularities as much as a sort of self-protection. Simulation and lying are violent means, symptoms of a flawed mind and a weakened soul. They break the social pact and render odious those who stoop to them. In extreme cases, one might say that dissimulation, habitus of the conduct of virtuosi, releases them from the simulation and lying to which the weak and clumsy are reduced. In a letter of January 15, 1748, earlier than those we will be citing here, Lord Chesterfield writes to his son:

> It has long been said: *Qui nescit dissimulare, nescit regnare* [Whoever does not know how to dissimulate, does not know how to rule.] I go further and say that without some degree of dissimulation, no affair of any importance can be properly concluded. It is simulation that is false, low, and criminal. Dissimulation is a shield, as secrecy is an armor.

Dissimulation and secrecy presume the soul's strength, but a strength known only to itself. What mask is more innocent, more agreeable to another, more delicious for society, more refreshing for oneself than that of the "Graces"? It is here that the Parisian "art of pleasing," refined in the company of ladies, becomes indispensable to the "hero of monarchies."

A diplomat himself, as much as a courtier and a skilled conversationalist, Chesterfield is an initiate of this casuistry of social forms. For him, "drawing," in his great work as educator, is that work's severe, learned, moral part of education, responsibility for which he left to Philip's two successive tutors, learned men of the first order, Pierre Mattaire and William Harte. They had created the character of the child, then of the young man, had provided him with literary and historical knowledge, elements of piety indispensable to his inner construction and capable of providing him resources for the rest of his life. Chesterfield himself was concerned to complete such knowledge by directing the studies of his son's "political sciences": the character of the different nations of Europe, the political regimes of the different states, the nature of their wealth, and the weaknesses of their military traditions. A good student, young Philip Stanhope had even become something of a specialist in international law, notably that branch that governed the internal affairs of the Holy Roman Empire, of which the king of England was one of the electors. He was in possession of all those elements of the soul's strength that can be acquired.

But now, one arrives in Paris. Something entirely different is involved: one must learn to cast a seductive veil over that morally well-formed character, over that solidly constructed mind, in order to play the game well and to win. One must learn to dissimulate that solidity beneath the Graces, that drawing beneath colors. In order to apply and to color such a veil, Chesterfield took up the paint-brushes himself. He replaced William Harte, the learned tutor who had hitherto accompanied Philip and had made his charge almost too learned; it fell to the father to complete, in this final stage and at long distance, the most difficult task of all, the portrait of the *Man with a Glove* that he had long been concerned to bring to an appropriate finish. It is this decisive phase of the correspondence that is our focus here.

A sort of anxiety now makes its nervous presence apparent in Lord Chesterfield's letters. It is controlled and balanced by a form of cheerfulness. Philip's arrival in Paris in 1750 causes his father to relive his own experience of the French capital where he still has many close relationships, masculine and feminine. It was here that he experinced the revelation of what Gracián called the secret of "heroes," and La Rochefoucauld of *honnête gens*, and Titian "of the Graces." For his son and for himself, Chesterfield reopens Watteau's *Enseigne de Gersaint*. If he had known this masterpiece, he would have seen not only the anti-Hogarth, the antithesis of *The Rake's Progress*, but the enchanted reflection of elegance, of gallantry, of the refinement of Parisian worldliness. He would have understood Watteau as he understood Titian and Guido, a symbol, this time French and contemporary, of the enigmatic seduction that can array the true man of the world who, far from referring to the void and to vice as puritanical Hogarth sees it, dissimulates and reveals the superiority of a civil wisdom and a complete character. If Lord Chesterfield had known in Paris the roses of *la douceur de vivre*, he had also experienced, during the negotiations in which he had taken part and that always had ramifications in the most elegant salons of Paris, the thorns that such flowers conceal, even for those who suspect their presence. At The Hague, in 1745, he had been swindled by the charming Abbé de La Ville, the envoy of Louis XV, who had nonetheless become his friend in later days. Of these two faces of the "great world" of France, of her alluring power that makes her such an "artist," he recalled a motto that he often repeated to his son: *Suaviter in modo, fortiter in re.* In other words, the iron hand in the velvet glove: the former is brutal and clumsy without the latter; the latter solo is empty and futile.

So now is the moment, on this pilgrimage to the Parisian Cytherea, to pull on the velvet glove. Without it the iron hand, however well tempered it has been, will rust. Now the rhythm of paternal objurgation accelerates; the moment Philip takes the road to the French capital, Lord Chesterfield ends his letters with a leitmotif in Greek: *Charites, Charites* (the Graces, the Graces). As if one were hearing Mephisto making Faust's ears ring with the strange invocation "the Mothers, the Mothers." Without the Graces, there can be no question of succeeding in French Europe, even if one were the shrewdest politician and the most determined of diplomats. Neither Frederick II nor Choiseul would have contradicted Lord Chesterfield.

THE SECRET OF FRENCH ASCENDANCY

For Chesterfield, then, Paris was the school of the Graces, Paris was Cytherea. The city's salons, suppers, theaters, parties, the veritable science of gaiety and pleasure, the *intrigues galantes*—for him all these were still, in 1750, so many paradoxical symptoms of a dissimulated superiority, all the more striking in that it could assume, with disarming naturalness, the feminine mask of voluptuous grace. The Japanese *onagata* is that actor of genius who, at the price of an iron training, manages to assume all the most delicious charms of the geisha, abandoning them if necessary at the least-expected moment, like Judith or Clorinda, suddenly drawing his sword and dealing death. For Chesterfield, Paris was an academy of *onagatas*, even if in his day the training was no longer of iron and the surprise of strength beneath gentleness much rarer. For his son, whom he had trained so long and so severely, he dreamed of seeing the young man assume the French "Graces," if only to turn them, at a given moment, against France.

So many years of labors and studious journeys would have meaning only if young Philip emerged victorious from this supreme initiation. In the correspondence the gravity of this stage is marked by the change of salutation: the hitherto invariable "My dear boy" becomes "My dear friend." This is the signal of the transition from school to real life, from sheltered childhood to adulthood and its odyssey. But it is also an invitation to the young man to deserve the title of friend, and to show himself capable of entering with his father and following him into the close community of the samurai of European aristocracy, as capable of drawing the sword of wit as of deploying the charms of seduction and civility. But to succeed in the school of the Graces is "no small affair." Chesterfield does not conceal this from himself, or from his son.

Try as he would to assure himself on the ground, in Paris, of the complicity of experienced and reliable women friends like the Marquise de Monconseil, or of first-rate auxiliaries such as the Abbé de Guasco, Montesquieu's friend, or the Abbé de La Ville, his old adversary at The Hague; and familiar as he was with the terrain, able to foresee all its trials, he knew quite well he was no longer entirely master of the game. He had collected on the spot all the conditions favorable to the initiation. But if the enterprise was to succeed, it was still necessary that his son's nature cooperate. And here the father held no winning cards. To don the mantle of the Graces, one must have some natural genius, some *ingenium*. One can grow into the Graces, but one must first be capable of doing so and of finding in oneself the seeds of such efflorescence. This gift of social artistry is not to be learned, only recognized. What was it then that Chesterfield meant by "Graces"? The classical moralists' je ne sais quoi, Castiglione's *sprezzatura*, Moncrif's "art of pleasing": in all these one discerns an erotic element that relates to magical contagion more than to any semiotic code. The secret of success in the theater of the world is a sort of second state, enchanted and enchanting, that men and women cannot resist: but this enchantment, if it passes through the requirements of gestures, through the correctness of movements, through the dance itself, is due above all to a natural charm that cannot be invented or learned. It is simply discovered. Here again, we confront a paradox, a union of contraries and incompatibles: the supreme art of pleasing achieves its effect only if it is first a spontaneous desire and a natural talent to please. In this great divergence of which the courtier must be capable, nature and culture overlap and sustain each other inseparably.

How to produce the spark that would make Philip what Henry James would call "a success" in Paris? Lord Chesterfield set turning all the wheels of the academy of Graces, of which the theater was one. The stage taught that "the matter," the text, even of a great writer like Corneille, was insufficient to transport the spectators. For the performer, and therefore for the man of the great world as well, "the expression, the gaze, the gestures, the movements, the enunciation, the harmonious accent were as necessary as the matter itself." The theater of the French salons corresponded to that of the stage. The form of which its actors were capable produced a magical effect on its spectators.

"The French," writes Chesterfield, "it is only to do them justice, are much concerned with purity, precision, elegance, and style in their conversation and in their letters. *To tell properly* for them is an object of study: and though they sometimes carry things to the point of affectation, they never express themselves in a vulgar fashion, which is much the worst of such extremes."

This tone of good company is to be learned only by impregnation and by mimicry. But the comic stage, like the theater of society, is also the occasion of a study quite as indispensable for a superior savoir vivre: that of "characters." The art of making oneself agreeable actually supposes a fine discernment of the differences that separate men, differences that must be known and recognized in order to avoid clumsy collisions: "With very little knowledge and experience of the world," Chesterfield writes to his son,

> one may recognize determined, striking, colorful characters. These are not common, and make an immediate impression: but in order to distinguish both nuances and the almost imperceptible shades, the finest gradations of vice and virtue, of reason and folly, of strength and weakness, of which such characters are commonly composed, one must have had some experience, must have observed a great deal, and paid wonderful attention. In like cases, most men do the same thing, but with a difference that is responsible for success. A man who has studied the world knows the time and occasion for action; he has analyzed the characters with whom he must deal: to them he adapts his means and puts his reasoning within their reach. But the man who has only what is called common sense, who has reasoned only from his own experience, and who has not struggled against the world, endangers what he says, hurries precipitously to his goal and breaks his head before reaching it.

Worldliness is a science, studied in the mirror of human characters and actions, and it is this science as well that gives its possessor the artist's conviction, his infallible effect on others. Chesterfield becomes an actor and a dancer himself in order to set his son on the path. Miming in his letters the knowing and gracious flight of Watteau's *Indifférent*, he invites Philip to imitate him in his letter of February 14, 1752: "There is a court garment, as well as a wedding garment, without which you will not be received. That garment is the *volto sciolto*; an imposing air, an elegant politeness, easy and engaging manners, universal attention, an insinuating gentleness, and all those je ne sais quoi that compose the Graces."

One must shine. But how to give the meaning of the wedding

dance? Lord Chesterfield does not hesitate to contradict the morality that his tutors have hitherto taught to his son and that, with the weight of the learning with which they have burdened him, has now become a danger. He literally flings his son into the arms of those Parisiennes to whom he owes his own enlightenment. He offers praise to Venus and Cupid, setting aside Juno and Minerva. "Women," he writes to Philip on April 15, 1751,

> are the only refiners of the merit of men; it is true, they cannot add weight, but they polish and give luster to it. Apropos, I am assured that Mme de Blot, although she has no great regularity of features, is, nonetheless, excessively pretty; and that, for all that, she has as yet been scrupulously constant to her husband, though she has now been married above a year. Surely she does not reflect that woman wants polishing. I would have you polish each other reciprocally. Force, assiduities, attentions, tender looks, and passionate declarations on your side will produce some irresolute wishes, at least, on hers; and when even the slightest wishes arise, the rest will soon follow.

Elsewhere he writes to Philip, certain that his son's already formed character has nothing to lose from such exercises, and that he has been sufficiently forewarned to choose properly: "*Nocturna versate manu, versate diurna*, which may be translated in English: *Turn men by day, and women by night.* I speak only of the best editions."

It is passages such as this one that compelled Samuel Johnson, questioned at the table of Sir Joshua Reynolds about the recently published *Letters*, to declare: "They teach the morals of a whore, and the manners of a dancing master."

So much the worse for puritans and pedants. It was no longer the time, in Paris, to study even Ariosto and Tasso, but to pass on to action and to become gallant. If the classical and the Italian poets had not roused desire, let the French tellers of tales whip up an appetite! Lord Chesterfield recommended to his son that he read *Les*

Égarements du coeur et de l'esprit by Crébillon fils. Success in love, the masterpiece of gallant persuasion that prepares it, the intermediary state that renders it irresistible, become the grand metaphor, but also the grand vehicle, of the Graces of a happy and general sociability. Cytherea is not a goal but a detour, an educative pilgrimage—but the most delightful in existence.

Working from the interior with Venus, Chesterfield is careful not to neglect the exterior: the "mechanics" of gestures, the second nature of bearing. He exhorts his son to repeat the exercises of M. Marcel, who has henceforth taken the reins from Dr. Harte, now returning to England. He counts as well on M. de La Guérinière, a distinguished riding instructor, to impart suppleness, resilience, and precision to his son's actions. He gives him meticulous lessons in physical cleanliness, entering into details (nails, mouth, nose) that suggest the suspicions he harbors as to the inadequacies of the pedantic education hitherto dispensed by Mattaire and Harte. But once again this coaching of the body, of attitudes, of movements relative to another body, supposes in the young man the appearance of a new internal *morbidezza* to be awakened only by women. Pygmalion can do nothing to animate his statue without the aid of *Vénus toute entière*.

Yet however vigorously this father employed all his talent and all his devotion to complete his son's education, he did not really make contact. At a distance, certainly, but with the Argus eyes of his many informants, he had studied Philip since his early childhood, had spied on him during his Grand Tour, and now redoubled his ubiquity during Philip's sojourn in Paris.

"Remember," he writes on November 8, 1750, shortly after his son's arrival there, "that I shall know everything you say or do at Paris, as exactly as if, by the force of magic, I could follow you everywhere, like a sylph or a gnome, invisible myself."

Why all this anxiety, this pressure, which he affectionately makes up for by trying to create between his son and himself, man to man, a climate of confidence and trust?

THE NATURAL SON

Hitherto Philip had not, strictly speaking, disappointed him. Docile, praised by his tutors, enjoyed by the foreigners he frequented, the child and the young man after him had made an excellent student. Never had Philip surprised his father. Never, furthermore, had he driven him to despair. But this decent modicum no longer sufficed. Would the charms of Venus, concentrated and refracted by the mirror of the arts, would the contagion of the capital's salons succeed in granting this excessively diligent student access to true superiority? The stake was not merely the success of an enterprise begun fifteen years before. A born gambler, Chesterfield was a good loser, and he was prepared to lose. But he was committed much too seriously.

If the undertaking had required it to this degree, and in a fashion so persistent and impassioned, it was because success, if obtained, would prove that Philip was indeed his son and worthy to bear his name. Lord Chesterfield did not have, in fact, a legitimate son. Philip, whom he had acknowledged, was nonetheless a bastard in the world's eyes. He had fathered him in The Hague, on a lovely Huguenot woman, Mlle du Bouchet, who was too impecunious for him to marry. When he did marry, in 1733, it was to George I's natural daughter, her mother the king's former mistress, Countess Ehrengard Melusina von der Schulenburg, raised in England to the rank of Duchess of Kendal. This marriage, a Whig affair if ever there was one, was less political than financial: Chesterfield had been the Prince of Wales's gentleman of the bedchamber, but George II, acceding to the throne in 1727, had preferred to him the eternal Robert Walpole. Petronilla von der Schulenburg, Lady Chesterfield, was extremely rich herself and had hopes of being even richer. Until her mother's death she continued to live with her in a mansion neighboring Chesterfield's in Grosvenor Square.

"Marriage," he had written in his *Stray Thoughts*, "is the cure for love, and friendship is the cure for marriage." To avoid excessive mockery of such a union (which moreover aggravated the irreconcilable animosity of Queen Caroline, the veritable king of England after the accession of her husband, George II), Chesterfield immediately chose as his mistress a "great beauty," Fanny Shirley, for whom he composed, seconded by his friend Alexander Pope, certain *galant* verses. His marriage remained childless.

The hope of his line, but also all that remained of his tenderer feelings, was therefore focused on the natural child, whose mother he may have actually loved. This raised certain practical difficulties. Even acknowledged, Philip (like Rousseau's Émile) had of course been raised as an orphan. For him there was no family milieu that might transmit by example, oral tradition, and contagious mimicry the appropriate form of a rank that he looked to his father to secure for him in an England that did not smile, or perhaps only smiled, at illegitimacy of birth. This situation, which literally distanced father and son, explains the necessity Lord Chesterfield had faced of resorting to correspondence in order to inculcate in the boy and the young man the imprint of tradition. The father deployed his talent as a writer and a conversationalist in order to be seen, heard, and loved by his son as if he were there, at his side. But this exploit of epistolary art had not sufficed to overcome the handicap of bastardy or of absence. In certain respects, the excessiveness of this remote father's generosity and attention emphasized the malaise still more. Philip responded uneasily to his father, and never spontaneously. Lord Chesterfield complained. The tutors were obliged to write at great length to make up for this mutism. And this obscure resistance kept the paternal letter-writer's powers of persuasion from achieving their full effect. Lord Chesterfield counted on the erotic sorcery of Parisian "Graces," the euphoria of freedom, and the pleasures of French high society to dissipate this secretive reserve and this secret reproach. Social talent, if it revealed itself in Paris, if it made itself known even in London, might finally overcome the disadvantage of the young man's birth.

It is apparent to us now that the Parisian experiment had been a failure. On the whole Philip had remained sulky and dull. In a letter he writes in French on February 25, 1751, to the Marquise de

Monconseil, Lord Chesterfield begins to doubt of success. He replies to a clearly indifferent accounting the marquise has sent him concerning his son's reactions to Paris.[1]

The ingenious stratagems Chesterfield devised with his correspondent to amend his son's unpromising nature have their singular analogies with Rousseau's ruses to accommodate his Émile's natural proclivities. The former remained without effect. Their consequence is to be found in his father's letter to Philip of February 4, 1751.

The Grand Tour was over. Now Philip would be launched on a political and diplomatic career. But Lord Chesterfield must count on himself alone to combat the force of the prejudice standing in his son's way. In 1754 George II and the Duke of Newcastle, his prime minister at the time, had opposed, despite the latter's promise, the nomination of Philip as unsalaried legation secretary at Venice. The argument was his illegitimate birth.

Chesterfield then managed to get his son elected to the House of Commons. From his maiden speech, Philip's stammering timidity disqualified him for a parliamentary career. His father obtained for him the mediocre position of English Resident at Hamburg (1756), then at Dresden (1764). The young man's health was failing. In 1768, during a vacation in France, he suddenly died in Avignon. Chesterfield then discovered that his son had secretly married an "undistinguished" woman and that he had fathered two children. This was the only respite Philip granted himself in an existence of entire goodwill toward his father. Chesterfield dutifully took responsibility for this unexpected family. Upon his death, despite the resistance of his other heirs, Philip's widow, Eugenia Stanhope, sold the letters to the publisher Dodsley for £1,500.

Long before Philip's death, Chesterfield had become conscious of his failure. In 1759, without interrupting his correspondence with his natural son, he undertook the education of another Stanhope, he too named Philip, the legitimate son of one of his cousins: Lord Chesterfield, already his godfather, became his adoptive fa-

---

1. See the text of this letter at the end of this chapter, beginning on page 213.

ther. This child was then four years old. With the same rhythm, and following the same progression, Chesterfield undertook by letters to draw, all over again, the *Man with a Glove*. Two hundred thirty letters remain of this second education undertaken by his Lordship. This time it was the adoptive father who died too soon to judge of his success. In 1773, this other Philip Stanhope, who became the fifth Earl of Chesterfield (1755–1815), was only fifteen years old. Rich and favored by George III despite or because of his bad manners, he managed to have an adequately honorable career in diplomacy and the civil service, then retired nobly to his London mansion and his estates at Bretby. Gainsborough painted a splendid portrait of him as a hunter posing with his dog.

The mold, twice over, had not found wax worthy of itself. At least in Lord Chesterfield's letters to his natural son, the contours of the mold subsist, with the precision and the relief of a classical medal. It is, first of all, the self-portrait of Lord Chesterfield as a perfect gentleman, provided with all the advantages of birth, fortune, and familiarity with the inside story. It is also the ideal portrait of the European courtier, of his brilliant sociability and his encyclopedism. The two portraits coincide, not without an effect of cruel irony when they are brought close to their intended recipient, the docile son of Mlle du Bouchet. Another effect of irony, with which Chesterfield deliberately toyed when he joked about the small stature of the Stanhopes, emerges from the contrast between this portrait of a courtly orator, by definition handsome, tall, and well formed, according to the canon of Polyclitus recommended by Quintilian, and his Lordship's physical appearance: George II, dispensing with his services, readily described him as the dwarf baboon. But Chesterfield's disproportionate head and nose and his harsh voice contributed to his authority and his wit, giving a particular savor to his perfect manners. The Hapsburgs painted by Velázquez may have been prognathous; they were nonetheless, according to an adjective dear to Henry James, magnificent. Chesterfield doubtless believed that these handicaps, which he had so ingeniously contorted in his favor, were no more serious than the one he invited his son to surmount.

THE MAN WITH A GLOVE AGAINST THE NOBLE SAVAGE

Contemporaries were shocked, as was Samuel Johnson, by the shamelessness of the incitations to pleasure (but not to debauchery) this father addressed to his son: no one paid attention to the involuntary and inevitable ferocity of the educative enterprise itself. Far from "corrupting" his son, this father, who had done his best, had perpetually driven him into a corner. There is the sketch of a sort of eighteenth-century *Bartleby* in the sententious commentary that Boswell, in his *Life of Johnson*, makes on the doctor's famous epigram against Lord Chesterfield's *Letters*:

This collection of letters cannot be vindicated from the serious charge of encouraging, in some passages, one of the vices most destructive to the good order and comfort of society, which His Lordship represents as mere fashionable gallantry; and in others, of inculcating the base practice of dissimulation, and recommending, with disproportionate anxiety, a perpetual attention to external elegance of manners. But it must, at the same time, be allowed, that they contain many good precepts of conduct, and much genuine information on life and manners, very happily expressed; and that there was considerable merit in paying so much attention to the improvement of one who was dependent on his Lordship's protection; it has probably been exceeded in no instance by the most exemplary parent; and though I can by no means approve of confounding the distinction between lawful and illicit offspring, which is, in effect, insulting to the civil establishment of our country, to look no higher, I cannot help thinking it laudable, to be kindly attentive to those, of whose existence we have, in any way, been the cause. Mr. Stanhope's personality has been unjustly represented as diametrically opposite to what Lord Chesterfield wished him to be. He has been called dull, gross, and awkward; but I knew him at Dresden, where he was envoy to that court; and though he could not boast of the *Graces*, he was, in truth, a sensible, civil, well-behaved man.

A novelist's compassion would certainly discover more than one abyss under the surface of that "sensible, civil, well-behaved man," exhausted by the educative storm unleashed by his father. Readers of the *Letters*—continually republished well into the twentieth century in England, translated several times in France and elsewhere in Europe, often alluded to by American writers, notably Henry James—have all tranquilly forgotten their initial addressee.

One should undertake to expatiate on everything James's *Ambassadors* or his *Princess Casamassima* owes to Chesterfield's *Letters*. One should study, in the prosopography of certain rich Americans (and American women: Natalie Barney, Winaretta Singer), who had made their Grand Tour and had "lived nobly" on the margin of the democratic run-of-the-mine, the overpowering influence exerted upon them by the masculine model, however embellished with femininity, that the great eighteenth-century Whig lord had drawn and painted. With Henry James, with Bernard Berenson, they had discovered in the *Letters* the most complete and for them the most accessible expression of one of the most fascinating myths that the history of Catholic and monarchical Europe had invented: that of the *Man with a Glove*. And one is entitled to wonder, observing the new and surprising vitality with which they endowed it well into the twentieth century, if the noble savage, as revealed to the world in Rousseau's *Émile* and his *Confessions*, is indeed the antithesis of Chesterfield's *Man with a Glove*. Is this noble savage not in reality the last avatar of the *natural* liberty and independence of the grand seigneur, released at last from all monarchical loyalty and livery, and determined to blaze a trail under a new enticement, no longer in the jungle of courts but in that of the new social and political regime?

And what if, long before Henry James and the splendid snobs of an America corrupted by Europe, the most paradoxical graft of the noble savage onto the *Man with a Glove*, the first and the exemplary one, had been the author of *Les Natchez* and the *Mémoires d'outre-tombe*, the Enchanter, the Vicomte du Chateaubriand?

LETTERS IN FRENCH FROM LORD CHESTERFIELD

To the Marquise de Monconseil

Bath, November 1, 1750

Consider, Madame, the silence I have kept so long by the power of will alone, despite the impulses of my heart, which so frequently protests against my will, and which constantly desires to share a few words with you. Here is the situation: toward the end of autumn, my spells of vertigo, my migraines, and indeed everything that can distress a mind, combined and united to overwhelm mine: surely it was not necessary to raise such forces to achieve such an end. Yet this being the case, that same mind, which knows the respect owed to your own, and which, even when it is quite well, ill withstands the contrary, sagely decided to take cover, until better times. This better *has at last occurred; I have brought that mind to this document, its preferred resource, which I have revived by a good deal of drinking—the local waters, of course. Here it is then, very respectfully presenting itself to yours all over again, which is to say, I am much better, and to reiterate the assurance of those sentiments of esteem and friendship, which are proof against all spells and sicknesses in the world.*

So you have found the means, as I never doubted you would, to keep Mme d'Hervey in Paris all winter: you are quite right to do so, as is she. Her letters are so many eulogies of France and the French, to the point of being injurious to ourselves. She reports that she often enjoys the pleasure of seeing you, which of itself suffices me to say as much, or more. For the rest, I have no hopes of being so frequently the subject of your conversations, since favorably as the two of you may be inclined toward me, you both know me too well for there not to enter several buts *in those very conversations; preferably, I would have each of you speak of me separately to such as do not know me at all, and then each of you might—and I flatter myself that she might indeed consent to this—lie with impunity on my behalf and to my advantage.*

Your student is at this moment in France, roving in Languedoc, Provence, Dauphiné, etc. He will have the honor of waiting upon you before Christmas. He seeks the Graces in Paris; I have informed him where to find them; if you judge I am mistaken, be so kind, Madame, as to indicate their abode to him; at least I have acted in good faith with him in this matter.

I hear from Berlin that Voltaire has made a perpetual farewell to France, and has settled in the new sojourn of the Muses, under the Augustus as well as the Maecenas of the north; but it must also be confessed that he has displayed more than an ars poetica in the bargain he has driven with this prince; for he has the Chamberlain's Golden Key, the Order of Friendship, five thousand écus to begin with, and as much again of a life interest, of which two thousand, in case of his death, are to be substituted upon his niece. Such conditions have an aroma that is more that of some mountain of Peru than that of Parnassus.[2] *He has already acted his Ciceronian part by an appeal, actually more of an infringement, of France's poetic tribunal of France to that of Berlin, and your judgment has thereby been quashed; yet you have so many fine wits in Paris that you will not be sensible of this one's loss. The ladies themselves will make it up to you. Mme de Graffigny's touching comedy is excellent along these lines,*[3] *and Mme du Bocage's Milton has, I can assure you, a great deal of merit. She has abridged him a good deal, but with judgment; and her translation of Pope's* Temple of Fame *is of an astonishing accuracy. I wish you a good evening, Madame.*

---

2. "Do you know, Monsieur, what most proves to me the superiority of your mind, and permits me to find you out a great philosopher? It is that you have become rich." Mme du Deffand to Voltaire, October 28, 1759.

3. She was the author of *Génie*.

To the Marquise de Monconseil

Bath, November 5, 1750

Our last letters have crossed, Madame. I received yours two days after sending my own; so that my justification was trotting on its way at the same time as my accusation. The latter will therefore be only my thanks for the attention you were so good as to pay to my silence, which deserved neither your regrets nor your reproach.

This link of our commerce, this child indeed, the object who has given rise to terms likely to be suspect to those curious parties who might open our letters, will soon have the honor of paying his respects. He will have much more need of your succor than he would have had were he the object of a well-founded suspicion; such a birth would have rendered a good half of my concerns supererogatory. Correct the defect, Madame, by your own concern, and render him at least worthy of a nativity that had made him worthier of your attention. You can accomplish this, you who are capable of allowing to friendship what others can give only to more violent sentiments. Truly, I count on you alone to make the fortune of this being whom I entrust to you; others will show him a certain amount of kindness, will tell me pleasant items about him, but will care very little, if anything, about all the rest. He would be precisely where he is now, and at his age one retreats if one does not advance. Yet I am convinced that you will behave in an entirely different fashion. You will inform him of his defects with that authority that always accompanies the accuracy of your criticism, and the manner with which you express it. It is inevitable that he should be clumsy and awkward: Germany does not confer the Graces, and Italy scarcely more. It is only in Parisian good society that one may acquire them: permit him, then—not only permit, but order him—to frequent your house of an evening, which is to say when there will not be too many there, and if you were to comfort him on occasion, thrust him into other society as well; it will be a very gentle constraint, and one entirely advantageous for him. He possesses indeed a great fund of knowledge; I do not know if there be much wit to accompany it, but I am sure that if he has any, you will put the crowning touch to his char-

acter by imparting manners and those Graces that embellish the best characters, and that expiate somehow the faults of the worst. In the ordinary course of the world, how many people do we not see who survive only by the good fortune of their manners, and how many others who, possessing very solid merits, are unable to reveal them for lack of just such manners! It is all very well to have knowledge, yet it is the je ne sais quoi that makes it worth having; only savages wear precious stones uncut and unpolished.

Farewell, Madame, I'm leaving here three days hence; and it will be from London that you will have the first news of your very humble servant.

To the Marquise de Monconseil

London, February 25, 1751

You are the only one in the world who knows how to combine true and solid duties with all the delights of friendship; others sacrifice, all too often, by certain impulses of self-love, the former to the latter; they suppress what they should express, in order not to say what will displease, however necessary it is that such things be known. You, Madame, on the contrary, acquit yourself of the true duties of friendship, laying bare the truth, however disagreeable it may be, rather than leaving us in ignorance of an evil to which one might find some present remedy, but one that in a short while might become incurable. There are, in the portrait that you have written for me, and that, I am convinced, is a very good likeness, certain features that shock me no end, and that quite disfigure the whole, despite certain good features that are certainly present as well. I fear, indeed, that it will be difficult to correct the original, since hitherto your efforts have been in vain, and since, for the last three years, I have labored without cease and apparently without success. I am sending him by this same post a letter, but one very emphatically expressed on this subject: and in order not to compromise you in his regard, and not to chill his feelings toward you, which would be to lose the sole remedy in which I have any hope, I am telling him that at the same time that I have received from you a letter extremely favorable to him, I have also received another, about him as well, from one of my friends in Paris, of a very different nature, which I go so far as to describe to him; after which I describe him according to the notes you have provided, and I finish by the strongest remonstrances, which he will be certain, of course, not to show you. To confuse him even more, and to put you in a position to speak to him even more strongly about these matters, I tell him that I am sending you, at the same time, a copy of this description so that you can tell me if it is like him or not. Be so kind, Madame, as to tell him you have received such a letter from me, and that you find yourself extremely embarrassed as to what answer you should make to me; that you see clearly that I am outraged by the suspicion that this description is an accurate one: How would it be, then, if you were to acknowledge such a likeness? This will give him a good scare, and at the same time will provide you with an innocent occasion to tell him some strong facts of worldly life, with the excuse that you are helping him to confront me somewhat more effectively. The fact is, he is lost if he does not utterly correct these bad manners of his, that inclination to disapprove of everything, and that penchant to argue so harshly and so righteously. That he has some wit, that he even has a good deal, if you say so, is a good beginning; but also you know better than I that it is a beginning that will come to nothing if not cultivated by good manners, civility, the amenities, and the Graces, in short by everything that distinguishes you from everyone else. He is still young, it is true; but also, for the last year and a half, he has frequented all the best company in Italy, and for all the time he has been in Paris, he should have assumed a certain amount of finish, considering the good company he has frequented the last two months, to say nothing of your precepts, and your example. With all this, you must admit, and I am sure you are putting matters as favorably as you can, that his progress is very slow; which is to say, that he has made none at all. I am by this reduced to something like despair, and I can hope for no remedy, if I hope for any at all, except from you. For about you, at least, he thinks as he should, and this being so, he must naturally hope to think as you do on all other subjects. To bring you even closer to him, if such a thing is possible, I have informed him that it was entirely at your urging that I finally brought myself to the point of sending him the sum of money he was to expend monthly, which he had so often desired; that I found fifteen hundred francs a month a quite reasonable sum, but that we would not quarrel over a possible expense of two thousand; of course, as you had suggested to me, he must not take this allowance as an excuse for a tone of superiority or of scorn for those who might have no such resources. Given all these circumstances, you have nothing to fear by not humoring him; tell him these truths freely, from you he will listen to them patiently and attentively: his fortune is absolutely in your hands; if he improves, it will be all your doing. Independently of any personal tenderness, he has been so long the object of my concern, and I have to such a degree flattered myself that I had made something of him, that it would be extremely disappointing that he should fail so near the end of the journey; which would be precisely the case if, with a good deal of natural intelligence and the acquisition of much learning, he should fail to have the manners so necessary to prove their worth.

Forgive me, Madame, all these details, and forgive me all the trouble I am causing you. I know that you will do so, since I know that our friendship is without limit; my gratitude will have none as well, and will come to an end only with my days on earth.

12. The Marquise du Deffand: From Voltaire to Walpole

AT THE CENTER of Enlightenment Europe, in the same little apartment in the rue Saint-Dominique where the disgraced Marquise de Montespan ended her days, a blind woman held court from Monday to Sunday, from five until midnight, always receiving her guests in the same canopied armchair (this singular piece of "conversation furniture," famously known as the "tub," seems to prefigure Magritte's right-angled coffin for a sitting corpse). This eighteenth-century Queen of Spades had lost her eyesight with her youth, in 1753.[1]

Immobile as a mummy, her only vital signs were talking, dictating, or writing on a carefully ruled desk. Nonetheless she was a lodestone, drawing company to her and holding captive the wittiest and most distinguished men and women of French Europe, then at its zenith. Her conversation recreated that *esprit de Mortemart* that had made formidable, even to Louis XIV, an entire generation of Montespans whose flashes of wit Marcel Proust was still searching for in *l'esprit des Guermantes*. To converse with the Marquise du Deffand was an ordeal as much as a fascination and a favor. One did not enter with impunity the room hung with yellow watered silk sprinkled with crimson knots where she received, as the afternoons darkened. Like the Danish baroness Karen Blixen, she would die in love with an agreeable man much younger than herself who man-

---

1. On the famous marquise, see the fine biography by Benedetta Craveri, *Madame du Deffand e il suo mondo* (Milan: Adelphi Edizioni, 1982), translated by Teresa Waugh as *Madame du Deffand and Her World* (Godine, 1994).

aged to get hopelessly tangled in her web by struggling to extricate himself from it. Karen Blixen's last love was a young Danish poet; Mme du Deffand's was a brilliant and eccentric Englishman, the third surviving son of Sir Robert Walpole who until his death in 1745 remained one of France's most formidable political enemies; his son, the Earl of Orford, was an infinitely talented man though no longer a young one, and regarded as something of a narcissist.

That this old woman, who had known all of life's pleasures and whose mind glowed against the background of an incurable ennui, should have incurred at seventy a *jeune fille's* violent and desperate passion, and that she should have incurred it for Horace Walpole, some twenty years younger than herself and whom she had never—could never—set eyes on, are the sort of enigmas that suggest the troubled and intimate "wrong side" of the decor of aristocratic Paris during the Enlightenment.

The French had discovered England in Voltaire's *Lettres anglaises*, and in Montesquieu's *Esprit des lois* they might have learned that, since 1688, the British constitution was the masterpiece of modern politics. But Mme du Deffand knew Voltaire all too well and had insufficient admiration for Montesquieu to be impressed. On the other hand, like her French contemporaries, she had allowed herself to be persuaded by Richardson's splendid novels *Pamela* and *Clarissa* that England, so much more primitive in worldly matters, possessed everything lacking in a refined and desiccated France, secretly haunted by decadence: a private life concentrated in the countryside, where strength of character and depth of sentiment were not eroded by the rapid grind of urbanity and wit. Perfectly impermeable to the Switzerland of Rousseau's *Nouvelle Héloïse*, Mme du Deffand could still be kindled by England, and Horace Walpole, who possessed the seductions of wit, talent, and manners and the trained tastes of a "virtuoso," was in a position to touch her imagination and to waken a heart cloyed by a mysterious gravity that owed nothing to pedantry and everything to a well-guarded intimate singularity. Here was a gentleman of a kind unknown in the country of *gentilshommes*.

As in those plays where the protagonists' drama is reproduced in another style in the servants' quarters, the witty Marquise du Deffand's conversion to passion was reflected in that of her provincial niece and companion, Julie de Lespinasse. Unable to bear another whiff of the too-rarefied air she had long been obliged to breathe in the shadow of her aged patroness, she left her, created her own "society," and secretly abandoned herself to torrents of sopping passion à la Rousseau: she fell in love with a young Spaniard, the Marquis de Mora, then, and somewhat simultaneously, with the Comte de Guibert, all unknown to d'Alembert, who was pining for her in vain. How many sighs and cries, muffled or otherwise, how much furtive and cruel wasting away! Mme du Deffand, who would never hear another word about that ingrate, endured to the end the pangs of her dry and precociously desperate passion for Walpole, cut from the same cloth as her ennui; she never yielded her dignity, without having anything to hide, and without interrupting the redoubtable and redoubted conversation whose tradition she maintained at an extremely high level.

"King Voltaire" and the Marquise

Voltaire himself, Voltaire the monarch of wit, despite the insolent independence he had won for himself initially at Les Délices, then in his nobiliary fiefdom of Ferney, had not resisted the fascination of this sibylline Queen of Spades. He had known her well in days gone by, himself still a brilliant novice and she a ravishing young libertine at the regent's court, then in the circle of the Duchesse du Maine when it was reconstituted at Sceaux in 1720.

The still-adolescent Voltaire had already frequented the duchesse herself, a granddaughter of the Grand Condé known as "the blueblood doll" for being so tiny, so shapely, and so well-born. He had tasted Sceaux in its first splendor, at the decline of Louis XIV's reign: this château had belonged to Colbert; the duchesse could then hope for everything from the mutual passion of the king and Mme de Maintenon for the husband with whom she had entered into a *mésalliance*, the eldest of the Great King's legitimized bastards: the Duc du Maine. The duchesse believed she was closing in on the crown as one by one the legitimate heirs died off. The year 1715 dissipated this great hope. In 1718 the regent would hurl his thunderbolt at Sceaux, which the duchesse's chagrin had transformed into a conspiratorial furnace. Mme du Deffand (married that same year) had wasted no time in becoming one of the regent's mistresses and participated in the famous debaucheries of the Palais-Royal, the Palais du Luxembourg, and Saint-Cloud. In the household of the Duchesse du Maine (amnestied in 1720), the young woman had known, with Fontenelle and Voltaire, an Indian Summer of the Grand Siècle that would last until 1753.

Since their years of youth, the marquise and Voltaire had written to each other occasionally. Their correspondence became frequent only in 1754, and infrequent again in 1765. Not long before he died, Voltaire, exhausted by his Parisian apotheosis of April 1778, paid a final visit to his very old friend: "I arrive a dead man, and choose to revive only to fling myself at the Marquise du Deffand's feet." As soon as he turned to leave, she wrote to Walpole: "He is eighty, and I do believe him to be almost immortal. He enjoys the possession of all his senses, not one of which has weakened; this man is a singular being, and in truth, quite a superior one."

The great writer, during the ten years of his continuous correspondence with the woman who was becoming the blind queen-regent of the Parisian grand monde (their alternating letters are one of the supreme masterpieces of our literature), had all he could do to keep up with her. The marquise doubtless made an exception for him, but she did not care for the literature of her day, metamorphosed to her blind eyes into a sort of flashy boulevard philosophy. If only, she sighed, the Voltaire she genuinely esteemed would renounce the weakness of trying to be its coryphaeus.

At a distance from the event, both correspondents had had time to grieve together, in 1764, over the illness and death of the Marquise de Pompadour, whose wit and charm, to the very end of her life, had managed to dissipate the boredom that afflicted Louis XV's heart, and whose sharp edges they had both experienced. Only now they discovered that she had been a friend to them both, though to different degrees: the royal mistress had been Voltaire's protectress; Mme du Deffand had owed her certain "obligations." A solidarity of *vanitas vanitatum* united, at least on the surface, the two valiant survivors of the reign of Louis XIV, the Regency, and the brilliant years of Louis XV, le Bien-Aimé.

Yet Voltaire had derided Pascal and his *Pensées*, had rewritten Sophocles' *Oedipus Rex* as a *pièce-à-thèse*, and shamelessly flattered the declining century with his moralizing notions of reform, benevolence, and progress.

And indeed it was the trenchant lucidity of the Grand Siècle libertines, whom Pascal had addressed in his *Pensées*, that Voltaire would now affront in a correspondent ripened and deepened by the ordeals of a lifetime. Part of the authority that this "ignorant worldling" wielded over him, and that Voltaire was pleased to acknowledge, was based on her disabused mind, which esteemed in the great writer only the author of *Candide*, and for the rest discerned nothing but charlatanism.

In the letters she wrote him, she never fell into the commonplaces exchanged by laudatores temporis acti. Instead she caught Voltaire out, striking him at his most vulnerable point: "There is, taking it all in all, only one misfortune in life, which is that of being born." He refuted her, scolded her, defended himself by spasms of black humor, but ultimately dodged that blind gaze that dared to remain focused on the nothingness of human affairs and that all too closely resembled his own conscience. The sculptor Pigalle would represent him in the heroic nudity of a quasi skeleton, stripped of the stage finery in which he had enrobed and protected the royalty of his opinions. Mme du Deffand, content merely to move her goose quill, had already compelled him to know himself away from the mirror the public presented to forget himself in.

In reality, this "ignorant worldling," this *salonnière*, as American doctoral students call her, knew her great writers to perfection, not as authors but as masters of intelligence and life. In a few fillips and rebuffs worth entire libraries, she summed up for Voltaire's edification the "spirit" of Montaigne's *Essais*, source of Pascal's *Pensées* and breviary of the well-read French aristocracy for 150 years:

> Here one finds everything that has ever been thought, and no style is more energetic; he teaches nothing because he determines nothing; this is the opposite of dogmatism; he is vain, and are not all men so? And those who seem modest, are they not doubly vain? The "I" and the "me" are in every line, but what knowledge can one have, if there is no "I" and no "me"? Indeed ... he is the only good philosopher and the best metaphysician there has ever been. There are rhapsodies here, you may say, perpetual contradictions, yet he establishes no system, he seeks, he observes, and remains in doubt; he is of no use, I grant you, but he detaches one from all mere opinion and destroys the presumption of knowledge.

One is pulled up short (doubtless more than Voltaire liked) by this sovereign art of going straight to the truth with that natural facility of hers: Voltaire had no doubt caught something of this art in other writers who resembled the marquise, but he had made a profession out of doing so. For the marquise, it was a liberal art of thinking, of saying, of living against all hope, but boldly and brilliantly, among the peers whom she had chosen and who had chosen her, but above all for herself and for the sheer beauty of the thing.

Mme du Deffand wrote as she thought and as she spoke, as a Zen grand master of brevity. For her, taste, and therefore style, was neither a matter of exercise nor of aesthetics nor of the effect to be produced. It was the needlepoint of a mind that had survived an entire life, and these were the fine antennae of a judgment trained to discern on the spot what rings true and what rings false. It was on this sort of *bon bec de Paris* that the young Voltaire sharpened his wits in his adolescence. Now he could permit himself to dazzle a vast public by the pyrotechnics that impressed his interlocutrix as a rather demagogic waste. His correspondence with Mme de Deffand led him back to his sources, even if he refused to turn around as his dangerous friend courteously invited him to do.

On her side, the marquise, implacable touchstone of the *parole juste*, could indulge herself in the luxury, concealed under the figures of modesty, of keeping on the alert the only contemporary man of letters she had deigned to the end to take into consideration. D'Alembert, who collapsed when he left her for the Lespinasse creature, had been her only illusion.

THE BLIND WOMAN OF THE ENLIGHTENMENT

It was not only by form that this grande dame could triumph over a professional in every category. It was also, and especially, by spiritual courage and by "encounters" (to speak like Montaigne) of her own thought with that of greater minds of other times and places. She was no doubt entertained by the literary politics of the day and by the infernal game that had made Voltaire the master of public opinion. But such trifles won from her no more than a "distant glance." Her tragic sense of life, like that of Lucretius and Montaigne, established her feeling for form. Voltaire knew or divined the seriousness of this woman, and the energy of her despair; he did not want to live at this degree of danger.

When she indulged in the brief luxury of a comparison between Shakespeare and Homer, to which Baudelaire himself, a century later, might have subscribed, Voltaire pretended not to understand; narrowly classical, he identified this judgment of taste superior in its time with the bons mots of a witty woman. Though she evoked with feigned embarrassment the lively interest she had taken in Richardson's masterpiece *Clarissa*, this too wakened no echo from the author of *Zadig*, for whom the English novel, which is to say, at this period, the novel itself, was merely a sentimental pastime of women or madmen like Rousseau.

When she reaffirmed to Voltaire, who had chided her for the excessively black thought that "the greatest of all misfortunes is to be born," she commented on her own sentence as an auditor of Sophocles or Socrates, five centuries before Christ, might have done:

> I am convinced of this truth, and that it does not apply solely to Judas, to Job, and to me, but to you, and to the late Mme de Pompadour, to everyone who has ever lived, or who is alive, or who is yet to be born. To live without loving life does not make one desire its end, nor does it diminish the fear of losing life. Those whose life is happy have a very melancholy prospect: they possess the certainty that life will end. These are idle reflections, but it is certain that if we had not had pleasure a hundred years ago, we had neither pains nor disappointments. And of the day's twenty-four hours, those of one's sleep strike me as the happiest. You do not know, and you cannot know by yourself, the condition of those who think, who reflect, who have some activity, and who are at the same time without talent, without passion, without occupation, without dissipation: who have had friends, who have lost them, without being able to replace them; add to this some delicacy in taste, a bit of discernment, a good deal of love of truth: cover the eyes of such people and put them in the midst of Paris, of Peking, or wherever you like, and I'll warrant you it would be happiness for them not to have been born.

All the salt of this little epistolary controversy inheres in one fact that neither the marquise nor Voltaire dreamed of evoking, for fear of pedantry, but that was the point of departure (and of divergence) of their respective existential prejudices: at Sceaux, with the Duchesse du Maine, Voltaire from 1708 to 1715, and the marquise from 1720 to 1727, belonged to the circle of auditors of Nicolas de Malézieu, tutor and lover of the "blueblood doll": an excellent Hellenist as well as a good mathematician, a member of the Académie Française and the Académie des Sciences, Malézieu had improvised for his hostess and her guests certain translations from the Greek. This was his way of supporting Mme Dacier in the *Querelle d'Homère*, the final episode in the *Querelle des Anciens et des Modernes*.

What did Malézieu translate for these listeners whom today we dare to describe as "frivolous" because they also enjoyed the "vaudevilles" composed by the same Malézieu? The tragedies of Sophocles, notably *Oedipus the King* and *Oedipus at Colonus*. We know that it was directly from this source that Voltaire and, a little later, Mme du Deffand became familiar with the chorus's terrible words from *Oedipus at Colonus* that she had summarized for herself and taken as a life maxim.

Sophocles's chorus comments on the spectacle of the old blind king, now a dispossessed wanderer, supported by Antigone, joined by Ismene, and pursued to the outskirts of Athens by Creon's hatred and by the misfortunes of Polynices:

> Not to be born comes first by every reckoning; and once one has appeared on this earth, to return to where one came from as soon as possible is the next best thing. Indeed from the hour when youth ceases to bestow its light-headed thoughtlessness, what painful blow is far away? What hardship is not upon you?
>
> Murders, civil strife, quarrels, battles, and resentment! And then, the final disgrace belongs to much-dispraised old age, powerless, unsociable, friendless, when all evils are with us to the end.

From Sophocles' tragedy *Oedipus the King* and from his "Past Recaptured," *Oedipus at Colonus*, Mme du Deffand, who as a child had alarmed Bishop Massillon by her precocious incredulity, remembered the meditation of the Athenian chorus, which she associated with the lamentations of Job and Ecclesiastes. The words were all the more deeply impressed upon her memory because they were addressed to a king struck down by the gods, and because she had several times seen the thunderbolts strike close to her, before being deprived of sight like Oedipus. Already at the moment when Malézieu, renewing a Hellenistic tradition that goes back to the origins of the French Renaissance (Lefèvre d'Étaples and Marguerite de Navarre, Jean Dorat and Ronsard), recited Sophocles to his audience at Sceaux, that assemblage could not help applying the lines to their own circumstances.

In 1708–1715, at the end of the realm's "Great War" and after the series of bereavements that had stricken the royal family (the Grand Dauphin, the Duc and the Duchesse de Bourgogne), Versailles took on the tragic and accursed colors of Thebes. The old, stricken, and despoiled king had then raised himself to the grandeur of *Oedipus at Colonus*. The Duc du Maine and the Duc d'Orléans could pass either for Eteocles and Poynices, who consummated the disasters of the realm, or for one Theseus or another who would bring it to an end. The Duc d'Orléans, at the death of the Great King, had triumphed over the Duc du Maine, exiled in 1719. Such was, for Mme du Deffand, then preparing to enter the world as the regent's mistress, her first initiation into the vanity of life, as it was revealed in the tempestuous light of power.

Upon the regent's death, she found herself, as the intimate friend of Mme de Prie (mistress of the Duc de Bourbon, the prime minister "appointed" by Louis XV), associated even more intimately with the anguishes and intrigues of the court. Everything rapidly ended in disaster on June 10, 1726: the Duc de Bourbon suddenly disgraced and Mme de Prie exiled to Normandy, where she suddenly and mysteriously died before the eyes and in the arms of her dear friend, who never revealed what may have been the terrible secret of this death. The crucial scene of 1715 was repeated with her no longer as a spectator but as a confidante. Once again, when she was admitted, between 1758 and 1770, on account of her close friendship with Choiseul and his wife, into the intimacies of supreme power, she would be obliged to witness sudden disgrace and exile inflicted upon her friends.

In the Hellenist Malézieu's lectures at the Château de Sceaux, Voltaire, for his part, had found the subject of his first dramatic work: *Oedipe*. He was nineteen years old. Surpassing the Molinist rewrite of the Sophoclean tragedy that Pierre Corneille had dedicated to Foucquet in 1661, Voltaire had made his first tragedy into a protest against the "wicked" god of the Greeks (and of Pascal), and against the priests who made use of him to lead men astray. He inaugurated the Enlightenment by a public implication of *l'Infâme*, the modern name he would later give to the Greek Atê and to the "hidden God" of Moses and Saint Paul. Voltairean reason, like the Jesuit will, would acknowledge evil and misfortune only to challenge and reduce them to submission. Neither Voltaire nor any other modern dramatist has ever managed to take up the subject of *Oedipus at Colonus*, in which Sophocles raises the acceptance of man's fate to this oracular speech of Oedipus: "So then, it is when I am no longer anything, when I am nothing, that I become truly a man." Mme du Deffand was capable of standing unshaken on this inner precipice. She would never vary on this existential and political cogito. This Parisienne was of Athens.

The ironist feared by all Europe, without his realizing it, had met his master: in the author of *Candide*, Mme du Deffand had exposed a made-to-order optimist, an optimist for the gallery, who had nothing to envy in Pangloss's "best of all possible worlds," though he was less sincere than that Leibnizian pedagogue. In *Candide*, she recognized herself rather in the Venetian senator Pococurante, the great virtuoso of ennui. She could therefore thrust her dagger into her correspondent's contradictions: How could Voltaire, who knew like herself (and like Pococurante) the nothingness of things, so deceive his world by a show of humanist beneficence and pseudophilosophical zeal? How could he write "We must cultivate our garden" and assume the leadership of a universal philosophical crusade? Was there not here, beyond a logical fault, a straw in the metal of the classical "high taste" of which Voltaire claimed to be the heir and by which he limited himself to coining the small change scattered by his polemical and preaching mania? As an expert diplomat of the mind who advances under a mask, the marquise delighted in drawing Voltaire back to the truth, which indeed is sad, and which will not be altered any more than life itself. In vain. Voltaire pretended not to understand her, dodged her thrusts. Yet he joined her on the shared grounds (thereby saving himself and the members of his party) of a general decadence of taste and wit: "*Le raisonner tristement s'accrédite*," that is to say, "Nowadays, grim reasoning finds more and more credit."

The marquise would be the first to weary of this dialogue of the deaf. She had found in her melancholic's heart, in her absurd passion for Horace Walpole, a much more exciting diversion than the anti-Fréron pamphlets and the pro-Calas pleas of the patriarch of Ferney. Like Racine's Nero in the intervals of his arguments with Agrippina, the Enlightenment's emperor had to admit to himself, between two epistolary passages of arms with the invalid of Saint-Joseph: "Before hers, my shaken genius trembles."

THE ENGLISHMAN AND THE MARQUISE

Horace Walpole was quite the opposite of the libertine of the French Enlightenment. His sensibility and his senses, allegorized and sublimated by debauches of literature and art, were virgin when he arrived in Paris. He was fifty years old. Introduced into all the best circles, celebrated by Mme Geoffrin, he lost no time in settling down with her great rival, who summed up, in her basket chair and her black lace tucker, two centuries of urbanity, moral intelligence, and mental acuity. This English wit who had launched the Gothic craze possessed the sentiment of time and a sympathy for the bizarre. He let himself be captivated by the "ancient sibyl" who drew around her, in her "convent corner," the fine female flower of the Parisian grand monde; the Maréchale de Luxembourg, the Comtesse de Boufflers, the Comtesse de Forcalquier.... But their "liaison," at first daily, quickly passed from conversation to correspondence, for Walpole, alarmed and deranged, judged it more prudent to put the Channel between this Queen of Spades and his own bachelor egoism.

The "romance" between an old sibyl, yet still a queen of Paris, and a virgin graybeard, yet the fourth son of the Whig prime minister under two successive kings of England, outclassed the one that developed, on the same Parisian stage, between Stanisław Poniatowski, Catherine II's former lover whom the tsarina had made king of

Poland, and Mme Geoffrin, his "*maman*," who with great ceremony had visited her "son" crowned in distant Warsaw. Horace Walpole had made a reputation for himself as a wit, but no one forgot that he bore the name of a statesman who had long defied Louis XV. On his Grand Tour on the continent, in 1739–1741, the young gentleman had spent only three months in Paris, and his anti-Jacobite name meant that he spent even less time in Rome. He perfected his French in Reims, Dijon, and Lyon, and his artistic proficiencies in Florence.

Lacking any political ambition, this deluxe offspring of a utilitarian aristocracy occupied his leisure in putting the finishing touches on a virtuoso's education: in seventeenth- and eighteenth-century Europe this was the name for a rich amateur who cultivated arts and letters for his own pleasure. France, in the same period, counted innumerable examples, besides the famous Duc de Nivernais, the Comte de Caylus, the Receveur des Finances Claude-Henri Watelet; Italy boasted the Marchese Scipione Maffei or Francesco Algarotti among others. England did not lag behind, and many of its castles, which no revolution has burned down or despoiled, are even today the fabulous repositories left by several such refined collectors, indefatigable importers of Italian pictures and antiques. But we must distinguish the true virtuosi from the host of those clever dilettantes who contented themselves with showing off. The true virtuoso excels full-time in several disciplines at once, frequently more astutely than the specialized professionals. This was the case with Horace Walpole.

Until his father's death in 1745, he pursued his studies and his reading, most frequently in the paternal Orford Castle, in Norfolk, for which he established, in Ciceronian Latin, the catalog and description. In this castle Sir Robert had put together a wide-ranging collection of Italian pictures; Horace made explicit his father's ambitions by writing up and publishing (in 1747) his *Aedes Walpolianae* on the model of the *Aedes Barberinae*, which Pope Urban VIII Barberini had received in 1642 from one of his courtiers, written to the glory of his family palace, built on the Quirinal hillside, and of the collections the Pope and his nephews accumulated there in a very few years. Ironical precedent for a Protestant prime minister.

Empowered by the fortune Sir Robert had left him, the youngest of the Walpole sons emancipated himself, and this new autonomy was declared in the choice of a personal residence near Twickenham, in the environs of London: Strawberry Hill. It was here that all his "originality" was given free rein; quite openly, Horace diverged from the Italian fancy that had inspired his father. In 1750 Strawberry Hill launched a neo-Gothic fashion that France would adopt only some half a century later, under the Restoration. Crenellated, fenestrated with stained-glass Catholic subjects, furnished with a pseudomedieval cloister and a dungeon, this flabbergasting and monumental suburban pavilion sheltered a heteroclite collection of pictures, statues, enamels, porcelains, gemstones, coins, and seals, but also a vast library and a printing press. Walpole completed this Gothic folly with an English park strewn with "manufactures"— this was Des Esseintes's decadentism a century and a half ahead of the Continent. In perfect symmetry, but in secret polemic with what he had done for his father's Castle Orford, Horace published in 1774 a *Description* in English of his own masterpiece and its contents.[2]

A model for Leonard Woolf and the Bloomsbury presses, Walpole published his own works in limited editions but also the *Odes* of his friend Thomas Gray and certain new editions that bear witness to his disparate tastes: Lucan's *Pharsalia* annotated by Oxford's great Hellenist Bentley, Anthony Hamilton's *Mémoires du Comte de Gramont*, and an English translation of Voiture's *Histoire d'Alcidalis et de Zélide.* These aesthetic curiosities and feverish activities intensified in 1764: it was during this year that Walpole published his own masterpiece, *The Castle of Otranto*, inaugurating the Gothic novel. As he took care this time to entrust the novel to a London publisher, it was a success. This incunabulum of the European fantastic made him immediately famous on the Continent. The French had attuned European tastes to the pretty, the graceful, and

2. Walpole's *Wunder-* and *Schatzkammer* is better known now since an exhibition at the Victoria and Albert (March–July 2010) and the accompanying catalog, *Horace Walpole's Strawberry Hill*, edited by Michael Snodin (Yale University Press, 2010).

the *galant*. In the wake of Burke's *On the Sublime and Beautiful* (1757), Walpole fired a pistol into this concert and made the spared strings resound with a disquieting strangeness and a sense of terror. An attentive reader of Richardson, Mme du Deffand would not have failed to remark the "new frisson" introduced into European fiction by this amateur novelist.

It was high time, taking advantage of an armistice in the Franco-English wars, that he came to Paris to reap his laurels. And here he met Mme du Deffand: their two "sublimes" amalgamated. Until the marquise's death, in 1780, he maintained a correspondence with her of which only the letters she addressed to him remain. Most of Walpole's replies have vanished. They were returned to him in 1775 by his correspondent, and he burned them. At his request, she did the same for the later replies as well. This sacrifice gives the measure of the "moral torment," or as the American expression puts it better, of the "mental cruelty" that could be exerted over the most feared Parisian woman of her time by the better-schooled egoist of Strawberry Hill.

Why did he insist on this destruction? Did he fear the posthumous publication of a correspondence that would reveal him in the ridiculous or odious position of a Mr. Potiphar? Or else, justly proud of his reputation as a letter-writer in English, did he fear that his letters in French, especially in comparison with those of a modern Sévigné, would cast a shadow on his future complete correspondence? If he had profoundly imbibed the seventeenth-century moralists and the Saint of Livry, as Mme de Sévigné came to be called, if he was flattered to be received in the most brilliant salons of Paris, he was nevertheless not an admirer of the French language. In 1788 he wrote to one of his correspondents, Lady Craven, apropos of the *Mémoires* of Frederick II and of French poetry:

> German, I am told ... is a fine language; and I can easily believe that any tongue (not excepting our old barbarous Saxon, which ... I abhor) is more harmonious than French. It was a curious absurdity, therefore, to adopt Europe's most unpoetic language, the most barren and the most clogged with difficul-

ties. I have heard Russian and Polish sung, and both sounded musical—but to abandon one's own tongue and not adopt Italian, which is even sweeter and softer and more copious than Latin, was a want of taste I should think could not be applauded even by a Frenchman born in Provence. But what a language is French, which measures verses by feet never pronounced, as is the case wherever the mute *e* is found! What poverty of various sounds for rhyme, when, lest similar cadences should too often occur, their mechanic bards are obliged to marry masculine and feminine terminations that alternate as regularly as the black and white squares on a chessboard! Nay, will you believe me, madam? Yes, you will; for you may convince your own eyes that a scene of *Zaïre* begins with three of the most nasal adverbs that ever snorted together in a breath. *Enfin*, *donc*, *désormais*, are the culprits in question.

Despite his efforts and those of the reluctantly obedient marquise, several of his letters escaped the auto-da-fé. They date from 1774–1775. Ten years after the encounter, the "fire" had long been quenched, especially on Walpole's side. Mme du Deffand no longer held him except by a sort of long-distance conjugality, occupied by the news from Paris (this is the moment when her dear Choiseuls, "grandpapa and grandmama," have been able to leave their Chanteloup exile and make their Parisian *rentrée*) and by the hospitality she offered his relatives and friends traveling abroad or on duty in France. She concealed as best she could her tormenting desire for her friend's return. She confided to him in vain her great and only secret, which was also that of her century: "I suspect that all the care I take has no other motive than to arm me against boredom; this is a sickness within me that is incurable; everything I do is merely a palliative; do not be angry with me, I am not to blame; your cousin could tell you I am doing my best and that I give every appearance of enjoying myself and of being content." Ask as she will after his health and inquire into his every action, the object obsessing her seems not to notice this attention focused on him and sees to it that their long-distance conversation remains a double monologue. With pursed lips and a sulky tone, he describes to her as insipid the details of his own life, or of English public life (he reports to her, without yet understanding the consequences, the first signs of the war for American independence). He happens nonetheless (a confidence that touches her deeply) to copy for her a fragment of his *Journal*: the account of a dream he had while in Cambridge. It is as if at this stage of their "liaison," the two roles being stabilized, they remained united by the complicity between two superior interpreters of the art of letter-writing. And on this terrain, the old marquise, writing in her own language, regains the upper hand that Horace Walpole had opposed to her in the affective realm.

In his old age, his brothers' deaths having put him in possession of the paternal castle, Walpole deserted Strawberry Hill and moved to Orford. From here he followed the events of the French Revolution, which confirmed him in an execration of France, the French language, and French men of letters, in which Mme du Deffand would have enthusiastically joined. It was here in Castle Orford that this barricaded bachelor finally found a sort of happiness, in the innocent company of two *jeunes filles*, Agnes and Mary Berry, living with their father in a nearby house that Horace nicknamed "Little Strawberry." Adolescent daughters of the English countryside, Agnes and Mary were admitted to the interior of the enchanted castle at the door of which the old French sibyl had knocked in vain, but where, by her tenacious insistence, she had perhaps finally given her sleeping prince the desire to awaken to the life of the heart.

LETTERS FROM HORACE WALPOLE TO MME DU DEFFAND

London, December 26, 1774
What a curious friend you are! You seem quite pleased with my gout, for your first reaction is to derive two letters a week from it. Moreover you forget the first rule of all, which is that it is the patient who is to be cared for and not the patient who is to care for those who are well, a

maxim that has escaped no one since Adam, except for you. Here is the situation. Friday, I was obliged to dictate a long letter concerning my affairs, the moment after the arrival of your letter in which you ask for two letters a week, one for you, the other for my cousin. Your letter, moreover, being a great pleasure for me, I wanted to satisfy you then and there. But having no one about who could write French, I had to address myself to M. Conway. In short, this task so wearied me that I lost my voice, my wind, and my pulse. But to be brief: my gout gives me pain only when I am tired, and I beg you for the fourth time to remember as much.

Today, for a miracle, I am wonderfully well. The splints have surpassed all my expectations, and I intend to send you a pair as an ex-voto to hang in the organ loft of the chapel. My cousin will tell you the rest. I must make short work of this, for my secretary, who is merely visiting, has no time to spare.

I inquired of the jeweler this morning about the emeralds: they are cut, but not polished, and the workmen will not finish them until after the holidays. I shall be ever so grateful to you for the new Ninon, for which I am tremendously impatient. My thanks as well for the barley sugar, and a thousand more for the good news about Mme d'Olonne. I beg you to tell Milady Ailesbury that the best way for her to insure all the porcelain she has bought is to send it directly to our London customs, addressed to herself. I am extremely eager to receive word of the arrival of your kinsfolk and to hear about your supper. Do not fail to give a thousand kisses to the lovely little hand of our little grandmama for me, and if you can achieve this without bumping your forehead, to her pretty little foot as well. Do not kiss, but embrace Abbé [Barthélemy] as well. Good night, I cannot manage another word, and my secretary is glad of it.

P.S. I have no plans to write anyone before a week from today.

London, January 4, 1775
Your last letter was all I could desire, and I thank you for it: But Milady Ailesbury's, which I received with it, pleased me not at all. She says you were so exhausted by your party that you thought you might

die of it. I hope that your kinsfolk [the Choiseuls] will not again be exiled, if their return must cost you so dear. You may be entirely at peace about my condition; all I have left is the swelling in my right hand, and yet I am using it now, tied up in the splint: M. Wiart will not recognize my handwriting; because it is so difficult to write, it is easier to read. I walk without a crutch and without assistance, but it is true that I am still very weak, and much more of a ghost than your parliamentarians. But I am getting enough rest. The town is empty right now; and of those who are here, I receive no more than a modicum. It was fashionable two years ago to visit me. All the beauties, all the great ladies came here as the impulse took them: nowadays I claim weariness, and I am quite forgiven by all but my intimate friends.

Here it is Wednesday evening, and that devil of a fellow has not yet brought me the emeralds. I'm afraid of missing the Dover coach. Couty brought me this morning two gridirons and four pounds of tea, which will go into the same chest.

My kinsfolk will have told you about the grand party given for their niece, Milady Françoise, a charming girl and so pretty. As are all these cousins.

I have not been troubled by their absence. I like being quite alone in my suffering. I know exactly how I must be treated. Only silence is required, and an extremely light—cold—diet. In this country, everyone advocates the contrary, and lectures me. I like none but obedient servants, and I certainly have no desire to kill myself. You see that I know what I am about, and I have cured myself quite readily. And I am delighted with the stay the cousins have made in Paris: honors, ceremonies, kindnesses received. I am delighted that they have made your acquaintance, and that they have had the good fortune to please you. By now, I begin to desire their return, and shall be glad to have you take leave of them.

Since the Dover coach leaves tomorrow, and then not for another week, I fear the emeralds will not arrive on time—but here they are! The jeweler has brought them just this morning. I'm afraid you will not be altogether pleased with them. The lid of the bowl is very heavy and clumsily fashioned: but the bowl itself is fine without a lid, and all the rest is very well. Had I refused to accept the lid, we should have a wait of another six months or a year; it appears they very rarely melt glass for this purpose, the style is out of fashion. M. de Trudaine must send the chest, which he will leave with the Calais customs. As well as the glasses, you will find two gridirons and four pounds of tea; everything has been packed by M. Couty, whom I have had come to me for this purpose.

Selwyn has spent the whole of yesterday evening with me, and even stayed for supper, that is, eaten biscuits while I was at my stewed apples. Your little friend is roving around the countryside: today, at Milady Spencer's, tomorrow chez les Ossory. I have no plans to leave here before next week.

This Friday the 6th

The right hand is getting better; I have taken off the splint and write wearing a glove. You may credit M. le Duc d'Orléans for this new proof of the excellence of the splints. My case is the ideal proof: five weeks instead of five and a half months. You recently mentioned to me your plan of taking dinner instead of supper: I cannot concur with such a notion. You have so long been accustomed to your usual method that I cannot believe that such a change would suit you better. Perhaps if you took a cup of bouillon instead of tea, that would sustain you better and keep you from eating too much later in the evening; but I should not advise you to do anything suddenly. You are a very delicate creature, and you must not risk a major change all of a sudden.

London, January 19, 1775

I can truthfully assure you that not only are my kinsfolk quite delighted by you but that they admire and love you as much as you deserve. This is what they keep saying, too frequently for me to have any doubts. On their side, what reasons to be delighted! Never has so much been done for strangers. It looks to me as if M. Conway would be quite pleased to move to Paris. Yes, I shall ask them more questions; but they have moved out of the circle of my acquaintances.

Your polite response to my couplets has greatly amused me. I quite *expected to hear you announcing that they were the silliest, flattest verses in the world. You have never had to blame yourself for over-praising my productions—why spare my French verses? Do you suppose I thought them good? I am perfectly aware they are detestable. It is my cousin who writes lovely ones—I was really delighted by those he wrote for Mme de Cambis. I found the ones for your birthday very pleasing, but not what I should call admirable. But there is nothing about which we differ more than verses. I must be wrong, for certainly you can judge your own language better than I.*

Will you allow me, for lack of anything better, to fill the rest of my letter with political news for my cousin? It appears that things could not be going worse with our affairs in America. We are about to send three more regiments. Parliament, which meets today, will be asked for the six thousand sailors who were denied last month. That may not seem very important news—but this is what is so strange, and scarcely warlike: it was announced in the public press yesterday by the authorities, which means by his, that Milord Chatham is to present himself in the House of Lords to make a proposal. There is much curiosity as to what this proposal might be, and what I hear is this: authorized by Dr. Franklin (my cousin will tell you who that is), Lord Chatham will offer the King, on behalf of the Colonies, three hundred fifty thousand pounds sterling a year, for the abolition of taxes and edicts that are burdening America. It is claimed that such a proposal will be laughed at—yet such laughter will be on the wrong side of our mouths.

Milord North presented in the Commons an enormous dossier of American papers, and asked that they be examined within the next eight days.

Now you know as much as any politician in our cafés. Yesterday there was a celebration at Court: Queen's Day. The clothes were of an extraordinary magnificence, the ladies' feathers somewhat emulating yours. At three in the afternoon came a fog so thick no one could find her carriage, and great was the bustle and the confusion, which did a good deal of damage to the equipages. The Prussian ambassador's valet knocked down a grenadier at the palace gate; the ambassador complained to the colonel about what the grenadier threatened to do to his lackey. "Monsieur," said the colonel, "what do you think would be done to an Englishman who struck a grenadier at the Berlin palace gate?" We are courtlier than that; the servant was released.

You have had a sampling of an English letter. I do not imagine you shall be asking for another.

January 20

Everything has changed today: they say Milord Chatham will ask that both land and sea forces be augmented. I shall not know the truth until after the post has gone; what is most likely is that the Ministry has determined on war, and that we shall threaten the Colonies with a very severe punishment.

Your emeralds cost five and a half louis. It seems to me that my letters are like Courts, filled with great and little things.

London, January 27, 1775

My cousin will be expecting news of the Duke of Gloucester's death—but all is well. Saturday's chill was merely a portent of fever, and now the fever is past, and the danger as well, for the time being, as we hope and pray. Our physicians are like yours, which is to say, ignorant. There is every reason to believe that the sea voyage will take place, but it is being put off until the month of April, which seems to me an "ignorant" piece of news. Why put it off? I confess to you that I should not be sorry, for my part. Our court is quite small, yet my role is not a flattering one. Strictly speaking, I am not an official member, and though the interest I take in the Duchess's alarming position causes me to neglect nothing that might show her my zeal for her well-being, it is very painful for me to attend court once or twice a day. It does not suit my idle nature, or my amusements, or my occupations. It draws me into the world, and that is contrary to what I have always loved—in a word, to liberty. I was charmed when my father left the ministry; I myself left Parliament the first moment I could manage it, and certainly it is quite alien to my will to find myself, at my age, a courtier. I have no ambition for it, or interest, or desire, not the jealousy, not the duplicity; I should happily yield my place there to anyone seeking to have it.

I have just received from M. Conway a letter of the 19th written by a young English lord who says they will be returning on a specific date, but I have no idea what such a date might be. He tells me about a great revolution imminent in the fashion of dressing in your country, and consequently in ours. He says it is will mean putting on things worn by the Chevaliers du Saint-Esprit. Oh! For my part, I swear I shall put on no such thing—I am not so made as to dress like a rope dancer. Like an Armenian woman, well and good: I should rather like to wrap myself in a great cloak down to my heels. I think they did a poor job of showing Saint-Cyr to my kinsfolk. When I was there, the young ladies were made to rehearse scenes and dialogues by Mme de Maintenon; they performed them to perfection; and as you know, I was given an original letter from the foundress: I spent five hours there, to my great joy, though not of the extreme felicity I enjoyed with you at Sceaux, or on that day at Livry. After all, one must be possessed by certain visions, as I am—otherwise everything is drear. And then, such dreams occur quite infrequently, for they come only to the elect. One such came to me after I had written The Castle of Otranto. *Two or three years later, I was visiting Cambridge University, where I had spent three years of my youth. As I entered one of the colleges that I had completely forgotten, I found myself in what I recognized immediately as the courtyard of my castle. The towers, the gates, the chapel, the great hall—everything corresponded precisely. So then, the idea of this college had remained in my mind without my thinking of it, and I had made use of it for the plan of my castle without realizing it, so that I believed I was actually entering the Castle of Otranto—if you had been beside me, I would have struck you in ecstasy, like that time in the carriage when you told me about your visit to Mme de Coulanges. Hah! since then I never enter the Palais-Royal with pleasure!*

Couty has paid me for the emeralds: did they arrive in good health?

The English part of my letter will be very short today. Debate raged until late yesterday in the Lower House about the remonstrances of the American merchants—but I know no details, except that Charles Fox attacked Lord North very furiously, and that the Duke of Alba sought to be recognized at court. And also that there was an attempt to re-

move Charles I from the Martyrologie: Wilkes said he was in accord with that endeavor, having always observed the day of that death as a feast day, not a day of fasting: but the court prevailed in the one contestation as in the other, by a large plurality of votes. What is amusing is that the city of Birmingham voted for war because they manufacture swords and guns there. I am finished—there is no way of improving on that opinion.

13. Catherine the Great: Voltaire's Eminent Correspondent

IN THE EUROPE of the monarchies, equilibrium depended symbolically (but the symbols then carried immense weight) on matrimonial alliances between ruling dynasties. These alliances supposed careful calculations in which genealogy and family affinities played a notable role. Kings and queens, princes and princesses, and the vast tribal network of their collateral and allied relatives, their innumerable high-ranking "houses," but also jurists, men of letters, agents, lovers, and mistresses, frequently of modest extraction but ennobled by their service—all were participants in the great politico-diplomatic game in which all spoke the language: French. If we add that Europe was crisscrossed by ambassadors, agents on mission, spies, even by travelers of leisure frequently entrusted with some negotiation, however trivial, it is easier to explain the astonishing "universality of the French language" in the eighteenth century. The Republic of Letters—which the history of ideas too often tends to locate in a philosophical empyrean—was itself a conducting medium particularly propitious to that generalized negotiation and the circulation of information of every nature on which it fed. The great minds of the period—Locke, Leibniz, Du Bos, Voltaire—had been, to varying degrees, intermediaries in this gigantic uninterrupted struggle of which the stake was the maintenance or the reestablishment of the relative equilibrium of the European powers. Such an experience of international affairs had nourished their thought. One sees Montesquieu in his *Spicilège* readily citing one of the great diplomats of his time, Cardinal Melchior de Polignac, as an authority on the institutions, manners, and character of the various European nations.

If they did not all write in French, the masters of the European Republic of Letters spoke it, and it is in French translations of the works of Hobbes, Locke, and Leibniz that their conceptions were circulated. Even certain Parisian salons celebrated by literary history, such as those of Mme de Lambert, Mme de Tencin, and Mme Geoffrin, which not only welcomed foreign princes and ambassadors and their literary-minded agents but were also in continuous relation with the ruling administration of Versailles or with the royal mistresses, had been essential and sometimes determining links with grand as well as petty international intrigue.

To maneuver this Francophone "magnetic field," if such an association of words may be risked, was a great affair for the sovereigns and their chancelleries. It had been, as we have seen, an essential trump in the cards played by Frederick II to seduce "*le roi* Voltaire," whose prestige and network of influence were immense. By superior skill the king of Prussia managed to turn the philosopher into his "press attaché" with regard to international public opinion. Conversely, the journal *Correspondance littéraire*, founded by Abbé Raynal but continued by Melchior Grimm, was intended for the crowned heads of Europe. Grimm was actually a German and Russian diplomatic agent, who had cunningly marketed himself as a perfect mole and who very effectively furnished his "clients" at the courts of northern Europe with firsthand bulletins about the secret and current life of people, arts, letters, and ideas in that city. Here were any number of elements indispensable to the "conversation *à la française*" that the great ones of this world had to conduct with their peers and with the highest ranks of international diplomatic personnel. So well did Grimm succeed in this task that he received the title of Baron of the Empire in 1772. Henceforth he officially represented the Duke of Saxe-Gotha in Paris, leaving to others the ancillary labors of the *Correspondance*. An assiduous collaborator of this manuscript review for the *happy few*, Diderot had entered the vast circle of European diplomacy as early as 1759, and at a modest rank, by means of his critical accounts of the Louvre's Salons.

Since Peter the Great and his famous trip to Western Europe in 1697–1698, the Russia of the tsars had cherished an ambition to join the game of European equilibrium and to play a major part in its development. Yet it was not until the appearance of Catherine II (Sophie von Anhalt-Zerbst, a German princess and a passionate admirer of Frederick II) that this ambition could develop a true diplomatic savoir faire and manage with real dexterity to maneuver the French Republic of Letters, its stars, and its Parisian coteries.

The previous tsarina, Elizabeth Petrovna, had responded to Voltaire's advances with a disdainful silence. Even his *Histoire de l'empire de Russie* (1759), which the philosopher attempted to dedicate to her, failed to overcome the indifference of Peter the Great's daughter. The new empress who assumed power in St. Petersburg in 1762 was determined to make up for this absurdity. She let the Seigneur of Ferney know that under her rule Russia would conform to Enlightenment principles. She also turned her effort in the Encyclopedists' direction, proposing to d'Alembert that he was free to publish the *Encyclopédie* at Riga.

With "*le roi* Voltaire," Catherine II—whom the Prince de Ligne was to name "Catherine le Grand," instead of "la Grande," because she was a very male ruler—henceforth maintained a regular correspondence, between equals, in which she cajoled the philosopher and offered him, in the most flattering light, her own foreign and domestic policy. She went so far as to support the campaigns of public opinion the philosopher had launched against Catholic obscurantism in France and against the injustices of French magistrates. She signed a petition in favor of the Sirven family. She set herself up as a champion of the rights of man and of tolerance. Voltaire, subjugated, glowed with enthusiasm for the "Semiramis of the North" and for the war she waged against the Ottoman Empire:

> *Pupil of Phoebus Apollo, of Themis, and of Mars,*
> *Who shares your august throne with all the arts,*

Who thinks a great man's thoughts and, rarer still,
Permits the thought of other men to thrive....

Though the Abbé Chappe, whom Louis XV had sent to Russia to study this rising power more closely, had infuriated the tsarina by publishing his *Voyage en Sibérie* in 1768, the book would have disabused Voltaire, were there any such need, as to what was hidden behind the "Potemkin villages" his imperial friend dangled temptingly before him: the extension of serfdom, the Tartar barbarism of Russian manners, and the more than precipitate justice of the Russian state. But the philosopher would never forswear Catherine. Despite all the highly emotional efforts of the Princesse de Talmont, née Maria Jablonowska, to depict for him the rebellion of the Polish Catholic nobles in the Confederation of Bar against Catherine II's former lover Stanisław Poniatowski, whom the Russian armies had made king of Poland (1764–1795), Voltaire had no interest to spare for these "fanatics." The first and cynical partition of Poland between Frederick II, Catherine II, and Maria Theresa in 1772, which was to deprive the country of real independence for a century, did not for a moment disturb the wheedling chatter the philosopher exchanged with the two northern potentates. Moreover, Parisian opinion was largely on his side. Mme Geoffrin, dazzled *en bonne bourgeoise* by crowned heads, fiercely protected Catherine II, daughter of one of her hosts and friends, and all the more passionately regarded the tsarina's former lover, whom she treated as her own "adoptive" son.

If it is difficult to find a single letter from Catherine II to Diderot, it is because the tsarina had evidently taken no trouble for the encyclopedist. She corresponded with d'Alembert, perpetual secretary of the Académie Française and of the Académie des Sciences, and with "*le roi* Voltaire." And she condescended to make abundant use of Diderot, who helped endow her throne with the attributes of esprit indispensable, since the Renaissance, to every European sovereign. She purchased his library, leaving him the usufruct of it, and through him negotiated the purchase of the fabulous

Crozat collection in 1771: today these paintings embellish the Hermitage and, following certain Bolshevik sales, a portion of the holdings of the National Gallery in Washington. Diderot traveled with Grimm to St. Petersburg in 1773, but it was in the tsarina's correspondence with Voltaire that Europe was informed of the pleasure the enlightened sovereign took in the philosopher's dazzling conversation. Catherine was a poor speller, like most of the Francophone sovereigns of the period, but her vitality, her greatness of soul, and her vigorous and seductive wit wrought wonders in a language that was only, after all, her third, after German and Russian.

In the Kehl edition of Voltaire's *Oeuvres*, the correspondence between the tsarina and the philosopher fills a whole volume. Beaumarchais, overseer of this edition, which raised Voltaire's oeuvre to the rank of the major classics, but whom Catherine II took a dislike to, had insisted on the return of the tsarina's letters by Nicolas Ruault, assigned the role of "launderer," who frequently went so far as to rewrite the text "to bring it to a legible state." Once Catherine II managed to obtain, through her client Mme Denis, Voltaire's niece and "widow," the proofs of this volume, she flew into a rage and demanded countless suppressions, which obliged Beaumarchais to make a number of very costly off-cuts for which the tsarina refused to reimburse him. The gallant editor held no grudge, and went so far as to write in November 1791 to Prince Youssoupoff that the letters from his sovereign "did him more honor than all the crowns in the world."

This was already the sentiment of Voltaire and of Diderot, who had apprised all Europe of their attitude. There entered into it, certainly, a degree of courtly flattery; the lord of Ferney wrote, for instance, to Ivan Ivanovich Shuvalov on March 28, 1774: "The good is rare the world over. Few are the Ladies in France who write like the Empress." Informed by the enthusiastic Diderot of the progress of French at court in St. Petersburg, Voltaire wrote two days later to Mme du Deffand: "Nothing is more extraordinary than this assemblage of all the French graces in a country that fifty years ago was the realm of the bear exclusively.... French is spoken at the Empress's court—a purer French than at Versailles, because our fine ladies do not pride themselves on their knowledge of grammar. Diderot is quite amazed by what he has seen and heard."

Allowing for a certain degree of hyperbole, it is certain that Voltaire was convinced that the tsarina had become a powerful relay of his own "philosophical" propaganda: "It is from the North," he would write, "that the light comes to us today!"

The tsarina herself was quite skillful at holding up a flattering mirror to her privileged correspondent. To Voltaire, who had written "Our language is a proud harlot, she must be paid her tribute at all costs," Catherine made a witty reply in a letter of June–July 1776, with a comparison of his French and her Russian: "The latter language is so rich, so energetic, and suffers so much from the composition and decomposition of terms, that it can be handled anyhow, whereas yours is so poor and submissive that one must be you to have turned it to the advantages you have managed to make of it."[1]

In order to appreciate the tsarina's several letters to Voltaire quoted below, one must take account of the fact that they were "corrected" according to the orthographic and even syntactical norms of the eighteenth century, as well of ours, before being printed. Catherine's excellent French was above all a result of oral improvisation and, as will be seen, animated by an indefatigable apologetic energy.

LETTERS FROM CATHERINE II TO VOLTAIRE

Peterhof, July 14 (25, new style), 1769[2]

Monsieur,
I received, on June 20, your letter of May 27. I am pleased to learn that

---

1. See the fine introduction by Gunnar von Proschwitz to his edition of the letters of Catherine II and Gustav III, *Catherine II et Gustave III: Une Correspondance retrouvée* (Stockholm: Nationalmuseum, 1998), pp. 17–19.

2. Voltaire, *Correspondance and Related Documents*, edited by Theodore Bestermann (Voltaire Foundation, 1974), vol. 35, letter D15775.

spring has restored your health; though politeness obliges you to say that my letters have contributed to that circumstance, yet I dare not lay that virtue to my charge; you can be sure of that, for indeed you may receive them so often that they will eventually cause you some fatigue.

All your compatriots, Monsieur, do not hold me in such regard as you. I know some who choose to believe that it is impossible for me to do anything good or proper, and who torment their minds to convince others of that very prejudice, and woe to their satellites if they dare think otherwise than according to this inspiration, if I may call it such. I am sufficiently charitable to consider this an advantage they afford me over them, for one who knows matters only by the mouths of his own flatterers knows them ill indeed, sees by a false light, and acts in consequence; and since indeed my fame does not depend on them but on my principles and my actions, I am consoled by not having their approbation; as a good Christian I pardon them, and pity those who envy me.

You tell me, Monsieur, that you think as I do on various actions I have taken, and that you are interested in these matters. Very well, Monsieur, you should know, since it gives you pleasure, that my fine colony of Saratov now numbers twenty-seven thousand souls; that contrary to the gazetteer of Cologne, the colony has nothing to fear from the incursions of Tartars, Turks, etc.; that each canton has churches of its own rite; that the fields are cultivated in peace; and that no taxes on that account have been paid in thirty years; indeed that our taxes are to be found elsewhere and are so moderate that there is not one peasant in all Russia who fails to eat a chicken when he likes, and that for some time there have been provinces where the peasants prefer turkeys to chickens; that the wheat harvests permit, with certain restrictions that guard against abuse without damaging commerce, raising the price of grain, favoring the farmer so that his crops increase from year to year; that the population has likewise increased by a tenth in many provinces in the last seven years. We are at war, it is true, but Russia has known that métier for a long while, and has emerged from each war more prosperous than when it entered it. Our Laws proceed, we see to that; it is true that they have become secondary issues, but they suffer nothing thereby. These Laws will be tolerant, they will not persecute, or kill, or burn anyone. God save us from an affair like that of the Chevalier de la Barre, judges who dared proceed in suchwise would be sent to prison. Peter the Great judged it proper to imprison madmen in a building that had formerly been a monastery. If war diversifies my labor, as you observe, nonetheless my various establishments will not suffer from it. Since the war I have engaged in two such enterprises: I am building Azoph and Taganrok, where a harbor was begun and ruined by Peter the First. These are two jewels for which I have created a setting, and which may well not be to Mustapha's taste; it is said that the poor man does nothing but weep, his friends having committed him to this war against his will; his troops began by pillaging and burning their own country; upon the emergence of the Janissaries from the capital, over a thousand persons were killed, the Emperor's ambassador, his wife and his daughters were beaten, violated, dragged by their hair, etc. in the presence of the sultan and his Vizier, without anyone daring to put a stop to such disorders, so weak and poorly arranged is that government. So much for that terrible phantom raised to frighten me.

You will have learned, Monsieur, that according to your wishes the Turks were defeated on April 19 and 21. We captured ten flags, three horsetails, a Pasha's baton, and several cannons; two Turkish camps and approximately fifty thousand ducats have fallen into our soldiers' hands. As an initial enterprise, this seems to me quite respectable.

When the horsetails were brought to me, someone in the room cried out: no one will say those were bought in the marketplace. My officers claim, Monsieur, that since the invention of cannon, Solomon's twelve thousand chariots will not have witnessed so fine a battery; they add that the Turks must now count chariots, horses, and the men employed to drive such chariots as lost. What you have occasion to tell me, Monsieur, is a new proof of your friendship, of which I am very much aware and for which I am all gratitude.

One assumes that the human mind is ever the same. The absurdity of past crusades has not prevented the ecclesiastics of Padolia, encouraged by the papal nuncio, from preaching a Crusade against me, and the lunatics of the so-called confederacies have taken the Cross in one hand and with the other have leagued themselves with the Turks from whom they have taken two Provinces. Why? In order to keep a quarter of the nation from enjoying a citizen's rights. And for this reason they burn and sack their own country. The pope's blessing promises them paradise. Consequently the Venetians and the Emperor would be excommunicated, I suppose, if they took up arms against these same Turks defending today crusaders against someone who has touched the Roman faith neither in black nor white. You shall soon see, Monseiur, that it will be the Pope who will stand in opposition to the dinner you propose at Sofia.

Erase, if you please, Philipopolis from the list of cities. It has been reduced to ashes this spring by the Ottoman troops who have passed through that region because an effort was made to keep them from pillaging it. I am not informed as to whether the Jesuits participated in all the misdeeds of their brothers in arms; to me it seems that I have given them no excuse, and even when they were driven from the states of Portugal, Spain, and France, they struck me as pitiable as men and as unfortunates, most of them I believe being innocent; consequently I have said repeatedly to anyone who would listen that if there were those who sought to marry and settle in Russia, they would be assured of our government's entire protection. I still entertain the same sentiments; it seems to me that for anyone who does not know where to turn, such propositions are as hospitable as they are honest. Like you, Monsieur, I hope that all these turpitudes will soon cease, that my enemies and those who envy me will have done me much less harm than they had hoped, and that all their devices will eventuate to their shame. I am vexed by the accident that has befallen young Galatin. I request, Monsieur, that you inform me whether you have determined to send him to Riga or here, in order that I may keep my promises for your protégé. Your poor opinion of most universities confirms me in my own, all these establishments were undertaken in quite unphilosophical times, it would be an enterprise worthy of a man of genius to prescribe a reformation on which we might base the schools of the future.

Farewell, Monsieur, be assured of the very special considerations I have for you.

Catherine

St. Petersburg, March 3 (14, new style), 1771[3]
Monsieur, In the course of reading your Encyclopedia, I would repeat what I have already said a thousand times, that before you no one wrote as you do, and that it is very doubtful whether after you anyone will ever be your equal. It was among such reflections that I received your two last letters of January 22 and February 8. You can well imagine, Monsieur, the pleasure they have given me. Your verses and your prose will never be surpassed, I regard them as the non plus ultra, *and I stand by that opinion. When one has read you one seeks to reread you, and one is revolted by all other reading.*

Since the party I gave for Prince Henry met with your approval, I am prepared to regard it as a success; before that occasion, I had offered him another such festivity in the country where the candle-ends and the rockets had their place, but no one was wounded, all due precautions were taken, the horrors that occurred in Paris taught us our lesson. Besides, I do not recall having seen a livelier carnival season for many years; from October to February, there has been nothing but parties, dances, spectacles. I know not whether it was the past campaign that is responsible for this impression, or if a true spirit of joy prevailed among us. I hear that nothing of the kind has occurred elsewhere, though we have rejoiced in the blessings of uninterrupted peace for the last eight years. I hope it is not a case of the Christian delectation over the infidels' misfortunes. Such a sentiment would be unworthy of the posterity of the first crusades. Not long ago you had in France a new Saint Bernard who preached a crusade in spirit against us here, without I believe being himself aware for what purpose; but that Saint Bernard was as deceived in his prophecies in much the same way as the first; nothing of what he predicted has come to pass, he has merely stirred up men's minds. If that was his goal, it must be granted that he

---

3. Voltaire, *Correspondance*, vol. 37 (1975), letter D17081.

succeeded, yet such a goal seems quite unworthy. Monsieur, you who are such a good Catholic, persuade those of your belief that the Greek Church under Catherine the Second bears no enmity toward the Latin Church, nor toward any church whatever under cover of storm clouds; that the Greek Church intends only to protect itself. You will grant, Monsieur, that this war has shown our warriors to advantage. Count Alexis Orlov continues to undertake actions that are spoken of everywhere. He has just sent eighty-six Algerian prisoners to the Grand Master of Malta, requesting that he exchange them at Algiers for Christian slaves. It has been a long while since any Knight of St. John of Jerusalem has delivered as many Christians from infidel hands. Have you read, Monsieur, the letter from this Count to the European Consuls of Smyrna who were interceding with him to spare that city after the defeat of the Turkish fleet? You mention his return of a Turkish vessel in which were the furniture and the servants of a Pasha. Here are the facts: a few days after the naval battle of Tchesme, a treasurer of the Porte returned on a vessel from Cairo with his wives, his children, and all his possessions, and proceeded to Constantinople. On the way he received a false report that the Turkish fleet had defeated our own, so he hastened to land in order to be the first to bring this news to the sultan. While he was riding as fast as his horse could carry him to Stamboul, one of our ships brought his vessel to Count Orlov: the latter strictly forbade anyone to enter the women's quarters or to lay hands on the cargo. He had the youngest of the Turk's daughters, a child of six, brought to him, gave her a gift of a diamond ring, as well as some furs, and sent her back to Constantinople with her entire family and their possessions. All of which was printed in the gazettes, more or less, but what was not known hitherto is that Count Roumenzof having sent an officer to the vizier's camp, this officer was first taken to the vizier's kiaya, the kiaya inquired, after the first compliments: Are there certain Count Orlovs in Marshal Roumenzof's army? The officer said there were not. The Turk urgently inquired: Where are they then? The Major said that two were serving in the fleet, and the three others were in Petersburg. Indeed, said the Turk, you must know that I hold their name in veneration, and that we are all amazed by what we have seen. It is toward myself especially that their generosity has been shown. I am that Turk who owes to them his wives, his children, and his possessions, I can never acquit myself of the debt I owe them, but if in all my life I may be of service to them, I shall regard it as a benefaction. He added many other protestations, among others that the vizier knew and approved of his gratitude. In saying this he had tears in his eyes. There you have Turks touched to tears by the generosity of Russians of the Greek Religion. The scene of this action of Count Orlov may one day figure in my gallery along with Scipio's.

The subjects of my neighbor the king of China, since the latter has managed to be rid of certain unjust obstacles, engage in commercial relations with my people as if by magic. They have bargained for some three million rubles of goods the first four months that this commerce has once again been in effect. The manufactures of the palace of my neighbor are employed now in making carpets for me, while my neighbor is seeking wheat and sheep.

You often make reference, Monsieur, to your age, but whatever it is, your works are the same as ever, witness this Encyclopedia filled with novelties, one need merely glance at it to see that your genius flourishes in all its strength. In your case, the accidents attributed to age become mere prejudices. I am quite curious to see the works of your clockmakers. If you were to establish a colony at Astrakhan I would seek some pretext to go see you there. Apropos of Astrakhan, I can tell you that the climate of Taganrok is incomparably finer and healthier than Astrakhan's. Everyone who comes back from there says that the place cannot be praised enough, about which in imitation of the old lady mentioned in Candide, *I have an anecdote for you. After Peter the Great's first capture of Azov, he sought to have a port on this sea, and chose Taganrok for it. This port was built, after which he long hesitated whether to build Petersburg on the Baltic or at Taganrok, but finally circumstances of the time inclined him toward the Baltic. We have not gained much in the way of climate thereby, since they have virtually no winter there, while ours is extremely long.*

Do the barbarians, Monsieur, who vaunt the genius of Mustapha, also vaunt his prowess? During this war, I know of none, save that he caused several viziers to be beheaded, and that he could not restrain the populace of Constantinople, which before his very eyes bloodied with blows the ambassadors of several European powers, whereas mine was confined in the Seven Towers (the internuncio of Vienna perished of his wounds). If such are the features of genius, I pray Heaven to spare me all such and to reserve them for Mustapha and Chevalier Tot, his supporter. The latter will be strangled one day, as the Vizier Mahomet was, though he once saved the sultan's life and is that prince's son-in-law.

Peace is not so close as the public press has given out, a third campaign is inevitable, and Signor Aly Bey must still gain time to strengthen his position; ultimately, if he does not manage to do so, he will not celebrate the carnival at Venice with your exiles who have gone to spend the winter in that country.

I implore you, Monsieur, to send me your verse epistle to the young king of Denmark, of which you have spoken; I should regret missing a single line of what you write, as you can judge by the pleasure I take in reading your letters, and from the great store I set by the friendship and esteem in which I hold the holy Hermit of Ferney who is so kind as to call me his favorite. You see what pride I take in that distinction.

Catherine

March 27 (April 6, new style), 1771[4]
Monsieur, I have received your two letters of February 19 and 27, almost simultaneously. You request that I give you some word of the vulgarities and stupidities of the Chinese to which I referred in one of my letters. We are neighbors, as you know, our borders are populated on either side by pagan and Tartar peoples largely occupied in raising sheep. These tribes are much given to piracy, they steal flocks (often in reprisal) and even take human captives. Such disputes, when they occur, are settled by commissioners sent to the frontiers. The Chinese

---

4. Voltaire, *Correspondance*, vol. 37, letter D17127.

gentlemen are so deceitful that it is the devil's own work to be done with these wretched affairs, and it has happened more than once that having nothing more to ask, they insisted upon being given the bones of the dead, not in order to do them honor but solely to haggle further. Such atrocities have served them as a pretext to interrupt all commerce for some ten years—I say pretext because the real reason was that His Chinese Majesty had given to one of his ministers the monopoly of all commerce with Russia. Both Chinese and Russians complained of this arrangement, and since any "natural" business is very difficult to cancel, the two nations exchanged merchandise where there were no established customs officers and preferred necessity to risks. His Majesty's minister thereupon harassed the adjacent Chinese provinces and brought all commerce to an end. When from here we wrote them concerning this state of affairs, we received in reply extravagant missives of ill-arranged prose in which neither philosophical spirit nor politesse could be even glimpsed, and that were from end to end nothing but a tissue of ignorance and barbarism. We informed them from here that we were unable to adopt their style because in Europe and in Asia as well such a style was regarded as unmannerly. I know that it might be answered to these communications that these Tartars who achieved the conquest of China are not the equals of the ancient Chinese. I can well believe it, but nonetheless it proves that the conquerors have not adopted the manners of the conquered, and the latter run the risk of being swept away by the prevailing manners.

I come now to the article Laws *that you were so good as to send me, and that speaks of me so flatteringly. Assuredly, Monsieur, without the war that the sultan has unjustly declared upon me, a great deal of all that you say would be achieved, but for the present we cannot yet manage to do more than sketch certain projects for the different branches of the great tree of legislation, according to my principles that I have caused to be printed and that you know. We are greatly concerned to bring this conflict to an end, and this effort distracts us so excessively that we cannot proceed with the application of this enormous enterprise at the present time.*

I prefer your verses, Monsieur, to a body of auxiliary troops, the latter might turn their backs in a decisive moment. Your verses will constitute the delight of posterity, which will merely echo your contemporaries. Those lines you have sent me are graven in my memory, and the flame that pervades them is an astonishment, it gives me the enthusiasm of a prophet. You will live two hundred years. One dearly hopes for what one desires: accomplish my prophecy if you please, it is the first I have ever made.

Catherine

January 7 (18, new style), 1774[5]

Monsieur,

The philosopher Diderot whose health is still uncertain, will remain with us until February, when he returns to his own country. Grimm also plans to leave at that time. I see both of them very frequently, and our conversations are endless. They might tell you, Monsieur, the store I set by Henri IV and by the author of the Henriade *and of so many other works by which you have made our age illustrious. I know not whether the two gentlemen are bored with life in Petersburg, but for myself, I could speak to them every moment of my life without once wearying of doing so. I find in Diderot an inexhaustible imagination, and I regard him as one of the most extraordinary men who ever existed. If he does not love Mustapha as you command me to do, at least I am certain that he wishes him no harm, his good heart not permitting him any such thing, despite his energetic mind and his penchant for tipping the scale to my advantage. Ah well, Monsieur, one must console oneself for the failure of your projected crusade by supposing that you have had to deal with good souls to whom nonetheless we cannot concede the energy of a Diderot.*

As head of the Greek Church, I cannot see you in error without reproving you in good faith. You would have enjoyed seeing the Grand Duchess rebaptized in the Church of Saint Sophia. Rebaptized, you say! Ah, Monsieur! The Greek Church does not rebaptize, it regards as authentic every baptism administered in the other Christian commu-

---

nions. *The Grand Duchess, after having uttered in Russian her Or-thodox profession, has been received in the heart of the Greek Church by means of a certain sign of the cross made in fragrant oils adminis-tered to her person in high ceremony, which among us as with you is called confirmation, in consequence of which one is given a name. On this point we are stingier than you, who bestow such things by the dozen, whereas here each of us has no more than is needed, which is to say, just one. Having brought you up to date on this important point, I shall continue to answer your letter. Know herewith, Monsieur, that a separate corps of my army having crossed the Danube in October, fought a very considerable Turkish force and captured a three-braid Pasha who commanded it. This event might have had consequences, but the fact is (you may not be pleased to hear) that there were none, and that Mustapha and I find ourselves virtually in the very situation where we already were six months ago, save that he has suffered from an attack of asthma and I have not. It may be that this sultan possesses a superior mind, but he has nonetheless suffered from this affliction for five years, despite the counsels of M. de Saint-Priest and the instruc-tions of Chevalier Thott, who will do himself in casting cannons, training cannoneers clad in ermine caftans without for all that the Turkish artillery's becoming any more effective or better equipped. All of which are examples of childishness to which we attribute much more importance than they deserve.*

Where did I read that such a turn of mind is natural to the barbar-ians? Farewell, Monsieur, be of good health and be once again assured that no one sets greater store by your friendship than I.

Catherine

August 24 (September 4, new style), 1774[6]
Monsieur, although you are amused to claim you are in disgrace in my Court, I declare that you are no such thing. I have not brought you here in place of Diderot or of Grimm or of any other favorite. I revere you as always, and whatever you may be told, upon my honor I am neither

*fickle nor inconstant. The Marquis Pugachev has caused me great dif-
ficulties this year, and for more than six weeks I have been obliged to
pay uninterrupted attention to this affair, whereupon you scold me
and tell me that you no longer wish to love your Empress, yet it seems
to me that having made such a lovely peace, both for its form and for
its fashion, with the Turks, your enemies and mine, I should deserve
from you some indulgence and no hatred whatsoever. Despite my
Pugachev concerns, I have not yet forgotten the matter of your protégé
Rose, the Livonian. His safe conduct could not be sent to Lübeck as you
wished because Rose, aside from his debts, has made his escape from
prison and carried away several thousand rubles to various persons; I
assure you he would be immediately returned to prison despite a safe
conduct (which is hardly customary among us). I have not received any
other letters from you for several months except that one concerning
Rose, and consequently I have no knowledge of the Frenchman of
whom you speak in your letter of the ninth of this month. But in truth,
Monsieur, I might complain in my turn of the declarations of extinguished passion you tender me if I did not see through your vexation to
the interest that a certain friendship for me still inspires in you. Live
well, Monsieur, and let us make it up, for in truth there is no reason
for us to be at odds. I hope indeed that you will retract by a codicil in
my favor that so-called testament that is so lacking in gallantry. You
are a good Russian, after all, and you can never be the enemy of*

Catherine

*St. Petersburg, October 1 (12, new style), 1777[7]
Monsieur, To answer your letters in order, I must first tell you that if
you are pleased with Prince Youssupoff, I can return the favor by telling you that he is enchanted both with your kind reception and with
everything you have said during the time he has had the pleasure of
seeing you.*

*Secondly, Monsieur, I cannot send you a collection of my laws be-
cause such a thing does not yet exist. In 1775 I caused to be published*

---

7. Voltaire, *Correspondance*, vol. 45 (1976), letter D20847.

certain regulations for our provincial governments, but these are translated only into German. The principal text offers some account of the reasons for these arrangements, and has been esteemed for the precise and concise manner in which are described the historical facts of the various periods. I do not believe that these regulations can serve for the thirteen cantons, but I am sending you an example for the library of the château at Ferney. Our legislative structure is being gradually constituted, its basis is the instruction for the Code that I sent you some ten years ago. You will see that its regulations do not depart from our principles but proceed from them. These regulations will be followed by those of our financial, commercial, and police enterprises, and some others as well: these have concerned us for two years, after which the Code itself will be an easy enough undertaking.

Here is my notion for criminal justice: the crimes themselves cannot be very numerous, in proportion to the punishments; I believe that settling this matter will require a separate labor.

I presume that the nature and strength of proofs and presumptions could be reduced to a quite simple methodical form, of questions casting light on the facts. I am convinced and I have established that the best and the surest of all criminal procedures is the one that makes these kinds of matters proceed in a fixed period by three instantiations, without which personal security might be at the mercy of passions, of ignorance, of involuntary blunders, or of hot-headedness.

Such are the precautions that might well not please the so-called Holy Office, but reason has its laws, against which sooner or later nonsense itself must collapse. I flatter myself that the society of Berne, since you belong to it, will approve this way of thinking. Be assured, Monsieur, that in these matters as in all others my regard for you is subject to no alteration whatsoever.

I was forgetting to tell you that the experience of the last two years convinces us that the Court of Equity, established by my regulations, is becoming the very graveyard of all quibbling.

Catherine

14. Ekaterina Romanovna Vorontsova, Princess of Dashkova: A Russian Heroine at Home and Abroad

SALIC LAW in France forbade women to exercise royal power, except in cases of regency during minorities. This did not prevent women banished from dynastic succession from occupying a considerable place in the social and even the political life of the ancien régime. In eighteenth-century Russia, women did not even figure in the censuses of the tsarist administration. They had less civil existence than the "dead souls," those serfs whose decease had not yet appeared in the land registers and treasury records. Yet eighteenth-century Russia knew four tsarinas who exercised full power: Catherine I, Anna Ivanovna, Elizabeth Petrovna, and Catherine the Great. The latter assumed the imperial title in 1762 by means of a palace revolution that set aside her incapable husband, Peter III; a young woman of nineteen, Ekaterina Romanovna Vorontsova, Princess of Dashkova (or Daschkoff) by marriage since 1759, had headed the conspiracy. The friendship and gratitude of the new empress for her heroine were tempered by the jealousy of Catherine II's successive favorites (notably Alexis Orlov, the assassin of Peter III without the princess's knowledge and to her great indignation). The widow in 1764 of a husband she "adored," weary of the persecutions she was obliged to suffer, Ekaterina left Russia for two long journeys (Grand Tours) in close succession to French Europe.

The first (1769–1771) took her, under an assumed name, to Germany (Berlin, Hanover, Spa); to England, where she learned the language; then to France. She attended incognito a public dinner of the royal family at Versailles, but was carefully isolated from Parisian society life by the obtrusive Diderot, duly instructed by his master the tsarina. Then, after the pilgrimage to Ferney, taking a boat up the Rhine, she reached Baden and made for St. Peterburg by way of Düsseldorf, Frankfurt, Spa, Dresden, Berlin, and Riga. Everywhere, she wrote in her *Mémoires*, she spent more time visiting churches, convents, statues, paintings, and other artistic monuments than in mundane pursuits. Everywhere she made friends and eventual correspondents.

Again, from 1775 to 1782, on the excuse of completing her son's education, she left Russia and sojourned in various points of Europe: in Poland, where she became an intimate friend of Mme Geoffrin's "son," Stanisław Poniatowski; in England; and especially in Scotland, where she arranged for her son to be received as a master of arts at Edinburgh University. Then she spent a year in Ireland, returned to London, crossed the Low Countries, and stopped in Paris. Here she resumed her friendship with Diderot, who had written her admiring and anything but flattering portrait in 1770:

> Princess Dashkova is not at all a beauty; she is tiny; her forehead is high and wide; heavy, discolored cheeks and eyes neither large nor small but somewhat sunken in their sockets; her eyebrows and hair are black; her nose wide, and her mouth large, the lips heavy and the teeth imperfect; her neck round and straight, a shape typical of her countrywomen; her breast convex and her waist nonexistent; a certain promptitude in her movements, but no grace, no distinction, though much affability; the combination of her features produces the effect of a memorable physiognomy; her character is serious; she speaks our language readily; she does not say all she knows or thinks, but what she does say is spoken simply, readily, and with the accent of truth; her soul bristles with misfortunes; her ideas are powerful and strongly held; she exhibits a certain boldness, and proud feelings; I believe she has a deep love of honesty and dignity. She knows her nation's people and their interests; she is filled with aversion for despotism, or anything at all redolent of tyranny; when an action is great, she

cannot endure that it be diminished by insignificant political views. She reacts with the same sincerity to the good and the evil she perceives in her friends and her enemies. Disappointment has greatly aged her and quite ruined her health. She is thirty-six years old this December 1770, and looks forty.[1]

Marie-Antoinette was to insist on receiving this famous exile who prudently avoided worldly occasions. Through Switzerland the princess then reached Italy, where her enlightened curiosity lingered from city to city in libraries, cabinets of natural history, painting galleries, and collections of antiquities; in Rome she was received by the pope and made friends with the French ambassador, Cardinal de Bernis. She had acquired the status of an itinerant ambassador of Enlightenment Russia: in Vienna, on the return trip, she argued with Chancellor von Kaunitz about the merits of Peter the Great (for whom she had little esteem) and received as a present from the emperor certain specimens from his personal collection of natural history. In Berlin, Frederick II invited her to review the Prussian troops at his side.

A year after the princess's return to St. Petersburg, a reassured Catherine II appointed her director of the Academy of Arts and Sciences. The following year, the princess founded the Russian Academy, which under her presidency undertook the publication of a *Dictionary of the Russian Language.* This extraordinary authority assumed by a woman produced criticisms, insults, and calumnies to which the empress did not always remain deaf. Then the princess retired to her estates. Upon Catherine's death in 1796, she was stripped of her rank and exiled by Emperor Paul, who had not forgiven her involvement in the conspiracy of 1762. In 1801, Paul was assassinated and she could triumphantly attend the coronation of Alexander I, with whom she had maintained a close friendship. In

---

1. Diderot, "Mélanges de littérature, d'histoire, et de philosophie, in *Oeuvres de Diderot*, vol. 9, edited by J. A. Naigeon (Paris, 1798), pp. 409–420.

1804–1805 she wrote her *Mémoires* at Troitskoe, her country estate. She died in Moscow in 1810.

This thoroughly European woman was nonetheless fiercely hostile to the Westernization of her country. Diderot wrote of her: "She is Russian *intus* and *in cute*" (expression of the Roman poet Persius, meaning "in depth"). She blamed Peter the Great for importing and imposing foreign masters on Russia, an abstract model that, according to her, did violence to the country's true nature. By founding the Russian Academy, she sought to publish "the rules and a good dictionary to free our language from those foreign terms and phrases, so inferior to our own in expressiveness and energy, which some have had the absurdity to introduce."

From her earliest years, she claimed in her *Mémoires*, written in French, "Bayle, Montesquieu, Boileau, and Voltaire were among my favorite authors." Nonetheless, this complete mastery of the French language and French ideas received throughout Europe produced no indulgence in her toward France. For her son, she chose a British education. "She took," Diderot writes, "a great liking for the English nation"; she loved "this anti-monarchic people." "Frenchified" was a pejorative word from her pen, as it would be from Tolstoy's. Like Rousseau, she avoided "French politesse" and opposed Gustav III of Sweden's "partiality," which she claimed to be exaggerated, in favor of France and the French.

Her dialogues—reported by herself—with Diderot and von Kaunitz established the quasi-Herderian depth of national sentiment in a woman who sought to assimilate French notions of Enlightenment only to compel them to serve those notions she had developed of her own fatherland. Her feudal sentiment was no less deeply rooted. It impressed Diderot, and did not shock Voltaire, who, at Ferney, may have urged the liberation of the "serfs of Saint-Claude" subject to the canons' mainmorte, but at the same time criticized the Geneva magistrates "who allowed their servants to lay down the law" and wrote coldly: "When the populace bothers to think, all is lost."

CONVERSATIONS OF PRINCESS DASHKOVA[2]

With Diderot, on serfdom

One evening, when Diderot was having a conversation with me, a visit from Mme Necker and Mme Geoffrin was announced. With great vivacity, Diderot ordered his servant to say on my behalf to these ladies that I was not in the house. "But, I protested, I met Mme Necker in Spa, and the other one is in correspondence with the empress, so knowing her could not do me any harm." "You have only nine or ten days left in Paris," Diderot replied, "so they would see you only two or three times; they won't understand you, and I cannot bear my idols to be blasphemed. If you were to stay two months, I would be the first to have you get to know Mme Geoffrin; she is a fine specimen of a woman; but since she is one of the trumpets of Paris, I don't want her to see you in a hurry."

So these ladies were told I could not receive them, having a touch of fever at the moment. I didn't get off so easily. The next day I received a very flattering note from Mme Necker, in which she said that Mme Geoffrin could not endure the notion of being in the same city and yet unable to see me; and that she had such a lofty notion of me that she would be inconsolable if she could not meet me.

I answered Mme Necker by emphasizing my desire to keep these ladies' good opinion, which, if it was flattering and perhaps undeserved, could not be justified by the state of illness from which I was at present suffering; that it was therefore quite necessary for me to refuse the pleasure of seeing them, and that I begged them to accept my regrets.

I was therefore compelled to stay in my room for the rest of that day.

---

2 I borrow these two extracts from the recent edition, the first to date, of the Princess Dashkova's *Mémoires* in their original French text, under the title *Mon histoire, mémoires d'une femme de letters russe à l'époque des Lumières,* edited and annotated by Alexander Worontzoff-Dashkoff, Catherine LeGouis, and Catherine Worontzoff-Dashkoff, with a preface by Francis Ley (L'Harmattan, 1999). Hitherto these *Mémoires* were known only by a French translation (1859) from the English translation published by Miss Wilmott in 1840 and reproduced in the collection Le Temps retrouvé (Mercure de France, 1989, second edition).

Ordinarily, after my daily errands, which usually began at eight in the morning and lasted till three in the afternoon, I finished by ending at Diderot's door. He would get into my carriage, would dine with me, and often our conversations would last until two or three hours after midnight.

One day he spoke to me of the slavery in which he believed our peasants lived. I answered: "Since my soul is not that of a slave, you will agree that it cannot be that of a tyrant, hence I deserve your trust on this subject. I shared your ideas on this subject and to that effect had established in my Orel estate a particular form of government because I believed I could make my peasants freer and happier, and yet I found that such an arrangement no longer afforded any control over them for pillage or the embezzlement of even the most insignificant officer of the crown. The well-being and the wealth of our peasants constitutes our prosperity and augments our revenues; hence it would be necessary that a landowner should be arrested for trying to destroy the source of his own wealth. The nobles are, with regard to their peasants, intermediaries between them and the crown, and they find it to their interest to defend them against the rapacity of the governors and officers in the provinces."

"But princess, you cannot deny that with freedom their perspectives widened, from which expansion ensued wealth and abundance."

"If the sovereign," I say to Diderot, "by breaking some links of the chain that binds the peasants to the nobles, also broke some that bound the nobles to the will of the arbitrary sovereigns, I should sign such an arrangement with my blood rather than ink, and with joy in my heart. Moreover, you will forgive me if I observe that you have confused hell with its cause: it is those enlightened perspectives that produce freedom; the latter without the former would produce only anarchy and confusion. When the lower class of my fellow citizens will be enlightened, it will deserve to be free because it will be able to enjoy such freedom without employing it to the detriment of its confrères, or destroying the order and subordination necessary in any government."

"You develop your theme admirably, dear princess, but you have not yet convinced me."

"There are," I replied, "in our fundamental laws antidotes to the tyranny of the nobles; though Peter III annulled several of these laws, there is even a jurisdiction by which the serfs can set forth their grievances against their masters; under the present reign, the governor of a province, by conferring with the marshal and the deputies of his government's nobles, can compel them to withdraw a tyrannical oppression and cause these goods and subjects to be ruled by a guardianship chosen by the nobles themselves. I fear I am not expressing myself as I should wish; but I shall say that having frequently considered this subject, I have always believed I was seeing a man born blind placed on a high rock, surrounded by dreadful precipices; the privation of sight left him unaware of the dangers of his position: ignorant of these horrors, he was in good humor, he ate and slept in peace, he enjoyed birdsong and sometimes sang on his own. Then occurs an optical accident that restores his sight without his being able to escape his dreadful position. Now here is my poor clairvoyant more wretched than ever: he has stopped singing, he neither eats nor sleeps sufficiently; these abysses surrounding him, the power of the waves of which he knew nothing, everything terrifies him, and he ends by dying of fright and despair in the prime of life."

Diderot was lifted out of his chair as if by some mechanical power as a result of my little sketch. He strode back and forth, spitting on the floor with a sort of rage as he said, all in one breath: "What a woman you are! With one blow you collapse a structure of ideas I have been cherishing for the last twenty years."

I admired everything about Diderot, even that sort of frenzy caused by his passionate way of seeing and feeling. His sincerity and the true friendship he felt for his friends, his penetrating and profound genius, the interest and esteem he always showed me had attached me to him for life. I mourn his death and I shall never cease to regret no longer being animated by his inspired living example. Nowadays no one is aware of the quality of that extraordinary mind. Virtue and truth presided over all his actions, and the general welfare was his passion and his constant pursuit. If his vivacity led him into erroneous ways on occasion, he was sincere in those convictions, and was his own dupe.

But is not for me to produce a eulogy worthy of him: other pens more penetrating than mine will not fail to do so.[3]

With von Kaunitz on Peter the Great

I paid him [Chancellor von Kaunitz[4]] a return visit, and he invited me to dine at his home. I accepted this invitation with the stipulation that if, after arriving at his residence, I did not find him at home, he would not regard it as ill-mannered of me to wait longer than four hours, after which I should return to dine at my own lodgings, since I would not have lunched that day and could fast no longer.

The day was ending. I arrived at the prince's residence at half-past three. He was already in his salon; I believe nonetheless that he was more than surprised and even a trifle resentful that I should have dictated the schedule, leaving him at the mercy of my whims for his dinner.

At table he spoke continuously about my country, and leading the conversation around to Peter I, he told me that all Russians were greatly in his debt, for he had created us. I denied this assertion, observing that it was foreign writers who had assigned this distinction to Peter I, because he had invited several of them to his country, and that it was out of conceit that they had described him as creator of Russia, since they envisaged themselves, or their cooperating compatriots, in this so-called creation. Long before the birth of Peter I, the Russians had conquered the kingdoms of Kazan, Astrakhan, and Siberia. The most warlike nation, known under the name of the Golden Horde[5] (because it possessed a great deal of this metal and because their weapons were decorated with it), had also been conquered by the Russians long before the ancestors of Peter I had been called to the throne. The

---

3. Dashkova, *Mon histoire*, pp. 91–93.

4. Imperial chancellor since 1753.

5. A name given by the Russians to the Khanate of Kipchak, the westernmost of the Mongol Empire; in the sixteenth century, it was divided up and gave birth to the khanates of Astrakhan and Crimea. Kazan and Astrakhan were taken under Ivan IV, "the Terrible."

arts had taken their refuge in Russia, and there are still icons in our monasteries, masterpieces of painting that date from this remote period. We had historians who left more manuscripts than all of Europe can show. "Four hundred years ago, Your Highness," I added, "churches covered in mosaics were destroyed by Batû."

"You count for nothing, then, Madame," replied Prince von Kaunitz, "that it was Peter I who brought Russia closer to Europe and that it was only since his reign that we have known anything of Russia?"

"A great empire, Your Highness, with sources of wealth and power such as Russia possesses, has no need to be closer to anything. When a mass as formidable as my country is well governed, it brings whatever it wishes closer to itself. If Russia remained unknown until the period Your Highness indicates, you will forgive me if I conclude that this proves only the ignorance or the unconcern of the European countries that were unaware of a power so formidable, and to prove to you finally that I have no prejudice against Tsar Peter I, I shall close by revealing to you quite sincerely my notion of this extraordinary man. He possessed genius, a craving for action, a desire for perfection, but a total lack of education left his impetuous passion sovereign over his reason. Impulsive, brutal, despotic, he treated everyone without distinction as slaves who must endure everything; his ignorance failed to allow him to perceive that several innovations, violently introduced by him, were being gradually introduced by time, exchange, commerce, and the example of other nations. He would not have destroyed the inestimable character of our ancestors had he not prized foreigners so greatly above the Russians. He would not have weakened the power and respect owed to the laws had he not changed them, including his own, so frequently. He weakened the foundations of his father's government and code of laws; for them he substituted despotic laws only to annul some of these afterward. He abrogated almost completely the freedom and the privileges of the nobles and those of the serfs, who had a constitutional privilege to which they could appeal in case of tyranny. He introduced a military government, which is certainly the most despotic kind, and the vainglory of being a creator made him urge the completion of Petersburg by extremely tyrannical means: thousands of work-

men perished in the marshes, and he encumbered the nobles by the workmen they were compelled to furnish, while they themselves were forced to build brick residences according to his blueprints, whether or not they needed to have houses in Petersburg; this operation was to become odious. He created a navy there, though the Neva's waters were so low that in his shipyards were constructed only the carcasses of warships, which later, at great expense and manpower, were loaded onto camels and dragged to Kronstadt, a labor he should have spared, for he must have known that even medium-size or overloaded vessels could not reach Petersburg. Under Catherine II, the city has quadrupled in size; the royal buildings are much more splendid, and that has been accomplished without using forced labor, without special taxes, and without public discontent."

I realized that this conversation was making a considerable impression on Prince von Kaunitz. Apparently he was willing to let me chatter on, for he said then that it is a fine thing to see a monarch at work in a building site.

"I am sure Your Highness is joking," I replied, "for you know better than I that a sovereign's time is not to be employed doing the manual work of a mere laborer. Peter I could hire not only carpenters and builders but animal labor as well. He failed to attend to his duty and to operations or major tasks by remaining at Saardam in order to become a carpenter and to cripple the Russian language by Dutch word endings and terms, with which all his edicts and anything involved with the navy are stuffed. He had no indispensable need to send his nobles to learn the trades of gardeners, ironworkers, and miners in foreign parts, etc., etc. Each noble would have been delighted to send three or more of his subjects to have them taught these trades."

Prince von Kaunitz let this conversation drop, and changed the subject. I was glad to notice the fact, for I did not regret not saying all that was in my heart concerning the foreign reputation of Peter I.[6]

---

6. Dashkova, *Mon histoire*, pp. 139–141.

15. The Abbé Galiani: The Warmth of Naples and the Wit of Paris

THE ABBÉ GALIANI lacked the serene Fénelonian sweetness of the Abbé Conti, Mme de Caylus's friend, but in the following generation he was, according to Nietzsche, who on this point agreed with Sainte-Beuve, one of the most brilliant minds of the eighteenth century and perhaps the most electrifying. And what an example of the remarkable complementarity that has ceaselessly united Italy and France! Born in 1728 in Chieti, Ferdinando Galiani was brought up with his brother Bernardo in the house of their uncle Celestino, archbishop of Tarento and grand chaplain of the Kingdom of Naples; Monseigneur Galiani, a friend of Vico's, was a learned man in touch with all the cultivated and scholarly minds in Naples. At twenty, Ferdinando, who had been a child prodigy, took minor orders, according to the old humanist tradition that made the ecclesiastical condition and its perquisites the best choice for a life of literary leisure. His earliest productions were rewarded by the learned Pope Benedict XIV, for whom he would pronounce and publish a magnificent funeral oration in 1758, one all the more magnificent since he was quite aware of the vanity of such eloquence. In 1749 he had circulated a parody of a funeral oration: *Diverse Compositions on the Death of Domenico Iannacone, Official Hangman of the High Court of the Vicariate of Naples.* Catholicism for the Abbé Galiani was a principle of intellectual freedom and universal irony. At the age of twenty-three he published a treatise, *De la monnaie*, which Marx cites in *Das Kapital* as a classic of the theory of commercial value. Bernardo Tanucci, Ferdinand IV's prime minister, received him as a member of the Academy of Herculaneum, where he delivered various papers on the mineralogy of Vesuvius and the antiquities discovered during the excavations at Herculaneum and Pompeii. In January 1759, Tanucci, dissatisfied with his ambassador in Paris, Count Cantillana, sent Galiani, with the title of first secretary, to study Choiseul's intentions and the politico-diplomatic intrigues of the French capital. The Bourbons of Naples had been obliged to sign the Family Pact devised by Choiseul to unite the three main Bourbon kingdoms (France, Spain, and Naples) against the Anglo-Prussian alliance, and Tanucci had no interest in being dragged into war. As veritable head of the mission, Galiani was presented to the king at Versailles. When the noble lords around Louis XV smiled at his tiny stature, Galiani saved the situation with a witticism that established his reputation: "Sire," he exclaimed, "what you now see is but a sample of the secretary! The secretary will follow shortly."

His diplomatic correspondence with Tanucci attests to the subtlety and effectiveness of this ambassador in miniature. In 1769, however, Galiani spoke one word too many to Baron von Gleichen, the Danish ambassador, whose dispatches were seized and read by Choiseul. Declared persona non grata, the Abbé Galiani, to his great annoyance, was obliged to return to Naples for good.

During his Parisian sojourn, his intellectual vivacity, his comic talents, his agreeable manners, and his fund of solid knowledge had made him the "lion" of the most exquisite or the most exacting circles. His compatriots Cesare Beccaria or Pietro Verri, passing through the French capital, remained astonished and jealous of this favor that made the abbé the soul of every conversation. Indeed he represented the soul of the Italian Republic of Letters as much as the Kingdom of Naples. Galiani was not only a worldly star, received and celebrated by Mme Geoffrin, Mlle de Lespinasse, and Mme Necker. The philosophes took him up as well, and he became a habitué of the mostly male Helvétius and d'Holbach clubs as well as an intimate of Mme d'Épinay, at whose residence he became close friends with Diderot and Grimm. Mme de Choiseul said of him: "In France we have the small change of wit, Italy has the lingots!" Galiani for his part enjoyed to the point of intoxication that unique mixture of fine manners and fearless intelligence that constituted Parisian conversation, especially in the society of the philosophes, a high-altitude oxygen for the mind. Yet he was not himself a philosophe in the French sense of the word. His irony and his sharp sense of the human comedy protected this Christian Epicurean against all dictates of system and particularly against any party line. He was too deep not to be deeply conservative, and he was one of the first to anticipate that "grim reasoning" would ultimately ransack the world's gayest nation. But this Italian Montaigne loved "the art of conversing," excelled in it, and among the philosophes, especially with Diderot, found interlocutors worthy of his mettle: he left them soon enough to have savored no more than the hors d'oeuvres of the banquet of wit.

His obligatory return to Naples in 1769 initially depressed him greatly. "Yes, Paris is my homeland, exile me from it as they will, I shall return," he wrote on July 17, 1769. The following year he was heard to remark: "Plants are denatured by a change of soil, and I was a Parisian plant."

Yet his "exile" was the point of departure for an active correspondence with his friends, who missed him fiercely, and especially with the intelligent and sensitive Mme d'Épinay, whom Grimm increasingly neglected. Galiani's oral invention, deprived of direct encouragement, was henceforth expressed by written improvisation. We owe indirectly to Choiseul one of the masterpieces of this typically French art, the friendly letter, practiced here by an Italian virtuoso. Exiled from Paris, Galiani in Naples became for correspondence in French what Casanova was called to become later in the Dux castle for French *mémoires*: the supreme master in his genre, besides Voltaire.

And then, shortly before his departure, Galiani, after an animated conversation at the d'Holbach mansion, had written at Diderot's request a dialogue in which he refuted the free-exchange theses sustained by the physiocrats and argued, under the name of Chevalier Zanobi, for a more pragmatic approach to economic matters. This *Dialogue on the Grain Market*, edited by Mme d'Épinay, was published by Diderot in 1770 and enjoyed a lively success. Voltaire delighted in its piquant vivacity as much as in its ideas. "How can you suppose," he wrote to Mme d'Épinay, "that I don't know the Abbé Galiani? Have I not read and reread him? Therefore I've seen him. He must resemble his prose like any two drops of water, or rather any two sparks. Is he not lively, active, full of reason, of genius, of fun? Always profound and always gay? I've seen him, I tell you, and I'll describe him for you."

The letters to Mme d'Épinay reproduced here[1] reflect the excitement of this editorial adventure, which made the Abbé Galiani an author famous throughout Europe. Grimm, in his periodical *Correspondance littéraire*, destined for an exclusive public of crowned heads, published many of Galiani's letters to Mme d'Épinay. They were indeed a king's banquet.

Wealthy, admired, even influential in his birthplace, Abbé Galiani never returned to Paris. He reaccustomed himself more than he dared admit to Naples and its comparative simplicity, where he wrote several treatises concerned with politics, commerce, and education. He added the finishing touches to his *Commentaire des oeuvres d'Horace*. In 1775 he provided Paisiello with the libretto for his opera *Socrate immaginario*. Having translated Cardinal de Polignac's *Anti-Lucrèce* into Italian, this Epicurean Christian died in 1781.

Letters from the Abbé Galiani to Mme d'Épinay

Genoa, July 17, 1769

Madame,

I am still inconsolable to have left Paris and even more so not to receive any word from you, nor from the lazy Philosopher [Diderot]. Is it possible this impassive monster fails to realize how much my honor, my fame (for which I couldn't care less), my pleasure, and that of my friends (for whom I care a great deal) are involved in the matter I

---

1. From the most recent (and best) edition, that of Georges Dulac and Daniel Maggetti, vol. 1, 1769–1770 (Paris: Desjonquères, 1992).

entrusted to him, and how impatient I am to learn that the bundle of papers has finally rounded the cape and passed through the terrible ordeal of revision? For once that has been accomplished I am entirely at ease about all the rest.

My journey has been very agreeable, on land and by sea. It has even been of an inconceivable felicity. I was never too warm, and there was a constant breeze behind us on the Rhone, and out at sea as well. Everything seems to encourage me to distance myself from all I love in this world. My heroism will therefore be all the greater and much more memorable in overcoming the elements, nature, and the opposing gods when I manage to return to Paris. Yes, Paris is my homeland, and even though I am exiled, I shall return. Meet me in the last room of the fourth floor of the rue Fromenteau, the room of . . . a fine figure of a woman. Here the greatest genius of our age will reside en pension *on 30 sols a day, and happy to do so. What a joy to rave on like this! Farewell.*

Please keep sending your letters to the ambassador's residence.

Has Grimm returned from his journey?

Naples, January 20, 1770

Dear Lady,

In the depths of depression into which I was cast by the contretemps my employment endured, I had no heart to answer your letter of the 13th. I kept saying, "Let us wait and see how this will end." The courier leaving Paris on the 25th could not overcome the obstacles caused by the snow and the flooding rivers, so we remained incommunicado from France for an entire week, and I just received both your letters of the 25th and the 1st. I do not yet know if I have escaped all these disasters, and if I shall ever receive my wretched hundred louis. For that is my entire ambition, my glory, my virtue. Yet I note that it has been necessary to dismiss a government supervisor, to instigate enormous financial irregularities, to cause the state to collapse in order that my little book be published. The night that gave birth to Hercules was not nearly so long, nor so stormy. I beg you not to send me the criticisms; just send me the charges, and see to it that the bookseller joins forces with the postal collector. That is all that interests me.

I shall be sure to study the Gazette de Paris *on a regular basis and make arrangements with Suard. His rheumatism, and your colics are insignificant. Get over them as soon as you can, and without baths, if you please. Drink fresh milk with honey from Provence, and in three days you'll be cured. The Georgics are no longer a poetic subject for our times. A colonial nation must practice an agricultural religion in order to speak with proper dignity and grandeur about bees, turnips, and onions. What do you expect to accomplish with nothing more than your pathetic consubstantiality and transubstantiation? There are two sorts of religion. Those of "new" peoples are cheerful, and regard agriculture, athletic medication, and population growth. Those of "old" peoples are melancholy and consist of nothing but metaphysics, contemplation, rhetoric, and spiritual elevation. These must bring about the abandonment of cultivation, fertility, good health, and other pleasures. How old we are!*

I must tell you something about your first letter. In Voltaire's pamphlet Tout en Dieu, *you express amazement that he takes only twenty pages to speak of the Universal Cause and its effects. I, however, am amazed by just the opposite. Anyone who says* Tout en Dieu *says clearly and distinctly that God is Everything, for anyone who says that two and three are contained in five is saying that five is merely the composite of three and two. Whereby everything is said. How the devil might one find enough to fill a pamphlet with a thing I couldn't have managed to extend for twenty lines except by adding some elaborate comparison or other. This once, Voltaire has played us false. He wanted to play the deist, and found himself an atheist without even noticing it. Taking the pitcher to the well too frequently, etc. You must never rub up against these subjects, they're much too slippery.*

His rage against Lent and dried eel may have more to it. I don't like the latter, either. But his fury against holidays is ridiculous. He imagines they're a divine institution, which is why he takes against them so. But he's mistaken. They're a human institution. They're not for God at all, they're for mankind, and consequently Voltaire ought to respect them. Once again he's confused his ass with his breeches. As for Les Adorateurs, *according to the samples you've shown me, it might be good. In a dialogue, each speaker must stick to his notion. The letter from our dear marquis is better than all that. My compliments to Antoinette-Rose on her opening night. Grimm has gone to a lot of trouble looking for the corrections to be made in a text that may be dearer to my friends by its imperfections announcing that cruel precipitation of my departure. My health is still the same. My condition is still worrisome. But who knows anything about it? Farewell, my dear and lovely lady.*

Naples, January 27, 1770

Madame,

Your letter of the 6th has just arrived, and quite convinces me the dice are loaded despite everything the baron can say—he's kept double books all his life, whereas I have kept only aces up my sleeve. Please try to understand that the only thing that concerns me in this business— the business of my wretched hundred louis—is precisely what meets with unheard-of, inconceivable, inexplicable difficulties. Give me your oath, Madame, as I give you mine: there are certain saints who must be invoked with regard to what a certain notorious gout victim has said.

I am anything but surprised by Panurge's contradictions. He is a man who has his heart in his head, and his head in his heart. He reasons according to passion and acts accordingly. For just that I love him with all my heart, though I reason quite differently, and he loves me madly, though he believes me to be machiavellino. *Moreover I believe that his heart, which is as fine and fair as any in the known world, will always lead his head, and that he will end by not answering, and by loving me all the more. He will perceive upon a second or third reading of the work that Chevalier Zanobi neither believes nor even pretends to believe anything he says; that he is the world's greatest skeptic, and the world's greatest academic; that he doesn't believe a word he says, just as he denies every word said to him. But I beg you, Madame, do not utter the one word that is the key to the mystery. Let us wait and entertain ourselves by seeing how long Paris takes to abound in my sense, instead of getting all hot and bothered over an interminable* question. Grimm was the only one who understood me at first, and he realized that the book had no conclusion. A conclusion had to be added to win the favor of the Parisian good-for-nothings who insist on concluding. Furthermore the book really is the work of a philosopher, and Grimm is the only one capable of mixing a philosopher with a statesman, that is, a man who holds the key to the mystery and who knows that it all comes down to zero. The Abbé Raynal is quite right to say the work is deep—it is indeed devilishly deep because it's empty and there's nothing in it. People who have said its principles are diffuse have described the dialogue perfectly: but no one in Paris knows anything about the style of dialogues. Those who take the trouble to connect my ideas may—eventually—divine the work's intentions.

You've sent me the first success of the grenadiers' volley, and only from the front line. I'm curious to hear the racket that will be made by the dregs of the army, which will surely be diabolical. But don't forget to send me what Voltaire has to say. And you must send a copy on my behalf to my dear Prince of Saxe-Gotha. Encourage those of my friends who've read the thing to write me. On such an occasion I shall gladly cover the postal charges.

Apropos, since the author is known, I flatter myself that you haven't failed to tell my friends under what disagreeable circumstances this wretched child was conceived—and aborted. I myself haven't a clue as to what to make of the thing. I haven't been able to read it through with a cool head. I left the original manuscript in your hands, so I know nothing about subsequent developments. It will mean nothing to the public, but I hope my friends will read it indulgently, and what they read will remind them of the sound of my voice, of my dialogue, of my gestures—that's all I dare ask; to be loved. All I deserve, in fact, and it will be a long while before Paris sees a more lovable foreigner than yours truly.

Another thought. Please send on my behalf (since the author is known) a copy to the newly married M. Baudouin, Committee Chairman, Place Vendôme.

There is no question of a second edition if the first doesn't sell. But if it does, I'd like to add a dialogue explaining the system of the supply *depots, which is the only one that can make a wheat market possible in France.*

And while I'm still dreaming about money, the bookseller will pay me 25 louis for this new dialogue. But you'll protest: How can you write dialogues outside of Paris? Well, I can't. I'm struggling through the most inconceivable depression here. My trip to the Congo is quite unfeasible. Instead I've been offered a journey to Cuba. Which is not my direction, I sadly reply. Do you know what I'm doing right now? I am seriously spending my time organizing my juvenilia, to be printed under that very title: Juvenilia. *They're all are in Italian, and consist of dissertations, verse, prose, classical scholarship, miscellaneous speculations. A young thing indeed, but my own. Farewell, my incomparable Dulcinea. You do love me, don't you?*

Naples, February 3, 1770

Madame,
At last I've received a copy of that book that Paris has been discussing so feverishly. I read it with the greatest eagerness, for I'd almost ceased to remember what it contained. On the faith of a connoisseur, the book is good. If it pleased the Abbé Raynal and our dear Schomberg, I'm content, for I set great store by the judgment of these two men. As for Madame du Deffand, I'm quite certain she hasn't read it. And Duclos's opinion always indicates what is the opposite of everyone else's. So all's well.

I've found very few changes to be made in the text, but those few produce a great effect. For which I thank my benefactors. If only I could say the same for my proofreaders. I noticed four or five capital errors, which it's extremely important to correct, if only by hand on the copies not yet sold. If sales should necessitate a second edition, I beg you to pay close attention to these corrections, besides asking you to be good enough to remove the card game from the end of the fifth dialogue, if I'm not mistaken, and to restore the dinner. I don't know what madness made you so eager to present me as a gambler rather than a gourmand. I am surely the latter, not the former. What could be wrong with talking food when wheat is the entire subject? I earnestly request,

Madame, that you restore dinner and remove this subject of dissipation that clashes with the beginning of the next dialogue, in which the speakers are still at table, etc. Let's avoid handing a triumph to maniacs for consistency. I want to be what I am, and to employ the tone I prefer. And if I'm bought, that's all I (and my bookseller) can ask. . . .

I'm answering your letter of the 14th, which just reached me. Those who've objected to the double tax that my import and export duties would impose on speculators importing wheat from abroad are ignorant of their own country's laws. It's two years since this inconvenience was obviated by a royal decree. It existed, however weakly, by means of a one percent import duty, and of the half-percentage export duty that the decree had established. The decree states that the wheat entering the country must be bonded, so that the ports of France will be free ports for wheat, and this one percent duty will not be paid when the foreign wheat that has been imported is resold. Such a decree does exist. If my papers were in order, I could send it to you from here. You yourself purchased it from me for 44 sols. So I needn't have discussed a judicious decree already in effect. Furthermore, I'd have mentioned it when I explained my system of supply depots and free ports, or as we call them caricatori, *which must be established in France as they have been in Sicily—but I left, or rather I was extracted from Paris, along with my heart. What more do you want from me? The answer you should make to this objection is not the one you sent me in your letter, but rather to purchase this decree, and to display it. It will be seen that the disadvantage is nonexistent, since it has been determined that surcharges are not to be paid; that when a proper import is made not by landing these shipments of wheat in the warehouses of commercial cities but by selling them to the inhabitants of the country, and similarly, when an attempt is made to leave with the wheat that has been shipped, it suffices to show one's declaration made upon arrival, and one is free to leave with the quantity of unsold wheat, without paying anything. All this was already achieved, and very wisely arranged by the French government two years ago, with every precaution to avoid frauds. However I cannot thank you enough for having written me about this matter. It will furnish me the substance for a future dialogue.*

Please make sure I hear from Grimm, from Schomberg, from the baron, from everyone. This is necessary for my salvation. I am a damned soul, likely to perish in despair, if my friends forget me. A thousand thanks to Mlle. de Lespinasse for her persistence in enjoying my bad jokes. Farewell, lovely lady. I have no time to tell you anything more this evening. Embrace my dear Philosopher, and embrace yourself on my behalf. Has M. de Sartine received the page I sent him from Genoa about the Lombards' settlement? Farewell.

Madame, I beg you to send a copy of the Dialogues *as a gift from me to M. Pellerin, the former chief clerk at the Naval Ministry, rue Richelieu. A gentleman of the old school, of whom I'm extremely fond.*

16. Friedrich Melchior Grimm and the Strabismus of the Enlightenment

FRIVOLITY AND PHILOSOPHY are the two breasts of the Enlightenment. The true philosophy of the century of Louis XV was perhaps his amiable frivolity, and the worst of his frivolities was certainly his philosophy. In any case it was by frivolity and not philosophy that eighteenth-century Paris had managed, without firing a shot, to reduce the rest of Europe to the condition of a province, dependent on and subservient to the fashions, the scandals, the animated stage, and the incidents in the wings of the Parisian social theater. An aristocracy capable of being amused by wit set the tone, at a certain remove, for all the other European aristocracies, who, not being in on the secret of finding diversion, sought it in Paris.

A specialty of men of letters, as fashions in clothes were the specialty of tailors, an art of thinking as "philosophers" appeared in the panoply of Parisian exports in the 1750s. It found in frivolity but also, it must be said, in aristocratic generosity, the glamorous, nourishing, and contagious Parisian milieu it could not do without. In order to promote beneficence and tolerance, it hastened to assume the colors of amusement, politeness, scandal, and fashion, which gave its excitingly new ideas a favored presence among the pleasures in which the elegant frivolity of Paris glittered in the eyes of the rest of courtly Europe.

A JOURNAL FOR "DECIDERS"

No organ of the Enlightenment is so characteristic of the fundamental ambiguity that the philosophes toyed with and that toyed with them as the *Correspondance littéraire, philosophique et critique*, which from 1753 to 1790 was their interpreter to the courts of Europe. Its subscribers were for the most part crowned heads or, at the very least, imperial princes: Frederick II, Catherine II, Gustav III of Sweden, Stanisław Augustus of Poland, the Duke of Saxe-Gotha, Prince Heinrich of Prussia, Princess Caroline of Hesse-Darmstadt, the Princess of Nassau-Sarrebrück, etc. By comparison, Marguerite Caetani and Valéry Larband's *Commerce* (1924–1932) was a mass-medium magazine and today *The New Yorker* could pass for a pop review.

All these subscribers *de grand luxe* wanted to know what Paris was reading and talking about, and in the costly *Correspondance* (handwritten, the supreme luxury for a review), they found a zest supplementary to the household disputes that set the philosophes at one another's throats: after his breakup with Mme d'Épinay, Rousseau was trounced there quite regularly. Yet the powerful and wealthy readers of this philosophical review saw only one facet, the most seriously piquant but neither the most singular nor the most attractive feature of the great Parisian entertainment. Of course they could, along with *The Social Contract*, discover in its reviews *Easy Ways to Cleaner Teeth* and *A Sure Treatment for Corns*. Yet they had to look elsewhere to keep abreast of what the *Correspondance* did not discuss: the latest fashion in matters of language, dress, and jewelry, of furniture, cooking, and tableware, as well as the hottest gossip concerning their French rivals and the titled of both court and city.

In the *Correspondance littéraire*, indeed, a coterie "philosophy" screened from publicity and therefore from censorship, protected by the narrowness of its foreign crowned and mostly Protestant subscribers, could indulge quite openly, and on paper, in persiflage concerning the prejudices of the Roman religion and the injustices of the French monarchy. But such criticism had to be skillfully mixed with intelligent and more practical varieties, among which sparkled, retrospectively to our eyes, Diderot's "Salons." Subscribers to the *Correspondance* were not only devotees of new books (Grimm was an excellent reviewer), but collectors of works of art greedy for tips about this market of which Paris was then the main site and Diderot an outstanding commentator.

From Journalism to Diplomacy

Such a combination of talents was wielded with *maestria* by the journal's director, Friedrich Melchior Grimm. In 1753 he had adeptly replaced the Abbé Raynal, founder of the *Nouvelles littéraires.* The title was changed, and the new director recruited a new public of royal subscribers in his native Germany. He made this highly specialized newsletter the instrument of his prodigious social ascent in diplomacy, in business, and even in the lesser echelons of the nobility of the Holy Roman Empire. The distinguished connections that this journal of the *happy few* created for him was the making of Grimm's fortune as well.

Born in Ratisbon (now Regensburg), his father a superintendent of the town's Lutheran clergy, Grimm had been a serious student who secured a teaching post at the University of Leipzig. An admirer and disciple of Gottsched, the great Herr Professor of German letters of the period, Grimm initiated his literary career as a docile imitator of French classics. His five-act tragedy *Banise* was performed in 1747 in Strasbourg and Frankfurt.

Like Rousseau and several other "provincial masters," Grimm "climbed" to Paris by means of his tutorial duties. In 1748 he accompanied the sons of Count von Schomberg to the French capital. He took up residence there in the service of a nephew of Marshal von Saxe, Count von Friese, who soon discovered he needed a secretary. In the early course of his duties Grimm made friends with Rousseau, who like himself was living a bohemian life. The citizen of Geneva introduced him to his new philosophical friends: d'Alembert, Duclos, d'Holbach, and Diderot in particular, whose intimacy with Grimm lasted until 1781. When fortune began to smile, Grimm invited these philosophes for a weekly informal dinner, which did not prevent him from frequenting some fashionable Parisian circles, notably that of Mme Geoffrin. La Patronne, as she was called, who detested Diderot's verve and bohemian manners, became infatuated with Grimm's more formal demeanor, and with the flattery he was determined to shower upon her. In short order she undertook on his behalf a permanent campaign of subscriptions to the *Correspondance littéraire, philosophique et critique*.

The tutor and intellectual chronicler emerged from obscurity by means of a stormy liaison with the famous soprano Mlle Fel. In 1753 he assumed, by becoming the lover of Mme d'Épinay, a considerable importance in the "philosophical communion" of which this lady was the Egeria. She has left a flattering portrait of him in her memoir-novel in the third person, *Histoire de Mme de Montbrillant*, in which she provides her own version, against the one Rousseau proposed in the *Confessions*, of the break between the "communion" and the author of *Émile*. She describes Grimm as yet another good savage, though one more polished and more candid than the citizen of Geneva:

> His countenance appeals by a certain mixture of naiveté and finesse; it reveals precisely that degree of pride that arouses respect without humiliating others. In morality and philosophy his principles are severe, and he takes no occasion to modify and soften them according to circumstances, though he generally relaxes when it comes to judging others.
>
> He has a just, profound, and penetrating intellect. He thinks and expresses himself forcefully. Though he speaks without any special correctness, no one commands a more attentive audience. It seems to me that in matters of taste, no one has a more delicate, finer, or surer tact. His humorous tone is entirely his own, and would suit no one else.
>
> His character is a mixture of truth, sweetness, shyness, sensibility, reserve, melancholy, and gaiety. He cherishes his solitude, and it is easy to see that his taste for society is not a part of his nature but a preference acquired by education and habit.
>
> The frequentation of his friends adds to his happiness, without being essential to it. Confronted with the aspect of what is not familiar to him, his first reaction is to flee. It is only reflection, good manners, and a sort of silliness in his character that later prevails. Since he is fearful of giving offense, he often remains in the company of people he finds tedious or

frankly dislikes. On which occasions a profound silence and a distracted expression soon take possession of him.

A certain loneliness, along with considerable sloth, occasionally makes his opinions, when given in public, equivocal. He never quite contradicts his genuine feelings, but leaves them in some doubt. He loathes argument and even discussion, claiming that they have been invented only for the salvation of fools.[1]

Actually, except in music where this German had a genius all his own, Grimm was more or less an adept sponge who managed to parody the ironic temper of his Parisian friends in order to dazzle society and astonish foreign courts. He had "imperturbably" studied, writes Jean Fabre, the spirit of society with the same application he devoted to the lectures of his master Gottsched.[2] He disguised this pedant's imitation by deliberately playing the "German simpleton" and concealed his scorn of French frivolity by declaring, with no sense of paradox, "I've remained natural and German."

He first crept into the French Republic of Letters by publishing (in the Abbé Raynal's *Le Mercure*) some critical editions of German literary works and by contributing in a number of brochures to the cause of Italian music in the *Querelle des Bouffons*. During Wolfgang Amadeus Mozart's second visit to Paris, when he was Grimm's guest in Mme d'Épinay's home in the rue Chaussée-d'Antin, the young musician was left to make his own way in Paris; Grimm had shown great interest in him when he was a child prodigy over whom every European courts, including Versailles, had marveled in 1763. As an unknown young composer set down in Paris, Mozart merited no more from his worldly host than a charitable hospitality.

After 1753, strengthened by his nascent reputation as an ingenious literary and musical critic and by his takeover of the *Correspondance*

---

1. Mme d'Épinay, *L'Histoire de Mme de Montbrillant* (Mercure de France, 1992).

2. Jean Fabre, *Stanislas-Auguste Poniatowski et l'Europe des Lumières* (Paris: Les Belles Lettres, 1952), p. 344.

littéraire, Grimm could count on the generous and abundant collaboration of Mme d'Épinay and Diderot, while claiming to be "chained to his desk like a convict" and on every occasion cursing this "hateful métier" that shackled him to books, authors, and the vulgarity of journalism.

As a matter of fact, he gladly and frequently abandoned the entire editing process of the bimonthly review to his two voluntary collaborators and friends, leaving Paris in order to revel abroad in the favor—and the financial advantages—he enjoyed on account of the "importance" attributed to him in the capital. In 1757–1759, he followed, as the Maréchal-Duc d'Estrées's secretary, the French army's campaign in Westphalia; in 1761–1763, he accompanied the crown prince of Hesse-Darmstadt to England. In September 1769 and during the summer of 1773, he had the signal honor of bringing the Parisian temperature to Frederick II in his palace of Sans, Souci.

When Grimm left the *Correspondance littéraire* in 1773 to Henri Meister (who continued the enterprise, without Diderot and much less brilliantly, until 1790), he became a tutor once again, but of a much higher class, first accompanying the young prince of Hesse-Darmstadt to St. Petersburg, then busying himself there educating the sons of a princely Russian family. And he would return to Paris only in 1777, after a belated Grand Tour, which began with a cure at Karlsbad in June 1774, continued with a long sojourn in Italy (1775–1776), and ended after a detour in Denmark and Sweden. Everywhere in French Europe Grimm was received as a Parisian celebrity, coddled by each and every court in turn. As these peregrinations proceeded, he ascended socially. In 1755 he had managed to have the Duc d'Orléans bestow upon him the title and office of *secrétaire des commandements*. A little later, the city of Frankfurt put him in charge of defending its interests in Paris, an appointment worth 24,000 livres. He had already become, for a jeering Diderot, "Monsieur l'Ambassadeur." By dint of carrying out Parisian commissions for Louise of Saxe-Gotha or helping to marry off the daughters of Landgravine Caroline of Hesse, he was named counselor to the legation of Saxe-Gotha in France in 1769. On his passage through Vienna in in 1774, Maria Theresa made

Grimm a Baron of the Empire, and the Duke of Saxe-Gotha appointed the new baron his minister plenipotentiary to the court of Versailles.

The Parisian Agent of Catherine II

Yet his greatest protectress was Catherine II, to whom he had been introduced in 1763 by the obliging Mme Geoffrin. The tsarina had sought to draw the two directors of the *Encyclopédie*, Diderot and d'Alembert, into her orbit; she offered in vain to transfer their enterprise to Riga, or to some other city within her empire. Grimm took advantage of her chagrin by celebrating her good intentions in the *Correspondance littéraire*: "A passion for philosophers cannot be carried further." The "Semiramis of the North," as Voltaire had called her, found in Paris her man as docile as he could be. Henceforth, Grimm leading on Diderot, the *Correspondance littéraire* busied itself relaying Voltaire in the apology for Catherine's policy of "tolerance" carried out in Poland, and in harshly refuting the travelers who unfailingly, at this period, described (before Custine) the Russian regime and its methods in Poland; Caraccioli, who had seen the Russians in action in Warsaw and said as much in his brochures, was in the *Correspondence* castigated for his former and formal rank as a "Polish colonel," and therefore as a biased witness.

In 1768, against the naive Parisians who sided with the Confederation of Bar and stirred up public opinion against the Russian repression, Grimm's editorial dictated the appropriate attitude to Europe's elite: "Today Poland has been infected by that same dangerous and convulsive fever [papist fanaticism] by which Germany and France were so grievously stricken during the last two centuries; it is to be hoped that the Russian physicians will shorten the course of this disease."[3]

Along with Voltaire, Grimm can be counted among the inventors of "aggression disguised as humanitarian warfare."

---

3. Fabre, *Stanislas-Auguste Poniatowski et l'Europe des Lumières*, p. 330.

The Campaign Against the Physiocrats

Not content with unreservedly covering the realpolitik of the despots of Eastern Europe, Grimm made the *Correspondance littéraire* a combat weapon against the chief rivals of the "philosophical communion" in Germany, Tuscany, Austria, and Sweden: the Physiocrats or, as they sometimes called themselves, the Economists. The Marquis de Mirabeau's *L'Ami des hommes*, one of the manifestos of this school that today has been virtually erased from the Enlightenment's map, had become then the pillow book of many enlightened princes and countless landowners. Our current tendency is to sum up the economic doctrine of the Enlightenment in Adam Smith's *Wealth of Nations*; but in continental Europe during the eighteenth century, a strictly French economic theory had won many partisans, notably in Poland, whose agricultural and mining potential was evidently underexploited. It had spread even farther since d'Alembert's and Diderot's articles in the *Encyclopédie* were inspired by the views of Quesnay and his disciples. Surprisingly, this theory has not yet been the object of some degree of erudite rehabilitation.

Physiocratic theory was simultaneously modernizing and conservative. No campaign was mounted against *l'Infâme*, no crusade in favor of tolerance, except the kind that permits economic exchange and prosperity in "the natural and essential order of the political sciences." Furthermore, the Physiocrats held the French version of administrative monarchy to be the best system in Europe, and made no secret of counting on it to achieve what they regarded as true progress. Voltaire, after teasing them in *L'Homme aux quarante écus*, reversed his own biases and followed Physiocratic principles at Ferney, enthusiastically supporting the empowerment, under Louis XVI, of the "Economist" Turgot in a royal ministry. But Grimm, ever Catherine II's votary, espoused the tsarina's hatred of Physiocracy. He utilized the *Correspondance littéraire* to conduct a fierce campaign against these spoilsports. His hostility led him to publish in 1770 a *Sermon philosophique* crudely mimicking the irony of the Voltairean pamphlets and characterizing the Physiocrats as "Capuchins of the

Encyclopédie." He also launched an attack against Rousseau's inopportune *Considérations sur le gouvernement de la Pologne*, of an entirely different orientation, but similarly opposing the philanthropic gambit invented to legitimize Catherine II's oppression of Poland.

TARTUFFE'S STRABISMUS

It is difficult to find a more explicit Tartuffe in the eighteenth century than Friedrich Melchior Grimm. Even his surface "acculturation" to the French language and literature masked the camouflaged barbarian. To Catherine II, who dreamed of ruling the universe from a recaptured and imperial Constantinople, he could write: "And I foresee a day when fate will replace the Greek language by Russian, and Latin by German."[4]

Rousseau characterized Grimm as "a man of false character." As so often, he saw clearly: a servile courtier of the despots of Vienna and St. Petersburg, Grimm professed in France the most intransigent principles of ethics and philosophical criticism. He carried duplicity to the point of caricature, but it must be acknowledged that he acquired this art of double-dealing from his French models, friends, and frequent accomplices: Voltaire, Diderot, D'Alembert, Marmontel. None of them seemed troubled by the contradiction between the frivolity that applauded them and the Roman virtue they professed; nor did they remark the degree to which their criticism of the monarchy and religion in France failed to match their apology for foreign tyrants. Only Rousseau, in his *Confessions*, recognized this duplicity and, as always in his case, confession of sin equaled absolution: "When I played the anti-despot and the proud republican in Paris, I felt in spite of myself a secret predilection for the very nation I regarded as servile and for the government I affected to oppose."[5]

Furthermore, ever aspiring to be unique, Rousseau did not regard

---

4. Fabre, *Stanislas-Auguste Poniatowski et l'Europe des Lumières*, p. 348.
5. *Correspondance littéraire*, February 15, 1770.

such duplicity as a feature of the coterie to which he had belonged, but as a *bizarrerie* all his own: "I am surely the only man who, living in a nation that treated him well and that he adored, affected *in that very nation* to disdain it."

The great figures of the Enlightenment supremely lacked any historical and political sense of the tragic. They acknowledged this blind spot, but only in theory, within the limited context of literary poetics. In a discussion of La Harpe's tragedy *Mélanie*, Grimm wrote:

> True tragedy, which does not exist in France and which is yet to be created, can only be written in prose, and will never accommodate the pompous, flowery, and inflated style of alexandrine verse. It is impossible to give such verse less bombast, more strength and simplicity than is to be found in M. de La Harpe's work, and it is this verse that invariably destroys the tragic effect and prevents the poet from breaking my heart, from tearing my vitals.... So must we toss Racine and Voltaire into the fire? No, they are to be read and admired through all eternity; but we need not believe that in performance their tragedies can have the striking truth, or produce the terrifying impression of those by Sophocles and Euripides: the childish absurdity will always show through somewhere.

We need not see in this criticism of French classical tragedy, that national literary institution of the realm, a call for its political and historical dethronement. At the time such criticism was a commonplace of the poetics of the philosophes; Voltaire himself, in his *Lettres anglaises*, pitted Shakespeare against French classical dramatists, before thinking better of it. Diderot, Grimm's friend, had borrowed from Burke a poetics of the "terrible" sublime, making it one of the chief motifs of his dramatic and particularly of his art criticism. The young German generation of Sturm und Drang was even then hoisting its equivalent of a banner, but with a view to reforming a lyric and dramatic poetry just as circumscribed.

When Grimm despairs, in the *Correspondance littéraire* of September 1, 1772, of the "weak progress of the philosophic spirit," we must not be too quick to recognize him as an impatient revolutionary. The example he gives immediately reveals not an aversion in principle to the European ancien régime in general but a deep hostility toward monarchic and Catholic France: "How far we are," he writes,

> from that salutary reform of our manners [read "French manners"] in which the nation's public festivals will have as their object of commemoration the great actions of its ancestors, and in which public shames are expiated by solemn days of humiliation, which inspire a proper horror of the crimes that sully the nation's annals! Two hundred years ago a young king of execrable memory, driven to crime by a mother still more execrable than he, ordered the massacre of a host of his subjects, by the most infamous and cowardly of betrayals. And I spent the second jubilee of that dreadful night of August 24 in the heart of Paris without encountering on my way a living soul who shuddered with horror and dread to recall the event. Never, I believe, have I experienced a more grievous sensation than the effect of that universal silence, that total oblivion, a symptom worse than death befalling the entire nation. Finally the old man of Ferney sought to remind his country of that dreadful event, but by stanzas too weak to waken the land from its mortal lethargy:

> *And after two years, you return*
> *Ghastly day, day fatal to the world.*
> *Would that Time's eternal abyss*
> *Buried you in eternal darkness. . . .*

The old poet who wrote those lines did not feel the fever that scorches any soul sensitive to the memory of that fatal night; indeed the cruelest response to such verses is to find them charming, without comprehending the subject whose horror they were meant to retrace. Shameful, that the Académie Française had a poetry prize to bestow on the day after that fatal jubilee, and never once dreamed of assigning the Saint Bartholomew's Day Massacre as its subject!

Ready to storm the heavens and impose an annual commemorative contrition upon the nation that had made him what he was, our good compere Grimm "never once dreamed" of applying such standards of historical morality to the kingdoms and principalities of the Holy Roman Empire or to the Russia of which he was a pensioner. Yet neither their pasts nor Luther's (who approved, indeed demanded, the pitiless slaughter of Thomas Münzer's Anabaptists) was supposed by Grimm innocent of crimes comparable to the Saint Bartholomew's Day Massacre!

When the Princess of Hesse-Darmstadt, a fervent reader of the *Correspondance littéraire*, questioned Grimm about the dangerous ideas that her son might contract in his company during their projected visit to England, he was able to reassure his illustrious correspondent in perfect good faith: "Deign to be persuaded that the writer of certain pages and the man to whom Your Highness entrusts the Prince her son do not have entirely the same ways."

Diderot, far from being unscathed by this strabismus, had made out quite early the duplicity of the German neophyte he had befriended. On November 25, 1760, he wrote to Sophie Volland apropos of the *Correspondance littéraire*: "The severity of his principles collapses. He distinguishes two justices, one which applies to individuals, the other to sovereigns."[6]

In reality, that distinction acquired for Grimm the severity of a principle. Reviewing with sovereign disdain Rousseau's *Considérations*, he wrote in the *Correspondance littéraire*: "Men in general are no more made for liberty than for truth, though they have these two words constantly on their lips. Each of these inestimable goods

---

6. Denis Diderot, *Oeuvres complètes*, edited by Roger Lewinter (Le Club Français du Livre, 1970), p. 995.

belongs to the elite of the human race, with the express proviso that they be enjoyed without making the fact too well known. The rest of mankind is born for servitude and error."[7] So much for Grimm. Voltaire wrote once and for all, and his disciples agreed, "When the populace meddles with thinking, all is lost."

THE TEMPTATION OF THE PHILOSOPHES

In Grimm's person the masters of the Enlightenment had for a publicity agent a "philosopher" capable of harking back (in advance) to Joseph de Maistre! But Diderot, who detested Frederick II, also yielded to the seductions of the Semiramis of the North, and Mme d'Épinay's entire coterie cheerfully practiced the same "bifocality" as Grimm: merciless to the motes they discerned in the eye of Louis XV, they were strangely blind to the beams of Eastern despotism.

The same moral and political strabismus troubled the vision of many twentieth-century philosophers and "new" French philosophers, exterminating angels when it came to France and her history, yet ready for any sophism to justify or admire entirely comparable injustices, archaisms, even crimes beyond our frontiers. When the French past was not in question, this quite un-Kantian but altogether Sartrean partiality operated on the world stage. The successors of the philosophes, in this regard the pious restorers of an old Parisian tradition, cannot find enough indignation with which to condemn certain guilty parties, while exposing their indifference to certain others, whose culpability, according to the principles they advertise, should be no less.

Eighteenth-century French frivolity, which at its best lacks neither wit nor depth, if we are to believe Nietzsche, never took the trouble to perceive the duplicity of its beloved "philosophes": they amused it, it saw no further.

---

7. *Correspondance littéraire, philosophique, et critique par Grimm*, vol. 10, edited by Maurice Tourneux (Paris: Garnier Frères, 1879), p.129 (January 1773).

The Revolution forgave neither Grimm nor his Austrian title of "baron" nor his all too conspicuous attachments to the autocrat of St. Petersburg. In due time, he departed for Germany. Before his goods were seized, he returned briefly to Paris in 1791, stuffed all he could in his trunks, and left again forever. Catherine II had no use for him at close quarters, but she continued to subsidize him, appointing him her minister in Hamburg, one of the capitals of French emigration. In their correspondence they quite playfully anatomized the fate of Poland, and only a few months before her death, the empress replied to her factotum, who had invited her to "enlighten" that wretched country as she had so successfully enlightened Russia, assuring him that she had no intention of attempting the impossible: "Venal, corrupt, frivolous, impulsive, overbearing, allowing their private fortunes to be managed by Jews who bleed their subjects white and give very little in return: believe me, a speaking likeness of the Poles."[8] After Catherine died, Baron Grimm decided to settle in Gotha, where he "yawned away his life" until 1807 in a provincial obscurity even deeper than that from which Paris had rescued him forty years before.

Among the many brochures Grimm published during the *Querelle des bouffons*, the most characteristic is *Le Petit Prophète de Boehmishbroda*, where in a ponderous pastiche of Voltaire he managed to parody the Bible, ridicule the Jesuits, and produce a murderous portrait of French musical taste. Here are some passages from this many-faceted satire. A celestial Voice addresses the "little prophet" of Prague, a pupil of the Jesuits, and teaches him what is to be thought of the French and their deafness to anything musical.

From *The Little Prophet of Boehmishbroda*

Here Begins the Revelation (Chapter II)
O walls I raised with my own hands as a monument to my glory, O

---

8. Tourneux, *Correspondance littéraire*, p. 352.

walls once inhabited by a people I called mine because I had chosen them from the beginning, in order to make of them the first nation of Europe, and to bring their glory and renown beyond the limits that I prescribed for the Universe.

O city that calls yourself "the great" because you are vast; and "glorious" because I have spread my wings over you: hear me, for I shall speak.

And you, O square where they have erected the theater of the Comédie-Française, to which I have given both genius and taste, and to which I have said: You shall not have your equal in the Universe, and your glory shall be borne from East to West, and from North to South: hear me, for I shall speak.

And you, O frivolous and proud theater, who have taken unto yourself the title of Academy of Music, though you are nothing of the kind, and although I have permitted no such thing: hear me, for I shall speak.

O frivolous and fickle people, O people tending to defection and given over to the madness of your vanity and your pride:

Come that I may treat with you, I who, if I choose, may treat you as nothing: come that I may confound your eyes, and that I may inscribe with my hand your cowardice upon your forehead, which is so haughty in every European tongue.

The Transmigration (Chapter XII)

You wallowed in the mud of barbarism and ignorance, you groped in the darkness of superstition and stupidity; your philosophers lacked sense and your professors were fools. In your schools a barbarous jargon was spoken, and on the stages of your theaters were enacted mysteries.

And my heart stirred with pity toward you, and I said to myself: this nation is fair, I love its mind that is so light, and its manners that are gentle, and I wish to make this people my own, for that is my wish; and it shall be the first, and there shall be no nation so fair as this.

And its neighbors will see its glory, which they cannot attain. And it will divert me, once I have formed it according to my will, for it is kind and pleasant as to its nature, and I delight in my diversion.

And I have relieved the fathers from the nothing in which they were, and I have scattered the shadows that covered you, and I have summoned the day to enlighten you: and I have carried to your vitals the torch of the sciences, of the arts, and of letters.

And I have opened the gates of your understanding, so that you may comprehend what was hidden, and I have filed and fashioned your mind, and I have endowed it with every gift, and I have bestowed upon it taste and feeling and the sole gift of elegance.

And when I could enlighten with my torch the Breton as well as the Spaniard, and the German as well as the inhabitant of the North, for nothing is impossible for me to accomplish, even so I did no such thing.

And when I could leave the arts and letters in their haunts, for I had caused them to be reborn there, even so I did no such thing.

And I said to them: come away from Italy and pass among my people whom I have chosen in the plenitude of my kindness; and in the country where I intend henceforth to dwell, and to which I have said in my clemency: you will be the fatherland of all talents.

And I have given you this entire host of philosophers from Descartes down to the philosophers whom I have placed at the head of the Encyclopedia, and even to that one to whom I have said: Create Natural History.

And that entire host of poets, of subtle minds, and of artists without number.

And I have gathered them all into a single century, and it shall be called the century of Louis XIV. Until that day, in memory of all the Great Men whom I have bestowed upon you, beginning with Molière and Corneille who are called the Great, down to La Fare and Chaulieu who are called the Neglected.

And even though that century has passed, I feign not to have noticed, and I have perpetuated among you the race of Great Men and of extraordinary talents.

And I have bestowed upon you poets and subtle minds and painters and sculptors of great power, and artists without number, and excellent men in all ways of life from the great to the small.

And I have bestowed upon you philosophers of great repute, and I have opened their eyes that they may see what you could not see, and they saw indeed, for they said that they did not see distinctly.

And I created a man with express intention, in whom I assembled every talent and every gift, so that there should be none that was not within him.

And I created another luminous man, and I made him profound in understanding and sublime in conception, and to him I said: See, and he saw. And I inspired him, and I gave to him the Spirit of the Laws, and he gave it to you thereafter, and he made you see what you would never have seen in the littleness of your vision and the weakness of your eyesight.

And your glory has been preserved among your neighbors until this very day.

The Suppers (Chapter XIII)

And although my blessings have brought you to defection and to disobedience, although they have made you proud and although your vanity and presumption have greatly increased;

Although you mistook my voice that summons you, and although you have given yourselves up to the taste that is false, and pursue the thought that I do not call thinking and that is false, even as the voices that sing the secondary roles in your opera;

Although you have forsaken common sense and good judgment, and although you have flung yourself into frivolity and the dissipation of your ideas that are devoid of sense;

Although in your intoxication you daily decide matters on which you have never reflected at all;

Although you daily condemn and in the weakness of your thinking and in the profligacy of the dinners that you call suppers, you despise the authors I have created and who are all your glory:

I have derided your insolence in my great pity, and I have regarded your impertinences with the eye of my patience;

And your numerous rebellions have merely multiplied the miracles and the wonders that I still cause every day among you, and in the academies, and on the stages of your theaters, and before your eyes that were once sharp and clear-sighted, and that have become coarse and stupid.

And I have hidden your shame and your decadence from your neighbors, and I have inspired them with respect and admiration for you, as if you had not lost the taste for great and beautiful things.

And I have kept them from seeing you groveling in the littleness of your ideas.

The Florentine (Chapter XIV)

And just as I had brought the other arts from Italy in order to bestow them all upon you, I sought as well to bring music to your heart, and to adapt it myself to the genius of your language.

And I sought to create your musicians, and to form them and to teach them to create music according to my ear and my heart.

And you despised my graces, because I shed them upon you in abundance.

And you formed in your persistence an opera that for these eighty years has wearied me and become the laughingstock of Europe to this very day.

And in the stubbornness of your extravagance you have erected it into an Academy of Music, even though it is no such thing, and although I had never recognized it to be anything of the kind.

And without consulting me you chose the Florentine for your idol, although I had not sent him.

And because he had received the illumination of genius, you dared oppose him to me, because in my clemency I had given you my servant Quinault.

And you supposed that his monotony would try my patience and compel me to abandon you, because I am ready of decision, and because you sought to weary me by the multitude of your works.

And you cried out in the stupidity of your ignorance: Ah here is the creator of song, ah here he is!

And because, in the poverty of your ideas, he has done as much as he could, you call him to this very day Creator, when he has created nothing, and when the Germans weary my ears and break my brains these two hundred years in their Churches and in their vespers, by a singing that you call your own recitative, when it is theirs (although they do not boast of it, for they consider it a poor thing) and that in the imbecility of your ideas you believe was invented by the Florentine whom you call Monsieur de Lully to this very day.

The Precursor (Chapter XV)

And notwithstanding your stubbornness and the obstinacy of your madness, I have not rejected you in my anger as you deserved, and I have not delivered you to the scorn of your neighbors.

And I have taken pity on the childishness of your judgment and the defectiveness of your hearing, and I have undertaken to restore you to the right path by the very ways in which you strayed in the madness of your heart.

And I have undertaken to disgust you with the Florentine's monotony and with the insipidity of those who have followed him for more than forty years.

And I have formed a man with express intention and organized his mind, and I have brought him to life and said to him: have genius, and he has had it.

And when it was time, I sent him and I said to him: Seize the stage that they have called the Academy of Music, though it is no such thing, and purge it of all this bad music that they have commissioned by people whom I have never avowed, beginning with the Florentine whom they call great, down to the little Mouret whom they call gay and sweet.

And you will astonish them by the fire and strength of the harmony I have put in his mind, and by the abundance of ideals with which I have provided him.

And they will call baroque that which is harmonious, as they call simple that which is dull. And when they will have called you barbarous for fifteen years, they will no longer be able to do without your music, for it will have opened their ears.

And you will have prepared the ways that I have imagined, in order to bestow a music upon this nation that is not worthy of my benefactions: for you are my servant.

17. William Beckford: The Author of Vathek

THE CENTURY of the Enlightenment was often indifferent to religion, but never to education. From Fénelon to Rousseau by way of Condillac, pedagogues pullulated. Even the aristocracy, which hitherto had derided pedants, now sought from them patents of moral and intellectual authority for its children. Whereupon the pedants, egotists by profession, took themselves for reformers of the race and treated all humanity as they did their pupils—children and adolescents—with a cumbersome and peremptory solicitude. Nothing was more perfectly reasoned, and more precarious, than the educational programs published by the Abbé de Condillac and the Abbé Mably. Lord Chesterfield, in his disconcerting way, competed with them, while in a different register Rousseau deployed the antennae of a great novelist to mold his Émile according to the original model of the "natural man."

William Beckford (1709–1770), an extremely wealthy Jamaica planter who had somehow become lord mayor of London, had too many deals and too many mistresses on his hands, and died too soon, to concern himself with the education of his only son, born in 1759. It was William Beckford II's mother, a great Methodist lady of the very noble and numerous house of Hamilton, who from a great distance or at least a great height, but with great tenacity nonetheless, presided over the training of a son whom paternal wealth and maternal birth would appear to have intended for a statesman's career. She followed the advice of her cousin William Pitt, Lord Chatham, the boy's godfather and the lord mayor's friend, who had declared that young William, "a compound of fire and air," might well become "a perfect young man" provided he received "a just proportion of properly terrestrial solidity."

The boy was therefore instructed in Latin and Greek, Italian and French (as well as English) literature, and geography and arithmetic by a pleiad of tutors in an Eton all his own, the vast Palladian pile of Fonthill Splendens, embellished with Chinese and Turkish apartments and a prodigious Egyptian Hall, all of which William Beckford senior had called into being at the heart of a vast landscaped park in Wiltshire. Mrs. Beckford, who may have read Quintilian on the subject, feared for her son the promiscuity of public schools.

A governess, Lady Euphemia Stewart, a first tutor, Robert Drysdale, then a second, Reverend Doctor Lettice, directed this superabundant education on the spot. William's half sister, Elizabeth Marsh, daughter of Maria Hamilton's first marriage, was initially the little prince's sole companion his own age; the pair romped together in the manner of François-René de Chateaubriand and Lucile at Combourg. Elizabeth Marsh later became a best-selling novelist. Her even more gifted half brother was proclaimed a child of genius by his mother and quite determined to prove it for himself. The ideal of the "perfect young man" so dear to Lord Chesterfield, for once in perfect agreement with Lord Chatham, was immediately repellent to the boy. He showed quite early an unsettling disposition to endure no other company but that of geniuses of his own kind, who indeed sought him out in increasing numbers, defying the approved programs of his tutors and teachers. Mrs. Beckford was at times uneasy about this, but actually was flattered. Beckford, handsome as befitted a future model of George Romney, encountered Mozart in London; he received music lessons from this Orpheus some four years his senior. They found each other sympathetic. Mozart was even inspired, some years later, by a march his prodigious pupil improvised, to write the aria "Non più andrai" for *Le nozze di Figaro*.

In 1772, another genius, Alexander Cozens (1717–1786), imprudently selected by Mrs. Beckford, was installed at Fonthill to teach

William the elements of drawing.[1] He immediately gave the child *The Thousand and One Nights* in Galland's French translation, which Lord Chatham had forbidden him to read. The child of genius and the visionary painter were made to understand each other. Belatedly alarmed, in 1777 Maria Hamilton dismissed the dangerous artist and obliged William to burn the "Oriental drawings" he had eagerly produced under the direction of his senior preceptor. It was much too late. Pupil and master immediately commenced an ardent correspondence that only Cozens's death could interrupt in 1786.

With his ecclesiastical tutor, Reverend Lettice, William was then sent to Geneva. Maria Hamilton doubtless counted on the Calvinist Rome to moderate her William's "fire and air": she knew all too little Colonel Hamilton, her relative to whom she had entrusted the youth. The colonel had just returned from the Indies. His narratives utterly transfixed young William's Oriental imagination, already awakened by the suggestions of Cozens. In their correspondence, the two accomplices planned the construction of a tower in which they might "escape the land of men to some region where the air is not corrupted by the breath of wretches who constitute the entire object of our scorn and our disgust." From Geneva, of course, William, now twenty-three, paid a visit to the monarch of Ferney. The "living skeleton" was pleased to question the youth about his kinship to Antoine Hamilton, whose *Mémoires du Comte de Gramont* and *Tales* the author of *Zadig* admired. In Geneva, William was made much of by Horace-Bénédict de Saussure, a meteorological physicist who accompanied him on Alpine expeditions, and by the painter Jean Huber, the chronicler of Voltaire's last years. This highly gifted artist was fascinated by Montgolfier balloons, and shared William's taste for Ariosto and Shakespeare. At Évian, William encountered a well-born dwarf of talent, Pierre de Grailly, who entered his service on a permanent basis. Nero was beginning to appear under the façade of a pupil of Seneca. Everything that, at

---

1. Readers are urged to consult a splendid book written by Jean-Claude Lebensztejn on the painter Cozens, *L'Art de la tache* (Éditions du Limon, 1990).

this concluding eighteenth century, departs from "common sense" seemed invincibly to coagulate around the handsome William.

After a visit to the Grande Chartreuse in 1778, in the footsteps of Thomas Gray and Horace Walpole (the two famous friends had made this pilgrimage together in 1730), Beckford wrote for Cozens his first poem in prose, "The Vision," sometime before publishing fragments of his correspondence with his master under the title *Dreams, Walking Thoughts, and Incidents* in 1783. He was nourished not only on Gray's melancholy elegies but on the new thoughts of Edmund Burke, who in 1756 had published in London his *Philosophical Enquiry into the Origin of Our Ideas of the Sublime and Beautiful.* Puritan and utilitarian England was now no longer content to promote its political and economic system and its individualist philosophy: it had its own poetics.

Changing course, England could even pride itself on internal rebellions against its own conformism. It gave lessons in the novel and poetry to a Catholic France short on imagination, renegade to its own lyricism and mystical theology. The English "eccentrics" reinvented Saint Teresa's "castles of the soul," their lyricism rediscovering Mme Guyon's *Spiritual Torrents* and even the Fénelonian spirituality of childhood, and they did so with more ambiguous seduction than the Marquis de Sade. It was not until Chateaubriand, who on the spot had understood this private and poignant imaginative world, that this Anglo-Saxon illumination imparted a green glow to the French *clarté*.

The Symbolists, then the Surrealists, in Swinburne's footsteps, returned to the "black humor" and the delicious perversity of those "fiery souls" Beckford and Byron. They paved the way for the "American century" that majestically extends before our eyes its bizarre *imaginaire* actually rooted in the aristocratic eighteenth century of Horace Walpole, Anne Radcliffe, and William Beckford, which is also the century of Fuseli, Flaxman, and William Blake. By an enormous paradox, so enormous that we fail to see it, the myths of mass-media democracy are the universal extension of the private hallucinations of these favorites of fortune, who were as proud, scornful, and rebellious as Lucifer himself.

At the age of seventeen, the future author of *Vathek*, visiting the Grande Chartreuse, could identify with the silent brotherhood of Saint Bruno, after identifying with the vociferating Saracens of *Gerusalemme liberata* or with the moaning German in *The Sorrows of Young Werther*. The child of genius, who reveled in an unknown god hidden deep within himself, was also a superior actor prepared to play every role. During a journey to England, in the Courtenays' castle at Powderham, he experienced the revelation of a second self; this magical double was William Courtenay, known as Kitty, at the time eleven years old (George Romney had painted his portrait, too). Cozens was forthwith informed of this *coup de foudre*. Maria Hamilton and Reverend Lettice were in a state of wild alarm. Surely this was the right moment to have William take the Grand Tour. Beckford left for Italy, though not before publishing in London his *Biographical Memoirs of Extraordinary Painters*, a satirical guide that devalued the Dutch painters, too generously represented at Fonthill, and exalted the great Italians. Before reaching Venice, English tradition insisted that Holland, Germany, and Austria be traversed. Finally on August 2, 1780, William landed with his tutor and a numerous company in Venice. His hostess and confidante, Countess Orsini, gave party after party to divert the young "lion," who cut a terrible swath through the great families of the Serenissima. In the city before him he discovered the "antichamber of the Orient," writing to Cozens:

> I spend my idle mornings in my gondola, wrapped in furs, reading and uttering cries of delight. My body is frozen, but my ardent imagination wanders to the Indies and delights in the rays of its own sun. At night, I am in the cafés or at the opera, where Bertoni's voluptuous music, marvelously served by the talent of the world's finest singer, *effeminates* me more than ever.... Alas, music destroys me, and what is worse still, it is my pleasure to consent to my own destruction.[2]

---

2. Didier Girard, *William Beckford, un terroriste au palais de la raison* (Paris: Librairie José Corti, 1993), pp. 63–64.

What we call "culture," that permanent sale of fleeting raptures that prevent and replace any birth of durable admiration and love —religion, heart, mind, arts, letters, manners—finds its incunabulum in the ecstasy that transported young Beckford in the Uffizi in Florence:

> I thought I would go mad when I set foot in the Gallery for the first time. I saw so many rows of statues, so many treasures, precious stones, and bronzes, that I collapsed in a happy delirium which only souls like ours can know. Incapable of putting an end to this spell, I flew from one bust to the next, from one cabinet to another, like a butterfly dazzled by a universe consisting of nothing but flowers.[3]

He was twenty years old.

In November 1780, in Naples, he acquired a new confidante in his relative by marriage, the flamboyant Emma Lyons, wife of the English ambassador Sir William Hamilton. This enlightened amateur, insatiable collector of antiquities and Greek vases, was infected by the fervor that led all Europe to the excavations at Herculaneum and Pompeii. Henceforth Beckford would be counted among the firsthand initiates into the palingenesis of paganism from its millennial ashes. On the voyage home, he stopped in Paris, but his heart was too preoccupied for him to mingle in salon life. Germaine Necker vainly paid him court. This was the moment of his imminent majority, which he would celebrate in what would remain the culminating event of his life, the Christmas party at Fonthill in 1781 (the year of Romney's two portraits). He gathered here, secluded for several days of gallant witchcraft, luxury, sex, and dreams, all the handsome young people who were dear to him: his cousins Louisa and Harriet Beckford and George Pitt, and of course William Courtenay. Alexander Cozens had also been invited, and he came accompanied by Philip James de Loutherbourg, a master of stagecraft

---

3. Girard, *William Beckford*, p. 67.

and the inventor of a primitive form of the cinema, the Eidophusikon, ancestor of Daguerre and Bouton's diorama. Cozens and Loutherbourg staged this memorable, and highly personal, Pleasure Dome, the program for which Beckford had arranged some months earlier in one of his letters from Italy: "For my part, I should like above all things to immure myself with those I adore, to forget all temporal intervals, and to posses a theatrical sun and moon I could make rise or set at my will."[4]

He himself wrote the narrative of this party, which constitutes a date in the history of the British and American *imaginaire* and therefore in our "civilization of eternal youth and leisure":

Immured we were, *au pied de la lettre*, for three days following—doors and windows so strictly closed that neither common daylight nor commonplace visitors could get in or even peep in—care-worn visages were ordered to keep aloof—no sunken mouths or furrowed foreheads were permitted to meet our eyes. Our *société* was extremely youthful and lovely to look upon, for not only Louisa but also her great friend Sophia, perhaps the loveliest woman in England, shed a fascinating charm upon our company. There reigned throughout the vaulted galleries and spacious apartments a gentle, tempered light that Loutherbourg, himself something of a mystagogue, distributed with a supreme and superior art. The great property of Fonthill, which I had razed in order to be constructed anew and even more extraordinary, was perfectly conceived for the celebration of mysteries. The solid Egyptian Hall looked as if hewn out of a living rock—the line of apartments and apparently endless passages extending from it on either side were all vaulted—an interminable staircase, which when you looked down it appeared as deep as the well in the pyramid and when you looked up was lost in vapor, led to suites of stately apartments gleaming with marble pavements

---

4. Girard, *William Beckford*, p. 77.

as polished as glass and gaudy ceilings and their ceilings painted with all the licentiousness of Casali's brush in the brilliant colors that accounted for his fortune at this period so hostile to beaux arts principles. From here, another flight of thickly carpeted steps invited us to pass into another world: frescoed rooms, a gallery designed by Sir John Soane, and still farther on, another more secret one filled with curious works of art and precious cabinets to which access was granted by a spiral staircase. Through all these galleries did we roam and wander, too often hand in hand—strains of music swelling forth at intervals—sometimes the organ, sometimes concerted pieces in which three of the greatest singers then in Europe—Pacchierotti, Tenducci, and Rauzzini—for a wonder of wonders!—most amicably joined. Occasionally, without anyone's being able to determine the provenance of such sounds, a chorus was heard, its innocent and touching modulations expressing a heartfelt language that drew tears from our dearest and most sensitive companions. Delightful indeed were these romantic wanderings, delightful the straying about this little interior world of exclusive happiness surrounded by lovely beings in all the freshness of their early bloom, so fitted to enjoy it. Here nothing was dull or vapid, here nothing at all resembled in the least the common forms and usages, the routine of fashionable existence—all were essence. Here was no tolerance for any attitude that might be tinged with uniformity. Monotony, in any of its manifestations, was not admissible. Even the uniform splendor of the gilded roofs was partially obscured by the vapor of aloe wood ascending in wreaths from cassolettes placed low on the silken carpets in porcelain salvers of the richest japan. The delirium of delight into which our young and fervid bosoms were cast by such a combination of seductive influences may be conceived but too easily. Even at this long, sad distance from these days and nights of exquisite refinements, chilled by age, still more by the coarse unpoetic tenor of the present disenchanting period, I still feel warmed and irradiated by the recollections of that strange, necromantic light that Loutherbourg had thrown over what absolutely appeared a realm of Fairy, or rather, perhaps, a Demon Temple deep beneath the earth set apart for tremendous mysteries—and yet how soft, how genial was this quiet light.

Whilst the wretched world without lay dark and bleak and howling, whilst the storm was raging against our massive walls and the snow drifting in clouds, the very air of summer seemed playing about us. The choir of low-toned melodious voices continued to soothe our ears, and that every sense might in turn receive its blandishment, tables covered with delicious viands and fragrant flowers glided forth, by the aid of mechanisms at stated intervals, from the richly draped and amply curtained recesses of the enchanted precincts. The glowing haze investing every object, the mystic look, the vastness, the intricacy of this vaulted labyrinth occasioned so bewildering an effect that it became impossible for anyone to define—at the moment—where he stood, where he had been, or to whither he was wandering—such was the confusion, the perplexity so many illuminated stories of infinitely varied apartments gave rise to. It was, in short, the realization of romance in its most extravagant intensity.[5]

In the wake of this party lasting "three days and nights," Beckford became the author of *Vathek*. This time he wrote his imaginary autobiography in French, a "personal myth" in which he revealed even as he masked himself. With an irony never sparing the author, he makes his mother, that determined preceptress, the principal motor of his odyssey toward Eblis; *Vathek*'s Princess Carathis was Maria Hamilton, but a Maria who did not conceal from herself what she truly expected from her son's education. To tell the whole truth about himself, Beckford had chosen convention rather than

---

5. Girard, *William Beckford*, pp. 81–85.

confession, the convention of the "Oriental tale." The French, from Voiture to Voltaire, were past masters of the form. The classics of Orientalism, following the Paris–Constantinople alliance, were all French: Bernier, Chardin, Galland, d'Herbelot. Masking autobiography, this convention permitted a further and deeper foray into avowal, avoiding any question of pathos. *Vathek: An Arabian Tale* is thereby a classical French masterpiece, in which all the tempests of the Sturm und Drang thunder remotely, but treated with mockery, like an Italian opera buffa. Vathek, his mother Carathis, his erotic victims Nouronihar and Gulchenrouz, and his Lucifer the Giaour disguise the "troupe" of Fonthill and its *jeu d'enfer*, but they make that particular *vie de château* clearer to us than any barefaced account could ever have achieved.

There is something of Mozart in *Vathek*—a nuance of the colors of *The Magic Flute*, certain measures of the *Jupiter* Symphony. The rhythm and sonority of Beckford's prose would win the admiration of both Gautier and Mérimée (who wanted to reprint the tale). But it fell to Stéphane Mallarmé to give a second life, on the threshold of Symbolism, to this final British jewel of the French rococo. The Anglophile poet of "The Afternoon of a Faun" reprinted *Vathek* in 1876, with one of those glistening prefaces that were his secret specialty. Thereby he reestablished a fact hitherto forgotten or dubious: although the English translation of *Vathek* was first published in London in 1784, the original text was written in French; a little later its author sent it simultaneously to Paris and to Lausanne, where it was published in both cities that same year, 1797. Stéphane Mallarmé wrote proudly in his preface: "I am restoring *Vathek*, Beckford's alluring tale, to the French language."[6]

Vathek concludes Beckford's childhood and adolescence. In 1782–1783 he still had a splendid though brief "worldly period" in London (where he composed a short pastoral opera for children's voices) and then a "learned period" at Fonthill where, accompanied

---

6. See the edition of *Vathek* with Mallarmé's preface, edited by Didier Girard (Paris: Éditions Corti, 2003).

by Cozens, he began to accumulate a library and prepare his manuscripts for publication. In May 1783, he married Lady Margaret Gordon, chosen by Maria Hamilton. It was a couple without apparent drama, from which two daughters were born. The family sojourned in Paris, where this time Beckford made himself known to a much grander society. This was the moment of Mesmer's "animal magnetism" and of secret societies. The author of *Vathek* observed with detachment this capital enthralled by the occult and baptized it "the Metropolis of Lucifer." He would return to it invincibly until 1814, and then produced a critical portrait of the city that does honor to his moral penetration:

> Everything that can be seen, heard, or smelled in Paris, from painted faces to the protuberances on the soles of certain shoes, is entirely the product of the most artificial art. Rousseau's prose poems dedicated to Nature have been sung in vain. The natural has been forgotten or is unknown. I abhor this precious verbiage now enjoying such a vogue in the most rarefied circles, a vogue produced despite the demands of the populace and their political miseries, by the admiration for fine music and the scorn in which are held the Cathedrals and Palaces, including Versailles and Reims. This bombastic way of exhibiting sentiments that none of these scandalmongers of either sex of are capable of feeling to the slightest degree is to me quite odious. The sincerity of their liberal views and their good feelings for the people in general is so problematic that I am quite convinced that this philanthropic whey will soon turn to a poison fatal to the first popular manifestation of patriotic fury.[7]

Then in the course of a stay with the Courtenays at Powderham, the scandal exploded. Beckford's erotic relation with the very young Courtenay was discovered. The Beckfords were obliged to leave Pow-

---

7. Girard, *William Beckford*, p. 126.

derham precipitately and moved to Vevey, in Switzerland, where Mrs. Beckford II died of puerperal fever soon afterward. In 1787 William sought consolation in Portugal, where he lived extravagantly in every way; later he would derive two masterpieces from his Lusitanian sojourns, *Italy; with Sketches of Spain and Portugal* and *Recollections of an Excursion to the Monasteries of Alcobaça and Batalha*. Between 1788 and 1793, Beckford sojourned sumptuously in Paris, which the Revolution was gradually transforming into a vast flea market where he made a number of well-advised purchases.[8] In his correspondence he describes the capital of the Revolution with as much astonishment and much less disgust than Burke had expressed two years before in his *Considerations*. We may note that all these travels, and even the terrible scandal, had not prevented his being elected several times to Parliament in London, where he stayed on occasion until 1820.

After 1794 he withdrew almost definitively to Fonthill. He consumed his fortune in creating a fabulous palace and park worthy of *Vathek*. It was at once the model for Coleridge's "Kubla Khan," for the castles of Ludwig II of Bavaria, and for the architectural and acquisitive follies of William Randolph Hearst.

The paternal castle Splendens, the scene of the Christmas party, was razed. In its place, Beckford built an incredible and heteroclite monastery, Fonthill Abbey, of which he would be the father superior. He remodeled the park entirely to give it the simultaneously picturesque and primitive aspect of the Garden of Eden and a sacred forest. His colossal means and his vast culture allowed him to extend modern individualism to its final consequences: Fonthill Abbey and its park became the walled property of "the ego and its own," in Max Stirner's sense of the phrase. Contrary to Horace Walpole's Strawberry Hill, which Beckford detested and always referred to as "a mousetrap," Fonthill Abbey was no neo-Gothic monument. Here Beckford's Orientalist eclecticism combined "colossal

---

8. See the magnificent and learned catalog *William Beckford 1760-1844: An Eye for the Magnificent*, edited by Derek E. Ostergaard (Yale Uinversity Press, 2002).

Gothic" (a style whose future would be in Chicago and New York City) with memories of Paestum, the Taj Mahal, Santa Sophia, and the Italian baroque. It is the first draft not only for Ludwig II's castles but also for the monstrous hotels of Las Vegas, those Fonthill Abbeys for twentieth-century "lonely crowds," quite remote from the *savoir-vivre* that governed the imagination of the world's worst enemy of crowds. Beckford wanted to finish off the "abbey" with a tower like the one that rose in Samarah, Vathek's capital. No sooner was it built than it collapsed. A second version of this Tower of Babel managed to remain standing: the first skyscraper, some eighty-four meters high.

In the countless halls of what Beckford called with perverse irony "the Sanctuary of good taste," his collector's frenzy accumulated what would fill several Victoria and Albert Museums: all the elements of Henry James's *The Spoils of Poynton* and even the figure of the redoubtable mother were already united in the genesis of this composite oeuvre; to the furniture brought from Paris and that often came from the royal storerooms, pieces by Boulle and Riesener (notably the celebrated desk of the Comte d'Orsay), Beckford juxtaposed precious and bizarre suites from the British or Spanish colonies, from the baroque palaces of Italy, or else produced by English cabinetmakers to his own designs. His "neoclassical" bed is today one of the attractions of the Metropolitan Museum in New York. His prodigious collection of jewelry and porcelains rivaled the contents of his painting galleries. Beckford, renouncing his father's taste for the Dutch, shipped to Fonthill Abbey masterpieces by Leonardo, Raphael, the Carraccis, Claude Lorrain, Bellini, and Velázquez purchased in Italy, Spain, and the Paris of the Terror, which succeeded in transforming, as if by ricochet, Christie's London sale rooms into Ali Baba's cave. But everywhere at Fonthill Abbey, in the galleries named for King Edward (a Hamilton ancestor) or the Archangel Michael, in the central Octagon, in the Great Hall as in the many boudoirs, angels, saints, candles, and ciboria mingled the pomp of the Catholic liturgy with reminiscences of Oriental harems. Hazlitt called Fonthill Abbey "a desert of magnificence, a glittering waste of laborious idleness, a cathedral turned into a toy-shop, an immense museum of all that is most curious and costly, and at the same time most worthless in the productions of art and nature." This enormous and luxurious prison had several points in common with the imaginary château of *The Hundred and Twenty Days of Sodom*. For Sade as for Beckford, the sublime was oxygen inhaled from the flagons of blasphemy.

In 1810, his resources failing, Beckford was obliged to sell Fonthill (which threatened to ruin him) to a rich industrialist, John Farquhar, who rapidly dispersed the contents at public auction. William Beckford set himself up in more modest though still splendid quarters in Bath, along with his books and a selection of his objects and works of art. In 1826 he even built for his own use yet another castle keep, Landsdowne Tower. Here he was buried in May 1844. By one of his daughters, who became Duchess of Hamilton, he would transmit his blood to an unexpected descendant: Prince Rainier of Monaco.

In France the object of a veritable cult, to which the Surrealists, after the Symbolists, contributed heavily, Beckford (though treated scornfully in the *Dictionary of National Biography*) is a key figure of the Anglo-American *imaginaire*. The likes of Natalie Barney, Winaretta Singer, Nancy Cunard, and Violette Trefusis have venerated him as an ancestor and a prophet. Orson Wells's Citizen Kane is an offspring of Vathek. If Larbaud's *Barnabooth* is as delicious and poetic as it is, it is because it expressly aims to give a French version, à la Toulet, of those despotic and nonconformist millionaire egos of whom Beckford is the life-master, consciously or not, in England and America. It is good to record such a genealogy nowadays, when this composite *imaginaire* of sumptuous and lettered origin impregnates, thanks to the movies and to various rock groups, the youth of the entire world. The Librairie José Corti, in the rue de Médicis, is the Parisian temple of the rigorist Beckford cult. It has published the entirety of his oeuvre, the English originals available in the admirable French translations of Roger Kann.

I reproduce here a fragment of *Vathek* in which the Caliph arrives at the portals of the underground city of Eblis, that goal of the "journey to the end of the night" that Beckford's hero has undertaken far from his capital of Samarah. Jorge Luis Borges has called this fragment "the first truly atrocious Hell in literature."[9]

AT THE PORTALS OF EBLIS

The Caliph, devoured by the ambition of prescribing laws to the Intelligences of Darkness, was but little embarrassed by this dereliction; the impetuosity of his blood prevented him from sleeping, nor did he encamp any more as before. Nouronihar, whose impatience if possible exceeded his own, importuned him to hasten his march and lavished on him a thousand caresses to beguile all reflection; she fancied herself already more potent than Balkis and pictured to her imagination the Genii falling prostrate at the foot of her throne. In this manner they advanced by moonlight till they came within view of the two towering rocks that form a kind of portal to the valley, at whose extremity rose the vast ruins of Istakhar. Aloft on the mountain glimmered the fronts of various royal mausoleums, the horror of which was deepened by the shadows of night. They passed through two nearly deserted villages, the only inhabitants remaining being a few feeble old men who, at the sight of horses and litters, fell to their knees and cried out:

"O heaven! is it then by such phantoms that we have been tormented for six months? Alas! it was from the terror of these specters and the noise from beneath the mountains that our people have fled and left us at the mercy of maleficent spirits!"

The Caliph, to whom these complains were of evil omen, drove over the bodies of these wretches and at length arrived at the foot of the black marble terrace; there he descended from his litter, handing down Nouronihar; both with pounding hearts stared wildly around them, and awaited with an apprehensive shudder the approach of the Giaour; but nothing as yet heralded his appearance.

---

9. Jorge Luis Borges, *Other Inquisition, 1937–1952* (University of Texas Press, 1965), p. 200.

A deathlike silence reigned over the mountain and through the air; on a vast platform the moon dilated the shadows of the lofty columns which reached from the terrace almost to the clouds; the gloomy watchtowers, whose numbers could not be counted, were shielded by no roof, and their capitals, of an architecture unknown in the records of earth, served as an asylum for the birds of darkness which, alarmed at the approach of such visitants, fled away croaking.

The chief eunuch, trembling with fear, besought Vathek that a fire might be kindled. "No," replied he, "this is no time to think of such trifles; abide where thou art and await my commands."

Having spoken, he presented his hand to Nouronihar and, ascending the steps of a vast staircase, reached the terrace which was flagged with squares of marble and resembled a smooth expanse of water upon whose surface no leaf ever dared to vegetate; on the right loomed the watchtowers, ranged before the ruins of an immense palace whose walls were embossed with various figures; in front emerged the colossal forms of four creatures, composed of the leopard and the griffin, which though but of stone inspired emotions of terror; near these were distinguished by the splendor of the moonlight, which streamed full on the place, characters like those on the Giaour's sabers, which writing possessed the same virtue of changing at every moment; these, after vacillating for some time, at last grew fixed in Arabiac letters and prescribed to the Caliph the following words:

"Vathek, thou hast violated the conditions of my parchment and deservest to be dismissed; but as a favor to thy companion and as the meed for what thou hast done to obtain it, Eblis permits that the portal of his palace be opened, and that the subterranean fire receive thee into the number of its worshippers."

Scarcely had he read these words before the mountain against which the terrace was reared trembled, and the watchtowers seemed ready to topple headlong upon them; the rock face yawned wide, disclosing within it a polished marble staircase which seemed to approach the abyss; upon each step were planted two huge torches, like those Nouronihar had seen in her vision, the camphorated vapor ascending from which gathered in a cloud under the hollow of the vault.

Such a spectacle, instead of terrifying, gave new courage to the daughter of Fakreddin. Scarcely deigning to bid adieu to the moon and the firmament, she abandoned without hesitation the pure atmosphere to plunge into these infernal exhalations. The gait of these two impious beings was haughty and determined; as they descended by the effulgence of the torches they gazed on each other with mutual admiration, and both appeared so resplendent that they already esteemed themselves spiritual Intelligences; the only circumstance perplexing them was their not reaching the bottom of the staircase; on hastening their descent with ardent impetuosity, they felt their own footsteps accelerate to such a degree that they seemed to be not walking but falling from a precipice; their progress however was at length impeded by a vast ebony portal which the Caliph easily recognized; it was here the Giaour awaited him with a golden key in his hand.

"Ye are welcome," he said to them with a ghastly smile, "in spite of Mahomet and all his dependants. I shall now admit you into that palace where you have so highly merited a place."

Whilst uttering these words he touched the enameled lock with his key, and the doors at once opened with a noise still louder than canicular thunder and as suddenly sprang shut with the same sound the moment they had entered.

The Caliph and Nouronihar beheld one another with amazement to find themselves in a place which, though roofed with a vaulted ceiling, was so spacious and lofty that at first they took it for an immeasurable plain. But, their eyes at length familiar with the grandeur of the objects near at hand, they extended their view to those at a distance and discovered rows of columns and arcades gradually diminishing till they terminated in a point radiant as the sun darting his last beams athwart the ocean; the pavement, strewn with gold dust and saffron, exhaled an odor so subtle as almost to overpower them; however they proceeded on their way and observed an infinity of censers in which ambergris and aloe-wood were continually burning; between the several columns were placed tables, each spread with a profusion of viands and wines of every variety sparkling in vessels of crystal. A *throng of Genii and other fantastic spirits of each sex danced lascivi-ously in troupes to the sound of music issuing from below.*

In the midst of this immense hall a vast multitude was incessant passing, who severally kept their right hands on their hearts, without once regarding anything around them; all of them had the livid pallor of death; their eyes, sunk deep in their sockets, resembled those phos-phoric meteors that glimmer by night in cemeteries. Some stalked slowly on, absorbed in profound reverie; some, shrieking with agony, ran furiously about, like tigers wounded by poisoned arrows; whilst others, grinding their teeth in rage; all avoided each other, and though surrounded by an innumerable multitude, each wandered at random, heedless of the rest, as if alone on a desert where no foot has trodden.

Vathek and Nouronihar, frozen with terror at a sight so baleful, asked the Giaour what these apparitions might mean, and why these ambulating specters never took their hands from their hearts.

"Be not perplexed," he replied abruptly, "you shall soon be ac-quainted with all; let us hasten so that we may present you to Eblis." They continued their way through the multitude, but notwithstand-ing their confidence at first, they were not sufficiently composed to ex-amine attentively the various perspectives of halls and galleries opening on the right and left, all illuminated by torches and braziers whose flames rose in pyramids to the center of the vault. At length they came to a place where long curtains brocaded with crimson and gold fell on all sides in striking confusion. Here the choirs and dances were no longer heard, and the glimmering lights seemed to come from a great distance.

Vathek and Nouronihar perceived light brightening through the draperies and entered a vast tabernacle carpeted with leopard skins; an innumerable host of elders with streaming beards and Afrits in full armor had prostrated before the steps of a dais, at the summit of which, upon a fiery globe, sat the formidable Eblis. His countenance was that of a young man of twenty whose noble and regular features seemed to have been wasted by malignant vapors. Despair and pride glistened in his huge eyes and his flowing hair retained some resemblance to that of an angel of light. In his delicate hand blackened by lightning he held the bronze scepter which caused the monster Ouranbad, the Afrits, and all the powers of the abyss to tremble.

At this sight, the Caliph lost all assurance and prostrated himself face down upon the floor. Nouronihar however, though greatly dismayed, could not help admiring Eblis's person, for she had expected to see some terrifying giant. With a voice milder than might have been expected but which struck a deep sadness into their souls, said to them: "Creatures of clay, I receive you in my empire; you are among the number of my worshippers; enjoy all that this palace affords, treasures of the preadamite sultans, their dread sabers and the talismans which will force the Dives to open the subterranean expanses of the mountain of Kaf, which communicate with those you see; here, however insatiable your curiosity, you shall be enabled to penetrate even to the fortress of Ahuriman and the halls of Argenk, in which are portrayed all creatures endowed with reason and the various animals which inhabited the earth prior to the creation of that contemptible being whom you denominate the Father of Mankind."

18. Goya, the Marquesa de Santa Cruz, and William Beckford

IN THE LOUVRE'S Spanish galleries, we can encounter the Marquesa de Santa Cruz as Goya painted her. Coming from the Pierre David-Weill collection, her portrait entered the museum as a gift in 1976. It is difficult to forget this lady once she has appeared before us, insolently brought to life by the magic powers of a painter bewitched by his subject.

Firmly planted, almost in profile, on two charming little feet in silver-encrusted white silk slippers arranged at almost a right angle without much concern for verisimilitude, the marquesa arches her back against the sky above a low blue-green horizon, a bronze-green early autumn landscape, and a glorious twilight. She is dressed as a maja: a long skirt covered with black lace and a mantilla of the same color gathered around her shoulders and at the waist by her bare forearms, one covered with heavy gold bracelets, the other holding by her fingertips a tiny closed fan.

Into the abundant jet-black hair that helmets her head are woven the loops and knots of a broad pink ribbon. Her skirt and the diminutive silk slippers below it form the plinth, resting on its point, of the bust girdled by her forearms crossed over the twist of her waist and swathed by the loose lace mantilla that blends imperceptibly into the black helmet of her hair: an opaque, almost Muslim veil that frames the startlingly illuminated face. The landscape, the sky, and the folded wings of this big black bird ready to take flight at any second seem to be here only to explain the mettlesome creature's animal stare, which rivets the spectator.

Yet this broad, fleshy countenance, this almost mannish nose, these full red cheeks, these sensual lips that insinuate a smile are not those of a pretty woman. The painter has not attempted to flatter her features, or to make them appear younger than they are. At the time the portrait was painted the marquesa was thirty-six.

But Goya has perceived and revealed in her a "nature" quite the contrary of the stereotypically gracious prettiness of the contemporary grandes dames whom Mme Vigée-Lebrun in exile painted one after the other in Vienna or St. Petersburg, as if the court of Versailles still dictated its patterns to Europe. Sure of herself, of her rank as of her allure, this Madrilenian aristocrat has all the aplomb of a peasant girl or a fishwife. Her elegance and flamboyance are those of an eagle or a pink flamingo. Her vitality, her freedom, her senses have never let themselves be constrained by courtly conventions. She is to other women what Goya is to other painters. And Goya has given her eyes the pupils he gave himself in his self-portraits, black and dilated.

As a matter of fact, the marquesa's eyes were sea green, as we know from her own miniature self-portrait in the Uffizi (she was actually quite a good painter, a student of the French miniaturist Dubois) and from another very fine neoclassical portrait by Appiani, which can be seen at the Academy of Saint Luke in Rome.

One of the least perceptible dimensions of our rich and air-conditioned poverty is the disappearance of the art of the portrait. I mean of portraits painted or drawn. A photograph, however artistic its intentions, will never be anything but ersatz. Nadar's portraits, quite properly admired, are after all merely a distant reflection, in the darkroom's depths, of an intelligence of the human countenance sharpened in Paris by the French school of portrait painting that dates back to Jean Foucquet and that shines so brightly in Nadar's time, with the pupils of David.

How to explain in Daguerre's Paris, which is also Ingres's, at the beginning of the nineteenth century, the craving for photography? In other words, the appetite for the objective "real," freed from human "prejudices" but stripped as well of that sensual and imaginary act of love between painter and model, which makes the painted portrait a living progeny, and not a more or less cosmeticized anthropological record for the police officer, the judge, the criminologist, the archivist, the undertaker, and the biographer, which must always, ultimately, remain an automatic identity photo.

Like a nuclear explosion filmed in slow motion, the irresistible photographic invasion, vampirizing the human face, has defeated the painted portrait as it has triumphed over most genres of the imitation of nature by art. By repercussion and retrospectively, the triumph of these specters makes us understand what constituted the magic of the painted portrait, even when it is the work not of a great master but simply of an artist: it is a love child. The photograph will always be a motherless, fatherless clone, a replica sans interlocutor.

In a painter's portrait, the moral physiognomy of the "father," even when the portraitist is a woman, haunts the features of the model-as-mother—whether the latter is a man or a woman. As a son or a daughter reflects the paternal and maternal features on his or her countenance, mysteriously superimposed and unpredictably proportioned, the painted portrait no less mysteriously allies the painter's self-portrait and the features of his model. The more original the artist, the more such procreation gives birth to original children, endowed with an amphibious and autonomous life. Such is the case with the Marquesa de Santa Cruz painted by Goya. Her portrait is the daughter, as alive today as in 1799, of the great Spanish painter and a grande dame of the court of Spain. The rest of us, ephemeral shades doomed to be content with mechanical reflections on matte or shiny paper, will disappear without descendants.

One takes to the mother as soon as one has seen this love child Goya has given her. In order to know her better, art history, which has correctly identified the painter's model (for a long time she passed for a supposed "Marquesa de la Mercedes"), has also reconstituted her biography. But literary history, without even being incited to do so by Goya's portrait, and without art history having paid any attention to its discovery, has brought to light a document that permits us to understand from within the singular personality of the Marquesa de Santa Cruz, as Goya might have known her.

This unlooked-for document is a partial bundle of forty-five of the marquesa's letters, written in French and sent to Madrid or from Madrid in 1788 to William Beckford, who had published *Vathek* in Paris the year before, and who had left the Spanish capital for a long stay in Paris. This correspondence, for the most part unpublished, was preserved in the Beckford archives of the Bodleian at Oxford and has only lately been printed for the first time.[1]

From the perspective of a few years, indeed, this correspondence reproduces the situation of Potiphar's wife or Phèdre illustrated by Lady Montagu's letters to Francesco Algerotti or Mme du Deffand's to Horace Walpole: the same possessive passion on the lady's part, the same efforts to recall the missing beloved, the same suspicions of his indifference, and, on the part of the stubborn absentee, the same dilatory tactics, the same cruel distancing of replies.

Walpole (and Strawberry Hill), Beckford (and Fonthill Abbey): Mme du Deffand's Hippolyte and the Marquesa de Santa Cruz's Joseph are, a generation apart and before Byron, "lions" produced by the powerful and prudish English aristocracy, released from their cages and from their conventions but not from their fortune: each of them, as a Catholic by preference, had cultivated, a century before Des Esseintes, an ostentatious decadentism of taste that Beckford and Byron would extend to Rimbaud's *dérèglement de tous les sens*.

The analogy between the Santa Cruz–Beckford letters and the du Deffand–Walpole correspondence can be taken even further: in both cases, the love letters were for the most part preserved by their indifferent recipients, but the answers are missing. Walpole had persuaded Mme du Deffand to destroy his letters. Beckford, or one of his heirs, had done away with a portion of the marquesa's letters, while the latter does not appear to have preserved her tormentor's responses (though the Spanish archives may yet reserve a surprise for us).

---

1. See the edition produced by the late collector and scholar Roger Kann, under the title *Lettres d'amour de la Marquise de Santa-Cruz* (Oxford: Studies on Voltaire and the Eighteenth Century, 1986).

With the aesthete's cynicism of which he was entirely capable, Beckford briefly annotated (in English) several of the ardent letters the marquesa had sent him, as if each was an opera recitative of a different pathetic color: "gloomy, discontented, and vindicating," "short and a little embarrassed," etc.

But the analogy between the two couples ends there. The blind Mme du Deffand was a great deal older than Walpole when she fell in love with him; she could expect from such a beloved no more than a loving tenderness, however exclusive and attentive. In 1788 the Spanish marquesa was twenty-five and Beckford twenty-eight. These young people had, in all likelihood, had a brief affair during Beckford's stay in Madrid. The marquesa was desperately eager to bring about the return of a perhaps unforgettable lover, at the very least an irreplaceable confidant and corrupter.

Age aside, we cannot imagine a livelier contrast than between these two women. Mme du Deffand was above all a highly literary intelligence *à la française*, for whom the life of the senses and the life of the mind were worlds apart. The life of the heart, which she discovered so belatedly, was a revelation for her. Though very re-fined in her fashion, the young Marquesa de Santa Cruz invested all her wits in the life of the senses and of the heart, which were never separate for her. She existed passionately and continuously, like those "savages" Paris dreamed of so ardently at the same period.

Before presenting this amorous correspondence, one might say a word about who this Madrilenian noblewoman was and in what circumstances she fell in love with William Beckford.

Maria Ana, born the Countess von Waldstein-Wartemberg in 1763, daughter of a princess of Liechtenstein, had married the ninth Marquès de Santa Cruz, José de Silva y Bazan in 1781. She was eighteen and poor; he was forty-seven and wealthy, indeed a power at the court of King Carlos III of Spain. On the return journey from Vienna to Spain, Don José, his young bride, and their suite passed through Paris. At Versailles the couple repeatedly visited Queen Marie-Antoinette, who was quite familiar with Ana's aristocratic Austrian family. They reached Madrid in mid-July and determined to seek a breath of fresh air at Don José's country estate at Hortaleza, not far from Alameda d'Osuna.

From this union four children were born, three sons and a daughter. That daughter, Mariana, who would become Countess of Haro, inspired Goya, in 1802–1805, to another of his finest portraits of women.

At the moment when the young marquesa arrived at the Spanish court in 1781, the painter, "an artisan rather than an artist," "a semi-literate and vulgar provincial," as described by Ortega y Gasset, was in the process of breaking off his dependency on the Bayeu clan, a thriving family of mediocre neoclassical painters into which he had married and to which he owed what fame he then enjoyed in Madrid. He had been revealed to himself, and to Spanish genius, by Velázquez, well represented in Madrid collections but unknown to international European painting. Goya's instinct, his tastes, his sensual vitality, and his painter's vocation led him to the creator of *The Spinners*, an artist certainly more intellectual and "literary" than himself but whose plastic energy shared his own sympathy with the naturelness of animals and of the personnel of the great lords *à l'espagnole*, physically tallied with the earth, the light, the blood and sweat of Spain.

The young painter's ripening accompanied the current fashions of Madrid, an enthusiasm for bullfighting and for the costumes and festivals of all classes of people, and everything they revealed of the harsh pleasures of life snatched from ephemeral joys, from fortune, and from death. Goya's cartoons for the Royal Tapestry Factories had already given the aristocracy and even the royal family a sample of these strong flavors, which they savored but which etiquette and official conventions, dismissing them as "artifices," kept them from enjoying directly. Such appetites for traditional and popular *hispanité* in taste contradicted the ideas coming from France and propagated by the philosophers of the Enlightenment: criticism of traditional costumes, popular beliefs, and superstitions. Goya would remain torn between such ideas, which he increasingly espoused, and the roots of his art in the old Spain of devotion to the saints and the Virgin, of majas, picaros, and seguidillas. This was the Spain that interested Beckford.

After 1781, bypassing the Bayeu clan, Goya was increasingly favored by court circles; in 1786, besieged by the most flattering commissions, he was named painter to the king. This extraordinary appetite of Spanish high society for the "artisan" of the people as well as of genius would culminate in 1795, says a symptomatic legend, in the quasi-erotic intimacy, from painter to model, established for several months between Goya and the famous and newly widowed Duchess of Alba: the fruit of this encounter was *La maja desnuda*.

Very rapidly, the new Marquesa de Santa Cruz, whose birth, marriage, youth, and seductiveness made her a star of the court and of Madrilenian high society, adapted herself handsomely to the "perfume" of Castille. By her four maternities she had amply fulfilled her duties toward her graybeard of a husband. When William Beckford and his numerous suite arrived in Madrid on December 11, 1787, the marquesa was a woman ready at last to live her own life, though without the slightest intention of troubling the appearances of her marriage, or jeopardizing her lofty social position, or sacrificing the mundanities that diverted her. In Beckford she found an unanticipated accomplice who immediately recommended himself by his beauty, his wit, his sulfurous celebrity, his appetite for pleasures of all kinds, his bulimia for social sumptuosities.

Fleeing England once again, where echoes of his amours with William Courtenay (eleven years old!) had expelled him from respectable society since 1784, and liberated from his beloved wife who had died in childbirth at Lausanne in 1786, the young and incredibly wealthy British lord, ever original and beyond his times, had decided to explore the other, less familiar half of the Latin Catholic world, the Iberian peninsula. In adolescence he had already squeezed dry the Italian lemon, and began his new quest somewhat by chance with Portugal, where he spent six difficult but often delicious months. Two astonishing books were born of this discovery: *Italy; with Sketches of Spain and Portugal* (1834) and *Recollections of an Excursion to the Monasteries of Alcobaça and Batalha* (1835).

Outraged by the refusal of Robert Walpole, one of Horace's cousins and His British Majesty's ambassador in Lisbon, to receive his countryman and introduce him at court, Beckford, at the head of an endless retinue that included his physician, his chef, his steward, a library, and a fine cellar of burgundy and pink champagne, headed for Madrid.

Here, too, the same ostracism was inflicted on the scandalous traveler by Mr. Liston, the British chargé d'affaires. Beckford remained only six months in Madrid. But this time his successes in Spanish high society and among various foreign embassies made up for British disdain. He had long been attracted to Catholicism: in Lisbon he had declared himself a great votary of the city's patron saint, Anthony of Padua, and never failed to attend mass, which he followed with evident demonstrations of piety. In Madrid he redoubled his devotion, but the Marquesa de Santa Cruz's letters suggest the real reason: such Catholic zeal did not, in any case, prevent the author of *Vathek* from forming an intimate connection with the Turkish ambassador, Ahmed Vassif, to whom he sent croissants specially concocted by his French chef. Singularly explicit in writing, which is extremely rare in the period, Beckford reports in his *Journal* (finally published in 1954) the strong feelings he has for Mohammed, a young Tunisian from the embassy: "Even as he took my hands with an inconceivable tenderness, he continued to whisper in my ear in a voice which pierced my heart. I thought I was dreaming. I think so still. We continued, Mohammed and I, to drink from each other's eyes (as Hafiz would say) with such avidity that time passed without either of us counting the moments."

Wasting not another moment, he formed attachments to the Duca de l'Infantado (fifteen years old), the Prince (fourteen) and Princesse de Listenois (eighteen), the Prince de Carency (seventeen), children of the French ambassador, the Duc de La Vauguyon, and especially, as we learn from the letters of the marquesa herself, the less young wife of Don José de Santa Cruz. He was seen at every ball, at the opera, riding in the Prado.... It was a high life he was living, which yet left him time to visit monasteries, churches, and palaces and to relish the pictures of the Italian masters or the then fashionable Anton Raphael Mengs, former guest artist of the court of Madrid and unworthy rival of Tiepolo.

Like everyone of the period outside the circles of Spanish art lovers, he did not even suspect the existence of Zurbarán and Velázquez. It was hardly surprising that the young English "virtuoso" certainly knew nothing of Goya, a local dauber. What is surprising is that Napoleon's marshals, especially Soult, should have shown such predatory appetites for the masterpieces of Spanish art, which they brought home to Paris in great numbers in 1813. But they had had time in situ, at the ephemeral court of the *rey intruso* Joseph Bonaparte, to learn from the *afrancesados* courtiers to delight in the best of the local production and to invest in it heavily.

Suddenly, without warning or farewell, Beckford left Madrid for Paris on June 14, 1788. The English chargé d'affaires, or else the Duc de La Vauguyon, or perhaps even Don José de Santa Cruz had threatened to have him expelled. It was also possible that Beckford wanted to cut through an overly complicated knot of liaisons in which he had entangled himself within a few weeks. Paris, moreover, was his capital of choice.

The first letter preserved from the marquesa to Bedford, whom she believed to be still in Madrid, is dated May 30, 1788. Beckford would inform her of his Parisian address only after his abrupt departure from Madrid, and they would continue to write to each other for several months over this great distance.

This correspondence suggests that a close solidarity had been formed between them in Madrid, behind Don José's back, though known to many at court and in town. The couple shared a whole series of French nicknames designating the chief figures of Madrid society: the English chargé d'affaires was "the Fox"; the new English ambassador "the Monster"; the French ambassador "Papa Vaughion"; his wife "the Beanpole"; his son-in-law the Prince de Listenois "the Twister"; as for Don José de Santa Cruz, he was "the Bird" or "the Owl."

In the murmurs of her correspondence, the marquesa sought to restore Beckford's appetite for Madrid by chronicling the doings of high society and the court, already so familiar to him. In order to arouse his jealousy, she didn't fail to inform him of the new passions that she had inspired (and rejected for love of him). She also told him of the steps she had taken to enable his return.

First of all, there was the matter of persuading the new English ambassador to receive him if indeed Beckford should return to Madrid. The marquesa would apply herself ardently to the task. But she also reported the result of the visits she consented to make at his request, transmitting messages and even presents to the young protégés he left behind in Madrid. She obliges Beckford in this regard, but complains about the task. It appears that Beckford's Catholic zeal is addressed not only to Saint Anthony of Padua but also to a choirboy nicknamed Kiki, whose family he had circumvented and who belonged to the choir school of his heavenly patron's sanctuary. Still another choirboy, Gregorio Franchi, extracted from the patriarchal seminary of Lisbon, had already become a member of the insatiable lord's retinue. Beckford had brought him along to Madrid; lover, accomplice, procurer, business agent, Franchi would not leave him until his death in London in 1828.

Even so, the young marquesa remained no less passionately attached to her correspondent. It would take her another six months to admit that she had been abandoned without hope of comeback. The uninterrupted successes of her *galant* career allowed or compelled her to forget such a humiliation rather quickly. She quite turned the head of Felix Guillemardet, the Directory's ambassador to Madrid; in 1799 Goya painted a splendid portrait of this man (bequeathed to the Louvre in 1865), and in addition a tiny copy of the full-length portrait of the marquesa (also left to the Louvre).

The extremely friendly relations of the marquesa and her husband, a minister of Carlos IV, with Goya, the painter to the king, were much in evidence between 1790 and 1800. The period was one of celebration for the painter, invited to join the coterie of *Lumières* who, under the authority of Carlos IV and the queen's lover Manuel

Godoy, governed Spain according to the French doctrine of enlightened despotism.

Don José de Santa Cruz was a strong advocate of the reform party. His wife was by now the reigning mistress of the powerful banker Cabarrus (father of the future Mme Tallien, still later Princesse de Caraman-Chimay). Of him as well, Goya painted a fine portrait. Delacroix, who had family links with the Guillemardets, reports in his *Journal* that in 1792 the marquesa had sought, contrary to all the laws of prudence, to accompany her present lover, entrusted by Carlos IV with bringing three million livres to Paris to pay for Louis XVI's escape: the couple was arrested en route and obliged to return to Madrid without being able to rescue the king of France.

In 1800 the first palace revolution occurred; the party of the *Lumières* was driven out of the government. Cabarrus, the Spanish Necker, was thrown into prison, and that same year Lucien Bonaparte replaced Guillemardet at the Madrid embassy: he resided, as a young widower, at the Santa Cruz palace and of course had an affair with the mistress of the house, who had no motive for showing him hostility. In July 1801 the marquesa was in Paris, alone, writing passionate letters and exciting news to Lucien, still posted as ambassador in Madrid. She was widowed two or three months later. Her French lover left Spain in November and the same month they met and stayed in his country house, Plessis-Chamant, near Paris. She went back to Madrid in the spring of 1802, for what she believed to be a short stay. At the beginning of the summer Lucien met Alexandrine Jouberthon in the park of Méréville. He fell in love with her on the spot and married her in spite of Bonaparte's wrath in 1804. The couple was then forced into exile in Rome.[2] The marquesa had to content herself with a gift of 500,000 francs. The French invasion of Spain compelled her to flee to the Italian city of Fano in 1805 where

2. See Marcello Simonetta, "Lucien Bonaparte ambassadeur" in the catalog *Lucien Bonaparte: un homme libre* edited by Maria Teresa Caracciolo (Milan: Silvana, 2010), pp. 70–79.

she died in the same year (1808) that Murat's troops entered Madrid. Goya recorded for eternity the resistance of the Madrileños in his historical painting *Dos de Mayo*; that resistance had been inspired by Ferdinand VII, son of Carlos IV, and by everyone in patriotic Spain who opposed the French representatives of the Enlightenment.

By a paradox that long marked Spanish history and tormented Goya's genius to the point of nightmare, the party of the *Lumières* (which had all the painter's sympathies: he had engraved his *Caprichos* in that spirit) was compromised by the painter's collaboration with the French invaders. And Spanish patriotism, which Goya had in his blood, would henceforth identify itself with its autochthonous traditions, Catholic, feudal, and popular. The Marquesa de Santa Cruz, with all her talent and thirst for survival, was extinguished by this drama like a wisp of straw.

I have reproduced three letters written in French from the marquesa to Beckford, disregarding the extravagant orthography of the original manuscript, to which I have added Beckford's only letter to the marquesa that has been preserved; it dates from his stay in Madrid.

From the Marquesa de Santa Cruz to William Beckford

Madrid, Thursday, June 5, 1788
I visited Kiki[3] first thing, without knowing why or wherefore, but who could guess that the child had any business being there—enough on that subject, I am too uncomfortable to discuss it further—I took a solitary walk this morning with my Don Pedro[4] to Sitio, over the hills that surround Aranjuez. I sat there studying the scenery, thinking continually of you, I was quite tired of walking and very sad to boot, keep-

---

3. An unidentified person, doubtless a choirboy to whom Beckford seems to have been quite attached.

4. Don Pedro de Silva, a priest, brother of the Marquès de Santa Cruz.

*ing in mind the reflections I made the while. Yesterday I saw Sir Fox[5]
as soon as I went to the House of Portugal,[6] I gave him the passport,
remarking that it could serve as an example, we shall see what he has
to say to me this evening, when I shall attempt to make him undertake
a particular conversation on our subject; he has already mentioned to
Clavel[7] what I told him about my conduct with the sensitive household[8]: I know they were quite aware of it and supposed to sound me out
on the matter. I plan to tell the Mqis this evening that the new opera is
on Saturday and that I plan to leave here Sunday morning if God
permits everything to work out, but it doesn't matter, nothing will prevent me from seeing you. I hope you will await my arrival with as
much impatience as I feel about seeing you, for I am happy only when
I am with you. You will have no difficulty crediting such a thing,
knowing how much I love you, passionately indeed, with all the tenderness of my heart and soul, and I have no hesitation about assuring
you that such sentiments are for life.*

Friday, June 13, 1788 [the eve of Beckford's departure]
*In all my life I have never experienced such a cruel situation as today's
separation from you, who have meant all my happiness. I cannot describe how my heart aches, how inconsolable I am, at this very moment my tears scarcely allow me to see what I am writing, I am in my
bed where I immediately sought refuge in order to write to you and to
comfort my poor heart, farewell, I lack the strength to tell you anything
more. Love me, that is all I ask of you, nothing can compensate me for
my loss of you.*

---

5. Sir Robert Liston (1741–1836) inaugurated his diplomatic career as embassy secretary at Madrid (1783), a post he left in 1788. He subsequently remained ambassador to Turkey at Constantinople until the age of eighty. He died at ninety-two,
dean of the world's diplomatic corps.

6. Don Diego de Noronha e Menezes, Portuguese ambassador to Madrid from
1786. In 1792 he played an active part in concluding an alliance between his country and Spain against France.

7. William Carmichael, American chargé d'affaires in Madrid.

8. The English ambassador to Spain at Madrid, William Eden, and his wife.

Madrid, June 16, 1788

More and more I feel the effect you have had upon my heart, it is only now that I know what it means to love someone—happy as I was all the time I spent with you, so unhappy am I now. I have invited Liston the Fox to visit me, he will ask the minister for a letter of recommendation to M. May, governor of St. Ildephonso, so that you can see everything there. I've especially recommended that they keep the fountains turned on, which they are usually quite reluctant about, and you must also visit the mirror manufactory. As for Segovia you won't need special permission, you can even inspect the military college, and then, above all, remember your poor little creature here who lives only for you. The Fox was supposed to send me that letter today or to give it to me at the House of Portugal, and I'll answer it as soon as I have it, we talked about you and I told him that I absolutely counted on seeing you again, that I would be attached to you for the rest of my life, because he was joking that I would choose someone else, he actually mentioned several individuals, among others de Carency, saying that he was returning next September, but that means nothing at all to me, these people have no idea how much I love you, however everyone does notice my sadness and my depression. Portugal says he dares not approach me because I am in such a terrible mood, I have also told Liston about the Vaughion business because of his daughter, he knew nothing at all about it, I hope you are having a better journey than theirs, they found the roads very bad and were stuck in a hole that they couldn't tell was filled with water so they couldn't get pulled out despite the efforts of all the mules and oxen that could be found on the road, they left the carriage and continued on foot, but on their way they encountered a cart and all of them got into it, and in this fine vehicle they arrived, I don't remember the name of where it was, the Princesse de Listenois terribly frightened and distressed by the rain and the damp, she caught a fever, which compelled them to remain two whole days in that place, after a lot of work and time the carriage was pulled out of that hole, luckily, I'm sure you'll laugh at the idea of seeing Papa Vaughion on a cart, I had to laugh myself despite my sadness that gives me so little desire to laugh. They gave Cavallerizo's[9] rank to Count de Montijo, Hariza's brother, he won't be pleased about that, for his rank as captain of the Halbardiers is much more advantageous. So you'll be leaving tomorrow according to what you told me the other day, my distress will be even worse then, for knowing you were still in Madrid it seemed to me I hadn't lost all hope, since afterward the satisfaction of hearing something about you every day was a great consolation and now I'm going to be deprived of that for a long time, it's a cruel prospect, my eyes keep filling with tears and my only satisfaction is to be alone and give myself up to my grief. Farewell to all that is dearest to me in the world, you whom I adore and will love all my life. Love me too, for that is the one way of making my situation more endurable.

All of Portuguese society was at the Beneventes,[10] which wasn't to my taste at all since I would be meeting Liston there, I had gone to his place but he wasn't there and I left one of my servants who waited for him to this very moment, and here's his answer....

Monday, July 28, 1788

Heavens how sweet you are my darling to write me in such detail about everything you're thinking and doing, but you must know for whom you're taking all this trouble and how grateful my poor heart is for the tiniest signs of your attachment, your letter gave me so much pleasure I couldn't contain my joy and my gratitude, so that at that very moment I did everything you asked me to do for Kiki. Afterward I thought better of it, but in spite of all my repugnance, your power over me was too strong to resist, and so yesterday I went to hear mass at Kiki's little church, he and his Father came right away to the sacristy door to see me, you can imagine how I felt at that moment but I over-

---

9. Equerry to the Princess of the Asturias, the future queen of Spain Maria Luisa, Godoy's mistress.

10. Countess of Benavente, a sharp-tongued old witch, according to Beckford's *Journal intime.* Her salon was a gambling den where she drummed up players for her faro bank.

came all my feelings and when mass was over I sent to the sacristy and asked for Kiki ... and requested to see his room; he led me to it and introduced me to his mother who is a tiny round woman, tiny and ugly too, I said I had news of you and that you had given me lots of messages for the child whom I was speaking to and who answered me when I said I had come on your behalf to give him word of you and I went white as a sheet then and a cold sweat covered my whole body. And that's not all, that was when the father and mother spoke of all the kindness and affection you had shown their son, that was the term they used, and that they didn't know what he had done to deserve it, to the point where you wanted to take him away with you, to which they couldn't consent, having only this one child; and my heart started pounding so dreadfully I couldn't speak and I left right away to revel in my own grief; and when I got home I was somewhat consoled, having received your letter from Bayonne, which a servant of Papa Vaughion brought—he said he had been sent there on purpose, I don't suppose that was your doing because you hadn't mentioned anything about it to me, but all the same it was very careless of him to not have spoken of it to me, well, better late than never, for I thought he was the same kind as the first one; you're furious, you say, about Ver[11] and the people who made you leave Spain. That way of expressing yourself is quite sincere since I am not the only one whom you have abandoned, and whom you regret, for that damn Kiki cares about you almost as much as I—you are still talking about him and fearing I won't do everything you tell me to do for him. Which is how I'll behave from now on, I won't be nice the way I was yesterday, enough is enough and I don't want to bore you anymore with my complaints, which merely stir up my jealousy and drive me crazy, but considering how much I love you and how it consumes me—about the portrait I don't want to go into all that I'd rather believe you about it, but I'm going to tell you how I know what I told you; it was through Beuste to whom I spoke of your portrait that I have, and he asked which one, the first or the sec-

---

11. Dr Verdeil, a Genevan, Beckford's personal physician. He often tried to get his patient out of the scrapes in which he was so frequently embroiled.

ond, I was surprised but pretended nothing had happened and all I said was that I didn't know which; at which point he said, ah, well, one is a better likeness than the other, I didn't lose my courage and I told him that was the one I have, and the other one is the one you sent to Mariala, which could have been true since that was your first intention, however I didn't believe it and a thousand upsetting ideas came into my mind and I wanted right away to tell you how upset I was, because I always tell you everything; that gives me some comfort and often I feel consoled and you really do everything you can to make that happen, what you tell me frankly about things you have done makes me feel a lot calmer but wouldn't it be to make way for someone else and not to be bothered, now you're going to say I'm always jealous and you're right but I can't help it, it's more forgivable than any other feeling, which only comes out of conceit and that certainly isn't what upsets me. It's a very different feeling. I would be delighted to receive your Agnus Dei *and the* Coplitas al Santissimo,[12] *but I don't like the words you have chosen, or that you prefer to compose church music, and with good reason, I'm having Beuste send you two Gally arias for the Deluse piece,[13] it's just your kind of music, especially the rondeau; I'm sure I heard you singing something very much like it; the words are* resta in pace, amato ben, mio dolce amor *[peace be with you, my dear beloved, my tender love]; I'm also sending you* Gil Blas de Santillane, *which has just come out in Spain and, as they say, transposed into its first language in which it promises to be much more interesting, I thought such a thing might give you some pleasure, but about my portrait in oils, I still have no news but I'll do everything I can to get it back. It's tonight that Beuste will be leaving, he'll stop at Bagnières and won't reach Paris until September 15, I've told him to talk to you quite regularly about me. He's a good devil of a fellow and I'm sorry that he's leaving, I trust him completely, we talk about you all the time and he was often good company, he was always in my box at the opera and on other days we used to take*

---

12. The *Stanzas to the Highest* (pieces of music composed by Beckford: see Timothy Mowl, *William Beckford Composing for Mozart* [London: John Murray, 1988]).

13. *Les Intrigues dévoilées*, most likely the title of an opera.

*our afternoon walks in the Prado together, and Perico too, but now I
don't know what I'm going to do, I don't want to go alone with Perico,
not because I'm afraid of anything he might try to do, but it would cause
talk if I were seen alone with him. C——* [14] *has written to me, I'm sending you his letter that I don't intend to answer, the grand beau he men-
tions is probably that tall Valon, but he's mistaken, I have no intention
of seeing him again, so you've been. . . . [the end of the letter is missing]*

From William Beckford to the Marquesa de Santa Cruz

Tuesday May 27, 1788

*What are you telling me now—What indeed?—some nonsense about
Papa Vauguyon, Mr. Kauff quite crazed, and dear Carency doused
with a big glass of water to put out the conflagration—how charming—how picturesque—I almost broke a rib laughing—I've often told
you that dear Twisty did not always sacrifice to nymphs and naiads
exclusively—Despite all the blossoms he managed to scatter so prettily
at the feet of the Sabatinis, the Galves, and the Villamayors—fauns
and even satyrs are the delighted recipients of his firmest homage. A
prophetic frenzy has seized me—I see him in the remote future sur-
rendering to the furies of the Greek delirium, despite the formidable
Beaupère, the tender Felknaman woman, and the virtuous Duchess—a nice list for you—already I hear the sound of households col-
lapsing, proud exclamations in the highest French style—shrill cries
and a tiny rather melodious voice persisting in its own defense. The
weather has not allowed me a single horseback excursion, this morning I went to Carmona's* [15] *and from there with Verdeil to the rue de*

---

13. The Prince de Carency, son of the Duc de La Vauguyon. "Twisty" is his brother-
in-law, the Prince de Listenois.

14. Manuel Salvador Carmona (1734–1820) came to Paris to compete his studies in
the art of engraving. He was admitted into the Académie des Beaux-Arts for his
portrait of Boucher. One of the finest engravers of his time, he married the daughter of the Austrian painter Mengs.

Tolède in order to worship at the shrine of Mengs's Virgin[16] that we viewed together. Ask Silva, who is not deaf as you well know, if by the ambassador's intervention I might get this picture out of Spain—it is sublime—the Virgin is more heavenly than all of Raphael's together.—No one has ever combined the majesty of a guardian Divinity with the graces, the candor, and the innocence of a mortal maiden—hence I am mad for her and ready to abjure all my sins and begin a novena in honor of the holy and compassionate Mary—I shall fulfill your request with regard to the Imperiali, *which you know only by very bad translations. I assure you that in Italian or better still in Neapolitan it is quite endurable—the arrival of the Penafiel creature pleases me enormously—she must be cultivated with great care and put in mind of all the cruel nastiness of our enemies.—I trust you will frustrate any liaison between her and the English Matron. Yesterday V. took her Bine to my little concert, she is not without her graces.— The singing was pitifully bad: if I may say so, there was only the Duo of your innocent and mine which was worth something. My ears still ache with the yowlings of Rubio and the basso continuo of the gracious Don Pepe.—The instrumental part was more successful than the vocal. The transports of the grand gala must pass before I show myself in the green streets of Aranjuez.—You wouldn't want me to go begging an invitation from these people who have wearied me with neglect and suspicions as ill-founded as they are absurd. I extended my morning ride to the Prado today.—The palace is of a matchless melancholy and heaviness, but the prince's pavilion has a merit all its own.*

---

15. Anton Mengs (1728–1779), born in Bohemia, is known chiefly as a portrait painter and pastelist. Following a stay in Rome, he imitated Raphael and professed great enthusiasm for the ancients. Creator of a new "neoclassical" school, in 1761 he became court painter to Carlos III in Madrid.

19. Louis-Antoine Caraccioli and "French Europe"

AFTER 1764, there were two Marquis Caracciolis in Paris, which was one too many.

The more recent arrival was the Marquis Domenico Caraccioli, ambassador of the court of Naples. This grand seigneur was not handsome; of him Marmontel wrote: "His features had that thick and massive expression that heralds stupidity." But he was endowed to a superlative degree, like his Neapolitan collegue Ferdinando Galiani, with what eighteenth-century Paris appreciated above all else: esprit. His witticisms were soon repeated throughout the capital. To Louis XV, who, aware that the ambassador worked late after a whirlwind of worldly diversions, had courteously inquired if he had time, at least, to make love—a civilized question if ever there was one—this Caraccioli replied: "No, Sire, I buy it ready-made." This spark and many more opened wide the doors of the most tightly sealed salons, even that of Mme du Deffand. At Mme Geoffrin's, he conquered the Encyclopedists at once; the Neapolitan grand seigneur diplomatically entered into their views and was of course rewarded for doing so. Grimm, d'Alembert, and Marmontel sang his praises, and all have left enthusiastic portraits of him. Recalled to Naples to become viceroy of Sicily, the marquis saw to it that like Catherine of Russia in St. Petersburg, he ruled in Palermo according to the enlightened directives of his Parisian friends and correspondents. And by doing so he showed himself to be an excellent and popular administrator. When he died in Naples in 1789, he had been the kingdom's minister of foreign affairs for several years. He belonged to one of the most ancient and illustrious Neapolitan families, fecund in admirals, cardinals, princes, statesmen, poets, and superior women, whose magnificent funerary chapel, recently restored in his Parthenopean church, honors a long heroic tradition.

The other Caraccioli, Louis-Antoine, was a descendant of the same family, but by a collateral branch that had taken root in France after being ruined by William Law's bankruptcy. Brought up in Le Mans, in 1739 he had entered the French congregation of the Oratory, one of the great spiritual families of the French Counter-Reformation, which had been founded by Cardinal de Bérulle and from which had emerged an entire lineage of great minds: Condren, Malebranche, Thomassin. Louis-Antoine taught rhetoric at the Collège de Vendôme, which in the nineteenth century would be a moral torture chamber for Balzac's Louis Lambert, but which even before the Revolution, unlike Juilly, the other great Oratorian college, was not to be the most agreeable of those nurseries of young minds in which France had so abounded since the seventeenth century; yet by the primary teaching they dispensed in the villages of the realm, the Brothers of Christian Doctrine had made France the most broadly literate and cultivated nation in Europe. Young Caraccioli's good humor and social talents (he performed fabulous imitations) were quite wasted in the métier of a provincial pedant.

Was it his Italian ancestry that impelled him, or did his superiors discover good reasons to offer him gentle encouragement to leave the priesthood, or to exercise it elsewhere than among schoolboys? He journeyed to Rome, the first stage of a long European peregrination. His name, his brilliant conversation, his social talents, and his literary acquaintances gave him every reason to enjoy the great world of Roman society. Popes Benedict XIV and Clement XIII received him with honor. Several Italian cardinals formed lasting friendships with him, and he remained in correspondence with them after his departure from the city. Very likely he obtained from the ecclesiastical authorities the dispensations he had come to seek. He then set out for Germany and continued on to Poland, where General Rewski appointed him his children's tutor. To be entitled to sit at this prince's table, the quite secular ecclesiastic received the rank of colonel *in partibus*. This employment included a lifetime pension of five thousand livres, which assured him a certain independence as long as it was paid, which is to say, until he left Poland in 1772. A witness to the Polish realities, Caraccioli vainly attempted, not without courage and by several leaflets, to combat the pro-Prussian and pro-Russian prejudices of the philosophes whose firing power silenced his voice.

Returning to France, he spent several years in Tours before settling in Paris, where he led the life of a man of letters and of a worldly abbé. His gaiety, his experience of foreign countries, and his amenity made him a valued guest of many societies, yet he became neither a renegade nor an apostate. Quite the contrary, the numerous works he published in various parts of Europe all reveal a pastoral Christian fervor; he composed a *Life of Bérulle* and a *Life of Condren* (1764), which attest to his fidelity to the Oratory. Might he have left the ecclesiastical condition (it is possible but unverified that he actually did so) for a better knowledge of "the world" and to enjoy more freedom to convert it with the most appropriate means?

Neither Bérulle's *Grandeurs de Jésus* nor Pascal's *Pensées* nor Bossuet's *Oraisons funèbres* nor even the eloquence of contemporary sermons could any longer affect the faithless or the faithful of the rococo period. No one more accurately than Caraccioli had measured the worldly distance from austere devotion that in France affected the aristocracy of both the court and the town, and of which men of letters hastened to construct a theory to suit themselves. How to keep such an example from spreading its contagion among a wider population of average Frenchmen? Caraccioli chose to be the interpreter of an Enlightenment religion that he knew to be everywhere present and latent, in France and in Europe, despite the atheism or agnosticism that was de rigueur or paraded in Parisian circles. And yet, to the applause of the most distinguished levels of society, it was precisely by attacking and intimidating this latent religion, accumulated and stabilized by a century and a half of militant Counter-Reformation, that the philosophical coterie, underhandedly electrified by Voltaire's cry of "*Écrasez l'Infâme*," sought to disconcert by every weapon at its disposal.

The Anger of the Philosophical Party

Voltaire and his friends never forgave Rousseau his "Profession of Faith of a Savoyard Vicar," which brought the fresh waters of sentiment to Christianity's old prayer mill. The work of the Counter-Reformation had succeeded: its missionary and polemical age had passed, its stable and benevolent age had arrived. The sweetness and joy of Saint Philip Neri and Saint François de Sales had entered into manners. Caraccioli intended to complete this success. But the philosophes' propaganda contrived to represent this Christianity without anguish as the instrument of despotism, a nightmare of inquisition and fanaticism. The eloquent Savoyard vicar imagined by Rousseau, thoroughgoing deist that he was, embarrassed too such antireligious propaganda.

All the more reason that the ex-Oratorian Caraccioli, now a Catholic publicist, could not long escape the whipping-boy's fate awaiting anyone in France, after 1750, who dared side publicly with moderate Christianity.

The European success of his numerous works was in fact considerable enough for someone in Liège, in 1763, to compose and indeed publish *L'Esprit des oeuvres de Monsieur le Marquis Caraccioli*, the sort of work that at the time testified to a distinguished or even an eminent rank in the European Republic of Letters. Voltaire had already had a comparable work produced in Amsterdam. Faithful daughter and guardian of the Enlightenment, America in our own day and age perpetuates this tradition: one finds in campus bookstores a *Foucault Reader* or a *Derrida Reader* that follows the same anthological formula and indicates the elevated status of these foreign thinkers in the university commerce of tenure.

This indeed was too much. The thunderbolts of Voltaire and his

Parisian confederates, La Harpe and Grimm, were directed against the intruder. To extinguish him by ridicule, it sufficed to reveal the disparity between this worldly Oratorian's literature and the title of marquis that his Liègeois anthologists had attributed (or restored) to him, or that other title of colonel that had been granted him in Poland. The opportune arrival of the brilliant ambassador from Naples, the year after the publication of the Liègeois volume, furnished the requisite occasion. The "real" marquis, when properly instructed, presented himself in all the places and on all the occasions where the "false" one had made, or could have made, his entrances, asking that the utterance of his name and his quality by the usher be followed by the shout "He's not the other one," followed by a good deal of laughter. The nasty crack, spread throughout Europe by Grimm's *Correspondance littéraire*, doubtless closed more than one Parisian door in the French Caraccioli's face and limited his frequentations. Voltaire released a veritable campaign of insinuations against his journalist foe, poor wretch, like the one he had decided in the past to wage against the Abbé Desfontaines, and that this time too could have had the "false" marquis jailed for "Italian vice." Caraccioli felt neither upset nor compelled to silence. His real and widespread public was not that of the philosophes. He continued publishing books and receiving bookstore successes. Literary history, eyes invariably fixed on the only stars made much of by Mme Geoffrin or by Mlle de Lespinasse, has been all too willing to espouse their sectarianism ever since.

Caraccioli had begun publishing in 1751, in the context of Voltaire's *Le Siècle de Louis XIV.* His earliest work, appearing in The Hague, touched on one of the dire shadows of the French Enlightenment: the anxiety of decadence. This alarm had surfaced in 1714, even before the death of the Great King, in the resounding essay of Anne Dacier, the knightly advocate of Homer against the moderns: *Of the Causes of the Corruption of Taste.* It had then taken a still more anxious turn in 1734, in the book of another ancient, Toussaint Rémond de Saint-Mard, entitled *Three Letters on the Decadence of Taste.* It had become almost aggressive in 1747 under the pen of an art lover, Lafont de Saint-Yenne, who created a scandal with his pamphlet *The Shadow of the Great Colbert, the Louvre, and the City of Paris.* Invoking the "great works" of the Grand Siècle, the author covertly accused Louis XV's administration of negligence and dereliction: the new Louvre remained unfinished; the royal collections, stored in Versailles, remained invisible to artists and public alike; Parisian urbanism had remained at a dead level since Colbert.

Against this background of nervousness Voltaire made in 1751 his own salvo from Potsdam, conceiving his *Le Siècle de Louis XIV* as an enormous amplification of Charles Perrault's famous panegyrics to the glory of the Great King that had, in 1687–1694, inaugurated the *Querelle des Anciens et des Modernes.* The Voltairean apology for the classical century was bound to irritate the anxiety of the ancients for having to live in a "decadent" century; it also fed the reproaches Lafont de Saint-Yenne addressed to Louis XV's administration. In any case, it suggested that the century of the Enlightenment would never bear the name of Louis XV.

DEFENSE OF LOUIS XV

Caraccioli had clearly perceived the Voltaire project's subtly perfidious intention and sought to come to the defense of Louis XV. It was not the result of a commission, and the court never showed him the slightest gratitude. But he was sincerely preoccupied by the difference between the Christian "grand style" of the seventeenth century and that which he himself felt bound to adopt in an utterly different period. His book, almost a brochure, was called *Dialogue Between the Age of Louis XIV and the Age of Louis XV* and was dedicated "to Time." It took up one of the great Augustinian themes of preaching and classical art, the fleeting "vanity" of human affairs, which must incite the Christian to make urgent use of the moments left to him here on earth. The preface touched on another great classical and Christian theme, illusion and disillusion, the play of flattering appearances that turns into harsh truth. At every age in life man is a Proteus who strives to avoid the awareness of his own lack of being and who must be guided to self-knowledge. The "progresses" of civilization that Perrault had vaunted and that had subsequently accelerated were actually limited, if Caraccioli is to be believed, to rendering ever more obvious, more rapid, and hence both more illusory and more revealing that wheel of Time on which all men in all centuries turn as straw. The "decadence" deplored by the ancients was in Caraccioli's Christian eyes merely another phase, more ambiguous but no less providential and however less brutal, of humanity's journey to its ultimate encounter with its final truth.

The allegorical dialogue that constitutes the body of the work is a classical school exercise, in a livelier variant of the "parallel" dear to Plutarch and to Montaigne. Caraccioli had only to look inward to know that in the age when he was writing the tone was set by hurried and frivolous worldlings whose attention, mobilized by a thousand different objects, was difficult to capture and to focus. More often than not he avoided a frontal attack upon such "dissemination," though he found it appropriate to publish, in 1766, *Contemporary Christian's Defeat by Those of Earliest Times*: this was a much mitigated version of a huge work published a century earlier by a Capuchin monk, Father Bonnal, in 1657. The adapter had retained the keen barbs, typical of the sacred eloquence of the seventeenth century, against "those who seek a Christianity without Calvary, a Calvary without a Cross, a Crown without Thorns." But he also admitted that such a severe manner could no longer be risked, save in tiny doses, and that a prudent laxism was preferable to the Jansenists' disheartening rigorism. Caraccioli was thus early convinced—and this would remain the rhetorical principle of most of his writing—that formal concessions to the rococo "flutter" (*papillotage*: the word would appear in 1764 in an anonymous satire against fashionable dandies), in order to attract versatile modern sinners, would allow Christian wisdom to be heard and perhaps followed in times of dissipation. This was the strategy already envisaged in 1642 by another forgotten Christian moralist, François de

Grenaille, in a book that introduced into French the word *mode* and that was entitled *De la mode, ou des caractères du temps* (On Fashion, or on the Characteristics of the Time). The Paris of Louis XIII's *ruelles* (fashionable ladies' "alcoves," hence literary cliques) had prefigured the boudoirs and high society of the Paris of Louis XV. Caraccioli's continuity with the French Counter-Reformation of the Grand Siècle is patent. But his orthodoxy did not exonerate this Enlightenment moralist from adapting his parenetic method to the very excesses that the successful Christianization of the realm had allowed, and from trying to afford them palliatives and vaccines duly adjusted to the new types of spiritual patients.

The "Pocket Book"

In 1760, inspired by the Jesuit scientist Father Castel's optical theories, Caraccioli did not hesitate to publish one after the other *Le Livre à la mode*, printed in green ink; *Le Livre à la mode, nouvelle édition polie et vernissée*, printed in pink; and *Le Livre des quatre couleurs*, printed in green, pink, blue, and beige, so many rhetorical and optical traps adapted to a sensual and sensualist public. His zeal, but also his eccentricity, anticipated Surrealism's most unbridled typographical whim.

Reviving the original ambition of humanist printing (to save the classical texts from the effects of time by engraving them on paper, as the ancient inscriptions had been eternalized in marble), Caraccioli revealed by this ironic and bizarre inking the frivolity of the modern "pocket book," an object of hurried and disposable consumption. He imitated it to the point of caricature, not in order to flatter or condemn it but to compel it to acknowledge what it reluctantly sought to overlook: its own principle of vanity.

"A medley of colors," he wrote,

is so fashionable that this book is entitled to offer itself to the hands of high society. It will not replace the *Dictionnaire encyclopédique*, so varied according to the matters it discusses, but it moves much more rapidly. Our minds today, changing like barometers, will not be at all shocked by the sight of a work that represents them, and our hearts, restless as quicksilver, will relish the moral it contains.... Today's world wishes to see everything in a magic lantern.... It has but a glance to spare, and books of every sort, and their authors too, must pass rapidly as they form a few shadows and a few pleasing suggestions.... I do not offer this book to posterity, for beyond the fact that it would not reach its addressee, it would then be "the Gothic Book" and no longer correspond to its title. I desire only that it should have the honor to rest a few moments on the sofa of the Duchess of —— and on the bureau of the Knight of ——. This enchanted pair, who remind us of Venus's doves, which like that goddess sigh so winsomely, displays a ravishing propriety [read: "elegance"] and daily soars into the region of the most delicious pleasures. My book will have made its way if such happiness were to befall it. But what glory would it not have if, ultimately serving as a pastime for Dorine, her charming little dog, it were elegantly dismembered page by page and thereafter collected to serve as curlpapers to some charming head quite devoid of good sense but embellished with locks artistically tiered. Such is the most brilliant success to which it might aspire. Would to Heaven that the majority of our writers might form no other ambition!

Introduced by the privilege of its shimmering hues into a boudoir à la Boucher, the book, as an object, becomes a *Vanity*, a *Soap Bubble*, testifying, at the price of its own destruction accepted in advance, to the illusion prevailing in our modern gardens of delight. But the text itself, printed in cosmetic colors, or the tints of a fan, is conceived to lead its deluxe recipients, if they have taken the time to read it through, to reflections that the frivolous aspect of the physical object could not anticipate. As for the less fashionable reader, he will be all the more delighted to realize, at the heart of this apparent trinket for idlers and triflers, the substance of the sermons he devoutly heard every Sunday:

> How times have changed! Our fathers never sat down to a meal without invoking God; today a person of repute would immediately lose it by crossing himself. Our fathers believed quite simply in a religion that begins with the world; we desire nowadays to have one that changes like our fashions. Our fathers were seriously convinced of the immortality of their souls, we delightedly adopt the rabbits and the woodcocks as our brothers and sisters; we claim to be of no different substance from theirs. Oh! what a lovely age we live in!

Tertullian disguised in the liveries of sylph and page tears off his mask, yet the moralist is nevertheless careful to brandish the skull upon which Mary Magdalene was once urged to focus her prayers. Even unmasked, this new Tertullian—Heraclitean, Epicurean, and Christian—refuses to scare us: melancholy and anguish are not, in his eyes, evangelical preparations. The devotion to which he seeks to convert us is of a joyous nature, the faith to which he would lead us is a principle of "delight": that is the real secret that comforts the modern layman for the painful instability of moods, tastes, and opinions that exasperate, conceal, multiply, and subtilize, in a complicated civilization, the sadness inherent in a human nature widowed of God.

A CHRISTIAN OF THE ENLIGHTENMENT

Between 1753 and 1764, Caraccioli published in Rome, Frankfurt, and Utrecht as well as Paris a series of spiritual treatises (*Conversation with Oneself, The Joy of Oneself, On Gaiety, On Greatness of Soul*) in which he strove, for a wide French-speaking public, to tame to a basically classical doctrine of moral analysis and spiritual life a "spirit of the times" that evaded any and all preoccupation with oneself. *Le Livre des quatre couleurs* belongs in this series of parenetic essays, even if it takes a singular path to reach the same end. "I know persons," Caraccioli writes, "who see everything in black, persons who would buy anxieties if they did not already possess some, and if they could be purchased in open markets. They find the world's surface a sort of lugubrious crêpe, or rather a winding sheet." Such is the reverse and neurotic side of that other modern and worldly vice, euphoric addiction:

> I know of others who would tickle themselves at eventide in order to laugh, and if one had not laughed during the day, who would not give up their lovely castles in Spain for a hundred thousand ecus rent, who stuff themselves with the most delightful chimeras, who then reject them, and who always have five or six charming colors at hand in which to dress any melancholy and depressing objects. This way of being will perhaps not be in fashion; for today it requires continual doses of hypochondria, especially among our sages of twenty, and stores of vapors among our prudes of seventeen. One sickens without knowing where the pain is, one suffers without knowing one does so, but one confesses it, and, the countenance adjusting itself to what is said, one dies every quarter of an hour; even as one continues to eat, and to live on.

Christians are children of Paradise and not of Hell. Christian optimism is closer to the truth than Christian pessimism and angst. Jansenist obsession with sin and rarefaction of grace is an offense to God's creation and image. It leads human souls to a perverse enjoyment of melancholy and doom. Faith is an experience of delectation. Caraccioli cannot therefore be an adept of "decadence," that black notion which shadows a frivolous and nevertheless enlightened century. Christians have to take their own sinful time as it comes and as it is, trying to convert it, here and now, without despairing of it.

The dialogue between the age of Lous XIV and that of Louis XV, the parallel between "our fathers" and "ourselves," is thus the very point of departure of the itinerary marked out by Caraccioli,

Christian moralist of the Enlightenment. It is also the terminal point of the quarrel between the ancients and the moderns. In his brochure of 1751, the tyro essayist lends to the personification of the Grand Siècle the discourse that Charles Perrault had employed in his poem and in his *Parallels*, and that Voltaire, to the sound of trumpets, had himself adopted for his tableau of the reign of Louis XIV: the seventeenth century had been the point of perfection attained by modern civilization, effacing all previous great ages, beginning with the most famous one of antiquity, the Age of Augustus. But Caraccioli, rejecting the idea of "perfection" that sets up the apology for the Grand Siècle's modernity by Perrault and Voltaire and that insists on the idea of decadence spread by the ancients, gives the eighteenth century's modernism every chance to prove its own merits and even its advantages, above all when considered from the vantage point of the Christian faith.

Defense of a Catholic Eighteenth Century

The spokesman for the contemporary age, in this dialogue, is more than willing to acknowledge the personal merit of the Great King's warriors, but only in order to reveal all the more clearly the progress of strategy and of technology, which have rendered the armies of Louis XV more effective and less destructive. Caraccioli's plea *pro domo sua* of the eighteenth century holds some surprises for the modern reader conditioned by the historiographical vulgate. Who ever studied sacred eloquence in the age of Louis XV and Louis XVI? Even the Abbé Bremond wavered from the task.[1] For Caraccioli, his century is a Christian age, mature fruit of the Catholic Counter-Reformation, and he can avail himself of great sacred orators, "the

---

1. The most comprehensive study of French Catholicism in the eighteenth century is actually the work of the late Anglican parson and outstanding historian John McManners, *Church and Society in Eighteenth-Century France* (Oxford University Press, 1998), which does not extend to literature and doctrinal conflicts.

illustrious Polignac," "the celebrated Duguet," who made fashionable an apologetics of Nature's spectacles:

> When he describes for us the Universe in its cradle, he sets before our eyes all the riches of Heaven and Earth. Sometimes he calls the firmament the first preacher of the Truth, representing it as a Book written in letters of light in which man, no more than a savage, learns to know his creator; sometimes he accumulates the waves of the sea, gathers them up with foam and shells to show the majesty of this proud element.

Other names unknown to literary history are cited following that of the great Massillon (Chateaubriand's favorite reading as a student at the Collège de Dol): "the admirable Ségault, the famous de La Neville, the learned La Bretonne." And of the "Eighteenth Century" he adds: "It is in this School embellished by the graces of an ever decorative style that the heart learns to think nobly, the mind to judge soundly, the senses to act with decency." What we cruelly lack here is a Bremond of the Enlightenment.

To the great Seventeenth Century, which proposes a Fénelon, the Eighteenth Century can offer Fontenelle, the modern par excellence, orator of the Cartesian cosmos: "More of an oracle than even those of antiquity, he employs the true language of the Gods; bolder than the famous Columbus, who discovered a corner of the Earth beyond the seas, he ascends to the stars, seeking among the planets themselves a world hitherto unknown."

The Seventeenth Century invokes Descartes and Malebranche. Its younger interlocutor reacts by citing Descartes's errors latterly divulged and the excesses of metaphysical imagination into which Malebranche had fallen. Never have mathematics and geography been cultivated as brilliantly as today; contemporary historians, antiquarians, jurists, and physicians have outstripped their predecessors by their knowledge and their talent. To the poets vindicated by the Seventeenth Century, the new age can oppose Jean-Baptiste Rousseau, Voltaire (the Voltaire of *Alzire*), Crébillon père, Louis

Racine, and Peyron, in whose hands "religion deploys its most sumptuous wealth."

To the great artists of the classical age, the reign of Louis le Bien-Aimé proposes their equals, the sculptor Edme Bouchardon, the painters François Le Moyne, Quentin de La Tour, Carle Van Loo: "What proportion in their works, what grace, what nobility! Are they truly men who are suddenly born from their hands? Are they mere figures? We cannot believe our eyes." Lully gives way to Rameau and Blamont, whose interpreters oblige us to forget those of the previous century:

> Under the clemency of the laws, under the tender modulations of Blavet, the flute becomes a voice that distinctly articulates words of grief or of love. At each stroke of Mondonville's or Guignon's bow, the senses waken, the heart redoubles its palpitations, the soul is in ecstasy. The outbursts of Jélyotte, like the rolling of subterranean waters, summon the gods, penetrate the Heavens, evoke the dead, open the infernal regions, lull Cerberus to sleep, and touch Pluto himself.

Louis le Bien-Aimé, aureoled by his victories in the course of the War of the Austrian Succession, a benevolent Apollo ruling over a supremely brilliant Parnassus where several women (Mme du Châtelet, Mme de Graffigny, Mme du Bocage, Mme de Puisieux) can rival Scudéry and Sévigné of the previous reign, has therefore no reason to envy, quite the contrary, his Jupiterian great-grandfather of illustrious memory. The scandalized Seventeenth Century then draws a formidable trump out of its sleeve:

> Most of your pupils are mere imitators; their productions are the work of superficial men. Who now has the courage to open an *in-folio*? That word alone is likely to bring on a headache; mere brochures have succeeded those enormous tomes that men of my era consulted with delight, that they leafed through with avidity. Youth now knows only books that may

be read in the space of two hours. It is with works as with bouquets: one is satisfied if they last a day.

The Eighteenth Century personified must confess that in the modern rage to publish, many trifles are created. But is that not the price to be paid for the wider diffusion of Enlightenment, which has now reached the "plebs" and to which attests the number of those who write as well as the success of excellent periodicals and dictionaries? One could hardly read the *Journal de Trévoux* "in two hours."

But what can be said about manners? The Seventeenth Century insists on this point and becomes severe:

> I see that this word leads you to that relish of fashions, of frippery, that nowadays confounds the two sexes, that submits all you undertake to the Reign of Frivolity. In my time who ever saw the male compete with the female in the matter of adornment, of beauty marks, of powder and rouge? Did my pupils have rules for their outfits, did they spend their days between the comb and the mirror? Who could castigate them for seeking to adorn themselves with a proper jewel, for painting their nails, for the right way to carry a parasol? Had they any other cosmetic than a noble perspiration excited by fatigue, did they argue about the merits of a frivolous adornment? Where today is that male spirit, the suitable concern of those who are truly men?

This disorder of the sexes is contagious. Politeness has become duplicity. A morality is now professed that would bring a blush to pagan Rome. The Supreme Being is treated as "a dream embellished by politics." Education is no longer what it was. Luxury has corrupted everything. Simplicity has vanished. Mere wit has replaced good sense.

The Eighteenth must concur that none of this is false, yet the previous century already had its *précieux ridicules*, its libertines, and even its transvestites: the Abbé de Choisy. Modern education, reformed by Rollin, provides manuals as excellent as that of the Abbé Batteux and, dispensed in a civil and vivacious manner, possesses graces and comforts that guide a young soul more effectively than the old severity. The recurrent revolutions of arts and fashions have the charms of variety, like the seasons of Nature. And luxury is a principle of a universal commerce that unites the most far-flung populations into a single humanity. In addition, does it not become the true Christian to derive good from evil? "I profit by my shadows," declares the age of Louis le Bien-Aimé, "in order to create a splendid light.... Let us agree in good faith that each age has its defects, nothing is perfect in this earthly world. It is not for us, mere transitory beings, to shine without casting a shadow. Eternity alone has that glorious privilege." Arbitration of the dispute, mediated by Time, renders an ideal justice to the two centuries, both "refulgences of the Universe." But a final point settles the affair differently: "Time continues on its way, even as did the seventeenth century, and 1701 vanishes from view. Soon no vestige of it will be seen."

Paris and Rome

A quarter of a century later, in 1776, Caraccioli returned to the astute parallel he had drawn in 1751, but this time without an outraged specter opposing the success of Christian modernity. The moderns have definitively triumphed over the ancients, and the century of Louis XV has kept all the promises of the century of Louis XIV, inclining them to joy, peace, and humanity. The essayist, at the peak of his verve, tallies the European advances of a double-sourced Continental civilization: Paris and Rome. It is a pity that this book is victim of *damnatio memoriae*.

In favor of Rome, and of a Catholic doctrine of the Enlightenment, the fecund writer published in 1766 at Liège his *Éloge historique de Benoît XIV*. Ten years later he produced a best seller in Paris, the *Lettres intéressantes du pape Clément XIV Ganganelli: Traduites de l'italien et du latin*, republished several times and translated into

German. Voltaire, before violently denouncing the letters as a forgery, was initially surprised and enchanted by them.

In favor of Paris, and of the Christian civilization of which the French capital was another radiant focus, Caraccioli published a little duodecimo simultaneously in Turin and Paris: *L'Europe française*. A second edition the following year modified (and specified) the title: *Paris capitale de l'Europe, ou l'Europe française*. From this book Rivarol took inspiration in his celebrated dissertation crowned in 1784 by the Berlin Academy, *De l'universalité de la langue française*.

Caraccioli did not use the word *civilisation*, which had just entered the language, but employed the verb *civiliser*, and it is certainly civilization in the profane and secular sense that is constantly invoked in this schema, in which the author, according to his own preface, sought to represent "Europeans by the French costume they have adopted." The universality won by the language of the realm is here described ahead of Rivarol:

> The courts of Vienna, of Petersburg, of Warsaw converse in the same language as the court of Versailles. One hears the same expressions, the same accent....The Parisian on his travels scarcely realizes he has left Paris, for he comes to no city where he is not answered in his own tongue.... Some time ago, illustrious Leibniz, you called for a language that would be shared by all the learned, that might be understood in every country. Return..., and you discover that your wishes are fulfilled. There is no educated man who does not speak French today, or who does not read it; there is no gently reared woman who is ignorant of its expressions and who fails to admire its beauties. This language has the advantage of having provided the English with virtually all the terms of the arts and sciences. How many sentences, how many works, how many axioms owe to the French language their luster and their reputation.... Modifying itself according to circumstances, this language is admirable in the mouth of sacred orators, majestic on the tongues of kings, energetic in the

voice of magistrates, ravishing among the poets, and seductive when uttered by women.

The widespread usage of French is accompanied by the adoption of the "modes" and "usages" of Paris, and by the profound influence of French thought in all the orders of the mind. And this ascendancy, pacific but irresistible, practiced by the Paris of Louis XV throughout Europe, is essentially modern and Christian. For Caraccioli, the Age of Enlightenment is the marvelous flowering of the seeds sown by the Counter-Reformation, in Rome by enlightened popes, in Paris by the French monarchy, great under Louis XIV, gracious under Louis XV. It was in Paris that a secular society could flourish that, priding itself on neither sanctity nor devotion, quite humanely fulfilled the evangelical beatitudes by the gentleness and intelligence of its manners, with all its absurdities, its defects, and its excesses, but also with a certain humor à la Montaigne. This reading of the eighteenth century as a peak of European civilization countermands many of today's received historiographic schemes. It agrees with the enthusiasm of the Goncourts and readily adapts to the notions of ancien régime *longue durée* maturity, defended in our days by Pierre Gaxotte, Michel Antoine, and Pierre Chaunu.

If the most Christian monarchy, by becoming an administrative regime, acquired a European diffusion and influence, it is because this stable regime permitted the realm's natural impulses to manifest all its positive moral qualities and to attenuate its political defects of querulous anxiety and abrupt changes of mood. Even the wars of Louis XIV, even the unjust revocation of the Edict of Nantes, Caraccioli recalls, became "occasions for distributing Frenchmen in every country" and for seeing their soldiers "transformed into kind warriors who, having fought, thereupon gave themselves up to the pleasures of society with a politesse that charmed the very peoples whose towns and fields had been devastated." All the more reason under Louis XV, when that king's temperament tended toward a "universal policy of peace," and when "several French writers" (homage to Voltaire) cast "an eternal ridicule upon wars and those who seek to wage them": now the magnetization of amenity, of gaiety, of the spirit of society, of gallantry, and of amity in the conduct of life itself as in the ordering of minds that characterized the "genius" of the French had become universal and irresistible. "The Europeans, almost universally on their guard, had become communicative only when they had assumed French manners."

This modern evangelization (so opposed to the sort that Chateaubriand would describe in his *Life of Napoléon*: "Like Muhammad with the sword and the Koran, we proceeded with the sword in one hand and the Rights of Man in the other") had transfigured the European Republic of Letters. Foreigners owed to French jurisconsults "the advantage of being more distinct, and consequently more precise, in their petitions and in their transactions." From the example France had afforded, European men of letters no longer conversed, as in the past, solely in order to dispute and to vie in erudition:

> Our books of every sort have much hastened the revolution that constitutes the subject of this work. These men who write so agreeably, and on such attractive subjects, so said the Europeans, must themselves be very agreeable, and we cannot do better than copy them. Whereupon once the Russian took up his pen, even as the Swede, we have seen coming from their hands books imitated from those printed in Paris.

What was true of books was quite as true of newspapers and periodicals:

> Question the studious men of Bohemia, Transylvania, Kurland, and they will speak of our authors as we ourselves speak of them.... It is the consequence of our newpapers and journals.... The ambassadors make them known, the foreigners who have traveled send for them, and communications occur with the greatest celerity. It was after the reading of our periodical literature that the Abbé Lami, famous for his erudition, produced a literary gazette in Florence, and thereafter

various journals, as lively as they were useful, appeared in Mannheim, Brussels, Liège, Bologna.... As for the gazettes, which were born in Venice, one observes that they are today almost all written in French: a great variety of voices indicating that the French language is truly universal.

Royal academies engendered, in imitation throughout Europe, "innumerable societies that now rejoice in a well-deserved reputation." French colleges inspired the reformation of their European equivalent: "The Theresian College of Vienna was founded in imitation of that of La Flèche, that of Warsaw resembles Juilly, and those of Rome bear a close resemblance to Mazarin, Harcourt, Lisieux."

FRENCH EUROPE

Borne by a rivalry of intelligences that carried on a dialogue in the same language and received an analogous education, the theses inspired by the "philosophic spirit," like the civil tolerance and inoculation the English had advocated coldly and without success, once they were taken up by the French, "were adopted everywhere, and it became a pleasure to profit by their example." The ephemeral and entertaining brochures, of which Paris was the horn of plenty, contributed in their turn to spreading among travelers, who devoured them eagerly and made them known throughout Europe, the vibrant spirit of the capital. For Caraccioli these essays of whimsical humor represented a further degree of that "philosophic spirit" that guides the advances of science and medicine and the general moderation of manners. In all its stages, the French spirit extended the sweet and loving "genius of Christianity" to the social, civil, and moral life of all peoples.

There is even something resolutely democratic in that sentiment of a spontaneous "plebiscite" that Caraccioli attributes to the general rallying of European opinion to the French gospel. "The greatest merit," he writes, is sustained much less by itself than by opinion, and certainly Europe would not have become French if opinion had not strongly contributed to its doing so. But the trumpet sounded with a flourish in favor of the French, and thereupon, the nations gave ear and were persuaded. Forthwith it was their amiability alone that was mentioned, and what was admired was all that they conceived with regard to the commodities of life and its pleasures. It was no use the German's creating masterpieces....

The vexed question Friedrich Sieburg would ask in 1927—"Is God French?"—had already been answered by Caraccioli.

But the most incontestable originality of *L'Europe française* is the paradoxical apology for traits of the French national character against which the philosophes, and not only Rousseau, protested as ardently as their theological adversaries: levity, a fervor for fashions, a preference for gaiety, amenity, and especially for whirligig frivolity that among the fops and dandies of Paris could verge on irresponsible extravagance. The moralist saw in this attitude toward life, which had irritated and fascinated the Europeans and which might seem incompatible with the severity of Christianity, a display of that supreme vice to which mortal humanity is vulnerable: blindness to truth about human nature and deep rooted self-satisfaction, pedantic or even wicked. That "diversion" reviled by Pascal, when pervaded by "wit," had become a superior exercise of humility and humor. This was a happy diversion, in France, of the temptations of intellectual pride and political frenzy. Even in themselves, the graces and social follies of the French have a power to soften hardened hearts and to advance the victory—in the absence of that sanctity reserved for certain rare great souls—of humanity over inhumanity. This Christian moralist of the Enlightenment was not really indulgent or laxist. He continued and carried out to their final consequences the Christian anthropology of Montaigne, Charron, and François de Sales.

The theater, and not only tragedy or serious comedy but the Favart *opéra-comique*, forebear of Offenbach or of Meilhac and Halévy, has contributed, Caraccioli boldy contends, to the conversion of Europe to *la vie en douceur:*

> Danes, Swedes, Italians, all return from Paris enchanted by the entertainments staged there, and it is not only the boulevard spectacles that seduce them. They take everything away with them, including the comic operas and the new comedies. Today there is virtually no court in Germany that is without its French comedy, and strange as it seems, in the very midst of Poland's devastation there is invariably some turn or other that seems to sweeten their miseries.... The Spaniard himself, so proud and so serious, pays homage to French comedy, for there is a *théâtre français* in Cadiz; and it is a consequence of this memorable fact that Spain can afford her plays a natural expression, doing so by bringing them close to the manners of Paris.[2]

The arts of the table, associated by the French with the art of conversation, have helped transform the Europeans from guzzling beasts into guests at profane feasts:

> [Nowadays] no one drinks more in Warsaw and in Prague than is consumed in Paris. Foreigners, either by frequenting the French ambassadors or by coming to France themselves, have finally learned that temperance is the particular virtue of well-bred persons. How embarrassing a Russian dinner table used to be, and nowadays what freedom, what pleasure! Everyone speaks there with interest, everyone laughs with restraint, everyone eats with delicacy, and this is yet another French miracle. One dines at Milan, ever since the Maréchal de Villars introduced the custom of giving dinners; one feasts

2. *L'Europe française*, chapter 25, "On Spectacles."

at Turin and one begins in Rome, according to the good example of the French ambassadors, to know what fine food is, and occasionally how to serve it.[3]

The apostolate of the French does not invoke the grim countenance or the sermons of professors of ethics: "Gaiety, more than any amount of lessons, has corrected the unsociability of most Europeans...."[4] "Any number of times, in the cafés of Munich as often as in Berlin, in Liège as in Rotterdam, the company assumes, upon the mere inspection of a Frenchman, his way of behaving, of presenting himself, of being."[5]

And Caraccioli does not hesitate to pronounce the most scandalous of his paradoxes: "Without his levity, the Frenchman would not have charmed the Europeans, would not have seduced them...."[6] Or better still: "Merit makes enemies only too frequently, and amiability reconciles all minds."[7]

It is a fact that this dancer's levity, alien to any idea of weight or effort, is not necessarily an absence of "merit." It is rather the attitude of a freedom quite determined not to concede anything to its chains. "The Frenchman," Caraccioli wrote, " would never have gallicized—and enfranchised—the nations of Europe had he been the slave of custom or of prejudice.... Any yoke but a rational obedience weighs him down, which is why he always seems to be doing just as he likes."[8] Anticipating Jean Cocteau or Jean d'Ormesson, to say nothing of Nietzsche's cherished notion of "freedom in chains," Caraccioli here defines what makes incomparable the true *politesse à la française*: "frank, at ease, granting each his own." It is not surprising that such an art of manners should have become, as well as an object of desire and imitation, a target of *ressentiment*.

---

3. *L'Europe française*, chapter 28, "Of Tables."
4. *L'Europe française*, chapter 30, "Of Gaiety."
5. *L'Europe française*, chapter 31, "Of Cafés."
6. *L'Europe française*, chapter 34, "On Levity."
7. *L'Europe française*, chapter 34, "On Levity."
8. *L'Europe française*, chapter 36, "On Liberty."

This has become a model, especially among the Poles, who, ever fawning on one another, used to express their attachment and their respect by bows and curtseys that were as painful as they were humiliating, but that today release them from such cruel shackles.... It was an ugly spectacle, before this last century, to see the crudity of the Germans and the Dutch. The manners of the nations have become civilized, and from that happy revolution has resulted an amenity that cannot be valued too highly.[9]

THE FRENCH TALENT

From the so-called levity of the French to their fashions, to their frivolity, to their talent for amusing themselves is only a step. Convinced that "evil, like good, enters into the order of events and is frequently its cause," Caraccioli ventures with assurance into those regions anathematized by theologians and disdained by philosophers. It is by their weakness, which they hitherto dared neither to acknowledge nor to accept, that foreigners have been converted by the French:

"I find the folly of the French inconceivable" is the grave utterance of a German nobleman of thirty-two quarterings, pulling on a pink suit of clothes trimmed with gold and applegreen braid. "They cannot be serious if they suppose they are setting an example for us." And simultaneously he orders his valet de chambre, lately arrived from Paris, to pick him out a sword-knot in the latest style.... What lectures had been unable to accomplish in the course of half a century, fashions achieve in a moment; nothing is so swift as that which is done in imitation.[10]

9. *L'Europe française*, chapter 39, "On Politeness."
10. *L'Europe française*, chapter 11, "On Fashions."

The Parisian dandies, to whom Jean Monnet insufficiently resorted in order to realize his postwar dream, in the eighteenth century had been the light cavalry of that first European unification that had also been a transition from barbarism to Enlightenment: "And behold the beings who have managed to transform Europe. When the need is great, everything serves. It required their whims, their simpers, their jargon in order to introduce amenity. True chameleons, they changed color moment by moment, and it was their variety, their mobility, their agility that produced their charms."[11]

The most magical embellishment of the Château de Versailles, Veronese's *Feast in the House of Simon*, a gift from the Republic of Venice to Louis XIV, represents Jesus, the Word incarnate, luminous with grave sweetness, in the midst of a sumptuous banquet where all the delights of color melt into a shifting array featuring apostles and tailors, lords and ladies luxuriously dressed in the latest fashions, valets and chambermaids, huge hounds and tiny lapdogs, and every kind of discourse, from the most profane to the most sacred. This riot of handsome creatures and elegant costumes, of glistening furs and luxuriant flesh, composes at once a splendid Christian *vanitas* and a fragile moment of Epicurian *voluptas* to which Christ's mercy grants the same grace as the painter himself. An unforgettable poem of humanity reconciled with its own carnal and ephemeral condition. Veronese had received objections—fortunately not implacable ones—from the Holy Office for having too intimately confused essential with innocent accessories. One might say that Caraccioli abounds in the spirit of *The Feast in the House of Simon* (one of the icons of rococo art) when he represented Europe united around Louis XV and converted to a conversation *à la française*:

> The world has been seduced by the way people talk in France.
> It is amenity itself speaking, candor itself that laughs, what is

---

11. *L'Europe française*, chapter 11, "On Fashions."

agreeable mingles with what is useful, what is news with what is unspeakable, and conversation moves from one subject to the next as imperceptibly as the most delicate nuances, among the tenderest colors happily blended.... An Englishman never used to have any subject but that which concerned his government; an Italian talked only about music; a Dutchman only about his commercial interests; a Swiss gentleman only about his country; a Pole about his freedom; an Austrian about his lineage. Now there is a unison of voices for the ways of conversation. We speak of everything, and we speak well.[12]

Nothing is known of Louis-Antoine Caraccioli's fate during the Terror, except that in 1795 the Convention of Thermidor granted him a pension of two thousand francs, which suggests the level of poverty to which he had fallen. Like all generous-spirited men, he welcomed the Revolution favorably. In 1785 he published a work entitled *Jesus Christ, by His Tolerance the Model of Legislators*, dedicated to the glory of Louis XVI, emancipator of Protestants and Jews. In 1789 he produced *The Magnificat of the Third Estate, to Be Sung on April 26 in the First Vespers of the States General*, as well as *On the Prerogatives of the Third Estate, by the Duchess of ——, Born a Commoner*, which is a sufficient indication of his hopes. In 1790 two more of his works were printed: *Abbé Maury, Hand on Heart, or the Passion of our good and humane clergy, the Office of Good Friday* and *La Petite Lutèce Now Great, wherein is to be seen her adventures and her revolution from her origin to July 14, 1790, the date of her majority and of a federative constitution*. Thereafter, silence until his death in 1803. Below may be read the conclusion of *L'Europe française*, a song of departure from a first "globalization" according to the spirit and the manners of the French realm, but that concluded so poorly for having renounced its evangelical inspiration.

---

12. *L'Europe française*, chapter 43, "On Conversation."

FROM *L'EUROPE FRANÇAISE* (1774)

I breathe at last! Europe is now the most agreeable abode in the entire universe.... Nothing is more advantageous than having crossed by means of public highways and public posts the enormous interval that separated the Europeans from one another.... Paris now touches Petersburg, Rome, Constantinople, and there is but one family that inhabits different regions....

I no longer meet with that fanaticism that seized upon the language of religion to set nation against nation....

The manner of study is virtually uniform.... Superstition hides its face, and religion shows itself.

If I examine society, I find it the same among all Europeans, always allowing for certain nuances. Gentleness constitutes the basis of this circumstance, amenity, and refinement. The same games are played, the same arguments are offered in support of the same ideas, the same sentiments. Women are educated in Naples as they are in Paris, in London as in Madrid; and they constitute the delight of all societies. The querulous wit that plays on a word's hidden meanings is no longer heeded. Only certain Italians preserve their concetti, *and will keep them because they cling to their language, of which they are properly proud.*

On all sides that work is sought out that bears the sign of delicacy and genius, and it is universally desired that such a work be written in French; that is the one language that is everywhere spoken with pleasure and that would become unique, if the majority of Europeans were consulted.

There are no longer any fashions but those that are French. The English go to enormous trouble to sustain theirs, but they are preserved only out of vanity.

One dresses in Vienna as in Paris, and one is coiffed in Dresden as in Lyon.

Italian exaggeration, German etiquette, Spanish arrogance have given way to French usages. No one cares any longer for what hampers and constrains, and the advantages of birth and of rank are sacrificed to the pleasures of sociability. Highness even as Eminence and Excellency, even as Grandeur, deign to laugh with persons who possess neither titles nor prerogatives, nor quarterings of nobility to display.... Happy transformation, which has reformed manners, by seeming to change no more than their garments!

There is now but one table among all the Grandees of Europe, but one and the same manner of dining. In every court is known that exquisite delicacy that affords almost as much pleasure from the sight of the dishes prepared as from their taste....

[At meals] people converse with interest, they... laugh freely. Certain literary disputes without bitterness, certain trifles without triviality, certain agreeable discoveries without indiscretion, enliven the diners and entertain them....

French politeness meets with no recalcitrance once it has been introduced among the nations. There is no one who fails to love ease and honesty.

Europe therefore is now a map on which all parts are admirably linked...; from which I conclude that the charms of amity and insinuation cannot be resisted, and that as the years accumulate, the more French amenity will prevail—that amenity that gives such pleasure to the most serious things as it gives interest to the most insignificant.

Inhabitants of the various parts of Europe, if this book should reach you, tell yourselves: it would not exist had we not desired it. What it discloses to the public eye is precisely what we do. It proves that we are French for our language, for our behavior, for adaptations, for readings, for opinions, and we unceasingly express that quality in our manners....

20. Gustav III of Sweden: A Parisian from Stockholm

IN THE MEMORY of Europe, of which Goethe was an irreplaceable witness, only ancient Rome has exerted an *étoilement*—what Hollywood calls a stardom—as far-flung and as ineffaceable as that of France. The imprint of Rome—its law, its language, its cities, and its vines—remains engraved even today within the *limes* that the Emperor Aurelian ordered built in the third century to protect the empire, an absurd military strategy but an irrefutable reckoning of an enduring configuration. The gentler degree of civilization represented by France presupposes the earthworks and the foundations left by Rome. The forms France introduced and spread are not so much mineral as they are moral. Its intelligence, less architectonic, is more subtly pliable, disposed to diplomacy and to happiness. Its language is less imperious than persuasive and luminous. France represents a certain progress in the seductive luxury of both heart and mind. Hence its expansion has been much greater. There is not nor can there be a French *limes* or a French Great Wall of China. The "doctrine of natural frontiers," and with all the more reason that of the Maginot Line, have worked against the deepest vocation of the realm, whose shifting and provisional form has never presented an obstacle to the attraction exerted by its most powerful magnets, neither power nor wealth for their own sake, but the art of rendering earth and our passage upon it more spiritual, that is to say, less ponderous, more enlightened. Thirteenth-century France, its knights, its poets, its *romanciers*, had impregnated with its heroic actions and its Frankish language not only the Mediterranean and the Near East but also a French Europe already more extensive than the Emperor Aurelian's.

Eighteenth-century France could lay a claim to Russia, insinuated itself into China, implanted itself in North America, and reigned over a French Europe without having to occupy the Continent in military terms. It even seduced Scandinavia where, already under Louis XIII, Christina of Sweden, daughter of Gustav Adolph Vasa, Richelieu's powerful ally, had given it in Stockholm a bridgehead of learned men, philosophers, and savants. Descartes came, and with him Claude Saumaise, Samuel Sorbière, Samuel Bochart, and the poet Saint-Amant.

Now that Sweden, along with Finland and Austria, has joined the new Europe, the moment has come to remember that "French influence" had already won over to Europe those Vikings whom Rome and its armies had not even dreamed of including in its vast empire. Gustav III of Sweden, born in 1746 and reigning from 1771 to 1792, incarnates, better than any other Enlightenment sovereign, that favorable climate of good manners, alert intelligence, and refined taste at the heart of which *le parler français* conducted European affairs and brought them to a certain maturity, often for the best and rarely for the worst.

A FRANCOPHILE PRINCE

Gustav III's mother, Louisa Ulrika of Prussia, was one of Frederick II's sisters, and like her brother, she had corresponded with Voltaire. With an older son brought up *à la française* by his first tutor, Count Tessin, and by his mentor, Count Scheffer, she might have found grounds for an affective understanding in their common passion for everything—books, periodicals, plays—that came from France; but this dry and haughty Prussian noblewoman of the old squirearchy harshly tried the prince's lively "sensibility" (the word then a neologism), though without managing to undermine his character, his intelligence, or his freedom. In 1778 he had been king for seven years, and succeeded in stoically withstanding the unprecedented scandal that the widowed Queen Mother created in the eyes of all Europe, and that fatally affected the Vasa dynasty, by publicly insinuating that her own son's firstborn was a bastard, thereby authorizing the rumor propagated by the anti-French Bonnets Party, according to which the king of Sweden, her husband, like her brother the king of Prussia, preferred men to women.

Gustav III's unqualified Francophilia declared itself very early, when he was merely the crown prince. This attachment to a distant France was the vehicle of the Chapeaux Party, of which the prince was the leader, and which regrouped at the court of Stockholm the adversaries of the influence and the intrigues of a too closely neighboring Russia, supported in the Swedish Diet by the Bonnets Party. In 1767, attentive to all the literary events of the French capital, the crown prince began a correspondence with Marmontel and enthusiastically praised his "philosophical" novel *Bélisaire*, condemned by the Sorbonne. The letters of Count Scheffer's pupil were spangled with all the neologisms then the passwords of "philosophy": beneficence, reason, humanity, sensibility, virtue, tenderness, and the adjectives attached thereto. In the *Bélisaire* controversy, in which Marmontel owed his salvation to Mme Geoffrin, the all-too-sensitive descendant of Gustav Adolph and Charles XII was carefully maneuvered. Marmontel was eager to have published, by a subterfuge that managed to keep him out of the limelight, the letter of sympathy from the crown prince thanking him for the gift of *Bélisaire*, which put the imprudent prince in difficulty in his own country, where the Lutheran clergy was up in flames against him. The poor fellow was already opposed by the pro-Russian party and now the pious were on his back as well.

In 1771, following the lead of his younger brother Charles, who was the first to visit Paris and Versailles, the crown prince was finally able to make a private visit to France. "I have arrived," he wrote on February 7 to his sister Sophie-Albertine, "in this city I have so long desired to see and that everyone is so concerned about at home." He was not disappointed. Louis XV received him at Versailles and Marly. He would never forget the gracious majesty of the king of France, whose support would never fail him. In Paris, he made the acquaintance of "almost all the philosophes: Marmontel, Grimm,

Thomas, Morellet, Helvétius." But at close range Marmontel did not correspond to the bucolic notion he had conceived of him from his works: "He is an energumen," he wrote his mother, "who talks with a kind of extreme enthusiasm and who is the greatest possible republican." He frequented the theaters, but his stay was interrupted by the news of the death of his father, Adolph Frederick. Gustav was now the king of Sweden and head of his country's Lutheran Church.

Preoccupied by the example of Poland, and by the parlementary *fronde* he had observed in France, the new sovereign, eager to be faithful to the inspiration of the Enlightenment, put an end to an "anarchy" whose principle, as in Poland, lay in the powers of an aristocratic Diet too readily swayed by Russian gold. A peaceful coup d'état, fervently accepted by the populace, suspended this nobiliary parliament. Gustav III reestablished in his own favor the equilibrium of powers, promulgating a constitutional law that limited the Diet's future jurisdiction (August 21, 1772). "Never," he wrote proudly to the Comtesse d'Egmont, the Maréchal de Richelieu's daughter, "has a revolution taken place more gently and peacefully than this one." This authoritative action was approved in Versailles as well as in Stockholm's streets, and the following year Louis XV would not hesitate to threaten Catherine II, who was preparing an invasion, that he would send a fleet and an expeditionary force of 15,000 to Sweden if that kingdom's independence were threatened. The tsarina understood the message and lay low.

Having become virtually absolute, the king intended to rule as an "enlightened" prince. He regularly notified Voltaire to witness the phenomenon, sending him his latest edicts and his court theater programs (in French) and announcements of court festivals: "It is chiefly to you," he wrote the philosopher,

> that the human mind owes the advantage of surmounting and destroying the barriers that ignorance, fanaticism, and a false political program have raised against it. Your writings have enlightened Princes as to their true interests. You have shown them, with that amenity that you alone can give to

even the most serious matters, that the more enlightened a people is, the more peaceful and loyal they will be with regard to their obligations. Hence it is only just that you should receive the first homage that reason renders to humanity.

In 1776, having learned of the first French victories in the service of the American insurgents, he wrote the Comtesse de Boufflers, morganatic "widow" of the Prince de Conti:

Furthermore, I congratulate you on the English losses in their colonies. As a good Frenchwoman, you must participate in them, and as a philosopher, such great events are entirely worthy of your attention. The spectacle of a state creating itself is of such interest that if I were not what I am, I should go to America to follow at closer range every nuance of the creation of this new republic.[1]

In 1777 the Francophile king made an official journey to St. Petersburg, where his cousin Catherine II received him with great ceremony, though without showing a trace of reciprocal sympathy corresponding to the public exhibition of good feeling. In 1783, his reign continuing successfully, he decided to draw tighter the bonds of friendship with France, now under a new reign. He had remained in daily relation with life in Paris and Versailles by reading the periodicals (Linguet's *Annales politiques, civiles, et littéraires* and *Le Courrier de l'Europe*, a pro-Insurgent journal created by Beaumarchais and published in London, like the *Annales*). He supplied them both with news of Sweden. His correspondence with his ambassador, Count Creutz, who would soon become his prime minis-

---

1. See the correspondence in French between Catherine II and her cousin Gustav III, collected by Gunnar von Proschwitz, in the splendid edition he edited: *Catherine II et Gustave II: Une Correspondance retrouvée* (Stockholm National Museum, 1998). It runs from 1771 to 1792, but is particularly intense in the years 1790 to 1792. (*Gustave III par ses lettres* [Stockholm: Norstedt/Paris: Touzot, 1986], p. 156.)

ter, kept him closely informed of the actual state of affairs at the court of France and the moods of Parisian opinion. Upon Necker's request, the count's successor at Versailles would be the insipid Baron de Staël-Holstein, engaged, on these conditions, to Germaine, daughter of the Genevan banker then director of the treasury, later of finance in 1777–1778. The king of Sweden also possessed at Versailles a young friend who was almost as dear to him as to Queen Marie-Antoinette: Count von Fersen, the son, however, of one of his bitterest political adversaries. On September 21, to the fury of his father, Fredrik Axel, Fersen *fils* was appointed proprietary colonel of the Royal Suédois, the regiment of the queen's personal guard.

Under the name of Count de Haga, Gustav III began his pilgrimage to the Latin south by visiting Italy, arriving in October 1783. Young Count Hans Axel von Fersen figured in his retinue. He made a long stop in Rome, where the French ambassador, Cardinal de Bernis, gave in his honor and in that of Joseph II, also journeying incognito, one of those French festivities of which his predecessors Polignac and Choiseul had set the inimitable tone; their successor Chateaubriand would awaken the nostalgic echo of them for a memorable evening at the Villa Médicis in 1828. Every subsequent evening of Count de Haga's sojourn, Cardinal de Bernis received the Swedes at supper as particular friends of France. The pope in person invited his Lutheran confrere along with his companions to visit the splendid collection of antiquities exhibited in the Museo Clementino.

The joyous company then turned back toward Paris, arriving in June 1784. The king was received quite fraternally at Versailles by Louis XVI and Marie-Antoinette, for whom, coached by Fersen, Gustav III immediately developed a sort of worship. He encountered in Paris his titled correspondent the Comtesse de Boufflers and this political schemer's noble friends, the Maréchale de Luxembourg, the Princesse de Beauvau-Craon, and the Comtesse de Forcalquier. He had the good fortune to arrive in time to attend, at the Comédie-Française, two performances of *Le Mariage de Figaro*, Beaumarchais's comedy first performed on April 27, which the king described, without a trace of reprobation, as "insolent": he soon engaged in a very friendly correspondence with the playwright. At the Opéra he attended the premiere of *Didon*, a work by a protégé of Marie-Antoinette, the Italian composer Piccini, on a libretto by Marmontel. His stay culminated in the party given in his honor by the queen at Trianon on June 24, 1784. To his prime minister Creutz, remaining in command at Stockholm, the king described the event as a diplomatic triumph:

> The queen's party at Trianon was charming indeed. In the little theater there, they put on M. de Marmontel's *Dormeur éveillé*, the music by Grétry, with all the scenery and the ballet from the Opéra production, combined with the forces of the Comédie Italienne. The awarding of the Diamond Ribbon ended the spectacle, supper was served in the pavilions of the gardens, and after supper the English garden was illuminated. It was a total enchantment. The queen had permitted respectable persons who had not been invited to supper to stroll in the gardens, and everyone had been requested to dress in white, which truly afforded a spectacle of the Elysian Fields. The queen did not sit down at table, but did the honors as they might have been done by any self-confident lady of the house. She spoke to each of the Swedes in turn and saw to their needs with extreme care and attention. The entire royal family was present, wards of the court and their wives, captains of the Royal Guards, leaders of the other troops of the king's house, and of course the Swedish ambassador. The Princesse de Lamballe was the only person of royal blood in attendance.[2]

The city did not lag behind the court. The king's correspondence singles out one by one the very women whose heads would one by one be cut off within a short time, as would be the majority of those of the ravishing models of Mme Vigée-Lebrun and David: "Mme de Pons," wrote the king to his prime minister,

---

2. *Gustave III par ses lettres*, p. 268.

gave in my honor, last Tuesday, a party with illuminations, performances, amusing varieties, and a balloon loaded with firecrackers. All the great nobility of the realm was present. One could not turn around without encountering some de Rohan, de Montmorency, or de Brissac.... Mme de Pons had made every effort to provide all the graces and all the attentions possible. Mme la Maréchale de Noailles took supper there and, for all her devoutness, attended Janot's performance afterward.[3]

Back in Stockholm the king revived the Swedish Académie de Belles-Lettres founded in 1753 by his mother. In 1786 he would create on his own initiative a Swedish Academy based on the Académie Française. He constructed on the model of the little Théâtre de la Reine at Trianon a playhouse in the park of his castle at Drottningholm. In 1932 it would be rediscovered intact and in working condition—costumes, sets, makeup, and machinery. No one since the king's death had ever entered this sleeping beauty of a theater; its very existence had been forgotten for a century and a half.

The war between Sweden and Russia of 1788–1790, from which he sought repose by translating into Swedish canto 2 of Voltaire's *Henriade*, did not keep Gustav III from following with tormented and perspicacious attention the first signs of a France *"anglisée,"* as he called it, and then the bloody progress of the Revolution. On August 7, 1789, he wrote to the Baron von Stedingk:

I shall now distress in you the French colonel attached to the queen and to France. Nothing more frightful can be described than what occurred at Paris on July 12, 13, 14, and 15. The Invalides occupied, cannon and arms employed against the Bastille, that fortress taken by assault, the governor M. de Launay dragged by the populace to the Place de Grève, decapitated,

---

3. Janot was a fashionable clown of the day. *Gustave III par ses lettres*, p. 269.

the head carried around the city in triumph, the same treatment inflicted on the merchants' provost.... Finally the king, accompanied only by Monsieur and the Comte d'Artois, went on foot, without retinue, amid the assembly of the States General to make something like honorable amends, requesting assistance in putting down the disturbances. That is what has occurred; that is how weakness, irresolution, and an unprepared and impudent violence will overturn the throne of Louis XIV.[4]

In September 1790, sated by Hans Axel von Fersen with the sinister news from Paris, he wrote to his old friend Baron von Taube: "It seems to me that the chaos [in France] is at its peak and that we must form a league like that of the Greeks against Troy in order to restore order and avenge the honor of certain crowned heads. I should dearly love to be the Agamemnon of such an army."[5] Indeed, immediately upon the conclusion of peace with Catherine II, he vainly solicited the French royal couple (utterly deprived of means), the attentive but laggard tsarina, Marie-Antoinette's brother Emperor Leopold, as well as his Chancellor von Kaunitz (who turned a deaf ear), and even the English government (which of course declared itself "neutral"), in hopes of devising a common strategy to arrange the flight of the French sovereigns and to offer the Revolution a united and resolute European front. His letters to Fersen show that the latter was his personal representative and his interpreter to the royal couple shut up in the Tuileries. As for himself, there was no limit to his will to save a dynasty to which he correctly assumed he owed a great deal. For lack of anything better, he did the impossible from Stockholm in order to support Fersen's impotent attempts with a view to organizing at least a second escape of the royal family. A letter from Fersen to the Baron von Taube, dated April l, 1792, is shaken with sobs mingling anguish for the queen's

4. *Gustave III par ses lettres*, p. 512.
5. *Gustave III par ses lettres*, p. 338.

fate and the horror of being forever deprived of Gustav III's support and affection:

> My friend, I am overwhelmed, I am alarmed, and I lack the power to express to you all that my soul is feeling. Your old valet de chambre Jean has arrived, he is going to Spain, and has told me everything. My condition can only be conceived by what must be your own, and this certainty further augments my distress. My grief is profound, and my uncertainty is terrible. You may judge of my suffering by the true attachment I feel for the king, which I shall endure and which I owe him in so many ways. Such sentiments can never fade from my heart, and my only wishes, those that I form in the best part of my heart, are that God will have the grace to allow me the possibility of proving such a thing to him.[6]

On March 16, during the fatal masked ball immortalized by Verdi's opera that bears this title, the king had been wounded by a pistol at the Stockholm Opera. He died thirteen days later. Fersen, on March 29, had just learned the news in Paris.

GUSTAV III AS A LETTER-WRITER

A few quotations suffice to measure the king of Sweden's talent as a letter-writer in French. Of all the crowned heads of the Enlightenment, only Stanisław Poniatowski can rival him for the vitality and the nuance of his French prose. Gunnar von Proschwitz, who has done so much to afford some justice to Gustav III and to the "golden age" he granted his realm, has written: "His natural style, lively, fresh, and witty, gives his correspondence an original physiognomy and assures Gustav III a place of his own among the cultivated men of his time. Even in the eyes of the French, severe judges not easy to

---

6. *Gustave III par ses lettres*, p. 375.

please in matters of style, Gustav III's French has found grace. Diderot makes a great case of one of his letters to Marmontel."[7] He wrote to Sophie Volland: "Our language must be in very wide use in all those countries of the north, for these letters, had they been written by our most polished courtiers, could not have been better." Similarly, Beaumarchais gives free rein to his enthusiasm, and a French official report offers this commentary: "His [Gustav III's] manner is agreeable, his gestures, all his movements are as lively as his discourse. He has nothing of the foreigner about him. He is a bit too fond of talking, but speaks well, pronounces French well, and one must pay very close attention to perceive whatever tiny faults he occasionally makes in our language."

To give some notion of this Swedish court where French was spoken, as well as of the king's style, here are some letters of his and of those close to him. The first, addressed to Crown Prince Gustav, then eleven years old, by his tutor, Count Scheffer, is a veritable initiation into the French civilization of forms. The next two, one from the crown prince, the other from his brother, give a lively image of the Paris of Louis XV, where they sojourned, one after the other, at the end of their father's reign. The last letter, from Gustav III to the Comtesse de Boufflers, shows the sovereign in full possession of his political judgment and of his stylistic instrument.

From Count Scheffer to Crown Prince Gustav

Monseigneur,
When I have the honor of proposing that Your Royal Highness might venture to write letters, Your Highness always raises great difficulties, and prefers to such exercise others that are actually much more difficult. However, I know that Your Highness is quite determined, as is quite natural, upon those projects that will cost him the least effort. I must therefore suppose, Monseigneur, that the composition of a letter must seem to Your Highness an extremely painful activity; this is an error,

---

7. *Gustave III par ses lettres,* pp. 11–12.

which doubtless proceeds from no more than the unjust notion Your Highness may have formed of the nature of epistolary style. I have no desire to offer Your Highness a dissertation upon this subject here; you will soon find as much difficulty in reading letters as in writing them. But if Your Highness wishes to know just what epistolary style is, you have merely to read the letters of Mme de Sévigné; you will have the sense of hearing a conversation, that of a mother speaking to her daughter as if they were together, face-to-face. If you find a good deal of wit in these letters, it is because Mme de Sévigné had a great deal of that characteristic, and because one speaks wittily when one has wit. But these letters to which I allude were never praised because they were witty; those of Voiture and Rabutin were quite as much so; rather they have been praised, admired, even adopted as models for letters because they were simple and natural, not because wit was artfully inserted within them, but as it would be found in the mouth of a person to whom it has not even occurred to possess such a thing. From this you may conclude, Monseigneur, that with regard to letters, it is no more difficult to write them than to speak. All that resembles conversation is good, all that has a more prepared and affected quality good taste will infallibly condemn. I daresay that after learning this Your Royal Highness, who speaks with such ease, will write in the same manner when you choose to do so. As an experiment, Your Highness will permit me to request a response to this very letter, and that without giving it another thought you will tell me quite naturally what you would have answered had I expressed aloud what I have just had the honor to write to Your Highness. If you follow such advice, Monseigneur, you will be surprised by the facility of what you presently regard as so difficult, and I wager that you will succeed, to the point of exclaiming: Is that all it is?

I should similarly rejoice to succeed in convincing you of all the sentiments by which I am animated in your regard, and which authorize me not only to speak to you with the profound respect that is your due and with which I shall be, my life long, Monseigneur, Your Royal Highness's most humble, obedient, and faithful servant.

Ulricsdal, April 7, 1757
Carl Fr. Scheffer

From Prince Charles to Crown Prince Gustav[8]

My Dear Brother,
I have at last left this Paris so vaunted, so desired, and so loved. What
an assemblage of pleasure, of amenities, and what a contrast of beauty
and villainy, of slovenliness, vices, and profligacy. To know this place,
it must be seen from all sides. Paris is a city that is very large, very
populous, but the beauties of which do not strike you at the first glance,
the houses and palaces being surrounded by walls, one sees their archi-
tecture only in the courtyard, and the street is embellished only on the
outside of the walls. The populace, which is to be found every hour of
the day at various entertainments and promenades, makes one judge
of the great number of folk that happen to be kept in this place, but
when one sees their poverty one judges that they pay very dear for the
pleasures and the movements of the great ones. What is to be admired
in Paris is the perfection of the arts and sciences, the paintings of all
kinds; what is to be seen at the Salon suggests the skill of the French
and the perfection of their genius, the literary abilities, and the good
taste that prevails in everything that is done, which justly deserves the
approval of the foreigners who try to imitate such models.

But when one regards the confusion of manners, the depravity and
libertinage prevailing everywhere, one finds our fatherland fortunate
in being ignorant of such dreadful customs, and one hopes never to
acquire here at home perfections so notably wicked and depraved. Cer-
tain gatherings where women of quality mingle with whores are left on
occasion by elegant gentlemen in order to venture to associate with the
latter. This occurs quite shamelessly, and no one is embarrassed by the
least irregularity. I have seen the Duc de Chartres with the Duc de
Lauzun, the Duc d'Aumont, and several other dukes showing them-
selves with Mme de Mirepoix, Mme de Villeroy, and Mme de Mont-
morency and then leaving them in order to chat with whores, taking
them by the arm, walking with them, and going off to dine with them,
while the other ladies merely laugh at the incident and say: Where do

---

8. *Gustave III par ses lettres*, p. 90–92.

you suppose they're going, those wild fellows? and then continue on their way. That is the kind of thing that has greatly surprised me and to which I cannot become accustomed during my stay in this city.

The Duc de Choiseul, who has shown me many kindnesses, has twice had me to supper, along with the Comte de Sparre, colonel in the Royal Suédois regiment. Other days have been spent visiting châteaux and palaces, private collections, academies, theatrical performances, and splendid drives.

Two days before I left, I received my audience with the King, not being able do so previously, he being occupied with Parlements and internal affairs, sessions of Justice, etc.

I have not seen Mme du Barry, out of regard for the Duc de Choiseul, who has refused all contact with her, and no minister or other foreigner has seen her at home or at the theater or at Fontainebleau, only Count Hassenstein has done so, but having decided not to concern himself with what people will say, he may do anything he likes. The other day he made a very clever remark in her boudoir, and that has somewhat compensated the Duc de Choiseul for the frequent visits he used to make to that lady.

Being at her toilette, she put on her most imposing airs, since several persons were present, and declared that she would buy a tiger and place it in her antechamber, but requested the company to inform her what the creature should be given to eat. Each person offered his or her opinion, some suggesting vegetables, others advocating a chicken, and other such nonsense. When she asked the advice of Count Hassenstein, he said: "Feed it a courtier, Madame. That won't cost you much." This remark was greeted with a good deal of laughter, though it was hardly agreeable to the lady.

I left Paris three days ago. Traveling night and day, I arrived here yesterday, where the most urgent of my tasks was to remind you of my existence, my dear Brother. I shall remain here several days, and then move on to Cassel, and from there, after passing some while in Brunswick, I expect to spend a month or perhaps only three weeks in Berlin. In this fashion, I expect to be seeing you soon, and early in November I hope to be in Stockholm, where I shall embrace a beloved Brother and enjoy among my family those pleasures that have been unknown to me during my journey and that cannot be compared with anything else in the world.

Let the pleasures that are to be enjoyed in Sweden—and their reputation has spread as far as Frankfurt—not cause you to forget me, my dear Brother; each word I receive from my fatherland is so dear to me that I gulp down all the news I read, and when I finish I wish I were starting all over again. There is nothing like the pleasure of receiving news from home. It is much greater than the mere distraction of seeing novelties that are almost immediately forgotten once they are out of sight.

But I shall not detain you any longer, dear Brother, with all my chatter, which you will soon find to be your own case, once you share my circumstances, undertaking your first expedition. I seek to possess this moment in your recollection and your tenderest friendship, begging you to be convinced of my perfect friendship and the attachment with which I am,

My dear Brother,
Your best friend and tender brother, Charles
Frankfurt-am-Main, September 20, 1770

From Crown Prince Gustav to his mother, Louisa Ulrika, Queen of Sweden[9]

Madame,
I have just made a journey to Marly, where the King received me even more graciously than the first time. We were lodged in the apartments of the Children of France, which is a great honor and a particular mark of the King's kindness. He treats us with the greatest friendship, as if we were his own children, and he often jokes with my Brother, whose behavior is perfection itself—all the ladies here are charmed by him.

Tomorrow we go to Versailles, to participate in the King's hunt—he has sent us his own hunting uniform, as he did for the King of Den-

---

9. *Gustave III par ses lettres*, pp. 107–108.

mark. It has grown bitter cold these last few days, a winter as fierce as in Sweden, and the snow has fallen in such abundance that we rode in a sleigh all the way to Versailles.

I have already made the acquaintance of almost all the philosophers: Marmontel, Grimm, Thomas, the Abbé de Morellet, Helvétius. They are more agreeable to read than to see. It is extraordinary that Marmontel, who is so charming in his tales and so gay, should be altogether otherwise in conversation; he is an energumen who speaks with extreme enthusiasm and is the greatest republican possible. My dear Mother may well believe that it is only to Her that I dare say such a thing, and scarcely dare think it here. It would be a dreadful blasphemy for which I should never forgive myself. As for Grimm, he is more agreeable, though more reserved. Thomas speaks as forcefully as he writes, but what strikes me as a general rule among all of them is a dreadful defect, which is that they have no modesty whatsoever, they all praise themselves with as much complacency as their admirers could ever do. As for d'Alembert, I am told that he is as modest as a great philosopher should be, but I have not yet been able to visit him. Rousseau is also here, and he is no longer an Armenian but, people say, a sociable being. I have been promised that a meeting with him will be arranged.

A new play, The Ill-Natured Man, has recently been put on here, its first performance a success, but only because of Molé's acting and certain mannerisms that do not strike me as impressive at all. The piece has since been performed several times, but yesterday when it was put on again it had no success at all, and no one applauded. As soon as it is printed, I shall have the honor of sending it to you. It might do better with us, but here it is a real problem.

There is a terrible dearth, right now, of novelties and on stage nothing has been performed but The London Merchant, which was hissed. That was before I arrived. The play has just been printed, but I haven't read it yet.

I've just seen Le Kain play Nero in Britannicus. Nothing finer or more admirable can be imagined. Brizard is also a splendid actor, but for the rest we have nothing to complain of at home, and it would be wronging our ladies to find them inferior. Mme Dumesnil, who is so *highly praised, falls into the familiar style in each verse, and there are only a few moments when she is fine, but then, it is true, she is sublime. As for the rest, it is better to say nothing about them, though there is still Mme Drouin for the roles of the ridiculous countess, in which she is very good indeed. But I haven't yet seen anyone who outdid Mme Baptiste.*

As for the Comédie Italienne, it is much superior in all respects to our troupe and to that of the Comédie-Française, but I must confess that the comic operas amuse me no better here than in Stockholm.

There has just been published here a manifesto of the Confederates of Poland, which is quite well written and, curiously enough, the speech of the bishop of Kraków, for which he was dismissed, is translated in the justificatory texts. The representative of the Confederates, a very worthy fellow, has distributed the manifesto here.

They have also published Voltaire's Questions on the Encyclopedia by Admiring Readers, *but this is such a scarce item that I had the greatest difficulty even borrowing a single copy.*

The post hasn't left the last two days, which troubles me greatly: nothing is so dreadful as absence, and when I think of how many leagues separate me from all that I hold dear, and how much time remains before I return, I feel a pain that all the pleasures I enjoy here cannot make up for. That sweet emotion one feels at the heart of one's family with a Father and a Mother so rightly and so tenderly adored—such a feeling, I say, which is so natural and to which I was so accustomed, leaves a terrible void in the soul that no other feeling can replace, and renders any other quite insipid for me.

My dear Mother will forgive me this digression, but it is so sweet to be able to express in writing the feelings I find impossible to speak, everything that my heart feels, and to give way to sentiment a little when I am alone like this, in a separation that is so hard for me and to which all the time in the world cannot accustom me. I have the honor to be, with the tenderest attachment and the deepest respect, madame, the very humble and obedient son and servant of Your Majesty,

from Paris, February 17, 1771

Gustav

From Gustav III to the Comtesse de Boufflers[10]

Stockholm, June 14, 1772

I have received, Madame, two of your letters at once, one from January 12 and the other dated February. I indicate the dates to clear myself of the blame for not having responded since then. Your friendship is too precious to me for my delicacy not to be wounded by the idea that you could have easily imagined some negligence on my part—as for forgetfulness, such a thing is impossible for anyone who has known you.

Since my last letters, many things have occurred that might interest you: the spectacle that my poor fatherland affords at this moment may well deserve the attention of a person who reflects as deeply as you do. The shock of democracy against the expiring aristocracy, the latter preferring to submit to that democracy rather than to be protected by the monarchy that opened its arms—that is the political horizon that this winter would have afforded you. It is virtually the same scene that I observed in France. Here it was the aristocracy struggling against the older monarchy. But what might have consoled you is that, whatever way the scale tilted, your government would have been properly balanced, whereas here we are rapidly approaching anarchy. There are some people who would have me believe that this is for the best regarding my particular interests, but, accustomed as I am to envisage only those of the State as a whole, I groan as a good citizen over the fate of a people who deserve to be happy, who desire to become so, but whom some fanatical and ambitious demagogues are leading into every imaginable disaster by denaturing the truest and most salutary principles. The spectacle of Poland ought to open their eyes to what an ambitious Princess can undertake.

The sacred names of religion and of liberty have reduced the Poles to the condition they now are in. The abuse of the most salutary things is injurious. As a spectator of every sort of shock, I await in fear and trembling the moment I see approaching, when neighboring powers will seek to profit by our difficulties to overcome us. I should at that

---

10. *Gustave III par ses lettres*, pp. 126–128.

juncture believe myself free to do anything in order to save my country from the yoke to which it will be subjected. I assure you, Madame, that I do not feel the phlegm of the king of Poland, who calmly sees his provinces divided up among other Princes, without even seeming tempted to offer any opposition whatever.

M. the Prince de Conti, who is so frequently regarded as being raised to a position of which he was much worthier than he who has arrogated it to himself today, must be painfully affected by the present condition of a realm that he has long regarded as belonging one day to his own patrimony. I judge by the sensation I myself experience how much his soul must be suffering to see this fine nation abandoned by its allies, and a victim of its neighbors. Perhaps too the relation obtaining between my country's situation and that of Poland renders my sensations more raw and my interest more sensitive.

The affairs of your country, Madame, now seem to me calmer and, if one can judge from such a distance, the ministerial conduct of the Duc d'Aiguillon entirely erases the unfavorable reports that had been circulated against him. Indeed it seems to me that he displays an uncommon moderation, quite different from the general opinion of his character. I may be mistaken, it is hard to judge accurately at a distance of six hundred leagues. What most concerns me is to know how the princes of the blood will behave. You flatter me, I must say, in remarking that your trip to Sweden was merely delayed by this event. One more reason for me to hope for their reconciliation.

I am enclosing a translation of the speech I gave to the States General, the day they took their oath. There are two copies, please give one to the Prince de Conti on my behalf. His approval would mean a great deal to me. At least, everything I said to the States General is the unvarnished truth, which it would be very expedient for them to believe, but unfortunately personal interest is the most destructive factor among the States General.

The ceremony of homage is one of the most august I have ever seen; it took place out of doors, and is the remains of the ancient way of electing our Kings. I've had a drawing made of the event, and once it has been engraved I'll be pleased to send it to you. The coronation was on

May 29, and according to the superstitious (every country has such people) there were fewer unfortunate accidents on this occasion than since that of Charles XI. I'm waiting for an opportunity to send you the print.

As I'm writing for your eyes alone, I count on your friendship and your indulgence to forgive the mistakes and oversights that escape my notice in writing in a foreign language, though as far as feelings are concerned, nothing regarding your country is alien to me, but such indulgence, which I claim as a consequence of your friendship, I cannot and must not expect from those who would read me before you, if I sent my letter by the post. Hence, do not be surprised by the old date.

I conclude all this chatter by hoping you believe how sincerely I regret having known you if I am never to hope to see you again.

If Mme the Comtesse Amélie should sometime recall Count von Gotland, I beg you, Madame, to tell her that he has requested me to give her all his compliments, and that among all the agreeable memories he has brought from France, her graces, her charming naiveté, as well as his affection for her dear mother, and the friendship for him that she was so eager to share with you will always remain engraved on his grateful heart.

21. A Romance in "The Cyclops' Maw": Hans Axel von Fersen and the "Austrian Woman"

"SURELY NEVER LIGHTED on this orb, which she hardly seemed to touch, a more delightful vision. I saw her just above the horizon, decorating and cheering the elevated sphere she just began to move in, glittering like the morning star, full of life and splendour and joy." Chateaubriand repeated to himself these lines of Burke in 1821 in London, in the presence of his embassy secretary the Comte de Marcellus, to whom he had just described once again his last encounter with Marie-Antoinette on June 30, 1789; he had already entered the passage in the *Mémoires d'outre-tombe*:

> She gave me, with a smiling glance, that gracious greeting she had already given me the day of my presentation. I shall never forget that glance that was so soon to be extinguished. Marie-Antoinette, whenever she smiled, drew the outline of her mouth so clearly that the memory of that smile (fearful thing!) made me recognize the jaw of the daughter of kings, when that unfortunate's head was discovered in the exhumations of 1815.[1]

This is the first occurrence, in the *Mémoires*, but also in Chateaubriand's intimate experience and in our literature, of what has been called that "involuntary memory" associating the sweetness of recollection with the anticipation of death. Preceding the "thrush of Montboissier" (the incunabulum of the famous Proustian "mad-

---

1. *Mémoires d'outre-tombe*, edited by J.C. Berchet (Garnier, 1989), vol. 1, p. 308.

eleine of Combray") there was the jaw of the queen exhumed in the presence of Chateaubriand, who with a delegation from the Chamber of Peers had participated in the macabre ceremony of disinterment.

The noble vicomte was given the responsibility of describing the incident to his confreres of the chamber, and in his account may be found the first sketch of the narrative in the *Mémoires d'outre-tombe*:

> I have seen, Gentlemen, the skeletal remains of Louis XVI mingled in the open grave with the quicklime that had consumed the flesh but that had not caused the crime to disappear! I have seen Marie-Antoinette's coffin intact under the shelter of a sort of vault that had formed above her, as though by some miracle. The head alone had been displaced! and in that head's shape could be recognized, O Providence, the features in which had breathed with the grace of a woman all the majesty of a queen.

Historians can debate forever the errors and delinquencies of the last queen of France. Some, like the American Lynn Hunt, can apply the grid of historical psychoanalysis to the torrents of obscenity and filth that Paris disgorged upon the involuntary heroine of the Affair of the Necklace, and then upon the prisoner of the Tuileries, the Temple, and the Conciergerie.

That is not the heart of the matter. Chateaubriand, like Burke, felt as much and said as much. With the "Austrian Woman" it was woman par excellence that a witch-hunting hatred pursued to the last echoes of the kill in the person of the queen of France.

How could a nation known throughout Europe since the twelfth century for its chivalrous and hospitable disposition have denatured itself to the point of treating the most gracious of all its queens, as well as cartloads of other female victims, with that "barbarism in civilization" that has had no equivalent, even among the fiery autos-da-fé of the sixteenth century, except in the camps and gulags of our iron century?

Chateaubriand, ahead of the Goncourt brothers, Léon Bloy, and Stefan Zweig, made Marie-Antoinette's fate in 1789–1793 the testimonial par excellence to the paradox of the French Revolution: the crime against humanity contemporary with the proclamation of the Declaration of the Rights of Man, and committed by several of the authors of this modern Tablet of the Law.

There was a precedent for the execution of Louis XVI: that king, a great reader of Hume's *History of England*, knew better than anyone that the sacerdotal vestments in which he was clad exposed him to capital punishment. Yet the death of Charles I on the scaffold did not suffice to denature England. That king's wife, Henriette of France, the sister of Louis XIII, did not suffer the fate of Mary Stuart, which concluded the Tudors' bloody sixteenth century. The treatment the French inflicted upon their queen created something irreparable. The "trail of blood never to be effaced," in Chateaubriand's words to the Chamber of Peers, linked political modernization in France to a crime that summarizes, along with the unspeakable and silent disappearance of the orphan Louis XVII, all those the Terror was to multiply.

In the queen's person, every natural sentiment that constitutes humanity—pride, dignity, maternal love, the heart's impulses, along with beauty and grace—were trampled upon and publicly defiled by her executioners.

The tender attachment that united the queen to Count Hans Axel von Fersen afforded her, in the first days of her misfortunes, her last earthly joys. One is reminded of the couple formed, during the Fronde, by Anne of Austria and Cardinal Mazarin. But Mazarin was a statesman; Fersen was a gallant gentlemen who counted for nothing in the French political scheme of things. Neither of these foreigners, initiated into the agreeable manners and the *douceur de vivre* of France, but mistaking (like all of Europe) the character of a nation that Fersen, in his *Journal* written in French, qualified in 1785 as "frivolous, immoderate, filled with vanities and pretensions," at all suspected, before the fall of the Bastille, the savage innermost depth of French ideas and passions.

For a long while the queen tried to believe, even after her forced departure from Versailles, that the French people would overcome the demagogues who were deceiving them. In 1793, Count von Fersen, horrified by the hatred that had attacked the royal family, which had been betrayed by its own relatives and abandoned by its friends, wrote in his *Journal*: "I detest, I abhor this nation of cannibals, they are all weaklings, cowards, with neither heart nor soul." When the volcano had exploded and torn to pieces the Pompeian vestiges of the grand French society that had long deceived them, the two friends remained united in the cloud of death that enveloped them.

Born in 1755 to a noble Swedish family as profoundly Francophone if not as Francophile as the Tessins, the La Gardies, or King Gustav III, Fersen had arrived in Paris in November 1773. He had met the dauphine during a masked ball early in 1774. It was only in 1778, after a second presentation, that the exceptionally handsome young officer entered the circle of Marie-Antoinette, who had meanwhile become queen of France. To cut short the gossip about some idyll or other concerning which the Swedish court had sounded the alarm, Fersen gallantly enlisted in the expeditionary corps Louis XVI was sending to the aid of the American rebels and did not return to Paris before June 1783. It was in September of that year that he became a colonel of the Royal Suédois, assigned to the queen's own guard. The following year he accompanied King Gustav III on his journey to Italy and returned with him to Paris in June 1784.

The love he had generated in Marie-Antoinette's heart exalted him sufficiently for him to be content with burning words. Moreover he had had a long liaison with the lovely Eléonore Sullivan, whose favors he shared with Quentin Crawfurd, another foreign habitué of the queen's circle. In his letters (in French) to his sister Countess Sophie Piper, before and after the queen's death, he analyzed, distinguished, and justified his two loves: love for Elle (the queen) and love for El (Eléonore Sullivan). He did not consider them incompatible but partly explicable by one another. It seems indeed that Louis XVI in particular—in the terrible years 1789–1792—saw nothing irreconcilable between the conjugal affection that closely united him to Marie-Antoinette and the attachment that the queen might feel for the young Swede, one of the very rare unbroken loyalties, along with that of the Englishman Crawfurd, that endured for both of them.

Fersen was not a Galahad, but he also had nothing of the Chevalier de Faublas about him. His romance with Marie-Antoinette was closer to Marivaux and Mozart than to Louvet or Laclos. It is hard to know if, as Napoleon believed (one might not have thought him so prudish or bourgeois: the husband of Marie-Louise of Austria refused to negotiate with Fersen at Radstatt on this pretext), the handsome Swede had "been to bed" with the queen.

Fersen and the heirs to his papers have done all they could to suppress anything that might have tended in this direction. The (very hypothetical) possibility of sensual consolations was hardly left to the two *amis* except during the sojourn of the royal family in the Tuileries between 1789 and 1791, far from the lynx-eyes of the old court, less easy to deceive perhaps than the national guards.

After the arrest of the royal family at Varennes on June 20, 1791, Fersen (who had prepared the flight with Crawfurd, but had not guided them beyond the gates of Paris) was to take refuge outside of France. From abroad he would devote all his activities, his credit, and his fortune to construct a means of salvation for the king and the queen. He would even risk, against the advice of Marie-Antoinette, a trip under an assumed name to Paris in February 1792. He succeeded one last time in reaching the queen's apartment in the Tuileries. "Went to her," he writes in his *Journal*, "taking my usual way miraculously enough, fearing the nat. gard., to her quarters. And," crossed out, "Stayed there." He would leave only the next day at midnight, after a consultation with the king whose serenely despairing remarks he reported.

He survived only in appearance the queen's torment. In his *Journal* returns like a leitmotif the exclamation: "Oh, if only I had died for her on June 20!"

Without seeking honors, he received them. King Gustav Adolph IV (who in 1792 had succeeded his father, assassinated during the fatal masked ball at the Stockholm Opera) made him a Grand Marshal of the Realm, chancellor of the University of Upsala, and his most trusted counselor. The rumor spread in Sweden that, out of hatred for revolutionary France, Marshal Fersen urged the king into war with Napoleon. When, on May 28, 1810, Prince von Holstein-Augustenburg, heir apparent to the throne, died suddenly, rumor had it that Ferson had poisoned him in order to take his place and have a free hand against France.

On June 20, the day of the heir apparent's funeral, the marshal's carriage was assailed by the populace. Dragged to the city hall, Fersen was massacred by stones and canes, as he doubtless would have been nineteen years earlier in Paris had he returned beside Marie-Antoinette and Louis XVI in the carriage from Varennes.

Three unpublished letters, one from Marie-Antoinette to the Austrian ambassador in France at the moment of the royal family's forced transfer to the Tuileries in October 1789 (with a veiled allusion to Fersen), the other two from Fersen to Lady Elizabeth Foster, dating from 1793, give some sense of their use of the French language, and a notion of the scheme that saved neither the Austrian queen nor her Swedish friend from a history of France that Poussin, in his letters to Chantelou, had already compared during the Fronde to "the maw of a maddened Cyclops."

FROM MARIE-ANTOINETTE TO THE COMTE DE MERCY-ARGENTEAU

Versailles, October 10, 1789
Only today, my dear comte, did I receive your letter of Tuesday the sixth, and I can easily imagine your anxieties, never having had a moment's doubt of your sincere attachment. I hope you did receive my letter of last Wednesday that will have somewhat reassured you, I am feeling quite well and despite all the unpleasantness to which I have

constantly been subject, I hope nonetheless to restore the healthy and honest status of the bourgeoisie and of the people, though unfortunately a great number of them do not have the upper hand, but with an unconquerable gentleness and patience we must manage to overcome the horrible mistrust that existed in so many people's minds and that has constantly dragged us into the depths where we are now. You write at the appropriate moment, yet I myself do not believe it is prudent to write him at this moment, even if it is only to tell him that I am all right.[2] The Assemb. will be coming here, but I am told there will be no more than 600 deputies, because of all those who have gone to calm the provinces rather than stirring them up over the situation here, for anything is preferable to the horrors of a civil war. I was greatly relieved that you managed to get away from Versailles, everything that has occurred in the last 24 hours is quite incredible. Nothing one can say would be an exaggeration, quite the contrary, everything that could be said would be less than what we have seen and endured. You would do well not to come here for some time, for that would still arouse feelings. Moreover, I may not see anyone in my own apartments, all I have is my little bedroom upstairs, my daughter is sleeping in my dressing room next door and my son in my main bedroom. Though it is awkward, I prefer to have them with me: at least I shall not be accused of receiving people chez moi. *Farewell, monsieur, the more unhappy I am the more I feel how tenderly I am attached to my true friends, and I am happy that for a long time I have counted you among them.[3]*

FROM HANS AXEL VON FERSEN TO LADY ELIZABETH FOSTER

Brussels, October 3, 1793

I cannot imagine, Milady, what mischance has delayed the kind letter you were good enough to write me from Lausanne on August 30 and

---

2. Very likely an allusion to Fersen.

3. Manuscript letter, private collection, Paris.

that I received only a week ago. Such negligence has deprived me of the pleasure of knowing sooner that you think of me and that you take an interest in my fate. I cherish such knowledge, and you must not doubt how much the assurance of it delights me: one is always comforted by discovering one's friends, but it seems that one has even greater need of them when one is in distress. Mine is occasioned by the fate of the Royal family. Their situation grieves me greatly, and haunts me at every moment. I do nothing but dream of some means of rescuing them, alas at present there seems little hope of any such thing; just yesterday we learned of the retreat of the combined armies before Verdun and probably out of France altogether, so there is less hope than ever now, the sign of disaster seems to be on everything we try to do for this unfortunate family, nothing has any effect, and it is only villains and scoundrels who succeed. Even as regards the weather, everything conspires against us, for it has rained continuously for the last two months, which has so damaged the roads that provisions could no longer reach the army. Dysentery was also beginning to inflict terrible ravages, and it is doubtless these two causes that persuaded the Duke of Brunswick to make a retreat that has proved so disastrous in its consequences. The poor Émigrés will be in despair, they have no resources and their position is dreadful, yet they are not in a such bad state as their King, for at least they are free men.

I have not left Brussels for a year, nor shall I do so this winter, my health has not been good and is not yet right, I am almost always sickly without being exactly sick. The B. de Breteuil has been with the King of Prussia for the last three weeks, but I should guess that he will be returning here shortly. Count Esterhazy is still in Petersburg where the princes had sent him last year. Such, my dear friend, are all the details about which you had questions, you cannot believe my delight in seeing that you are still concerned and that you have not forgotten a friend whose tender feelings for you will end only with his life.

Farewell, my dear friend. You may rely on these feelings of mine. In return, you might send me your news from time to time. Tell the Duchess how deeply I share her delight in Lady Duncannon's recovery, and let me know something about the latter. Farewell.

My dear Duchess, a thousand thanks for the note you wrote me, and the kind interest you take in my affairs. I feel more deeply than I can express how much it affects me. I hope you will continue to entertain such feelings, I am worthy of them on account of all those which I have sworn to you, for life.[4]

FROM HANS AXEL VON FERSEN TO LADY ELIZABETH FOSTER

Brussels, October 22, 1793

I did not realize, kind lady, upon receiving yours of the 10th of this month, that my answer would have to inform you of a piece of news so painful to my heart. You doubtless know already that the Queen of France, the paragon of Queens and of women, is no more. It was at eleven-thirty in the morning of the 16th of this month that this crime was committed, which makes both nature and humanity tremble, and my heart is cruelly torn. Yours is too sensitive not to share my grief, which is lightened only by the notion that at least this unfortunate princess is delivered from the disasters and dreadful sufferings that she endured for four years and that only such courage as hers could resist. Mme de Fitzjames is extremely distressed. We mourn our common loss together. I try to console her, but alas, my own need for consolation is too great to be able to give any to her. I lack the strength to provide you details concerning this sad occurrence, moreover those we possess are anything but precise. Farewell, my dear friend, pity me, give me your news and believe in the tender friendship I feel for you.

A thousand thoughts to our good and kind Duchess.

I have just now received your parcel from Count Elliot, and I shall give your letter to Duchess Fitzjames.

Count Elliott arrived yesterday evening and leaves this morning.[5]

---

4. Manuscript letter, private collection, Paris.
5. Manuscript letter, private collection, Paris.

22. Benjamin Franklin, Frenchmen, and Frenchwomen

SUBJECTS AND OFTEN SLAVES of fashion, the French have always been considered spirited, curious, versatile, defenseless in the face of novelties, and easily infatuated by their foreign guests.

In the sixteenth century, Henri Estienne cursed the fashion that outrageously favored Italians in France. In the seventeenth century, John Barclay, a great traveler, could write in an essay on the national characters of Europe:

> The world can never be grateful enough for French hospitality, which seems to open the temple of humanity in order to welcome the fortune of any and all foreigners. It is men's wit that is valued here, not their country.... Foreigners need not forget the manners of their own land nor bend them to French ways; suffice it that there be no pride on their part, nor too provincial a barbarism. Indeed the affections of this curious nation may in fact be gained by professing a foreign fashion, for France judges foreign costumes more candidly than its own: one may say that the French relish a certain imperfection in life or limb, provided they come from afar.

In the eighteenth century, Montesquieu's Persians had no reason to complain of Paris. In the nineteenth, neither Heine nor Turgenev and in the twentieth neither Hemingway nor Richard Wright nor Picasso suffered to the slightest degree in Paris from their exotic birth.

Could the French have suddenly gone into reverse? They are accused of doing so, and nowadays readily accuse themselves of inveterate xenophobia. If there is xenophobia in France, it is the be-latedly cast shadow of a long and extraordinary tradition of xeno-philia, indeed of xenomania, unexampled elsewhere in the world. The career of Benjamin Franklin in Paris would suffice to attest that Barclay's observation, a century and a half earlier, identified a long-lasting French habitude.

Born in Boston in 1706, the last of a tallow-chandler's brood of fifteen, this self-made man, who ultimately created a prominent posi-tion for himself in the world of Philadelphia printing, was nonethe-less treated on his two sojourns in London as a classless outcast. Even when he returned there in 1755 with the triple title of director-general of His Britannic Majesty's Post on the American continent, mem-ber of the Legislative Assembly of the Pennsylvania Parliament, and head of that assembly's mission to the Crown and to the honorable owners of the province, the Penns, he was never anything there but a morganatic diplomat, doomed to obscurity and rebuffs. He had dealings with the English aristocracy, and on some occasions be-lieved he had made friends there and even allies, but was obliged to face the facts of a contempt that ultimately blew up in his face. This neither surprised nor discouraged this mild but deeply radical Whig, who attributed all his English disappointments to the scien-tific absurdity of the existence in England of a hereditary nobility.

Such social thorns only toughened him, indeed made him formi-dable. They did not prevent him from gaining, against the edifice of pride and ruse that was the British establishment, surprising successes in defending his mission's interests. Yet scientific glory (attested none-theless by the Royal Society's Copley Medal), which the discovery of the electric nature of lightning and the invention of the lightning rod had won (1748–1751) for the virtuoso artisan and autodidact of genius, did not afford this commoner even a makeshift sort of title in London. In aristocratic France, Franklin's experiments were re-peated in the presence of Louis XV, and in his own hand the king of France wrote a congratulatory letter to the Boston tallow-chandler's son. Enthusiastic French disciples made him their prophet: Had not this new Prometheus stolen the thunder from Jupiter himself?

During his second London sojourn, which lasted ten years, Franklin nonetheless did his best, while quite effectively protecting the interests of the English colonies, to favor their maintenance under the British Crown, stipulating self-government in fiscal and tariff matters. It was certainly contrary to his efforts that there developed in New England and Virginia a movement of armed rebellion and a demand for independence. Yet it was Franklin who, on January 29, 1774, suffered a scapegoat's fate in the eyes of an exasperated England: before the Privy Council of the Crown, a tribunal presided over by the prime minister, Lord North, Great Britain's public prosecutor covered Franklin with scornful insults before the most elegant assemblage of the realm, including numerous lords who were his "friends." Stripped several days later of his position as director-general of His Majesty's Post, there was nothing for Franklin to do but return, an unwilling martyr of independence, to a rebellious America.

From London, he had made several forays onto the Continent, notably to France in 1767. Paris's well-administered sanitation services and its excellent system of distribution and filtration of water appealed to this practical mind, a friend to comfort and commodity. Like everyone else, he was dazzled by Versailles where he was invited to attend the *souper du roi*: Louis XV exchanged several gracious remarks with him. Everywhere he was received with politeness and even honor. He pleased everyone. He applied himself to pleasing, wearing a becoming suit and a light wig *à la française*. He felt quite at home in the circle of Physiocrats formed around Monsieur Quesnay and the Marquis de Mirabeau (author of *L'Ami des hommes*), seduced by their ideas of general prosperity through rational agriculture, fiscal reform, freedom of commerce, and free-trade policies: all grist for an American mill hampered by an urban England insatiable for indirect taxes. He published articles in the Physiocrat journal *Les Éphémérides du citoyen,* which by its European circulation became a precious organ of propaganda for the cause of King George's transatlantic colonies. He returned once more to Paris in 1769, though briefly.

The friendships Franklin had made in France during these two visits designated him in 1776 to represent to the French government the new federal state (in gestation, in revolution, but still nonexistent in the eyes of international law). France, supported in the Mediterranean by the Family Pact and in Central Europe by an alliance with Vienna, was at this time by far the greatest and most prosperous European power, the only one moreover whose public opinion manifested a veritable enthusiasm for the "Rebels." The reign of Louis XVI had begun as a golden age. All of revolutionary America's hopes turned to France.

At the age of sixty-nine, accompanied by two of his grandsons, the Patriarch of Philadelphia set off on this great adventure, on which depended the entire future of the American Revolution.

On December 3, 1776, a storm forced him to disembark at Quiberon and to reach Nantes by coach; on those muddy roads he may have encountered the future Chouans. In the century of the Enlightenment, these medieval peasants must have struck him as just as backward as the Delaware Indians his compatriots were cheerfully dispossessing and liquidating. Immediately reported in Paris, Franklin's arrival in Nantes became the news of the day. On December 20 he reached Versailles, where he registered at an inn. Officially at peace with England, France had hitherto responded to the American Congress's requests for supplies through the mediation of an engaging commercial agent: Beaumarchais. Such contraband was covered by a firm entitled, doubtless in homage to *The Barber of Seville*, Rodrigue Hortalez et Compagnie. The British ambassador, Lord Stormont, discovered these sinister French maneuvers and peppered Vergennes, the minister of foreign affairs, with protests. Franklin's appearance in Paris, and the success he became there, utterly transformed the Anglo-Franco-American situation.

In one of his *Lettres anglaises*, Voltaire had portrayed the Quakers as a heartwarming society. *Le Quaker* had become a French myth, related to the Noble Savage subsequently accredited by Rousseau. Philadelphia, whence Franklin had come, was a Quaker foundation; this time the American envoy took great care not to dress and wear his hair *à la française*: his "citizen's" garments, his republican manners, and his rustic simplicity embodied both American myths at once. Though anything but a Quaker, Franklin assumed the character and appearance of one, cultivated the misunderstanding, and did so with such guileless amiability that he also passed for the Noble Savage of the American forests. Whereupon Voltairians and Rousseauans, enemies in all other respects, fell into each other's arms to idolize him.

With a shrewd sense of the scene and of public relations, Franklin immediately made three visits that were as many test cases; and three times over he carried off all the honors. The first was of course a private audience with Vergennes, Louis XVI's minister of foreign affairs, a cultivated and generous grand seigneur, who was touched by the modesty and competence of the good fellow delegated by the American Congress. His colleague Malesherbes had been moved in the same fashion, several years earlier, by Rousseau, that plebeian of genius, and had taken him under his protection permanently. Behind the scenes, Vergennes saw to it that two million livres were advanced to the insurgents.

More formidable was Franklin's appearance before the supreme tribunal of Parisian high society, the salon in the rue Saint-Dominique presided over by that blind regent of the Enlightenment, the Marquise du Deffand. Franklin was presented after dinner on December 29, 1776, to the marquise enthroned in her basket chair, the famous *tonneau*. A brilliant areopagus was gathered around her: the Vicomte de Beaune, the Chevalier de Boutteville, the Abbé Barthélemy, the Comte de Guines, former French ambassador to London, the ex–prime minister the Duc de Choiseul, and the young Englishman called Eliott.

The worst might well have been expected. The marquise was in love with Horace Walpole. Lord Stormont, the present English ambassador, was one of her habitués. In principle, she ought to have sided with the British government. Franklin's democratic and commercial notions, had she known them, would have horrified her more deeply than Voltaire's paradoxes, which she disdained, or d'Alembert's logic, which she detested.

Yet everything happened for the best. Franklin spoke little, listened a great deal, smiled and exclaimed at the right moments. He was declared altogether an honnête homme. It must be supposed that Choiseul, who tugged against his reins and dreamed of a comeback as prime minister, had personally organized this visit to his hostess and great friend and made certain it did not turn into a disaster: one unfavorable word from the formidable marquise could have ruined Franklin. As a matter of fact, the American cause was already so popular in France that even candidates for the ministries made it a duty to provide the new nation with funds.

Then Franklin paid a visit to the Marquis de Mirabeau. He had known him since 1767 and was well aware of the Physiocrats' sympathy for the American cause. But the Physiocrats, including Turgot, the most famous of them all, were also pacifists. Franklin was a pacifist too, but his mission compelled him to plead for war. The affection of the "Friend of Man" for Franklin, the solidarity of the Physiocrats with this foreign brother, moderated and even neutralized their reservations. Only Turgot, who was not present at the interview, remained intractable.

Franklin was above all determined to raise to a white heat the public opinion already disposed in his favor. Starting on January 15, 1777, he regularly attended the Académie des Sciences, of which he was a corresponding member. He visited the great Parisian libraries: that of the king, the Sainte-Geneviève, the Mazarine, etc. His delighted confreres and the entire Republic of Letters declared themselves his servants. The French and foreign grands seigneurs who prided themselves on erudition or scientific knowledge lined up to meet the great man: the Duc de Croÿ, the Duc de Chaulnes, the Comte de Lauragais, Prince Galitzin, Baron Blome, M. Eyck. The last three, diplomats of European scope, became serious trumps in Franklin's hand.

The worlds of high society and fashion flung themselves at his feet. The young Duc de La Rochefoucauld, who knew English, obtained the favor of serving as secretary to the American *grand homme*. His entire illustrious, powerful, and ancient family immediately became the megaphone of Franklin's fame and the American cause. Nor did the tribe of the Noailles hang back. The son-in-law of the Duc d'Ayen, the Marquis de La Fayette, once the formalities were over, begged Franklin to facilitate his engagement as a volunteer on Washington's staff. Despite Louis XVI's opposition, the marquis embarked in May. The Comte de Broglie dreamed of becoming the William the Silent of the new "United Provinces"; so the illustrious and powerful de Broglie family adopted Franklin and his cause.

But it was a mere tycoon, a sort of disciple of Franklin, Le Ray de Chaumont, who lodged him in the outbuildings of his Hôtel de Valentinois, in Passy. This breezy neighborhood was the rendezvous of French Freemasonry, which the Duc d'Orléans was busy reviving at this time. In this milieu Franklin found friends, allies, and access to a huge network of the French press, published in France or abroad. Excellent journalist that he was, he made the most abundant and efficient use of these relations.

The velvet that yielded most eagerly to Franklin's caresses was the women, who had always played an exceptional role in French public life, and at this time reigned as never before.

They became infatuated with this pseudo-Quaker, sensual and sentimental, doughty and cunning as a peasant, but a good companion and a gentle shepherd, not eloquent but generous with his cajoleries. In Paris Franklin experienced much more than what Roland Barthes called a "fragment of a lover's discourse."

So many supports and such a variety of comforts permitted him to withstand without flinching the grim news that reached him at first from America and that made Lord Stormont swagger. Then, when the rebels' first great victory was announced—the capture of Burgoyne and his army, which had marched south from Canada—Franklin displayed his vulpine capacities. Pretending to negotiate with London, he convinced Vergennes that it was vital that France speedily seize this shadow of peace and engage openly in war. On February 8, 1778, Franklin finally wreaked his brilliant revenge on Lord Stormont and English arrogance: in the Hôtel des Affaires Étrangères, formerly the Hôtel Lautrec, on the Quai des Théatins, he and Vergennes signed a Franco-American treaty of alliance. On March 20, Louis XVI officially received at Versailles the American delegation led by Franklin.

The legend spread that the wigmaker had been unable to find a *perruque* big enough for the great American. All France chorused: "He has a big head, a great big head." Actually he presented himself to the king coiffed in his own scattered long white locks, without a court sword on his hip. One could hear the whole court, under the spell, murmuring: "He's dressed like a Quaker!"

Thus the inventor of the lightning rod and the slow-combustion stove was also the creator of "self-promotion" and "the look." Further, on that day, in the finest theater in the universe, the grand apartments of Louis XIV, the young troupe of the "Fifteen United Provinces," flanked by their patriarch and presented by Louis XVI in person, made a sensational entrance on the world stage. The next day, the American delegate received a very kind welcome at the queen's *lever*; then *chez* Monsieur, the king's brother; then *chez* Madame, the Comtesse de Provence; and lastly *chez* Madame Élisabeth, the king's sister. One understands why the Château of Versailles has remained dear to the United States. It is their other Cape Canaveral: from here they were launched into world history.

Henceforth, as official ambassador plenipotentiary of the Congress of the United States, Franklin knew true glory. Even more than from Louis XVI, he received it from the hand of the dying Voltaire, who had arrived just in time to enjoy his own apotheosis in Paris. Accompanied by his grandson William Temple, Franklin did not miss the opportunity of paying Voltaire a visit at the Hôtel de Villette. The two "stars" conversed at first in English, then, to general amazement, in French, after which Franklin pushed his grandson William Temple toward Voltaire, asking the latter to bless him: the king of the Republic of Letters extended his skeletal hand over the youth's head and pronounced his benediction "in the name of God and Liberty." Everyone burst into tears.

Several days later Voltaire and Franklin sat next to each other at the Académie des Sciences, in its formal session at the Louvre. The crowd compelled them to stand, to greet each other, and to speak together. Finally the public shouted: "An embrace *à la française*!" The tiny French skeleton hugged the tall, stout American, while the crowd applauded, wept, and shouted, "How delightful to see Solon and Sophocles embrace!"

The envious and the scoffers on the other side of the Atlantic frequently made things difficult for Ambassador Franklin. Nonetheless he led a softer existence than he had ever known, comfortably installed in his Passy residence, abundantly supplied with rare wines, many servants, an infirmary, a print shop, a laboratory, a studio workshop, and a carriage. The first American to enjoy Paris as a "moveable feast," he was much in demand with great ladies, beginning with Queen Marie-Antoinette, who consulted him as a sort of oracle and otherwise made much of him. All sought to embrace him, to call him "Papa," and he returned their favors in kind. The echo of these liberties, crossing the Atlantic, caused something of a scandal. To friends who informed him of the fact, he replied:

> You speak of the kindness Frenchwomen have shown me. I must explain this. The French are the politest nation in the world. The first persons you meet try to find out what you like, and inform all the rest. If it is understood that you like mutton, dine where you will, you are served mutton. Someone apparently let it be known that I liked the ladies; straightaway everyone offered me ladies (or the ladies offered themselves) to embrace (in other words, to kiss on the neck. For kissing the mouth or the cheek is not done here, the former procedure is regarded as uncouth, the latter spoils the rouge).

Never was an ambassador (and Franklin still held that office provisionally, on the dotted line, as it were) more wildly fashionable in his foreign capital of accreditation. Paris has frequently been subject to such frenzy, but for the most part in the democratic era following the Revolution, and for national political stars: Bonaparte, his nephew the future Napoleon III, General Boulanger. Ahead of his time, Franklin managed to excite ancien régime Paris as no one before him, taking the city and society at the secret point that makes every man and especially every woman thrill, and transforming them, all at the same moment, into an ecstatic crowd. This American democrat invented and released the rock-star phenomenon in the midst of aristocratic Paris! Louis XVI, subtler than historians have often described him, detected in this phenomenon a whiff of the trouble that lay ahead. Exasperated by the extraordinary merchandising of Franklin himself, of his portrait on snuff-boxes and fans, on clocks and medallions, Louis XVI ordered the Manufacture Royale de Sèvres to produce a chamber pot at the bottom of which gleamed the famous medallion of Franklin, with its celebrated caption. He sent this household utensil as a gift to one of the great ladies of his court who was fanatically enthusiastic about the American. This was Mme Campan, reader to the king's aunts and author of entirely reliable memoirs reporting the incident. The "caption" she alludes to was in fact the Latin inscription that Turgot was said to have composed in Franklin's honor and that figured under his heroic bust carved by Houdon, another key item in his publicity campaign: *Eripuit caelo fulmen sceptrumque tyrannis* (He has wrested lightning from heaven and from tyrants their scepters). Sufficient, indeed, to irritate and even to outrage the king of France.

A few years later, in 1784, when the ambassador of the quite young federal republic, mission accomplished, came to make his farewell to Louis XVI, the latter finished the charade that had begun with the portrait in the chamber pot: according to a tradition dating back to *le grand monarque*, Louis ceremoniously offered the departing diplomat, as a signal honor, his own portrait in full court costume, a work of the famous miniaturist Louis Sicardy, mounted in an oval gold case engraved with the royal initials and set with splendid diamonds. Did Franklin compare the two halves of the mute symbolic message, on one hand the profane effigy of the self-advertising plebeian, on the other the icon of the sovereign crowned at Reims, each in its appropriate frame? Did the ambassador understand the lesson in hierarchy articulated by the monarch though concealed beneath the most exquisite forms of etiquette and politesse? Improbable, but not impossible. Franklin had at least as many antennae as the king, and the rumor of the first initiative that the latter had taken with regard to portraiture may very well have reached his ears. Whatever the case, the ambassador's family inherited the precious object that, from generation to generation, lost its diamonds, which were sold to finance journeys and useful acquisitions.

Since 1959, the king's ambiguous gift, minus its crown of diamonds, has been in the collection of the American Philosophical Society, which Franklin founded after his return to Philadelphia. None of the *douceurs de vivre* of the French ancien régime's autumnal season was denied to Franklin's vigorous winter. M. and Mme d'Houdetot, joined by Saint-Lambert, poet of *Les saisons* and Madame's lover in the bargain, gave in his honor, on April 12, 1781, a fête champêtre at their Samois estate. Franklin had to step out of his carriage a kilometer from the château, welcomed by choruses in praise of liberty. He advanced through the park and gardens decorated with garlands and floral arches of triumph to the table where a delicious supper was served. Between courses, the guests sang a set of verses composed for the occasion:

> *We celebrate the genius of Benjamin,*
> *And the benefits linked with his name:*
> *In America he shall have altars,*
> *In Samois we drink to his fame.*

After the meal, Franklin was invited to plant a Virginia chestnut in the garden, with a votive inscription on a marble plaque attached to its trunk. Returning from the ceremony, an orchestra accompanied the procession of guests who sang in chorus:

> *This seedling, planted by his favoring hand,*
> *May raise its nascent trunk to stand*
> *Above the sterile elms, soon making sweet*
> *The welkin of this rural seat*

Where Lightning can no longer set at naught
All that frail mankind has wrought,
For Franklin's genius has devised a way
To cancel or direct its sway,
Sparing thence the coming human race
Endless disasters else to face.

In Passy, Franklin enjoyed, successively, two idylls with two adorable women, Mme Helvétius and Mme Brillon de Jouy, his neighbors. The extremely wealthy widow of the farmer-general and great philosopher before the Eternal, Mme Helvétius had been one of the most ravishing young beauties of France and Lorraine, her native province where her family, the Lignivilles, were among the oldest stock of the duchy. In her salons at Auteuil, she had regally received all the talents and great names of Paris and indeed of Europe, and preserved as well the fine remainder of her glorious looks. The old American ambassador delightedly inhaled the fragrance of this autumnal rose of the French aristocracy, and she did not resist the great and glorious Wasp who had crossed the seas to reach her. Her salons, entrée to which had always been greatly coveted, had now become a slightly passé Noah's Ark; still lovely, distinguished, witty, and tenderhearted, she now found herself besieged by kittens, puppies, birds, and young abbés. She coddled Franklin, making much if not everything of him. He wrote tale after tale for her in French, calling her "Notre-Dame-d'Auteuil." In 1780 he went so far as to make her an offer of marriage. Turgot, whom she had loved in her youth and whom she consulted on this point as on all others, scolded her severely for having indulged the weakness of considering such a proposition for even an instant. And then, for all her efforts at coddling and cleverness, something cracked between them. One wonders what would have become of M. and Mme Franklin in Auteuil in 1793?

His appetite whetted for French felicity, Franklin turned in the direction of another neighbor, Mme Brillon, née Hardancourt, wife of the receiver-general of bills of Parlement. Still young and extremely pretty, she had grown up reading *La Nouvelle Héloïse*. The pair spent very long evenings together, in music, conversation, and innocent caresses, like Julie and Saint-Preux at Clarens. Together they visited Moulin Jolie, the famous English gardens of Watelet. Did Henry James recall this "conversion" of the old son of Boston to the charms of Paris when he described in *The Ambassadors* the elderly American bachelor coming to Paris to wrest young Chad from the arms of the lovely Mme Vionnet and falling himself into the snares of a French Armida? Franklin, emboldened, went so far as to envisage a marriage between his grandson, William Temple, and one of the Brillon daughters, a proposition that M. and Mme Brillon politely evaded.

This new laceration to his amour propre was blessedly drowned by a deluge of joy: news of the crushing Franco-American victory at Chesapeake Bay was announced on September 5, 1781. England was obliged to make terms.

Franklin was a significant pivot of the negotiations. When the treaty's preliminaries were finally signed, at Versailles on January 20, 1783, the hour of his own apotheosis had struck. All France, indeed all Europe, appeared to have made the pilgrimage to the Hôtel de Valentinois, the main portion of which the ambassador now occupied. His portrait was reproduced in even the smallest market stall, alongside those of Louis XVI and Washington. Every scientific academy in the provinces and Europe conferred membership upon him, if this had not already been accomplished, and requested documentation of the experiments and discoveries he continued to make in his workshop-laboratory in Passy. His advice was decisive in the disqualification of Mesmer and his famous bucket by the Académie des Sciences. The Lodge of the Nine Sisters made him a lifetime "Venerable."

He had become a living messiah heralding humanity's salvation by science and morality. His authority was such that it planted deep in the soil of the French public an Enlightenment catechism (*Poor Richard's Almanack*, 1748) that neither Voltaire's nor Rousseau's writings, both addressing a cultivated elite, had managed to popularize on such a scale. The young Comte de Mirabeau volunteered to translate and also to circulate in France (with Franklin's consent as well as Chamfort's) the first frontal attack against hereditary nobility ever to be printed in Europe: *Considerations on the Order of Cincinnatus*. Franklin had devised this pamphlet to silence the veterans of the War of Independence who were seeking to constitute a hereditary order. Mirabeau adapted and amplified the text to produce a firebrand against very basis of the French monarchy. Franklin may have seen no harm in the thing, which abounded in public declarations of admiration for Louis XVI and did not skimp on praises (which cannot be read retrospectively without a shudder) of the French national character:

> In manners and civility the French have surpassed the English by many degrees. I find here a nation entirely congenial to those from other countries who live here. The Spanish have a reputation for pride, the Scotch for insolence, the Dutch for avarice. But I believe the French can be reproached for no national vice. Perhaps a certain frivolity, which is of no real gravity. To dress one's hair so that one is unable to wear a hat, and then to carry that hat under one's arm; to fill one's nose with tobacco—these may be called follies, but hardly vices. In short, nothing good is lacking in the French character, among all that may contribute to make a man agreeable and estimable. These people have, merely, a handful of excessive bagatelles that they might readily eliminate.

Whatever Franklin's afterthoughts might have been about the "bagatelles" to be eliminated in France, he was not excessively rewarded by the United States, of which he had literally been the midwife. "Released" on May 2, 1785, he was replaced by Thomas Jefferson. Back in Philadelphia he played no more than the part of an elderly sage in the Constitutional Convention of 1787, respected for his popularity but mocked behind the scenes by the real bosses of the new political system. At least he successfully opposed the persistence, in this new America, of the teaching of Greek and Latin, which he characterized as "charlatanism in literature" and in which he saw the roots of a possible American aristocracy, as useless as it would be idle; a moral monstrosity that as late as 1889 the puritanical sociologist Thorstein Veblen was to fustigate in his famous *Theory of the Leisure Class*.

Franklin applauded the news of the French Revolution, though deploring its excesses. He died on April 17, 1790, in his big house in Philadelphia, surrounded by his books and the machines he had invented and constructed. His will created two foundations to assist the artisans of Boston and Philadelphia. He was eighty-four years old.

When news of his death reached France, the young Comte de Mirabeau gave his funeral oration at the National Assembly and saw to it that a vote passed for three days of national mourning. In a work published in French in Washington in 1927, Gabriel Chinard collected all the speeches and descriptions published of the ceremonies performed in Franklin's honor by a unanimous France (including future victims of the Terror such as Vicq d'Azyr, Marie-Antoinette's doctor, and future advocates of the guillotine such as Robespierre): the first version of those revolutionary pantheonizations of which Jean-Claude Bonnet has lately become the enthusiastic historian.[1]

Franklin spoke and wrote an estimable French. I reproduce here the letter that he wrote to Mme Helvétius after her refusal of his proposal of marriage and that he himself printed on the embassy presses in an amusing collection of his gallantries entitled *Les Bagatelles de Passy*, as well as an exchange of letters between Mme Brillon and himself, reproduced from the manuscript of the American Philosophical Society.[2]

FROM BENJAMIN FRANKLIN TO MME HELVÉTIUS
(PRINTED IN *LES BAGATELLES* AND NOT DATED)

Desolated by your barbaric resolution, pronounced so positively yesterday evening, to remain alone all your life in honor of your dear

---

1. *Naissance du Panthéon* (Fayard, 1998).
2. *The Papers of Benjamin Franklin*, vol. 28 (Yale University Press, 1990), pp. 464–465.

husband, I withdrew to my residence, flung myself on my bed, suppos-
ing myself a dead man, and found myself in the Elysian Fields.

    I was asked if I desired to see any particular personages. Bring me
among the philosophers.—There are two of them who reside nearby in
this garden, they are fine neighbors and close friends of each other.—
Who are they?—Socrates and Helvétius.—I esteem them both prodi-
giously; but let me see Helvétius first of all, for I understand a little
French and not one word of Greek. He received me with great courtesy,
having known me by reputation, he said, for some time. He asked me
a great many questions about the war, and about the present state of
religion, of liberty, and of the government in France.—Then you do
not seek to be informed about your dear friend Mme Helvétius; yet she
still loves you exceedingly, and it is only an hour since I was with
her.—Ah! said he, you make me recall my former felicity.—Yet one
must forget such a thing in order to be happy here. For several of the
first years, I thought only of her. Finally I found consolation. I took
another wife. One as like her as I could find. She is not, it is true, alto-
gether so beautiful, but she has as much good sense, a little more wit,
and she loves me greatly. Her continual study is to please me; and at
this very moment she has gone to find me the best nectar and the best
ambrosia with which to regale me this evening; stay with me and you
shall see her.—I perceive, said I, that your former companion is more
faithful than you: for she has been offered several good matches, all of
which she has refused. I confess that I myself have loved her madly; but
she was severe in my regard, and rejected me absolutely, for love of
you.—I pity you, said he, for your misfortune; for truly, she is a good
and lovely creature, and lovable indeed. But are not the Abbé de la
R—— and the Abbé M—— still with her on occasion?—Yes certainly,
for she has not lost a single one of your friends.—If you had lured the
Abbé M—— (by giving him a café à la crème*) to speak in your behalf,*
perhaps you would have succeeded; for he reasons as subtly as Duns
Scotus or St. Thomas; he places his arguments in such good order that
they become almost irresistible; or else by presenting the Abbé de la
R—— with some fine edition of an old classical author, you might have
persuaded him to speak against you, and that might have succeeded

even better: for I have always noticed that, whenever he counsels some-thing, she shows a very strong tendency to do the opposite.—At these words there entered the new Mme Helvétius with the nectar: at once I recognized in her Mme Franklin, my old American friend. I protested to her, yet she said to me, quite coldly: I have been a good wife to you for forty-nine years and four months, almost half a century; content your-self with that. Here, I have formed a new relationship that will last for eternity.

Vexed by this rejection by my Eurydice, I immediately resolved to quit these ungrateful shades, to return to this good world, to see the sun once more, and you yourself. Here I am!

Let us take our revenge!

From Madame Brillon to Benjamin Franklin

May 11, 1779

You are quite right, my dear Papa, we must envision true happiness only in the peace of our souls; it is not in our power to change the char-acter of those with whom we live, nor to prevent the course of the vexa-tions that surround us; these are the words of a sage who seeks to console his daughter, excessively sensitive about teaching her the truth; O my Papa, I beg your friendship, your healthy philosophy, my heart hears you, and submits; give me the strength that may take the place of an indifference your child can never feel; but my friend, concede that for one who knows love, ingratitude is a dreadful evil; how hard it is for a woman who would unhesitatingly give her life in order to assure her husband's happiness, to see herself stripped of the fruit of her concerns and her desires by subterfuge and duplicity—time will mend all, as my Papa has said, and I believe him; but has not my Papa also said that time is the substance of which life is made?[3] Well, my life, my friend, is made of a fabric so fine and light that grief lacerates it cruelly. If I were

---

3. An echo from Franklin's *Poor Richard's Almanack* (1748): "Dost thou love life? then do not squander time; for that's the stuff life is made of" (III, 64).

to have reason to blame myself, I should have ceased existing long ago! My soul is pure, simple, frank, I dare say as much to my Papa, I dare claim that soul is worthy of him; and I dare assure him that my conduct, which he has declared to be wise, shall not belie itself, that I shall await justice with patience, that I shall follow the counsels of my respectable friend with dignity and trust—farewell, my well-beloved Papa, never call me anything but your daughter: yesterday you called me madame and my heart sank, I searched my soul to find some way I may have wronged of which you were reluctant to tell me—forgive me, my friend, this is nothing I blame you for, it is a weakness of mine, I was born much too sensitive for my own happiness and for that of my friends; cure me and pity me, if you can do the one and the other as well. Tomorrow is Wednesday, you will be coming for tea, will you not? Believe me, my Papa, the delight I take in receiving you is shared by my husband, my children, my friends, I have no doubt about it and I assure you it is the truth.

From Benjamin Franklin to Mme Brillon (the next day)

You tell me, my dear girl, that your heart is too sensitive. I can certainly tell, from your letters, that this is all too true. To be truly sensitive to our own faults, that is good; but to be truly sensitive and pained by the faults of others, that is not. It is their responsibility to be sensitive to such things, and to be pained by the wrongs they had committed. We ourselves must remain at peace, which is the fair share of innocence and virtue. But you say that "ingratitude is a dreadful evil." That is true—of ingrates—but not of their benefactors. You have conferred benefits on those you believed worthy of them. So you have done your duty, for it is our duty to be beneficent; and you must be content with that, and happy in the consciousness of having done so. If they are ingrates, that is their crime and not yours; and it is they who will be unhappy when they reflect on the turpitude of their conduct in your regard. If they do you harm, reflect that though they may have previ-

ously been your equals, they have, by their behavior, placed themselves beneath you. If you revenge yourself by punishing them properly, you will restore them to the state of equality they had lost. But if you forgive them, without administering some punishment, you will perpetuate in them that low state to which they had fallen and from which they can never emerge without true repentance and true reparation. Follow, then, my very dear and forever lovable girl, the good resolution you have so wisely taken to continue to fulfill all your duties, as a good mother, a good wife, a good friend, a good neighbor, a good Christian, etc. (without forgetting to be a good daughter to your Papa) and to overlook and to forget, if possible, the harm that may be done to you now. And rest assured that in time, the rectitude of your conduct will win over the hearts and minds of even the wickedest persons; and even more those who are basically good-natured and who show good sense, though for the present perhaps they are a little misled by the wiles of others. Thus, all of them will ask of you with compunction the return of your friendship, and they will become for the future your most zealous friends.

I am aware that I have perpetrated here a lot of very bad French; this may distress you, who write that charming language with such purity and elegance. But if you can manage to decipher my obscure expressions, gauche and incorrect as they probably are, you may have at least that sort of pleasure one has in explaining riddles or in discovering secrets.

23. A United States Ambassador to the Rescue of Louis XVI: Gouverneur Morris

IN THE ABUNDANT LITERATURE on the French Revolution, one frequently finds cited the testimony of one Gouverneur Morris,[1] concerning whom the learned authors provide remarkably little information, either because such details appear to afford little of interest or because certain incongruities had better remain unexamined.

This faceless witness, who must be cited even so, then passes in many readers' eyes for the "governor" of some state of the American federation who must have retired to France at the worst possible moment. Jean-Jacques Fiechter's excellent biography[2] therefore filled, somewhat ahead of the French Revolution's bicentennial, a real lacuna. Fiechter instructs us that Gouverneur Morris's French given name has nothing to do with the title of "governor," which he had never held. He was born in 1752 to a Morris family of English origin, whose installation in New York, on an estate baptized Morrissania (today reduced to a charming museum in Harlem) dates back to the seventeenth century: the family had avoided Charles II's Restoration and the repression against Cromwell's partisans that followed. His mother, Sarah Gouverneur, sole daughter of Huguenots escaping the Revocation of 1685, had given him a first name that was that of her own family, which she thus sought to perpetuate somewhat longer. It was also she who chose, in order to provide

1. 1752–1816.

2. *Un Diplomate américain sous la Terreur: Les années européennes de Gouverneur Morris, 1789–1798* (Paris: Fayard, 1983).

him an excellent classical (and French) education, the Calvinist Academy of New Rochelle, created on the model of the Académie de Saumur by a colony of Protestants fleeing the persecutions of Louis XIV. He brilliantly passed his lawyer's examinations at the age of twenty.

Tall, powerfully built, the young American had regular features, a proud gaze, and a magnificent voice. One of Washington's officers has left this portrait of him:

> Mr. Governeur Morris is one of those Genius's in whom every species of talents combine to render him conspicious and flourishing in public debate:—He winds through all the mazes of rhetoric, and throws around him such a glare that he charms, captivates, and leads away the senses of all who hear him. With an infinite streach of fancy he brings to view things when he is engaged in deep argumentation, that render all the labor of reasoning easy and pleasing.

All these gifts were eventually to win him the liveliest successes in Paris, at a period when male beauty rediscovered for criteria the canon of Polycletus and the Roman ideal of the orator. George Washington, twenty years his senior, with whom he formed a close friendship, belonged physically to the same neoclassical type, in perfect agreement with the "colonial" colonnades and pediments of Palladian architecture. The sculptor Houdon, in order to complete successfully the general's full-length statue, at the moment he had been elected president of the United States in 1789, arranged for Gouverneur Morris to pose for him in his Parisian studio, at the request of Thomas Jefferson, who was struck by the resemblance between the head of state and his young friend.

With such advantages, Gouverneur Morris, well before seducing the salon sirens of France, quickly became in his own country, and not without scandal, a great lady-killer à la Kennedy or Clinton. The jealous gods of the Protestant ethic begrudged him this talent: in 1780, escaping a little too rapidly from a Philadelphia mansion where the man of the house had surprised him, Morris fell under the wheels of a carriage and had to have one leg amputated at the knee. His wooden leg in no way clouded his agreeable temperament, in fact rather adding to his attraction for the ladies. In 1792, threatened in the streets of Paris by a crowd shouting its hostile feelings against the "aristocrat," Morris emerged from the episode with great aptitude indeed, brandishing his wooden leg as a trophy and exclaiming: "I won this on the battlefield of American independence!"

In 1775, making a choice contrary to that of his brother, an officer loyal to the British Crown, Morris was elected to the first New York Provincial Congress of the insurgents, then again, in 1777, to the Continental Congress that voted for and led the Revolution. It was at this point that he became intimate with Washington. After the victory of 1783, he was made secretary of the treasury of the provisional government; in these functions he sharpened his experience of Franco-American economic and financial realities, in which the questions of the considerable debt contracted by the new nation to the French monarchy (it rose further in 1793 to 16,835,000 livres) and the American exports of cereals and dried beef (vital for France during this entire period) were of great importance.

In 1787, elected deputy to the Philadelphia Convention, he was one of the members, at age twenty-three, of the committee appointed to draw up the Constitution: he played a preponderant part in it, entering in his own lifetime the legend of the Founding Fathers for having polished and written out in his own hand the final text of both the Bill of Rights and the Constitution.

In these practical exercises of constitutional law and political philosophy, Morris was on the side of the moderate editors of *The Federalist Papers*; this legislative activity revealed, but also sharpened, his superior gifts of analysis and foresight, which justified Washington's deep sympathy for him and which found occasion to function on an infinitely more difficult and dangerous terrain in France and in Europe between 1789 and 1794.

This profound political wisdom afforded him the right to judge without indulgence the constitutional metaphysic of the intellectuals then dominating the Parisian scene. In his diary, one of the live-liest and best-informed accounts we possess of the Paris of the Revolution, Morris writes: "Go to dine with Madame de Staël, who is not yet come in.... The Abbé Siéyès is here, and descants with much self-sufficiency on government, despising all that has ever been said or sung on that subject before him, and Madame says that his writings and opinions will form in politics a new era, as that of Newton in physics."

This theoretical and decisive turn of mind was not unknown among Americans on the scene. Gouverneur Morris (anticipating the severe judgment of Conor Cruise O'Brien in his book *The Long Affair: Thomas Jefferson and the French Revolution, 1785–1800*) reproaches his predecessor in the American embassy in Paris (and his republican friends in the United States) for allowing themselves to be guided in their analysis of French events by blinkers that we would readily describe as ideological (O'Brien recalls that Jefferson, eager for equality—for France and in theory—was in fact coldly racist and pro-slavery in his personal behavior). Of such American members of the Montagne, Morris would write, before July 14, 1789: "They imagine that everything will proceed all the more smoothly the further they depart from present institutions. In their cabinet they see men insofar as they are necessary to their system. Unfortunately, such men exist nowhere, and even less in France."

And on June 19, 1789, aiming still more directly at Washington's future successor in the White House, Morris wrote: "[Jefferson], with all the leaders of liberty here, is desirous of annihilating dis-tinctions of order. How far such views may be right respecting man-kind in general is, I think, extremely problematical, but with respect to this nation I am sure it is wrong and cannot eventuate well."

On June 21, he declares to La Fayette, who does not even under-stand what his interlocutor means: "I am opposed to the democracy from regard to liberty." And a little later that year, on November 26, he writes: "[La Fayette] says he should like two chambers, as in America. I tell him that an American constitution would not do for this country, and that two such chambers would not answer where there is an hereditary executive; but that every country must have a constitution suited to its circumstances, and the state of France requires a higher toned government than that of England."

Gouverneur Morris had arrived in Paris in February 1789 to head the American economic and financial mission. He quickly found himself at home, introduced into Parisian high society and at Versailles by the many connections he had made as Washington's close friend, during the War of Independence, among the French *noblesse d'épée* that had flocked to the support of the insurgents. Even as he struggled under the British yoke, this good reader of Montesquieu had come to know well both the French aristocracy— with its weaknesses but also its inherited strength of a civilization of old and refined manners (quite superior in this regard to the harsh British gentry)—and the old French monarchical structure, it too a work of art secreted by the ages and fashioned by the nature of a great people: after all, it was to this ancient monarchy and to this no less ancient nobility that the United States owed and still owes its existence. Morris would have preferred that each be allowed to evolve with a certain prudence, without awakening the barbarous passions of civil war and the temptations of despotism. Such sentiments were shared by the most enlightened Founding Fathers, and not only Washington: John Adams, Alexander Hamilton, and even Jefferson's "spiritual son" William Short,[3] chargé d'affaires in the interregnum between his "father" and Morris—this young man went so far as to demand (in spite of Jefferson and naturally without success) the signature of Louis XVI, already imprisoned in the Temple, on the bottom of the receipt for a repayment of the American debt contracted by the young republic to the king of France. One would have to wait for Edith Wharton, Henry Adams, and Henry James (whose work has recently been reread from this viewpoint by Mona Ozouf) to locate among Americans a disabused

---

3. The correspondence between the Duchesse de La Rochefoucauld and William Short has recently been rediscovered and published in the collection Le Temps retrouvé, edited by Doina Pasca Harsanyi (Paris: Mercure de France, 2001).

complicity with the human success represented by the French *longue durée*.

Gouverneur Morris's Epicurean attitude (in the philosophical sense) toward life had given him a whiff of brimstone in his own country. In Paris, however, in the last days of the *douceur de vivre*, it found a climate that suited it. "Indeed," he writes, "pleasure is the great business." Or again: "Here, we are in the country of Woman. Women enjoy a virtually limitless power, and seem to take an extreme pleasure in it, though I am not sure that the country is extremely comfortable about the fact."

Even when the repeated massacres had begun, filling him with horror, the diary's author finds respite in the contemplation of that "dream of stone," trees, and light that French history has imagined and named Paris. The evening of the bloody day July 17, 1791, he notes: "I think one of the finest views I ever saw was that which presented itself this evening from the Pont Royal. A fine moonshine, a dead silence, and the river descending gently through the various bridges, between lofty houses, all illuminated . . . and on the other side the woods and distant hills. Not a breath of air stirring. The weather has this day been very hot."

He has his entrée at Mme Necker's and at Mme de Staël's, whose cult to her brilliant father he did not share: "He has the look and manner of the countinghouse, and, being dressed in embroidered velvet, he contrasts strongly with his habiliments. His bow, his address, etc., say, '*I* am the man.' . . . If he is really a great man I am deceived, and yet this is a rash judgment. . . ."

He makes friends with the great Malesherbes (who has become, these same years, the mentor of young Chateaubriand); in a letter of March 7, 1790, Morris writes of him: "He has so much goodness and so much serenity that is is impossible not to feel a very sincere affection for him."

From the start, this disabused analyst of situations and circumstances is convinced of two things: on the Continent the "European system" created by the treaties of Westphalia is ruined, and France has every means of designing another that will be even more favorable to her future. But this would require a Richelieu, and the monarchy's structural crisis under a wavering king (on July 1, 1789, Gouverneur Morris writes to John Jay: "The sword has slipped out of the monarch's hands without his perceiving a tittle of the matter.... My private opinion is that the King, to get fairly out of the scrape in which he finds himself, would subscribe to anything") and a politically crippled aristocracy merely delays this inevitable redistribution of the cards. Within the country, the absence of will at the head of the state will make impossible any moderate and reasonable solutions to the regime's crisis and will create a dramatic situation from which France will emerge, after many convulsions, only by a military dictatorship that will impose order internally and intervene in Europe by means of an empire. Has anyone proved a better prophet?

Gouverneur Morris's short-term pessimism will not keep this great heart from doing everything in its power to prevent the worst. He was partially in agreement with an "ultra" like Baron de Besenval, who found the convocation of the States General to be a disproportionately dramatic gesture for a bagatelle like the budget deficit (a very modest deficit by our own standards, 160 million on a budget total of a half-billion livres). Chateaubriand, in his *Mémoires*, will express the same retrospective bewilderment. Hence the "economic attaché" of the American embassy proposed to Necker an ingenious financial framework that could allow the anticipated repayment of the federal debt, reduced (according to the interests of the United States) but capable of relieving the famous deficit that was one of the origins of the French political crisis. Necker refused.

For lack of anything better, Gouverneur Morris made himself the intermediary of massive imports of flour and rice from the United States, payable on the terms of the debt (they later saved the Revolutionary governments from hunger riots), but he also oriented the transatlantic property investments that many Frenchmen—including Talleyrand and the Necker family—chose to make, not without risks of disappointments when they were not well advised. His own funds (which he had greatly improved by the commissions that such contracts assured him) were generously opened to hard-pressed French nobles (the first rank of these would one day include the wife of General de La Fayette).

But Morris's role in French affairs soon exceeded the limits of his mission. He was too astute in political analysis not to be tempted to intervene in a chess game as unusual and unpredictable as what was being played before his eyes, in the center of the universe, since his arrival.

Was it an accident that this ladies' man fell in love with one of the most ravishing and talented women of Parisian society, but also one most closely linked to politics (after, of course, Germaine de Staël)? Adèle de Flahaut, wife of the Comte d'Angiviller's younger brother, the director of the king's buildings and thereby provided with a large apartment in the Louvre, was already the official mistress of the bishop of Autun, M. de Talleyrand (by whom she had a son, Charles, who was to become the lover of Queen Hortense of Holland and father of the Duc de Morny), when she fell into the vigorous American's arms. Initially, Gouverneur Morris, jealous and disconcerted, felt for Talleyrand the aversion of a "noble savage" for the *diable boiteux* of old Europe: "He appears to be," he wrote, "a sly, cunning, ambitious, and malicious man. I do not know why conclusions so disadvantageous to him are formed in my mind, but so it is, and I cannot help it."

Mme de Flahaut having ultimately yielded to the newcomer, and the bishop of Autun having accommodated himself quite gallantly to this *ménage à quatre*, Gouverneur Morris, unaccustomed to finding political genius in the French nobility, inevitably soon recognized Talleyrand's and granted him the estime that a chess champion cannot deny a champion of another category. Since Talleyrand took a small revenge on Adèle de Flahaut by consoling Mme de Staël for the Comte de Narbonne's infidelities, Morris thereby entered the most brilliant society of Paris, and revealed himself quite competent to take part, if not in terms of cynicism (for example, Talleyrand, weary of Louis XVI, briefly allying himself with the extreme republican left), at least in the exercise of wit.

Though he had no illusions as to Louis XVI's will, or that of his most loyal minister, the Comte de Montmorin (the ill-fated father of Pauline de Beaumont, the survivor of the Terror whom Chateaubriand would canonize in the *Mémoires d'outre-tombe*), Morris indefatigably offered them his lucid analysis of the situation, enlightened by the information he was given concerning the projects of the Girondins and the Jacobins. When the king made up his mind to accept the Constitution of 1791, Morris composed in English, a language the king possessed, and made Mme de Flahaut translate for the queen, an acceptance speech to the assembly: Mme de Beaumont was in on the secret, and Mme de Staël managed to find it out. The speech was ultimately not retained. Fortunately nothing was ever discovered of this princely counselor's role played by the American diplomat. Discretion of this kind would make possible Gouverneur Morris's nomination, in January 1792, to the rank of ambassador plenipotentiary. Washington, who had imposed Morris on Jefferson (now secretary of state), strongly advised his friend to cultivate prudence and reserve.

Nevertheless, perhaps having read the president's real intentions between the lines, Morris did his best to collaborate with Montmorin on the second attempted escape of the royal family, who had become increasingly unpopular since the start of the war against Austria and whom the Duke of Brunswick's stupid manifesto had practically condemned. The conspirators combined their resources; Gouverneur Morris became the depositary of a certain fraction of this money, for which he accounted in a letter to Madame Royale in Vienna in 1796. Other escape projects, conceived by Mme de Staël or by the queen's friends Crawfurd and Fersen, were much discussed. As if fascinated by their imminent disaster, the king and the queen were still in the Tuileries, defenseless, when the enraged populace, on the indicated day, invaded the palace and compelled them to take refuge in the lodge of the logographer of the Assembly, from which they were led to the prison of the Temple.

On that day the American embassy (rivaling Sweden's in compassion) became the refuge not only of Adèle de Flahaut and her son but also of numerous other noble families entitled to seek the gratitude of the United States. In his report of August 16 to Jefferson, the ambassador paid homage to the king's dignity in misfortune; he nonetheless added: "The republicans had the good sense to march boldly and openly to their object, and, as they took care not to mince matters nor embarrass themselves by legal or constitutional niceties, they had the advantage of union, concert, and design against the disjointed members of a body without a head."

On September 10 Morris informed his minister of the bloody week:

> We have had one week of unchecked murders, in which some thousands have perished in this city. It began with between two and three hundred of the clergy, who would not take the oath prescribed by law. Thence these *executors of speedy justice* went to the Abbaye, where the prisoners were confined who were at Court on the 10th. Madame de Lamballe was, I believe, the only woman killed, and she was beheaded and disembowelled; the head and entrails paraded on pikes through the street, and the body dragged after them. They continued, I am told, in the neighborhood of the Temple until the Queen looked out at this horrid spectacle.

Montmorin had suffered an even more savage torture: covered with blows, then impaled alive, the father of Pauline de Beaumont was dragged by the mob from the Abbaye prison to the National Assembly. At this point Talleyrand decided to flee to England, where he made for Mme de Staël's country residence, Juniper Hall. Adèle de Flahaut, to earn in Hamburg her livelihood and that of her son, at this point entered upon a career as a popular novelist. Gouverneur Morris was the only ambassador who did not abandon his post in Paris. He managed to send, indirectly, some aid to the royal family. His sumptuous embassy (the Hôtel Seymour, in the rue de la Planche) was the last Parisian salon illuminated during the Terror, during which several temporary survivors sought relief by creeping along the walls to gain entrance. The furniture, silverware, works of art, precious books, and vintage wines bought at low prices from the royal cellars were conveyed here before being packed up and sent to Cherbourg. (At the same time William Beckford did the same shopping, destination Fonthill Abbey.) Gouverneur Morris planned to transform Morrissania, his family mansion, into an American museum of the French *art de vivre*, on the model of what Jefferson was undertaking in Monticello, his splendid Palladian villa in Virginia.

Morris's French country house in Sainville, where he spent most of his time during the Terror, was the refuge of the Comtesse de Damas, wife of one of his old military companions in the War of Independence (she bequeathed to her host a splendid portrait, reproduced by Fiechter), and of several other ladies rescued by the ambassador. He could do nothing more for Louis XVI except to bear witness, in his report to Jefferson, of the deployment of troops and the terrified abstention of the public at the moment of the execution on the former Place Louis XV.

On October 18, 1793, he described in a letter to Washington the radicalization of the new regime, and foresaw the quasi-genocidal law of 22 Prairial of the year II:

> The present government is evidently a despotism both in principle and practice. The Convention now consists of only a part of those who were chosen to frame a constitution. Those, after putting under arrest their fellows, claim all power, and have delegated the greater part of it to a Committee of Safety. You will observe that one of the ordinary measures of government is to send out commissions with unlimited authority. They are invested with power to remove officers chosen by the people, and put others in their places. This power, as well as that of imprisoning on suspicion, is liberally exercised. The Revolutionary Tribunal, established here to judge on general principles, gives unbounded scope to will. It is an empirical phrase in fashion among the patriots, that terror is the order of the day.... Whatever may be the lot of France, ... it seems evident that she soon must be governed by a single despot. Whether she will pass to that point through the medium of a triumvirate or

other small body of men seems as yet undetermined. I think it most probable that she will. A great and awful crisis seems to be near at hand.... Already the prisons are surcharged with persons who consider themselves as victims. Nature recoils....

Recalled on the insistence of the French Committee of Public Safety, Gouverneur Morris had time, before receiving the official letter of dismissal from Philadelphia, to witness the fall of Robespierre and the beginnings of the Directory. He left Paris on October 10, 1794, resuming his diary, which he had prudently interrupted on August 10, 1793. He lingered another four years in Europe, moving from court to court. He several times reencountered at Altona, near Hamburg (aside from his last Parisian mistress, Mme Simon), his dear Adèle de Flahaut, now a famous novelist, widowed since 1793 and engaged since 1796 to a young Portuguese diplomat, Count de Souza, who actually married Adèle only in 1802, so numerous were the former lovers who seemed to make their various rendezvous with the lady in this nest of émigrés: Talleyrand, back from America, Lord Wycombe, Gouverneur...

The diary as well as the private and diplomatic correspondence of Gouverneur Morris has been published, generally in English, but like most of the Founding Fathers, he spoke and wrote French very well. I limit myself to citing two of his letters in that language addressed to the Comte de Montmorin, Louis XVI's minister of foreign affairs, one in 1790 and the other in 1791, as well as the draft of a note addressed to the king.

LETTERS OF GOUVERNEUR MORRIS

To the Comte de Montmorin

January 26, 1790

The King is advised to present himself to the Assembly and to place himself (it is said) at the head of the Revolution. The métier of revolutionary, it seems to me, is hardly appropriate for a prince. I did not hesitate to say at the time that this was an inept and perfidious concept. These are bitter fruits that he has hitherto culled from his speeches to the Assembly. Inaction is for him not only the surest course but the only one not extremely dangerous. That those who fear the consequences of having driven matters to extremes seek now to take shelter from events in the shadow of royal authority is clear enough. Again, that those who began the Revolution and who, in attaining their goal, see themselves overtaken by their disciples, seek support against the violence they have provoked, is only natural. That the cleverest among them desired to preserve for some years the name of the monarchy in order to void it all the more completely of its content does not at all surprise me. But that the King should lend himself to this procedure, that he should lower his head and run right into the trap being set for him! Ah! That is a terrible pity.

Then what is to be done? Nothing. The Comte d'Artois's children are already well out of the realm, so that the royal family is no longer entirely in the hands of its enemies, who will be inclined to show more respect to those who still remain here for fear of reprisals from those who have escaped. Let them do their worst! In a short time, the whole social structure will be brought down, and the very persons who have poured insult on the crowned heads and instilled bitterness in their hearts will in their turn experience the very evils they have occasioned. War will come at the moment the general weakening will grant the enemy their certain prey. It will come to purge the State and set things on a new footing. Finance, in skillful hands, will gain certain advantages. It is not the means that France lacks, or the talent to employ them; but it must not be supposed that it will be possible to restore matters to their former condition. No, France must henceforth have a constitution that will assure its people all the liberty of which it is capable, or there will surely be a terrible tyranny. Such a circumstance is not at all within the powers of a wise and sensitive king. Therefore the latter possibility will surely come to pass, and there will be nothing to do but wait for its advent. Let the people be disgusted by the unprecedented novelties for which they are so greedy: time changes everything, and henceforth tranquillity will become, in its turn, the object most ar-

dently desired. Then men will come before the King to offer him the spoils of which he has just been stripped, and it will be in his power to assure the happiness of France forever.

To the Comte de Montmorin

May 25, 1791

I desire, my dear count, before I leave, to tell you something of the present state of affairs, and I must ask you to take the trouble of reading this letter rather than occupying a few more moments of your time in conversation. You gave me a very good response the other day when you asked: But who are the persons who at this very moment are regarded with favor by the people? If it were as easy as it is difficult to answer that question, it would still be impossible to know how long such persons would keep the goodwill of the people or, to put it better, of the populace. I am making no attempt to conceal the difficulty, as you see. But I wish to draw your attention to something else that is very clear. We know quite well the men, and the women too, who are detested— very unjustly, but heartily and frankly. Now, it is quite possible that we shall not choose very well, but it will still be a very good thing to change our choices. When the newcomers are depopularized, we shall have to change again, since by then the opposition will be to these new associates of ours rather than to the former leaders. I am strongly convinced that if the persons you favor now were to retain their positions for several months more, the political scene would be restored. Already we are beginning to see that anarchy will soon destroy everything if some remedy for it is not soon devised. This remedy is the authority of the leader, and since everything depends on public opinion, we require the time necessary to make people realize this great truth. Meanwhile I must ask you to consider that the Assembly and the departments have sought the dismissal of several persons; that the disorders inseparably connected to a paper currency[4] will continually affect the lower classes of society; and that we shall then see the emergence of a sort of struggle between the partisans of the old and the new regimes, perhaps

---

4. The assignats, promissory notes issued by the revolutionary government.

between the King and the Assembly. For it cannot be doubted that each will seek to cast blame on the other. If, at such a moment, the court were to find itself surrounded by those who have drawn upon themselves the quite unjust hatred of the populace, who is to answer for the consequences? Especially if, at the same time, France is threatened from outside her borders? You are well aware of the schemes long since devised by those I mention, and you will see that the good Father Duchesne, whom I have the honor of making known to you,[5] is already beginning to indoctrinate his beloved flock. I bid you farewell. I promise myself the pleasure of seeing you tomorrow at your café, when you shall return to me this and the other little papers that you know.

I am, with the sincerest attachment, M. le Comte, your humble servant.

G. Morris

To King Louis XVI

Paris, November 18, 1791

Sire,

It is a long while since M. de Montmorin left his post, and M. de Ségur accepted it only to resign the following day. Circumstances do not yet permit Your Majesty to fill the post with the proper person, indeed Your Majesty is experiencing great difficulty in making even a provisional nomination. Such a marked indifference to the first places of the realm thereby demonstrates the vices of the constitution. It must be very bad indeed for no one to be willing to serve under it, and it must be changed soon, since everyone realizes how unworkable it is. The republican party knows as much and sets great store by Your Majesty's inevitable impatience. That party is convinced that Your Majesty will give occasion to his enemies to raise themselves on the monarchy's ruins, and flatters itself that in the shocks inseparable from such utter anarchy the King will remain alone among the wreckage of his realm.

At such a moment, Sire, I dare address myself to Your Majesty. I

---

5. It appears that Morris helped launch a "false" royalist Father Duchesne to counter the attacks of Hébert's journal and of the *Enragés*.

shall not consider whether his old minister has served well or badly, because even supposing that he had been devoid of talent and zeal, it seems to me that the King's role is to regard himself obligated to make his gratitude evident to all. Certain unfortunate circumstances oblige him to oppose a representative Assembly. Now such Assemblies are always ungrateful, and consequently their members are moved only by a passing sentiment of enthusiasm. Yet a King, and especially a grateful King, commands hope, which is to say a universal human motive. As a result of which, everyone will sooner or later abandon the Assembly's cause for the King's. Thus, even if gratitude were not a virtue, it must always be a royal quality, for it is always a great means of governing. However, it does not fall to everyone, or on every occasion, to dispense largesse. In a royal lottery, it is only the greatest prizes that count, for little men and little services are rarely useful to kings. By distributing a host of small gratifications, one dissipates enormous sums to create a host of ingrates. By granting, on the contrary, great though few rewards, one excites the efforts of all by paying only one recipient, and thereby manages to reconcile the severest economy with great magnificence.

The moment is approaching, Sire, when the factions lacerating France will engage all their powers. If the émigrés remain calm until the Republicans have entirely broken with those who desire the conservation of what they call the monarchy, the latter will gradually unite with the aristocratic party, and then the Republicans will yield to the law of the stronger. In this union, there will be a question of the royal authority, and Your Majesty's rights will be supported only by those who hope to derive advantage from them. I am not offering the praise of humanity, sire, but a picture of France. May it be useful to Your Majesty. I desire his happiness and that of his august Queen with all my soul, and it is in accord with that desire that I dare communicate to them my reflections, convinced that they will pardon a perhaps importunate zeal.

24. *A Queen of England* in Partibus: *Louise Maximilienne Caroline von Stolberg-Gedern, Countess of Albany*

CHATEAUBRIAND ends his history *Les Quatre Stuarts* (1828) with this brief funeral oration for James II: "The tomb of the son of Charles I [at Saint-Germain] rises above our ruins, a melancholy witness of two revolutions and an extraordinary proof of the contagious fatality attached to the race of the Stuarts."

Louis XVI, reading Hume's *History of England* in the Tuileries and then in the prison of the Temple, meditated on the fragility of divine-right thrones, a fragility unknown to his ancestors but first manifested in the seventeenth century by the destiny of the Stuarts. The author of the *Mémoires d'outre-tombe* was haunted by the same parallel: the chronological displacement that made Charles I and his two sons, allies of Louis XIII and Louis XIV, a premonitory mirror of the French royal family's future, while revolutionary England offered an inverse image of the France of the Terror. On the other side of the Channel, the monarchy and the aristocracy survived the execution of Charles I and his second son's definitive exile, while in France—Chateaubriand had already reached this conclusion in 1828—not only was a dynasty too intimately associated with divine right no longer at home but the monarchical form itself could never again "take" after the execution of Louis XVI. Had the French martyr-king read in 1790 Burke's *Reflections on the Revolution in France*? Historian and statesman that he was, Chateaubriand paid close attention to the contrast the great Whig essayist drew between English continuity and French discontinuity. As a young émigré endeavoring to "think the Revolution," Chateaubriand had paid a visit to Burke in 1797.

The Penultimate Stuart

His narrative, in *Les Quatre Stuarts*, ends with James II's death in 1701 at Saint-Germain, "like a saint" (Dangeau *dixit*). James was indeed the last of the dynasty to have actually reigned, however briefly, rather like Charles X after Louis XVIII. In the *Mémoires* instead, Chateaubriand, with the same premonitory chronological displacement, describes the concluding history of the English Restoration—just as he gives, in his accounts of journeys to Prague and to Butschirad, the history of Charles X's abdication in 1830, the adventures of the Duchesse de Berry, and the twilight of the exiled court of the dethroned last Bourbon king and his family. He retraces the pathetic existence of James II's grandsons, "the Young Pretender," Charles Edward (Charles III *in partibus*), better known under the pseudonym the Count of Albany (1720–1788), and the obscurer life of his brother the Cardinal of York (1725–1807): these last two Stuarts never reigned and died without issue. The memorialist Chateaubriand also evokes the robust personality of Charles Edward's wife, whom he had met in Florence in 1803 and who survived her husband by nearly forty years.

Forgotten by French biographers since Saint-René Taillandier (1863) and surviving in English memory thanks to Vernon Lee, the Countess of Albany, like the Prince de Ligne, is a characteristic example of the continuity and the vitality of literary European high society between the Enlightenment and Romanticism, remaining outside of France, unscathed by the traumatism of the Terror and the emigration, which morally crushed so many of their French survivors. Much less affected than Germaine de Staël, that Genevan bourgeoise (though a Parisienne at heart), by the French drama and its ideologies, this cosmopolitan grande dame managed to escape the "contagious fatality" attached to the Stuarts, which spread to the French dynasty even before 1789. She separated as soon as possible from Charles Edward, and in 1792 she left Paris at just the right moment.

The European circle she gathered around herself in Florence, though unable to rival the grand occasions of Coppet, with which that circle was linked, enjoyed a longer life. During the Revolution and again under the Empire, Paris was no longer the "world capital" of French Europe: a constellation of cosmopolitan salons began to glitter outside of France, taking up the slack of Parisian salons with less worldly brilliance but already with the gravity of nineteenth-century Romantic ones. During the Terror, Adèle de Flahaut (Mme de Souza) transported her salon to Altona, outside Hamburg. Mme de Staël reconstituted hers at Juniper Hall, in England, then at her father's in Coppet. The Countess of Albany's Florentine salon, starting in 1792, was one of these delocalized nerve centers of European civilization. During the period between the two world wars, an analogous phenomenon was to be observed: Mme Mayrisch's circle in Luxembourg and the *Décades* of Pontigny in Burgundy endeavored to shield the conversation of the Republic of Letters from the racket of Paris. The history of "European salons" remains to be written, and the Countess of Albany, born a German princess and by marriage queen of England, though Italian at heart, would hold a notable place within it.

Her marriage to Charles Edward, celebrated at Macerata on April 17, 1772, occurred long after the great adventure of the Young Pretender's life: his attempt to regain the crown of his ancestors starting from the dynasty's fatherland, Scotland. This truly heroic attempt was the inspiring model for the Duchesse de Berry's 1831 escapade, which turned into opera buffa. The Pretender's landing in Scotland, his initial military successes, and the chivalric loyalties he aroused have remained the great legend of the ancient kingdom, immortalized by two of Walter Scott's most celebrated novels, *Waverley* and *The Fair Maid of Perth*, whose Restoration Romanticism worked a certain enchantment. Bonnie Prince Charlie, who counted on the support of Versailles (then at war with England), though he rallied the Jacobite Highlanders and made a foray that threatened London, gained no support from either French military or naval forces. The loyal Scottish knights were repulsed, scattered, and massacred at Culloden (April 16, 1746) by the Duke of Cumberland's army, and the Pretender barely managed to escape from one Hebri-des island to the next, regaining France at Morlaix.

In Paris, another humiliation awaited him two years later. By the Treaty of Aix-la-Chapelle, Louis XV agreed to expel from his realm the heir of the Stuarts and the great-grandson of Henriette of France. Charles Edward, regarding French hospitality as a family privilege, refused to leave Paris of his own free will. To general reprobation, he was arrested in his box at the Opéra and expelled *manu militari* in the direction of Avignon. It is likely that he almost immediately returned in secret to Paris; it even appears that he ventured incog-nito to London, where neither the Jacobites nor the Hanoverian police paid much attention to his presence. The crushed young hero had in effect become an inveterate and prematurely aged drunkard.

In 1776, his father, the Knight of St. George (James III), died in Rome. From Basel, where he heard the news, Charles Edward rode to the papal capital in order to be recognized as king of England by Clement XIII. The pope conspicuously ignored his existence. The following year, rebuked by his brother the Cardinal of York, he agreed, very much against his will, to present his respects to the Holy Father under the simple title of Count of Albany.

The young Princess von Stolberg-Gedern, daughter of a great Thuringian family of Austrian obedience and many Flemish pos-sessions, was an idea that occurred to the Duc de Choiseul.

He wanted the race of the Stuarts to perpetuate itself in order to keep an ace up Versailles's sleeve in the great Anglo-French game. Louise Maximilienne Caroline was not yet nineteen. Entirely French by education, this canoness of the Abbaye de Sainte-Vandru was pretty, witty, and cultivated, and in such a marriage the Hapsburg Fontevraud of Flanders saw a crown. On his part, Charles Edward was lured by the pension Choiseul had promised him. The couple made a royal entrance into Rome, which had no effect whatsoever on the papal resolution not to recognize "Charles III."

Never had Rome, on the eve of the suppression of the Jesuits, been a more brilliant European capital of the arts. Furthermore, Cardinal de Bernis, the French ambassador, brought there in Choiseul's wake

Parisian elegance and luxury, reflections of the sumptuous festivities of Versailles. Ignored, "Queen" Louise, unable to express her rank on any occasion, was doomed to abstain from them all. As the papal jubilee of 1774 approached, the "king" and "queen," to avoid a cascade of affronts, were obliged to say farewell to Rome and establish residence in Florence. Grand Duke Leopold, like the pope, ignored them. Charles Edward's impotent rage found expression only in his private life: dead drunk, he cruelly abused his young bride.

THE QUEEN AND THE POET

Two years previously, a young Piedmontese gentleman, virtually an autodidact but intent on becoming the new Petrarch *and* the new Dante, had made Florence his residence to rid himself of what in his autobiography he would call "French barbarism": he had determined to make himself a master of the Tuscan language. French Europe, unconscious of the fact, had already been undermined by the emergence of a Europe of the nations. By choosing to be "national," the Revolution and imperial France between them stripped away the "universality" of French language and manners, even as they claimed to replace it by the universality of great civic principles.

Impatience with the Gallic yoke suffered by Vittorio Alfieri (1749–1803) corresponded to analogous aspirations manifested in the same period by Germany, notably in Herder and Hamann, foremost apologists of the German race, language, and national spirit. Describing in his autobiography his first journey of Italian discovery, the Piedmontese poet would write:

> Furthermore, since in departing for a year's journey I had brought with me no other books than several Italian narratives, all in French, I was every day making new progress toward perfection in this barbarism in which I was already far advanced. With my traveling companions, conversation always occurred in French, and in the various Milanese houses

I frequented with them, it was also in French that we spoke. Hence this suspicion of certain ideas I was arranging in my little mind was never dressed in anything but French tatters; if I wrote some wretched child's play, it had to be in French— and of the worst sort—, for I had never learned this cursed language save by accident: if ever I encountered even the tiniest grammatical rule, I had taken no care to commit it to memory. As for Italian, I knew even less of that. Thus I gathered the fruit of the original disaster of being born in an amphibious country and then of the fine education I received there.

It was only in 1775, disgusted by the mediocrity of his first Italian tragedy, *Cleopatra*, and even more by the French prose tragedies stacked under his desk, that he took against "the paltry and unpleasant tongue" of the Welches (Voltaire's pejorative name for the un-Roman origins of the French); he then swore "to spare neither ink nor energy to put myself in a condition to speak my own language as well as it was spoken in Italy, convinced that, if once I managed to speak well, it would not thereafter cost me much to conceive and compose properly."

In Florence in 1777, all the future Dante lacked was a Beatrice. As soon as he set eyes upon the Countess of Albany—blond with black eyes, intelligent, and bookish—he knew it would be she:

> Having at last realized after two months that this was the very woman I was seeking, since, far from finding in her, as in the common run of women, an obstacle to literary glory, and in the love she inspired in me instead of a disgust for useful occupations inevitably diminishing my thoughts, here I found a stimulus, an encouragement, and an example for everything that was fine, I learned to know and to appreciate so rare a treasure, and henceforth I gave myself to her entirely.

A providential encounter. The young Italian aristocrat prefigured Chateaubriand, Lamartine, and Vigny, seeking in the writer's quill and laurels a substitute for the sword and wig of the old-fashioned court-and-battlefield gentleman. The Countess of Albany, too, was seeking a role of substitution. The ardent flame of this handsome red-haired cicisbeo, the sacrifice he made to her of his Piedmontese nationality (which for years cost him the income of a third of his fortune), and the many poems and dramas she inspired (notably *Maria Stuart*) ran too strongly within the current of her own desires for her to remain insensitive to the Italian poet's objurgations. Insulted and abused at home, she grew impatient with her reclusive situation. Alfieri himself took steps, obtaining the support of Grand Duke Leopold and the Cardinal of York in organizing the countess's escape from the conjugal domicile, now a prison familiar to all the world. At first she took refuge in a Florentine convent. A brief from Pope Pius VI approved the separation and designated a Roman convent where the countess might find asylum.

The scandal was enormous, and the rage of "Charles III" overwhelming. Alfieri turned into a bravo, arranging for a group of armed horsemen to protect the countess's carriage as it left for Rome. Then he turned back and, for decency's sake, waited several months in Florence.

In 1781, on the pretext of a journey to Naples, he again saw the queen of his heart behind her convent grille in Rome. To free herself from this new prison, the countess solicited Queen Marie-Antoinette, who granted her a generous pension, thereby freeing her from any financial dependence upon the cardinal her brother-in-law, now bishop of Frascati, who generally resided there. She took up residence in his Roman apartments in the Chancellery Palace, while the touchy Alfieri obtained, after a great deal of bowing and scraping for which he never forgave the Roman clergy, curial authorization to reside at last in Rome.

They were in the groping process of together inventing the Romantic adulterous couple, developing apart from conventional society a literary and artistic sphere inaccessible to scandal. In doing so they cleared the way for such legendary pairs as Germaine de Staël and Benjamin Constant, Chateaubriand and Pauline de Beaumont, Chateaubriand and Juliette Récamier, George Sand and Alfred de

Musset, Liszt and Mme d'Agoult; these became the new Europe's ruling couples. Electrified by his visits to the Chancellery Palace, Alfieri's talent made its definitive ascent, and the Roman salons where he read and even staged his new tragedies began to spread the news that a genius had been born to Italy. The vogue of the "return to the antique" was in full spate. The aristocratic poet's dramas were already being compared to David's *Oath of the Horatii*, everything in them exhaling passions of liberty, hatred of tyrants, republican virtue, and the stoic courage to confront violent death.

All the same, the situation was scabrous. The Cardinal of York, from his bishopric in Frascati, ended by realizing as much and being distressed. The pope informed the poet that he was an undesirable in Rome. In despair, Alfieri was obliged to leave. But he was henceforth a major figure of the Italian Republic of Letters, cherished in Milan by the old poet Parini, in Padua by the famous Cesarotti, Ossian's translator. In Florence Alfieri printed a select group of his tragedies. Yet he was gnawed by a certain ennui and decided to overcome it by journeying to England, where he would give himself up to another of his passions, racehorses. On the way, he made a long pause at the Fountain of Vaucluse, where he invoked Petrarch and Laura and in imitation of the fourteenth-century poet addressed versified maledictions to Paris, that "sink of iniquity," and to the "nasal jargon" of the French.

Meanwhile the countess enjoyed the official solicitude of Gustav III of Sweden, visiting Italy under the name of Count de Haga. Not content with soliciting from Baron de Staël, his ambassador in Paris, a supplementary pension for Charles Edward from the court of Versailles, the king took it into his head to unite husband and wife. The Countess of Albany managed to convince him instead to negotiate a separation in good and due form, which he obtained. Approved by the Cardinal of York, signed by Charles Edward, authorized by the pope, and sweetened for the Count of Albany by an augmentation of the pension provided by France, this document definitively emancipated the countess. She could henceforth rule in her own fashion and on her own account.

A Late Season in Paris

She agreed to meet her lover in Alsace, where they spent an agreeable two months; it was a spot from which Alfieri could easily run over to Kehl to check the proofs of his dramatic poems, printed by "Beaumarchais's admirable press," publisher as well of Voltaire's complete works. After this delay for propriety's sake, they moved on to Paris, which the countess had no reason to snub, and where the Imprimerie Didot would prepare yet another edition of Alfieri's tragedies. The year was 1787, and it was the late autumn of the menaced French ancien régime. We must concede this grand morganatic couple, in addition to the art of evading the faintest shadow of the demimonde, the further art of proceeding with a sure instinct for the apropos, always being present "where the action is" and promptly leaving when things go wrong.

But make no mistake: in their long shared adventure, it was the Countess of Albany who had a firm grip on the helm. She had the kind of mind analogous to the one that kept Talleyrand unsinkable in an age of revolutions. Like the bishop of Autun, she owed it to the iron discipline and infallible tact forged in the old courts of Europe. At Charles Edward's side, fallen as he was, she had been to the same school as Mme de Maintenon or Mme des Ursins. She therefore never dreamed of marrying Alfieri, which would have cost her a royal title. Intrepidly she pulled off the tour de force of always being greeted and treated as a queen, though publicly living in concubinage. She had assumed the tradition of the court of James II at Saint-Germain, but unconsciously she was preparing for the Récamier-Chateaubriand couple and their nest, the Abbaye-aux-Bois.

In the first Parisian residence she shared with her poet at the end of the rue Montparnasse, almost in the countryside, she had arranged a sort of throne room, all her silver was engraved with the arms of Great Britain, and her servants were trained to address her as Your Majesty. Mme de Staël always began her letters to the countess "Dear Majesty." Never for a moment did the countess lose sight of Florence where Charles Edward, assisted by an illegitimate daughter whom he had transformed into a Duchess of Albany, died with some dignity in her arms on January 30, 1788. In order to counterbalance this moral rehabilitation, she boldly emerged from the reserve she had hitherto preserved. Transporting her royal decor to the rue de Bourgogne, she took advantage of the great Parisian stage to declare herself the muse and sovereign of Europe's greatest living poet, permitting him to dedicate to her, with a fervor that eternally raised her above any vulgar reproach, the tragedy of *Myrrha* in the Didot edition: "You alone are the source of my poetry and of my inspiration, my entire life dates from the day when it was united with yours."

Thus she abandoned to his fate an illusory and narrow-minded king only to create out of whole cloth a prince consort who was also a prince of the spirit. The French public was well prepared by Rousseau's fictive trio of Julie, Saint-Preux, and M. de Wolmar to accept this legitimation of adultery in the name of poetic fecundity and spiritual supremacy.

Indeed Parisian high society rushed to accept the queen and her poet. Paris acknowledged a new salon, where great lords and high dignitaries such as Jacques Necker, the Comte de Montmorin, Malesherbes, diplomats like the Viennese minister Comte de Mercy-Argenteau, the Swedish minister Baron de Staël-Holstein with his young wife, and even the papal nunzio Monseigneur Dugnani regularly dined and conversed. A splendid revenge: never had the English court, even in the days of Charles I and Henriette, sported finer linen in its castles. Even if she had never been more than half-convinced of Alfieri's genius, Mme de Staël now established with the Countess of Albany a sort of power-to-power friendship that never altered. Beaumarchais came to the rue de Bourgogne, where the morganatic couple had their second Parisian address, to read *La Mère coupable* on February 5, 1791.

One of her masterstrokes was her brief sojourn in London. As the "legitimate widowed queen," she was officially received by the "usurping" royal couple George III and Queen Charlotte; she throned it in the royal box at the opera and on the ladies bench in Parliament. Horace Walpole commented on this enormous practical joke: "It is the great reversal of our day." In the diary she kept during this stay, the countess marveled like Montesquieu at "English liberty," but she considered English manners the least polite in Europe. She felt no desire, once her whim and her curiosity had been satisfied, to linger in London. Her salon, upon her return, shone with extraordinary brilliance: David, Marie-Joseph and André Chénier, the famous Hellenist and traveler Ansse de Villoison, the antiquaries d'Hancarville and Séroux d'Agincourt, and Alexandre and Joséphine de Beauharnais augmented the number of her habitués.

Alfieri could scarcely dream of a literary agent more effective than this new Beatrice. Yet the poet's biases against the French were not diminished, quite the contrary: political revolution, in which he had thought at first to recognize the shift to action of his aristocratic poetics of liberty, increasingly revolted him. Instead of the liberty of Miltiades and Cato, he saw the most jealous and ferocious of tyrannies being established before his eyes. He entirely agreed with Burke, who wrote eloquently in 1790:

> In such a popular persecution, individual sufferers are in a much more deplorable condition than in any other. Under a cruel prince, they have the balmy compassion of mankind to assuage the smart of their wounds; they have the plaudits of the people to animate their generous constancy under their sufferings; but those who are subjected to wrong under multitudes are deprived of all external consolation. They seem deserted by mankind, overpowered by a conspiracy of their whole species.

Along with André Chénier and Friedrich Schiller, this fierce "republican" passionately supported the cause of Louis XVI, for whom he composed an *Apologie du roi*. In private he no longer called the Revolution anything but *questa tragica farsa*.

The bloody riot of August 10 persuaded him to decamp, and the countess offered no objection. This tragedy was not theirs. On

August 18 they set out, duly armed with passports delivered by the section of their quartier. At the White barrier, the national guards let them pass, but the sans-culottes were alert and halted them with shouts of "Death to the aristocrats!" "Aristos to the Hôtel de Ville!" "The rich are leaving Paris with their money so the poor can starve!" The mob swelled, threatening to set the two carriages on fire. Alfieri, fortified by his up-to-date passports and arguing from his status as a foreigner, contended so effectively that the national guard came to the rescue, opposition was silenced, and they were permitted to drive out onto the high road. They had escaped just in time. Two days later, an arrest warrant for the countess would be pasted on her domicile, she had been added to the list of émigrés, and in the normal course of events would have ended hanging from a streetlamp in front of the Hôtel de Ville.

After these violent emotions, the Italian poet, already ill disposed, conceived an incoercible hatred against France. In 1804, his *Oeuvres complètes*, published under the direction of the Countess of Albany, would contain a collection of verse and prose entitled *Il Misogallo*, republished in London in 1814 but never translated into French. These *xenias* had been written in the heat of Alfieri's arrival in Flanders, where the couple found their first refuge.

Twilight of an Ideal Couple

By November 1792 they had returned to Florence. There the countess recovered the respect due her rank, and in her Palazzo Giantigliazzi on the Arno, equipped in 1794 with a theater for performances of Alfieri's tragedies, she resumed her role as Maecenas and hostess to the world of arts, letters, and diplomacy. But the poet's querulous humor, ravaged by taedium vitae, limited the new ascent of the countess's worldly vocation. In 1799 they were obliged to withdraw to the hills of Florence in order to remain apart from the French invasion, which Alfieri viewed with horror and rage. Yet the gallantry of Bonaparte's officers toward the countess and the connections she had recently formed with Josephine managed to save them from any damage.

By now the official grand amour, which Alfieri's writings had never ceased to exalt to the point of incandescence, was nothing but a social fiction as cold as that of *Les Yeux d'Elsa* for Aragon and Triolet or the Windsors' glamour for Edward VIII and Mrs. Simpson. Romantic passion, aimed against the conventions, in time becomes a convention itself, frequently one more rigid than marriage. Vittorio first suffered these constraints internally and in silence, just as in Paris he had suffered the no less disappointing political experience of liberty's mutation to license and to terror. He engaged in numerous brief and costly liaisons. Yet in his autobiography the idolatry of his queen and muse always remained at high pitch. He burrowed ever deeper into his laborious translations of ancient poems.

Little by little, a young plebeian painter, French into the bargain, a product of David's studio and of the Académie de France in Rome, François-Xavier Fabre (1766–1837), made his way into the couple's intimacy. He had begun in 1793 by giving the "Queen of England" drawing lessons and subsequently made a first portrait of the countess and the poet together. The secrets of this life *à trois* have been well kept. The correspondence between the new Petrarch and his Laura was destroyed by Fabre during the countess's lifetime and at her request. The formal executor of Fabre's will, a Jansenist, saw to it that none of his papers survived.

When Alfieri died on October 7, 1803, his "incomparable friend" had not left her poet's bedside for a moment. She had lost Marie-Antoinette's pension, but became the sole heiress of a Piedmontese fortune that her lover had recovered in its entirety. A widow's grief, and the tearful letters that made her a familiar presence throughout Europe, were worthy of the legend of Dante and Beatrice, of Petrarch and Laura, which the couple had reinvented together. A marble tombstone, the work of Canova, on which was engraved a Latin epitaph composed by Alfieri, eternally associated the great poet's name with that of *Aloysia e Stolbergis, comitissa Albaniae.*

This monument was inaugurated with great pomp in 1810 at Santa Croce, the Westminster Abbey of Florence.

Some months after the official period of mourning, François-Xavier Fabre had taken up residence near the countess *a casa di Vittorio Alfieri*, on the Lungarno. He presided, artist to artist, over the conception and completion of Canova's severe sepulchral monument to the poet's memory. He also superintended the typographical perfection of Alfieri's *Oeuvres complètes*, which appeared in 1804. He even borrowed the subject of a grand *tableau d'histoire* from one of Alfieri's tragedies. Chateaubriand, who claimed to have discovered the whole truth of the trio's relationships in 1803, during Alfieri's obsequies, nastily commented on the poet's Muse: "This lady, thick-waisted and quite expressionless as to countenance, made rather a common impression. If the women in Rubens's paintings were to grow old, they would resemble the Countess of Albany when I met her. It grieves me that this heart, fortified and sustained by Alfieri, should have required further sustentation."

A European Salon in Florence

It was then, nonetheless, that her great season as the hostess of Europe, long constricted by Alfieri's growing unsociability, could really flourish in Florence. All the new books published in France and Germany were read and discussed in the Palazzo Giantigliazzi. All foreigners of distinction passing through Italy aspired to be received there.

The Countess of Albany was too much a figure of the old courts to relish the ardent eloquence deployed by Mme de Staël against the Terror and the Empire. Such civic passion was too redolent, for her, of the France of 1789. On good terms with Josephine, she was also friendly with Elisa Bacciochi, the emperor's older sister, since 1808 the Duchess of Tuscany. But in her heart of hearts, and for quite other reasons than the chatelaine of Coppet, she was even more irreconcilable with the Empire.

Her Florentine salon was therefore not, like Coppet, a center of liberal thought and political resistance, but in her correspondence with Mme de Staël's guests, who were sometimes her own, like Sismondi and Bonstetten, she kept herself professionally informed of all that was said and read in her friend's establishment. This sufficed to concern the imperial police: the anti-French ghost of Alfieri might raise a suspicion that the countess's house had become a symbol, if not a rallying point, for an Italy rebellious to Napoleon's plans. In May 1809 the Countess of Albany received orders to move to Paris by autumn.

She left accompanied by Fabre. The emperor received her during an audience. He requested her, not without irony, "to satisfy her taste for the fine arts" in the French capital, without further troubling his own plans for the integration of Tuscany with the Empire. He had deracinated Mme de Staël from Paris, which she adored, and had forced her to occupy a residence under surveillance at Coppet. He deracinated the Countess of Albany from Florence where she ruled at her ease and confined her in Paris, for which she had lost all taste in 1792. Fabre of course could reconnect with David and his old studio buddies. After a year, the countess fortunately received authorization to return to Florence. All things considered, she was not a threat in the eyes of the police.

In 1815, Mme de Staël, in Pisa for the wedding of her daughter Albertine to the Duc de Broglie, exchanged many letters with the countess. It is easy enough to glimpse, behind the mundane graces, an essential political divergence: both women desired the failure of the Hundred Days, but one feared an antiliberal reaction and the other hardly concealed that she desired exactly that. Mme de Staël reached the point, the following year, of cruelly writing to the countess: "In this period of legitimacy, couldn't you become queen of England all over again?"

The countess concealed her sentiments well enough that as the widow of the "republican" Alfieri but also the widow of a Stuart, she could obtain the confidences of Italian liberals. What mattered to her was to remain in the movement and to attract to herself people who counted. A virtuoso of conversation *à la française*, she could not afford to flaunt convictions in any vulgar fashion. Hence the fine flower of liberal Europe, Adèle de Souza, the elder Bertin (the friend of Chateaubriand) Paul-Louis Courier, Lamartine, and Ugo Foscolo could be numbered among her guests and correspondents. But the Duchess of Devonshire, the Duchess of Hamilton, Cardinal Consalvi, ambassadors, ambassadorial secretaries, indeed the fine flower of the Europe of the Holy Alliance were equally pleased to appear with the countess and indeed at her home.

Fabre was of plebeian birth, but the countess, who had understood the social future of the arts, had not chosen a mediocre artist in order to exercise at his side the function of royal muse. Winner of the Grand Prix de Rome in 1787, this pupil of David was regarded by the master as the most gifted of his disciples after Drouais. Stendhal judged too quickly, as he frequently did, when he wrote, after visiting Montpellier: "Monsieur Fabre knew how to buy pictures, but not to make them." Fabre excelled in portrait, landscape, and history painting. Deprived of (or delivered from) Parisian competition, he painted relatively little, at intervals, but often with happy results. Like David exiled in Brussels, he adapted nicely in Florence, all things being equal, to an infrequent or visiting clientele.

Holding political views contrary to David's, he brought his parents to live with him in 1798, and his liaison with the illustrious and eternal émigré prolonged his own emigration. Paul-Louis Courier has left us incontestable testimony in favor of the countess's wit and that of her consort in a brief and sparkling dialogue entitled *Conversation chez la Comtesse d'Albany*, reporting three-way discussions at Naples in 1812. It fell to François-Xavier Fabre, who rather monopolized this "conversation," to establish—not without a polemical point against Napoleonic France and an indirect homage to Alfieri —the superiority of arts and letters to military heroism, and the fecundity of the wisdom of the ancients to the restless mind of the moderns.

The countess died in January 1824, leaving Fabre her sole heir. He took the time to have erected for her, according to his own design, a marble cenotaph in Santa Croce near Alfieri's tomb. That same year Fabre returned to Montpellier, the town of his birth, which after his death and according to his will made of his stately home a museum to contain the pictures by Renaissance and seventeenth-century masters that he had collected in the mansion on the Lungarno, as well as the countess's abundant epistolary archives and the contents of his own studio. In exchange for these considerable exports, he had given Alfieri's manuscripts to the Biblioteca Laurentiana.

To give some idea of the Countess of Albany's wit and animated style, here is a fragment of her London diary and a penetrating judgment on Mme de Staël's love-hate relationship with the Revolution and the Terror.

SPECIMENS OF THE COUNTESS OF ALBANY'S PROSE

Notes on England (1791)

I spent about four months in England, three of them in London. I had imagined this city quite differently. Though I knew that the English were melancholy, I could not conceive that a stay in their capital would be as sad as I found it to be. No sort of society, a great many crowds.... Since they spend nine months of the year en famille *with very few persons, they choose, when in the capital, to indulge themselves in what they call* flurry. *Consequently the women never stay home. The entire morning, which begins at two in the afternoon (for they rise only at noon, going to bed at four in the morning), is spent making calls and promenading, for the English need, and the climate necessitates, a great deal of movement. Coal smoke and the continual absence of sunshine, heavy eating and drinking oblige people to shake themselves up a lot; yet all this exercise does not save them from attacks of gout, which keeps them in bed for months and sometimes for years, for many people are crippled by this disease, which I attribute in large part to their intemperance.*

All the provincial towns are preferable to London, being less melancholy and less smoke-ridden; the houses are better, too. As everything costs a good deal of money, the windows, too, are taxed; consequently one has but two or three on the street, which renders the houses cramped and uncomfortable; and since property is extremely dear, houses are built straight up, story upon story. The one luxury England enjoys, and this an inappreciable one, is political liberty.... Their government being a mixture of aristocracy and democracy and monarchy, this latter element, though quite limited, is powerful enough to keep the machine running without the help of the other two, yet not enough to ruin the country, for though the prime minister may have a majority in the Chamber, if he seeks to undertake some enterprise harmful to the nation, his friends abandon him, as occurred in the war with Russia. The people have only as much government as is necessary, that is, of which they are capable, and though it is often claimed that the government is bought at elections, the offices invariably fall to persons who would not willingly dishonor themselves by supporting a bad cause, one harmful to the nation and contrary to their own interests. The aristocracy is also a part of the government, for a certain number of families compose the House of Lords; but that Chamber never inflicts damage, because the House of Commons is filled with the brothers of these lords, and there is not a single member of the lower house who may not aspire to become a lord, if the services he has rendered to the State should lead there. But there is no country where each order is so pigeonholed into classes as England. The populace feels at liberty, yet renders what is due to each individual; it is accustomed to this procedure, and the English people, while respecting their superiors, know that they are equal before the law. If England had had an oppressive government, this country, as well as its people, would be the last and least in the entire universe: bad climate, poor soil, and consequently produce that has no taste; it is only the virtue of its government that has made this country habitable. The English are a melancholy people, with no imagination or even wit; all are greedy for money, the dominant English characteristic; there is no one who cannot be bought by more or less of this metal. I attribute this vice to the extreme need felt in this country where, even with a considerable fortune, one is yet poor, a consequence of the enormous taxes that must be paid and the dreadful cost of even things of the mere necessity.

It seems to me that the good laws of this country have accustomed its people to justice; it similarly seems that the weak are properly protected; children running in the streets have never anything to fear. The English love their womenfolk for physical needs, but do not understand the necessity of living in society with them. They are severe and demanding husbands, and their wives are generally more obedient than in other countries, because they have more at risk; the arrangement of houses keeps them from receiving at home without the servants and the husband being informed. They are in general good wives and good mothers, though they love gaming, and the great ladies are excessively given to dissipation. There is nothing in London that could be called private society, nor the charm of such a thing; one lives in the constant company of one's family, which is to say with one's husband and one's children, for one grants nothing to one's father nor to one's mother, at least in the class which I have frequented.

"The English are not capable of responding to any of the fine arts, and still less of executing them; they buy many pictures and understand nothing whatever about them...."[1]

Observations on Madame de Staël's *Influence of the Passions on the Happiness of Individuals and Nations* (1797)

This book is a jumble of ideas plucked from hither and yon, seasoned by a careless and obscure style that is the product of the bad taste of the times. It is evident that the lady is much taken by the Revolution, which absorbs all her thoughts; that she flatters the powers of the moment in order to return to Paris, absence from which is her devouring passion. In the chapter "On the Love of Glory," she describes her father, for she believes him to be the greatest man of the age.... She also believes she knows love, though she knows merely the imagination's lapses.... Only the chapter "On the Spirit of Party" is interesting, for having lived among the plots of the Revolution, she knows their every intricacy. This

---

1. Saint-René Taillandier, *La Comtesse d'Albany* (Paris: Michel Lévy Frères, 1862), pp. 112–116.

is one of those books that will fall from one's hands, like so many others that are born during the troubles of the moment and perish with them.

Certainly it is difficult to express a more iniquitous judgment than hers. How many mistakes, how flagrant the injustices! Can it be that the introduction alone has not enlightened the author as to the true character of her book and the true mission of France? Mme de Staël, one is inclined to say, was a faithful representative of our genius, when she eloquently cried in 1796: "Shame be upon me if in the course of two dreadful years, during the reign of terror in France, I had been capable of such an endeavor, if I could have conceived such a plan and garnered such a result, involving the horrid mixture of every human atrocity! Generations to come will perhaps examine the cause and the influence of these two years; but we, the contemporaries and compatriots of the victims immolated during these bloody days—could we have sustained the gift of generalizing ideas, of meditating upon abstractions, of separating ourselves even a moment from our impressions in order to analyze them? No, even today reason can scarcely approach this incommensurable period. To judge these events, by whatever names one assigns them, is to force them back into the order of existing ideas, ideas for which there were already expressions. Confronting this hideous image, the soul's every agony is renewed, one shudders, one burns, one longs to do battle, one hopes to die; yet thought cannot yet grasp any of these recollections, the sensations to which they give birth drown any other faculty. Hence it is by averting this monstrous epoch, it is with the help of other main events of the French Revolution and of the history of all peoples that I should try to unite impartial observations as to governments, and if such reflections were to lead me to the acknowledgment of first principles on which the republican constitution of France is founded, I wonder whether, even amid the frenzies of the spirit of party that now lacerate France and, through her, the rest of the world, it might be conceivable that the enthusiasm for certain ideas does not exclude the profound scorn for certain men, and that hope for the future might be reconciled with the execration of the past."[2]

---

2. Saint-René Taillandier, *La Comtesse d'Albany*, pp. 144–146.

25. Charles-Joseph de Ligne: The Last Homme d'Esprit

THE PRINCE DE LIGNE belongs to that Enlightenment literary family to which not much attention has been paid, so jealously have the modern heirs of *les gens de lettres* and *les philosophes* secured the leading roles on our century's stage for their own ancestors. Yet this family of *hommes d'esprit*, and *femmes d'esprit* too, was precisely the one that set the tone and the style, if not the thinking itself, of the Enlightenment. Men of letters and philosophers dreaded that family's ascendancy, and competed with it by intimidating means (paradox, provocation, scandal, sarcasm) likely to rouse opinion and put the crowd of laughers on their side. The figure who today is sometimes called the "media intellectual" appeared in eighteenth-century Paris and took that century by surprise.

Esprit is not the same as intelligence that plays to the gallery. It is an ancient and aristocratic notion. *Ingenium*, by its etymology, is a natural gift received at birth. It is also a quality of the free man, the *ingenuus*, who dares to have his sentiment but expresses it apropos, without forcing the tone and taking care not to wound, to humiliate, or to provoke by vulgar outbursts. This confidential felicity of lively, rapid repartee, this sense of the mot juste and the right tone in the most delicate contingency, are social gifts and graces sparingly distributed, and their reputation is not cherished in the marketplace. In the sixteenth and seventeenth centuries, Castiglione, Montaigne, La Rochefoucauld, and La Bruyère had been the several Socrates of this aristocracy of esprit that is never identified with an "establishment," even if nothing keeps them from overlapping.

In 1713, Anthony Hamilton's *Mémoires du Comte de Gramont*,

which Chamfort would describe in 1787 as the "breviary of our young nobility," had sketched for the century of the Maréchal de Richelieu and the Prince de Ligne the typical portrait of a young gentleman, heroic on the battlefield, boldly amorous and adventurous in peacetime, but always an *homme d'esprit*, a cornucopia of diverting remarks, of piquant characterizations, of sharp and epigrammatic anecdotes. It follows that the "man of wit" caught by Hamilton in the fine flower of his age, all too busy living gaily and dangerously, has nothing of the man of letters or the philosopher about him. It was his brother-in-law, vain of his clever pen, who had taken the trouble to polish the *Mémoires* that the aging Gramont could scarcely be bothered to write but that he had nourished orally on memories of his younger days selected for the diversion of his friends. The young knight of the *Mémoires du Comte de Gramont* ends by finding a companion worthy of himself in Elizabeth Hamilton, a female equivalent of this male paragon. He will marry her. This book set the tone until 1789 for the style and behavior and conversation appropriate to the fierce male youth of the French nobility, a model for their European equivalents.

If education, study, reflection, and work can develop *ingenium*, it is crucial that such a help be neither known nor seen. Esprit is a casual improvisation, free of all the stigmata of effort on which the pedant prides himself. It has everything to do with charm, vivacity, the lovable ease that becomes as irresistible in love affairs as in the great world. Epigram, pun, the quick turn of phrase, the telling characterization, the racy story—everything that adds salt to dialogue and fire to life in society enters into the felicity of the oral expression of the man or woman of wit. Graces of speech and the social ballet, these talents for the joys of life signify only among those "wellborn," by blood or co-optation. They are inconceivable to the vulgar, as numerous among lords and squires as among commoners. In the *Mémoires*, Hamilton assails the dullards of the court of Charles II, though they bear the greatest names of England, for not divining the "smart set" with whom they come in contact. Wit (Pascal calls it *habileté*) invariably has that profound complicity with the real persons among commoners that he denies to the demi-habiles among the wellborn. The people have no acquaintance with the dullard's vanity and the parvenu's crude arrogance, possessing a natural common sense along with a spontaneous appetite for all the various gifts of nature. An *homme d'esprit* is at home everywhere. Knowing who he is but making no show of it, he acknowledges the diversity of conditions, of tastes, of manners without ceasing to evaluate them.

The misfortune that can afflict the heart of an *homme d'esprit* (and that eventually impels him, as in the case of Anthony Hamilton, to write) is not a reason for him to limit his *ingenium* and seek compassion. Like the warrior's valor and the lover's desire, his *esprit de joie* never slackens. Even when inspired by melancholy (the Prince de Ligne, belittled by his father, frustrated in the advancement of his military career, overwhelmed by the death of a beloved son, suffered many disappointments), the nonliterature of an *homme d'esprit* resists acknowledging that Rousseauan self-pity that the survivors of the eighteenth century censured in Chateaubriand. Such nonliterature has the gay naturalness of conversation, which it continues by other means. And like conversation, it discovers its reward in itself. Nothing is more odious to a man of wit than the label of "professional author," except perhaps that of the "successful author" who derives a profit from what he writes and from its eventual sales. The artisanal notion of a masterpiece is profoundly alien to him, for it presupposes hard labor, which destroys a natural style and offends liberty. That the Prince de Ligne was a European authority in the sphere of *gens d'esprit* is evidenced by the Comte de Tilly's *Mémoires*, dedicated to Ligne: "What little I've read to you from my *Mémoires* in Berlin [in 1805] seems to have gained your approval; you were indulgent enough to praise them so highly that I did not hesitate to continue to the end."[1]

---

1. *Mémoires de Comte Alexandre de Tilly*, edited by Christian Melchior-Bonnet (Paris: Mercure de France, 1986), p. 58. These *Mémoires* are dedicated to the Prince de Ligne, to whom the author writes: "How to explain the impulse that compels us to leave a memento to ruins and wreckage? Might we have an inclination to claim certain spoils from death, to leave certain traces of ourselves, to propagate the thoughts contemporaneous with our passage through life? We hope our writings will survive him for a time: we love to combat nothingness" (p. 57).

By beheading esprit's public as well as a good number of *hommes d'esprit*, the Revolution condemned the survivors to the sedulous toil of the "successful" text, to the histrionic and publicity-seeking strategies of the "genius" who must, like Napoleon, proceed from exploit to exploit, to the forced labors that must be carried out in order to achieve advancement, and for the losers to the sufferings of the crucified. Chateaubriand is the archetype of the noble young survivor who has broken with the Hamilton model and been compelled to accept the discipline and histrionism of the professional writer, living by his reputation and by his pen. The Prince de Ligne, ruined by the French invasion of Flanders, was by then too old to change his style, but was nevertheless compelled, in 1795, to sell his writings in a democratic market to a publisher and even, supreme shame, to write for his living.

Fouquier-Tinville could not arrange the execution of Charles-Joseph de Ligne, citizen of French Europe and the archetype of a former aristocrat. The Prince de Ligne had had the wit not to be born French, and not to have set foot in France after 1787. His very old feudal family from the Catholic Low Countries, of the same rank as the Arembergs or the Croÿs, caused him to be born a prince of the Empire. His natural capital was Vienna, though he spoke no more German than Frederick the Great. He was French by the language and education that a former student of the Jesuits of Louis-le-Grand had given him; Paris and France were for this grand seigneur—as much at home among peers and relations in Berlin as in Warsaw, in St. Petersburg as in Versailles—that second fatherland of every *homme d'esprit*.

Nor did the Prince de Ligne have occasion to distinguish himself and eventually to die during the Franco-Austrian wars of the Revolution and the Empire. The higher Viennese bureaucracy invariably denied him a military command and regularly preferred, for the conduct of absurdly conceived wars, nonentities whom Dumouriez and later Napoleon found an easy target of ridicule. Yet this born soldier had given his measure in his youth; he had brilliantly served Austria during the Seven Years' War, though Austria never afterward gave him occasion to deploy his military talents. He made up for this prematurely interrupted career in the imperial army with insatiable love affairs, that other aristocratic sport. He appreciated all its specialties, without clerical or bourgeois prejudice. All he excluded from love was marriage, that lineal duty that he ultimately fulfilled without any fuss. He was indeed an inconstant and even absent husband, but the best of fathers. When in 1794 he encountered Giacomo Casanova in the latter's melancholy retreat of Dux, in Bohemia, he formed a close friendship. Not surprisingly, Casanova's *L'Histoire de ma vie*, which Count Waldstein's old librarian was then writing as a cheerful recollection of a suddenly vanishing French Europe, delighted the prince, his colleague in letters and in regrets.

De Ligne enjoyed triumphs other than those of the alcove, particularly in the art of conversation, which won him the esteem of connoisseurs and champions as incontestable as Frederick II, Catherine II, Stanisław Poniatowski, and Germaine de Staël. Sénac de Meilhan has left us a portrait of his *ingenium* in action: "He gave the impression of a poet in the exaltation of his verve, and of a painter in the heat of composition. His countenance had a noble expression, his manner was somewhat distracted yet fond. He could embrace a man tenderly yet be at a loss to remember his name, and frequently would pass by one of his friends without seeing him."

Correspondence, for an *homme d'esprit*, is conversation continued by other means, yet with the same verve, in the same style. The Prince de Ligne was a peerless letter-writer. A convincing performer on *stages de château*, like everyone in the eighteenth century, he was also one in life, performing the most various roles in swift succession. He wore the most diverse campaign or parade uniforms of several armies: Austrian, Polish, Russian. Despite such dazzling sociability, this gift of ubiquity, and these metamorphoses, lacking a field of authentic action, he ardently engaged in writing, yet without succeeding in producing himself on the stage of the Republic of Letters. He did, however, visit Ferney to pay his respects to Voltaire in 1763, figuring in the almanac of eminent European nobility and crowned heads who corresponded with the patriarch. He clambered up to Rousseau's attic in the rue Plâtrière in 1767. Such gestures manifested an appetency for the philosophes, but hardly an allegiance.

Like all noble warriors with a taste for writing (Montaigne, who wore a sword in his portraits, was first to serve as a preeminent model), he wrote profusely as an amateur in genres that themselves were nonprofessional, and not only letters, for his personal satisfaction or that of his friends. The Comte de Caylus, who always published anonymously, and frequently in collective compilations, left an impressive quantity of manuscripts, *vers de société*, *comédies de château*, travel diaries, maxims, reflections, and tales, but a great part of them vanished in the revolutionary torment. Though two generations younger, the Prince de Ligne was seized by the same addiction to private and autobiographical writing and proved to be no less abundant than Caylus.

There is, indeed, a "literature of *hommes d'esprit*" that has its own features, its own genres. The difficulty that history and academic literary criticism (leaving aside the lesson of Sainte-Beuve) have persistently encountered in situating the prince's *Mémoires* comes largely from their not having taken the true measure of this literature of often very gifted amateurs, whose most misleading characteristic is a frequently and extensively postponed publication. The quite recent appearance of the unpublished (and hitherto unknown) correspondence of the Duchesse de La Rochefoucauld with William Short, between 1790 and 1838,[2] attests to the fact that the clandestine manuscripts of the eighteenth century are not always those of persecuted philosophers.

But as a consequence of writing drop by drop, as Jean Paulhan used to say, one acquires the knack, even the métier. Montaigne, here too, afforded the best of examples. An abundant and virtuoso letter-writer, essayist, moralist, historian, literary critic, poet, and

2. Edited by Doina Pasca Harsanyi (Paris: Mercure de France, 2001).

dramaturge, the Prince de Ligne excelled in the same genres as Caylus, but with different arborescences. Even when he determined to publish a great part of his production, he failed to create a writer's personality distinct from his persona of prince of the Empire. So he remained a grand seigneur, at once the most independent of men and the most perfect courtier, which obliged him not to publish under his own name, and not to expose himself to the judgment of the wider public. It also doomed him to remain marginal to the Republic of Letters. This grand seigneur preferred the company of writers to that of the majority of his peers, yet he did not privilege that company.

With time and disappointments, he developed a secret graphomania, like the Duc de Saint-Simon. The sequel to his *Mélanges* he called *Mes posthumes*, among which figure the *Mémoires* under the title *Fragments de l'histoire de ma vie*, written in Vienna and at Toeplitz between 1795 and 1814. Nothing was known of them until 1927; we have had to wait for the Jérôme Vercruysse edition to obtain the critical text.[3] The prince's work in fiction, thanks to the efforts of Roland Mortier and Marcel Couvreur, has begun to reach the attention of the learned. His *Livres rouges* or *roses*, a collection of delightful short stories, were for a long time condemned to darkness by his heirs. They are now at last printed in his *Complete Works*.[4] One discovers in the Prince de Ligne, nonchalantly sown, seeds that, carefully cultivated, would make the fortune of Chateaubriand and Proust: "Have I spoken on some occasion of the pain one suffers from recollections? The dinner bell of the château here [at Toeplitz] has the same sound as that of the Château de Bel-Oeil. This has on me the same effect as the cry of the peacocks that are kept in the Prater."

The same year he began writing his—by definition posthumous

---

3. *Fragments de l'histoire de ma vie*, vol. I, edited by Jérôme Vercruysse (Paris: Champion, 2000).

4. Now extensively published by Professor Roland Mortier and other scholars in a series that appeared from 2000 to 2007 (Paris and Geneva: Editions Champion). The complete *Correspondence*, in the same series, is a work in progress.

—*Mémoires*, in the deep shadow that the French Revolution had cast over Europe, the Prince de Ligne made up his mind to publish, but anonymously, in Dresden, at the publishing house of the Walther brothers, thirty-four successive volumes of *Mélanges militaires, littéraires, et sentimentaire* (an unhappy neologism destined to combat that other one: *sentimental*), from which he derived some income and that paid some of his eternal debts. This publication extended from 1795 to 1811. Other numerous manuscripts from his hand have slept for two centuries in the archives of the family château of Bel-Oeil in Belgium.The prince described this château along with his gardens and kiosks in a short essay that still remains his only famous text (because it was the first printed in his lifetime): *Coup d'oeil sur Bel-Oeil.*

At the beginning of 1809 he made another step outside the ancien régime of *hommes d'esprit* and penetrated somewhat further into the professional Republic of Letters. Mme de Staël, whom he had delighted in Vienna, published in Paris, with a preface-portrait, an anthology of his *Mélanges*. This work had a lively success and several editions. The name and title de Ligne, this time clearly avowed, thus made their belated official entrance into literature, and in the author's lifetime.

Almost simultaneously, Chateaubriand published his masterpiece, polished since 1804, *Les Martyrs*, an epic in prose. The book was lacerated by the Empire's official criticism, and the public remained aloof. Hence an ironic set-to between the two aristocrat-writers, one loyal to the amateurism of the eighteenth century, the other urgently seeking to adapt himself to the "age of revolutions." The Prince de Ligne's best friend, according to his own statements, was Alexandre de Laborde, son of Marie-Antoinette's banker (guillotined in 1793). By 1805 Alexandre de Laborde was closely linked to Chateaubriand, a guest at the family château of Méréville. There Lucien Bonaparte met Antoinette Jouberthon, and Chateaubriand met and fell in love with Nathalie de Noailles, Laborde's twin sister, his "best beloved." "Dear Francis," as Mme de Staël called Chateaubriand, was moreover on the best of terms with the Lady of Coppet, de Ligne's publisher and friend. The future author of the *Mémoires d'Outre-Tombe* could not have known de Ligne's *Mes Posthumes*, where the prince wrote, "This is a dead man speaking. "But he could have read in 1828 in the opening pages of Tilly's *Mémoires* the same preference for adopting a "ghost's voice" characteristic of the survivors of 1793: "I would not have let myself write if I were not dead to the world before having ceased to live."[5]

Of course, for the prince and for Tilly, "beyond the grave" meant the pastoral underworld of the *Dialogues des morts* of Fénelon and Fontenelle, where one perpetuated the conversation between *gens d'esprit* that had given life its savor. It had nothing in common with Milton's and his admirer and translator Chateaubriand's biblical and modern Hell.

While still an adolescent, the Prince de Ligne had been appointed chamberlain to Empress Maria Theresa at the Hofburg. He knew Marie-Antoinette before she left for France. In 1779 he appeared first in the dauphine's Austrian entourage, then in the queen's, still controlled by Ambassador de Mercy-Argenteau. In his memorable biography of the prince, Philip Mancel is not tender to the young princess, who managed to focus against herself and against French royalty the only strong religious sentiment the Enlightenment had left intact in France: patriotism. This biographer absolves de Ligne, who shone in the salons of Paris even more than at Versailles and who avoided participation in the intrigues of the seraglio. Counter to French opinion and the dauphine's attitude, the prince, like Gustav III of Sweden, had every indulgence for the old Louis XV's liaison with the exquisite Comtesse du Barry, and after the king's death paid several gallant visits to the ex–royal mistress at Louveciennes. In France, he sought above all to obtain from the queen and her ministers support in the various trials lingering under Parisian jurisdiction, whose financial stake was vital for this magnificent spendthrift.

Based mainly in Vienna after 1787, he demonstrated his political intelligence of French affairs in 1792, writing to his friend Ségur,

---

5. *Mémoires du Comte Alexandre de Tilly.*

who had rallied to the cause of the Revolution, he prophesied: "An iron scepter: that is the consequence of such liberty. You will become slaves, as you deserve." This was also the sentiment of Gouverneur Morris, American ambassador to Paris at the same period. And Bonaparte, even appearing under his name, was already on the vanishing point of revolutionary perspectives in the eyes of the sharpest observers.

As a grand seigneur spontaneously critical of central authority, the Prince de Ligne did not sympathize with Joseph II's enlightened despotism. In 1789 he supported the rebellion of Flanders against Viennese centralism. But as an Enlightenment layman and free spirit he took anticlerical positions and, like Voltaire, devastated hypocrites and bigots with his epigrams.

Without causing him to deviate from his fundamentally liberal turn of mind, the Terror restored simultaneously his sense of Catholic piety and of the monarchical ancien régime, both of which had hitherto been so patent and unshakable facts entirely susceptible to spirited mockery. When in 1814, at the age of seventy-four, full of renewed faith and hopes, he watched the proceedings of the Congress of Vienna, which would, it was believed, revive the spirit of the Europe of the treaties of Westphalia and, by a Holy Alliance, put an end to the nightmare parenthesis of the Revolution and the Empire, the handsome old man, as witty as ever, was enthralled by the fireworks of several imperial and royal courts concentrated in the same metropolis. For two years (1814–1815) receptions, balls, comedy and opera performances, and concerts made Vienna the artistic as well as the diplomatic capital of Europe, substituting itself for a parenthesis to Louis XVI's and Napoleon's Paris. As Ligne said: "The Congress does not walk, it dances." The recent literary fame he owed to Mme de Staël added to his reputation as an incomparable courtier and diplomat. He was the man of the day. Without realizing it, the grand seigneur had also become a glamorous star in the modern sense, spinning in a galaxy of kings, emperors, ministers, generals, and beautiful women. Chateaubriand, though he would claim to have become the leading man of the Congress of Verona

(1822), became its star only after the fact, in the narrative he published himself along with the acts of the congress.

The Prince de Ligne was accustomed to slow rhythms, to gradual advances in the relatively limited circles of ancien régime diplomatic life. He did not long resist the artificial (strictly speaking, already media) pressure that Napoleon had imposed upon international relations at Erfurt and Tilsit and that the anti-Napoleonic Congress of Vienna, that triumph of the French language and indeed of French Europe, had inherited. Exhausted, the Prince de Ligne died on December 13, 1815, fortified by the sacraments of the church. The night before, as his wife reported to him that all the sovereigns had inquired after his poor health, he made a last thrust: "Tell them to go to the devil, they're the cause of it all."

Never did the Prince de Ligne's talent for conversation appear livelier than in his letters to the Marquise de Coigny, the totality of which constitutes a complete reportage on Catherine II's show trip across Russia to the Crimea in January 1787 (the "Potemkin villages" were invented to decorate her progress). The tsarina was accompanied by ambassadors from France (Ségur), Austria (Cobenzl), and England (Fitz-Herbert), and she had invited the Prince de Ligne to accompany them as her particular friend and guest: his wit was to serve the diplomacy of the Russian autocrat. On May 18, Joseph II, traveling incognito, joined the empress. De Ligne made the third party in their discussions. This was the prelude to a Russo-Turkish war (1787–1792) in which the cosmopolitan prince participated in a Russian uniform: Catherine II had given him an estate in the region of Yalta.

It was appropriate that Mme de Staël published these letters in her 1809 anthology, completing them by the prince's portrait of the empress's minister and favorite Potemkin, taken from a letter to the Comte de Ségur. Germaine had erected a cenotaph to what she had most loved in the French ancien régime, to what she would have wished at all costs, like Stendhal, to transplant into the new grim regime *à l'anglaise* of the post-1789 moderns: the charm of *hommes* (*et femmes*) *d'esprit*.

Letters from Prince de Ligne To the Marquise de Coigny[6]

Barczisarai, June 1, 1787

Arriving in Tauris, I had expected to elevate my soul by the great things, true and false, that have occurred here. It was prepared, that soul, to take a turn to the heroic with Mithridates, to the fabulous with Iphigenia, to the military with the Romans, to the tender with the Greeks, to the piratical with the Tartars, to the mercantile with the Genevans. All such genres are quite familiar to me. But here comes one altogether other *than these, by my troth. They have all vanished behind or before the* Thousand and One Nights.

I am in the harem of the last Khan of Crimea, who was quite wrong to have broken his camp and abandoned to the Russians, some four years since, the loveliest country in all the world.

Fate has bestowed upon me the quarters of the loveliest of the sultanas, and upon Ségur those of the chief black eunuch. I have not yet seen him, for I am writing you at five in the morning; but I wager that, for reasons the contrary of my own, and out of fear, he has spent (as have I) a dreadful night. My cursed imagination is not susceptible to a single wrinkle, it is fresh, pink, and plump as the cheek of madame the marquise herself.

In our palace (which has a touch of the Moorish, of the Arabesque, of the Chinese, and of the Turkish) there are fountains, secret gardens, paintings, a great deal of gilding, and inscriptions everywhere, among others in the extremely entertaining and extremely splendid audience chamber, in Turkish letters of gold, around the cornice: "Despite the Jealous, one learns the world over that in all of Isfahan, of Damascus, of Istanbul, there is nothing to be found so rich and fair as here."

Since Cherson, we have found encampments magical by their Asiatic magnificence in the deserts. I no longer know where I am, nor in what age. When I suddenly discern mountains rising, which then

---

6. *Lettres et pensées du Prince de Ligne* (from the edition of Mme de Staël), edited by R. Trousson (Paris: Tallandier, 1989).

*march past, I believe it is all a dream: there are stud farms of drome-
daries, creatures that, when they stand up on their long legs, produce
the effect of a certain distance. Is this not the very place, I ask myself,
that furnished the stable of the three kings for their famous journey to
Bethlehem? I am still dreaming, I tell myself, when I encounter certain young Caucasian princes all in silver, mounted on steeds whose
flesh is finer and whiter than that of all our duchesses, with the exception of one or two. When I see them—these princes—armed with bows
and arrows, I believe myself to be in the days of old (or is it of young?)
Cyrus. Their quivers are superb. You know only the one Love bears,
and God be thanked your features are finer than his thereupon, gayer
and more piquant, for they are not so steeped in the anacreontic. Woe
to those who would find them fiery! For you would despise their cure.
Marquise of my heart, you disdain such means, which are in truth
quite familiar, and readily to be found almost anywhere.*

*When I come upon whole detachments of Circassians handsome as
the day, whose captive waists are even slenderer than Mme de Lauzun's[7]; when I encounter here certain Murzas better dressed than the
Choiseul girl at the queen's balls, or certain Cossack officers with more
taste in fabric than Mlle Bertin[8] and in colors more harmonious than
those ventured by Mme Lebrun in her paintings, I am seized by an
astonishment not to be gainsaid.*

*When, returning from Stare Kim to a palace for a single night's
sleep, I discover there the most interesting thing in half the globe and
almost as far as the Caspian Sea, I suppose that this is a parody of Sa-
tan's temptation, who never showed anything half so lovely to him
whom you know.*

*I saw from the same coign of vantage, leaving my bedroom, the Sea
of Asaph, the Black Sea, the Sea of Zabache, and the Caucasus. The
guilty Titan who was eaten here (eternally, I believe) by a vulture had
not stolen as much fire as you have in your own eyes and imagination,*

---

7. Amélie de Bouffers (1751–1794), granddaughter of the Maréchale de Luxembourg, married to the Duc de Lauzun.

8. Marie-Antoinette's milliner.

as your silly hunt-the-slipper Abbé d'Espagnac would say. If you were here, at Barczisarai, with us; and if you were a storyteller such as Dinarzade, I should not believe you; but instead of your letting me tell, I would tell you, dear marquise.

For it is still a dream, when, in a triumphal chariot set about with figures in precious stones, seated in the depths of such a carriage for six passengers, between two persons on whose shoulders the heat frequently overwhelms me, I hear, as I wake, one of my traveling companions say, "I have thirty million subjects, they tell me, counting only males." "And I have twenty-two," the other one replies, "all told." "I require," adds the first, "an army of at least six hundred thousand men, from Kamchatka to Riga, including the Hook of the Caucuses." "With half of that," the second replies, "I have just what I need."

Ségur will instruct you how much this comrade has pleased him. Ségur, on the other hand, has greatly pleased the emperor, who enchants everyone he sees. Released from the cares of his empire, he creates its felicity by his own society. He showed only a brief instance of temperament the other day, when he received news of the rebellion of the Low Countries. It was this one or all those who had land in the Crimea, like all the Murzas and those to whom, like me, the empress has given land, who have sworn an oath of loyalty to him. He came toward me and, seizing me by the forelock, said, "You are the first of the Order who has kissed hands with the long-bearded lords." "It would be better," I told him, "for Your Majesty and for me that I be with the Tartar gentlemen than with the Flemish gentlemen."

In our carriage, we passed in review all the states and the great personages. God knows how we managed to accommodate them! "Rather than sign the separation of thirteen provinces, like my brother George,"[9] said Catherine II quite sweetly, "I would have fired a pistol." "And rather than have handed in my resignation, like my brother and brother-in-law, convoking and naming the nations in order to discuss abuses, I don't know what I should have done," said Joseph II.

They were also of the same opinion about the king of Sweden, whom

---

9. George III of England.

they did not like, and whom the emperor had taken a grudge against in Italy, on account of a blue and silver bathrobe, he said, with a diamond plaque. They both agreed that he has energy, talent, and wit. "Yes, certainly," I replied, defending him (since his kindness to me and the great generosity I had seen him expend attached me to him). "Your Majesty might well prevent a scurrilous satire, in which one dares treat a kind, lovable prince possessed of as much genius as Don Quixote himself." "Such a man," I said to Joseph II, "would be from the Baltic, not from La Mancha, unless one were to add three letters more,[10] nasty jokers would add, who yet might have respected the crowned heads. Summon M. de Villette in order to explain what it all means, for one must have a good knowledge of French and of history for such a thing, and the ladies would have difficulty understanding a joke that employs such phraseology."

Their Imperial Majesties reflected for some time concerning the poor Turkish devils. Remarks were made in their own regard. As an amateur of classical antiquity and of some novelties as well, I spoke of reestablishing the Greeks; Catherine spoke of reviving Lycurgus and Solon. I mentioned Alcibiades; and Joseph II, who was more for the future than the past, and for the positive rather than the chimerical, said: "What the devil is to be done with Constantinople?"

In this fashion many islands and provinces were disposed of with no difficulty whatever, and I said to them, speaking for myself, "Your Majesties will merely be taking on misery after misery." "We treat them all too well," said the emperor, speaking of me in particular; he lacks all respect for us. Do you know, Madame, that he was once in love with one of my father's mistresses and that he kept me from managing a proper entrance into the world at the side of a certain Marquise de Prié, angelically pretty and indeed a first passion the two of us shared?

There was no reserve at all between these two great sovereigns. They told each other the most interesting things: "Has anyone ever attempted to take your life? Myself, I was threatened on one occasion." "Well, I

---

10. "Chevalier de la Machette," like the Marquis de Villette whom Voltaire nonetheless married off to his protégée, "Belle et Bonne" de Varicourt.

did receive anonymous letters." There followed a confessor's story and certain charming and unknown details of a whole world of people, etc.

The empress had asked us, one day, in her galley: "How does one write verses? Write me an explanation of such a thing, M. de Ségur." He wrote out the rules of versification with some delightful examples. And she set to work then and there, producing six lines with so many mistakes that all three of us burst out laughing. And she said to me, "To teach you to make fun of me, make some verses yourselves, immediately; I won't attempt any more, I'm thoroughly disgusted with such exercises for the rest of my life." "Well done!" said Fitz-Herbert[11]; "The two of you should have saved your talents for the grave of one of your bitches":

Here lies Duchess Anderson
Who bit Monsieur Rogerson.[12]

Then I was given rhymes to compose verses on, with orders to complete them quickly, here's how I met the challenge:

To the rules of verse, the laws of harmony,
Compel the strength of genius to submit.
In vain the neighbor states will sue for peace,
In vain your empire shows its golden face.
For rhyme, abandon glory for a while
And trace new paths to Memory's holy place.

This all came back to her at Barczisarai. "Ah, my lords," she told us, "I shall withdraw to my quarters, and you shall see the result." And this is what she showed us, no more and no less:

On the Great Khan's sofa, stuffed with down,
In a golden kiosk, all grilled with gold...

---

11. The envoy from London.
12. Catherine II's personal physician.

You can easily guess we covered her with reproaches for not having managed to go further, after four hours of pondering and making such a good start. For nothing ever gets done on a trip.

This country is certainly a land of dreams, but none of them ever comes true, one can never find a single woman with whom to make such things happen. The ones here are all locked up by these wretched Mohammedans, who never learned Ségur's song about the bliss of being deceived by your own wife. The Duchess of Luxemburg would turn my head if she were in Achmeczet; and I'd make a song to the Maréchale de Mouchy if she lived in Balaklava.

There is no one but you, dear marquise, whom one can adore in the heart of Paris: adore is the proper word—who has time for loving?

Hereabouts there are several sects of dervishes, each more entertaining than the next—whirling, screaming. . . . The latter are Jansenists, even madder than the medieval convulsionaries. They scream Allah! until their strength is exhausted and they fall on the ground in hopes of rising only to enter heaven.

I left the court here on the plain for some days, and risked my life to climb and then climb down from the Tczetterdar, following rugged streambeds instead of the paths I could never find. I needed to rest my mind, my tongue, my ears, and my eyes from the brilliance of the illuminations that every night contend with one another, wherever we may be, and from the sun, which is only too much over our heads all day. And at last I've found what I'm going to tell you, or rather to send you: which is that I've written on this very page in pencil what I've just copied out properly in ink for you.

To the Comte Louis-Philippe de Ségur

Camp Otchakow, August 1, 1788

I see an army commander (Prince Potemkin [the favorite of Catherine II]) who has an idle look about him yet who labors night and day; who has no other desk but his knees, no other comb but his fingers; always in bed yet sleeping neither day or night because his zeal for his sovereign, whom he adores, continually torments him, so that a can-

nonball he does not receive disturbs him by the thought that it costs the life of some of his soldiers. Fearful for others, brave for himself; halting under the fiercest attack to give his orders, yet more for the purposes of Ulysses than of Achilles; anxious in anticipation of all dangers, gay when in their midst; sad in pleasures; unhappy by dint of happiness, indifferent to all diversions, easily disgusted, morose, inconsistent; a deep philosopher, a skillful minister; as a politician sublime or a child of ten; never vindictive, asking pardon for a misfortune he's caused, promptly repairing an injustice he hasn't; believing he loves God, fearing the devil, whom he supposes to be greater and grander than a Prince Potemkin; with one hand beckoning to women he finds alluring, with the other making the sign of the cross; arms outspread at the feet of a statue of the Virgin, or around his mistress's alabaster neck; receiving countless favors from his great sovereign, and immediately bestowing them elsewhere; accepting estates from the empress, returning them to her or paying what she owes without letting her know of it; selling and buying back immense domains in order to build there some great colonnade and an English garden, then immediately disposing of them; always gambling or never gambling; preferring to give to charity rather than to pay his debts; prodigiously rich without having a sou; suspicious or trusting, jealous or grateful, sarcastic or playful; easily influenced for or against, reversing himself at once; talking theology to his generals, and war to his archbishops; never reading but questioning those to whom he speaks, contradicting them to learn still more; pulling rude faces or kind ones; affecting the most repulsive manners or the most welcoming; having alternately airs of the proudest Oriental satrap or of the wiliest courtier of Louis XV; under a great show of harshness, actually very gentle in the depths of his soul; capricious about his moments of attention, his meals, his periods of repose, and all his preferences; eager as a child to own everything, and quite able, like a grown man, to do without; abstemious for all his greedy glances; gnawing his nails, biting into apples and turnips; grumbling or laughing, dissimulating or swearing on his honor, roaming the streets or praying, singing or meditating; inviting, dismissing; summoning twenty aides-de-camp without having anything to tell them;

tolerating hot weather better than anyone, apparently thinking of nothing but the choicest immersions; making light of the cold while seeming to be unable to do without his furs; barefoot or in spangled slippers, without cap or hat: I've seen him like that under rifle fire; sometimes in a filthy bathrobe or else a superb tunic, with his three medals, his ribbons and diamonds as big as your thumb set all around the empress's portrait, those diamonds apparently put there to draw enemy fire; bending over backward or curled up in a ball at home, and standing tall, nose in the air, proud, fine, noble, majestic, or seductive when in front of his troops like Agamemnon among the kings of Greece.

What is his magic then? Genius, genius again, and still more genius; natural wit, an excellent memory, a certain elevation of spirit, a kind of malice without meanness, cleverness without cunning: a happy mixture of whims whose good moments, when they occur, draw every heart to his; a great generosity, a certain grace and fitness in his rewards: remarkable tact, the talent to guess what he doesn't know, and a great knowledge of men....

26. An Enlightenment Test Site: Poland and Its Last King, Stanisław II Augustus Poniatowski

IN WHAT they regarded as the Far West, political thinkers of the Enlightenment ultimately located their promised land in a "virgin" British America. In Eastern Europe they sought, but much more distractedly, a test site in the ancient Catholic and nobiliary Republic of Poland, its fluid and spongy frontiers encircled by the Prussia of Frederick II, the Austria of Maria Theresa and Joseph II, the Russia of Catherine II, and the Ottoman Empire. The long reign of Stanisław II Augustus Poniatowski, the "crowned philosopher," lasted, for better or worse, from 1764 to 1795. For thirty years, this disarmed king, who had taken for his motto "Patience and Courage," was subject to a Russian protectorate even as he contended with a declared or masked civil war, and also had to endure a first unconscionable partition of his country among Russia, Austria, and Prussia. Without altogether succumbing, the king attempted to create a modern state in what remained of his realm and ultimately, incited by the enthusiasm of Polish youth for the French Revolution, dared to provide it with an English-style constitution. The entrance of Russian and Prussian troops into Warsaw in 1792 put an end to this experiment, which St. Petersburg regarded as Jacobin. Having survived the first partition, the amputated realm lost, under the Russian boot, its last semblance of independent political existence. Prussia and Austria received as their due an additional share of the cake, a situation foreshadowing Poland's in 1940. In 1798 the ex-king ended his days in a closely watched residence, an exile in the capital of the tsars.

If there was one country where the age's much-prized diplomacy, sensibility, and philosophy dropped the mask and revealed its underpinnings of realpolitik, cynicism, and sycophancy, it was certainly the remote Poland of Stanisław Augustus. And yet its player-king possessed enough of such diplomacy, sensibility, and philosophy, derived from his education and his travels in Western Europe, to survive for three decades amid a multitude of dangers, stubbornly maintaining, within his shrinking realm, the modernizing program of an "enlightened sovereign" despite the West's indifference and his neighbors' increasing military pressure, and enduring as well the frequent armed rebellions of compatriots with whom he nonetheless sympathized. On closer inspection, this reign was a sort of incomplete and inglorious masterpiece of the Age of Enlightenment.[1]

THE EDUCATION OF A FUTURE PHILOSOPHER-KING

Bonaparte, younger son of minor provincial nobility in Europe's oldest hereditary realm, was quite unlikely to become a king or, even less imaginably, an emperor. Similarly, nothing except perhaps prophecies invented after the fact predisposed the sixth son of Count Stanisław Poniatowski to become king of Poland. However his hand held several trump cards that Bonaparte would lack, and that Stanisław's relatives, teachers, and an imperious mistress managed to turn to advantage, somewhat against his will. Nobly born as he was, Stanisław's father had been a hero, fervently celebrated by Voltaire in one of his first masterpieces, the *Histoire de Charles XII*. Uniting, as Voltaire has it, the courage of Achilles with the cunning of Ulysses, Count Poniatowski had revealed himself capable of prodigious exploits that on several occasions had saved the life of his

1. On Poniatowski and his times, the basic work remains that of Jean Fabre, *Stanislas-Auguste Poniatowski et l'Europe des Lumières* (Paris: Les Belles Lettres, 1952), supplemented by Poniatowski's *Mémoires*, 2 vols. (St. Petersburg Academy of Sciences, 1907). For a more recent synthesis, including an up-to-date bibliography, see Adam Zamoyski, *The Last King of Poland* (London: Weidenfeld and Nicholson, 1992).

master, Peter the Great's impetuous adversary, and, being equally adept at diplomatic and political feats, had on several occasions at Constantinople, where Charles XII had taken refuge after the terrible defeat of Poltava, almost managed to launch the Ottoman forces against the tsar, thereby appeasing the king of Sweden's vengeful feelings. Hailed as a hero in Paris during the Regency (it was then that this eyewitness provided Voltaire with the elements of his *Histoire de Charles XII*), the "Handsome Pole" had returned to his own capital aureoled with the laurels of Mars, acquired beside Charles XII against both Russians and Turks, and sporting the myrtles of Venus won from the Duchesse du Maine and Mme de Tencin over any number of Parisian ladies, both high and low. This double prestige merited in 1720 a love marriage with Constanza Czartoryska, as well as the honor of entering the council of "the Family," as the Poles called the aristocratic Czartoryski clan, the most titled and powerful in the kingdom, sole hereditary rival of the more or less united clans of the Radziwills, Potockis, Branickis, and Sapiehas.

Unlike most of the crowns of Europe, that of Poland (as in principle that of the Holy Roman Emperor) was not hereditary but elective. The Polish Diet, which elected the kings of this nobiliary republic, was divided among irreconcilable clans wielding the *liberum veto*, which in normal times kept any decision from being made by this eloquent assembly, and in times of election opened a vast field to diplomacy, corruption, and military blackmail by the European courts competing for who would forge a majority for its candidate. In the sixteenth century, Henri de Valois (the future Henri III) had briefly reigned over Poland. In the eighteenth century, the grand electors of Saxony, Augustus II the Strong and Augustus III, had been kings of Poland in alternation. During the interregnums, Louis XV had intrigued in vain to have his cousin the Prince de Conti elected. A Polish nobleman, Stanisław Leszczynski, of modest standing but France's alternate candidate, had briefly managed to "rule" the Polish anarchy before restoring the throne to Augustus III and finding a comfortable refuge with his son-in-law, the king of France, in the Duchy of Lorraine. The "King's Secret" (the personal diplomacy of Louis XV) had determined once and for all, though without managing to provide the means, that Poland would remain a traditional nobiliary republic, i.e., a rubber-stamp state.

If a Leszczynski, more a less a "Family" client, had managed to rule, why not a Poniatowski, son of a Czartoryska? Favored by his parents among all their numerous progeny, young Stanisław, born in 1732, revealed precocious talents. He had received an education that, without openly preparing him for the royal métier, gradually placed him among possible candidates for an election that the death of Augustus of Saxony would eventually bring about. In a century rife with almost as many preceptors as diplomatic agents, the preferred and coddled son of Constanza Czartoryska responded to the teachings of the most heteroclite masters, before exposing himself to the tempestuous direction of numerous *mamans* who, each in her own way, succeeded the watchful and severe Constanza. This Telemachus lacked for neither Mentors nor Minervas of all nationalities, sexes, religions, and philosophic allegiances, which made of this passionately patriotic Pole the progeny par excellence of a cosmopolitan and variegated Europe of the later Enlightenment. This paradox earned him a good deal of hatred among a Polish nobility whose biased "republicanism" Rousseau admired, encouraging their partiality for a fiercely, jealous, politically imbecile nationalism, known as "Sarmatism."

Stanisław's mother, a devout Catholic riddled with quietist tendencies, put him initially in the hands of German Lutheran pedants who gave him the rudiments of Latin, Polish, geometry, and national law; thereafter he studied under Italian Theatine fathers who taught him an elegant French and gave him a taste for the theater, fine arts, and good manners. From the age of twelve, he was tormented by the theological anxiety the eighteenth century had inherited from the great disputes of the preceding age between Jansenists and Molinists, between Bossuet and Fénelon: Free will or predetermination? Voluntarism or submission to Providence? Several years later, Stanisław would rouse the anger of the master from whom he had learned most, defending against his libertine voluntarism the cause of "fatalities no human prudence can foresee." This preference brought him under the influence of a wavering and mystical optimist who led him, in such questions, to resemble Louis XVI. In 1745 the future tutor of the Duc de Chartres (Philippe Égalité under the Terror), the Abbé Allaire, took it upon himself to complete young Stanisław's training in classical rhetoric and French civility. It was from this perfect honnête homme that he acquired, despite his real mastery of Polish, German, English, Italian, and Russian, his avowed predilection for French and for the clipped prose style of La Bruyère, Anthony Hamilton, and Voltaire.

Simultaneously, Stanisław, devoured by the pride and timidity that made him an exemplary disciple of each and every hand extended to him, received certain lessons from his powerful Czartoryski uncles. Hoping to rally him to his idol Frederick II, Empress Elizabeth's ambassador to Poland, Count Hermann-Charles Kayserling, ex-professor at the University of Königsberg, initiated Stanisław into the subtleties and *distinguos* of scholastic logic, a truly useful casuistry in the juridical, political, and diplomatic labyrinth of Polish affairs.

In 1747, seeking to make his fortune in Poland, a Swiss military engineer who was also a secret agent of Louis XV, Lucas de Toux de Salverte, arrived in Warsaw and forthwith instructed the young nobleman in fortifications. This was the only military training ever received by Stanisław Poniatowski, the future defenseless king who thereby resembled Louis XVI even more closely. A high-ranking Mason, Toux de Salverte henceforth continually seesawed between Paris and Warsaw, though for whose benefit no one knows—the Lodges or the "Secret" of the king of France?

During the summer of 1750, the Polish Telemachus (then seventeen years old), on a visit to Berlin where Kayserling had sent him to worship his god Frederick, encountered the English mentor who was to take him under his wing for some years to come. To begin with, he inculcated Stanisław with his own scorn for the king of Prussia, "a perverse, barren, spiteful little wretch." In London the author of this conviction, Sir Charles Hanbury Williams, had been the scandalous prince of the *jeunesse dorée* of the Dilettanti Society and of the Hell-Fire Club founded by Lord Hervey. His friend Horace Walpole referred to him as "a bright genius, dangerously bright." His mordant wit, equally fit for satire and *vers galant*, had so well served Robert Walpole that the Whig prime minister had made him a baronet and an ambassador, first in Dresden, then in Berlin where Frederick II, envying his talents, took an instant dislike to him and heaped humiliations upon him. Voltaire, who was then at Potsdam, took a contrary fancy to Sir Charles's wit and his compliments; as he wrote to d'Argental: "The envoy from England has sent me some very fine English verses." The following year Williams managed to get himself sent back to Dresden, one of Augustus III's two capitals.

A liaison with Stanisław's older brother, the "handsome" Casimir, did not keep the irresistible Sir Charles from befriending the younger, whose wit and culture he greatly appreciated; he realized, a perception that made him a favorite of the Poniatowski parents, that their son had a royal future. He also planned to ensure a precious trump card for British policy in Eastern Europe. In Dresden, more agreeably than in Berlin, Sir Charles managed once more to construct around himself a minor version of the Dilettanti, with his secretary Harry Digby, several other young Englishmen, and Casimir Poniatowski. This too was a complicity with a view to a grand design, tacitly approved by the family, which made him Stanisław's guide on the precipitous paths of politics and diplomacy. With this new preceptor, Stanisław left the Arcadian terrain so dear to Fénelon for the troubled shores soon to be explored by Balzac: through the Mentor–Telemachus pair shines the Vautrin–Rubempré pact, sealed by Sir Charles, who would write to Stanisław: "I love and cherish you like my own son, always remember that," though without Stanisław, delighted by his impassioned preceptor, perceiving the slightest double entendre in such a sentence.

In the knight's company and that of his friends, Stanisław lost his timidity as well as his innocence. "My friendship with Sir Charles Williams," he wrote in his *Mémoires*, "became more intimate and was very effective in the world of society, affording me a consideration and the appearance of a mature man that my age did not yet offer me and that my very short stature, which developed only that very year by a quite sudden growth, had hitherto only retarded."[2]

During the splendid court—theaters, operas, ballets, concerts—that King Augustus held in Leipzig on the occasion of Saint Michael's Fair in 1750, Stanisław enjoyed the most magical hours of his life:

> This happy life lasted six weeks. I had health, not much money but more than I needed, no worries, I was living in a splendid place, in a lovely season, in very good company, I was almost in love but not at all libertine, I saw only people who seemed to me happy and appeared to have no other business than to enjoy themselves, I've never been so happy but when the six weeks were up, my good times vanished with them.[3]

During this visit, he found himself in great sympathy with the wife of Augustus III's omnipotent prime minister, Count von Brühl. The countess, a friend of Constanza's, took a great liking to Stanisław and "adopted" him. This was the first of his *mamans*.

A GRAND TOUR OF ENLIGHTENMENT EUROPE

Stanisław's parents, to keep him from losing his position in Poland, preferred that he make, instead of a single continuous Grand Tour, the usual thing for young English and Dutch aristocrats, a series of brief sojourns in the great European capitals, well prepared by letters of recommendation and interrupted by dutiful attention to obligations at home. Stanisław had already ventured to Flanders to

2. Poniatowski, *Mémoires*, vol. I, p. 42.
3. Poniatowski, *Mémoires*, vol. I, pp. 44–45.

meet the Marshal Maurice of Saxony in 1748. In 1750 he acquainted himself with the Viennese court, which he found stilted. A flirtation he commenced with a maid of honor of Victoria of Savoy, the niece and heiress of Prince Eugène, which was denounced to his family by the nuncio Serbelloni, provoked his immediate recall to Warsaw. He returned to Vienna in 1753 to attend Count von Kaunitz's ceremony of accession to the imperial chancellery on his return from his embassy in Versailles. He subsequently accompanied Sir Charles Williams to Hanover, the electorate of the king of England, George II, then visited The Hague, where he befriended Count von Bentinck, the torturer of a proud divorced wife and the real power of the court of Orange. At this point he left Sir Charles, who returned to London, and headed for Paris.

He remained there only five months, nor could he ever manage to return, yet this brief stay sufficed for him to consider himself henceforth a Parisian, whatever rebuffs he received from Choiseul and the king's secret diplomacy, whatever disappointments he suffered from French frivolity and the difficulty of being admitted into what was considered in Paris *extremely good society*. He had to content himself with entirely literary felicities. Recommended by the Countess von Brühl, he was received and adopted by the ancient Mme de Brancas, who had known Mme de Maintenon and who herself kept alive at Versailles, by her conversation, her style, and her kind of politesse, the memory of the court of Louis XIV. Faced with an utter lack of interest in himself on the part of political Versailles, Stanisław, whom the Abbé Allaire had brought up on French *mémoires*, revealed himself to be all the more sensitive to the "Proustian" dimension of the court of France and to personages there who restored the past in the present. Beyond the Duchesse de Brancas, he was quite prepared to attach himself to that other mine of memory, the ancient Maréchal de Noailles, Mme de Maintenon's nephew, had he not irritated the old gentleman at the very start by clumsily praising him in the same breath as Puisieux, his ex-colleague in the king's council, though unfortunately the maréchal regarded old minister Puisieux as, precisely, a valet. The same disappointment was encountered with regard to the king, to whom he was presented by the Maréchal de Richelieu, but who did not address one word to him. He was unable meet Choiseul. Instead of playing a political part in her country's favor, Marie Leszczynska, Louis XV's queen, who had retired from the conjugal bed and was living by her own choice in an agreeable little devout court of her own, could do nothing for Stanisław.

The city, in the person of his universal hostess, Mme Geoffrin, initially made much of him, then dealt with him as a scolding and irritable *maman* who could not forgive his gaffe with the Maréchal de Noailles. "I submitted to correction," he wrote in his *Mémoires*, "I tried to accustom myself to the different styles Mme Geoffrin employed according to the occasion."[4] In her salon he encountered Montesquieu, similarly reduced to servitude by La Patronne (whom he described *in petto* as "a fishwife of the beau monde"), and the leading survivor of the moderns, Fontenelle, next to whom Mme Geoffrin "insisted on placing a little iron stove to maintain him at the degree of warmth necessary to preserve him in his ninety-sixth or ninety-seventh year; he preserved to the very end of his career, despite his deafness, that witty coquetry and simpering expression of his better days. He asked me one time quite seriously if I knew Polish as well as French."[5] It was in the same rue Saint-Honoré salon that Stanisław also met the philosophers Grimm, Marmontel, and d'Alembert, to whom he had little to say for himself but all of whom he admired duly without reservation.

Brought up on La Bruyère's *Caractères*, Stanisław paid close attention to the *bizarreries* and innocent singularities in which Paris still abounded, which flourished as openly as they chose without troubling anyone:

I was presented to the Duc de Gesvres, governor of Paris, at noon. He was in his bed, whose curtains were folded back on either side to the wall, as might be those of a woman at the

---

4. Poniatowski, *Mémoires*, vol. I, p. 86.

5. Poniatowski, *Mémoires*, vol. I, p. 89.

end of her delivery who is now receiving society. He was sixty years old, wore a woman's coif fastened under his chin, and was actually making knots with a shuttle, like a woman. This was a man who had waged war, yet his effeminate manners astonished no one, and the public seemed quite pleased with him. And I said to myself: "One travels to see elsewhere what one cannot see at home, and externals do not always reveal what lies within, and one must learn not to be surprised by anything."[6]

Though the great affair of the moment must have been the exile of the Parlement of Paris to Pontoise, Parisian conversations were entirely concerned with the Quarrel of the Buffoons, which the encyclopedists, siding with Italian vaudeville against the opera of Lully and Rameau, utilized to further the theories advanced in their admired friend and new accomplice Jean-Jacques Rousseau's articles in the *Encyclopédie*.

Stanisław was received by the Prince de Conti, eternal and eternally disappointed candidate to the throne of Poland, henceforth in disgrace with Louis XV and weakening in public opinion. In the city, and in the country as well, thanks to the coexistence under the same families' roofs of several generations of forceful characters and varying stages of manners, today's fashion hugged the fashion of the past. The Duchesse d'Orléans, the Prince de Conti's sister, by her countenance, by her entire person, in repose and in movement, walking, riding, dancing, or seated, "continually recalled Watteau's most delightful paintings."[7] But "it was an equal pleasure for me," relates Stanisław in his *Mémoires*,

to encounter once again among the figures who composed the Duc d'Orléans's court, in the third and fourth generation, almost all the names that had become familiar to me by

6. Poniatowski, *Mémoires*, vol. I, p. 90.

7. Poniatowski, *Mémoires*, vol. I, p. 92.

the descriptions that the famous Grande Mademoiselle, of the era of Louis XIV, and the Cardinal de Retz have left us in their memoirs of the house of Orléans of their own day. An old Mme de Polignac, one of the Duchesse d'Orléans's ladies in waiting, dispensed by her wit almost as much pleasure in that court as did her niece, the Marquise de Blot, by the charms of her countenance.[8]

Since the cantankerous Mme Geoffrin's lessons counted for less than those of Sir Charles Williams, the Polish tourist was dizzied rather than dazzled by that "inexhaustible wealth of ever-new objects that constantly fed the frivolous attention of the French," and he was on the point of acknowledging his tedium, if family instructions to proceed to England had not left him the impression that he was nevertheless about to obtain that lasting "vogue" Parisians so easily granted to adopted foreigners. It was perhaps this curtailed accomplishment that would keep him on the qui vive with regard to the philosophes, "Maman" Geoffrin, and French public opinion, so powerful but so easily distracted and so wildly prejudiced.

In London, though he did not find Sir Charles there, his mission and the introductions he had received from "the Family," anxious to pit London against Versailles, brought him into relations with the highest level of English political life, from the old Duke of Newcastle, the prime minister, to the young Pitt, "tall, thin, with an aquiline countenance," on the brink of his great career. The brothers York, sons of Lord Chancellor Hardwick, with whom he had become acquainted during his stay in The Hague with Sir Charles, offered him the most affectionate and the most seriously intellectual company he had yet encountered. He learned English, discovered Shakespeare, landscape gardening, cockfighting, and the curiosities of English education, divided between caning and utter abandonment to savagery, a combination that encouraged each pupil to cultivate his "originality" if not his eccentricity. A more perspicacious

8. Poniatowski, *Mémoires*, vol. I, p. 93.

observer than Voltaire, the Stanisław of the *Mémoires* remarked that a calculating and utilitarian individualism had become the rule in Britain, according to the slogan *Primo mihi*, though without affecting respect for the law and a prudent sense of common interest. He was astonished by the quasi-instrumental array of well-groomed British sailors, functioning as if on springs in a naval review. This cold, very *Modern Times* specialization appeared to conflict with generosity and love of liberty, aristocratic conventions that Stanisław shared with Continental Enlightenment tastes. He discovered a similar Anglo-Saxon professionalism in the maniacal care Lord Chesterfield took in showing himself to be up-to-date in his Parisian conversation, unaware of the casual and offhanded essence of this supremely difficult art:

> Lord Chesterfield spoke the French language with much greater purity and even elegance than any Englishman I have so far encountered, in which an anti-Gallican wit and tone went much further than what one hears nowadays. But he was so fond of displaying his talent for linguistic novelty that he expressly paid a correspondent in Paris to send him all the words and new expressions that fashion continually produces. He had nothing more pressing to say, the first time I was presented to him, than to observe that "I must have seen this very morning not only many *poilus* but also *beaucoup de gens comme il faut en habits coquins* in St. James's Park." Yet since the same fashion that produces so many new words discards almost as many in succession, some future philologist, under whose eyes my manuscript may one day fall, will perhaps be much obliged to be able, thanks to me, to augment his vocabulary of *obsoletorum* of the mystical signification of these underlined expressions. *Poilu*, originally a hunting term, once signified a dog with a certain texture of reddish pelt; but in the figurative sense, fashionable speakers designated by this word any obscure fellow whose birth was quite unknown, as opposed to *gens comme il faut* who were all noblemen or at

least distinguished in their sphere. Now these *gens comme il faut* had already got into the habit of taking morning walks in the streets, but had not yet adopted the word *frac* for what they were wearing when they did so, though they already were making use of the thing. Now this thing in Paris in 1754 was called *un habit de coquin* [a rogue's suit], and it is the knowledge of this important truth that Milord Chesterfield zealously flashed before my eyes, or at least my ears.[9]

What Stanisław lacked—henceforth assured of British support, though disdained by France and by Frederick II, then allied with Versailles—was the indispensable accord of Russia. Providence willed that Sir Charles Williams be appointed in June 1755 to the embassy of St. Petersburg, and Stanisław's family was delighted by the notion that their son, under the guidance of this practiced shepherd, should proceed to make himself known in the capital of the Russian Empire, traditional protector of "the Family." Stanisław moved into the British embassy at the Russian court. Sir Charles had received his mission to seal the Anglo-Russian alliance and had taken it upon himself to make this alliance serve Stanisław's career somewhat beyond the reign of the Tsarina Elizabeth, daughter of Peter the Great, empress of all the Russias.

The future, for those who kept their eyes open, would belong to the Grand Duchess Catherine Alexeïevna, ex–Sophie von Anhalt-Zerbst, abused spouse of Grand Duke Peter Feodorovitch, Duke of Schleswig-Holstein, the German nephew Elizabeth had selected as her successor. The long-term seal of the Anglo-Russian alliance, as well as Stanisław's crown, depended on a spark passing between the reigning tsarina and the royal candidate. Eighteenth-century diplomacy preferred to light its fires with the tinder of elective affinities.

Sir Charles's perspicacity and discretion were manifested by the measure of his devotion to the interests of London and his passion

---

9. Poniatowski, *Mémoires*, vol. I, p. 129.

for the athletic young Pole. Like Vautrin, arranging Lucien de Ru-bempré's amours with the Duchesse de Maufrigneuse and his mar-riage with Clotilde de Grandlieu, Williams managed to have Stanisław noticed by the grand duchess, whom he knew to be in search of lovers as well as funds. He obtained for her the funds she lacked, neutralized Elizabeth's minister Bestutchev by paying him off, and with the help of Naryschkin, a gentleman of the grand du-cal bedchamber, he arranged for Stanisław a secret rendezvous, though one of high risk, since the grand duchess, kept under lock and key by her husband, was also closely watched by the reigning tsarina. No diplomatic immunity covered the young Pole: "I was forgetting," Stanisław would write, "that there was such a thing as a Siberia." He became Catherine's lover and saw her frequently. Wil-liams immediately obtained Catherine's entire trust—he was irre-sistible to anyone with high ambitions—and became the third party, both confidant and letter box, in the fiery liaison he had ignited. The success of this intrigue was darkened by the dramatic failure of his mission to the Tsarina Elizabeth. Alarmed by the triple alliance of England, Austria, and Russia that Williams had virtually con-cluded, Frederick II reacted strongly to the prospect, and managed to discourage Maria Theresa even while seducing the British cabi-net. Disavowed in England, despised in Russia, the English ambas-sador became persona non grata in St. Petersburg by the autumn of 1755.

Sir Charles's nervous reaction to his humiliating defeat became such that, driven to extremes one day by an argument with Stanisław over free will, he threatened to break off their sacred agreement. Catherine's lover momentarily faltered, so narrowly did the plot and his whole future seem to depend on the ambassador's genius. He toyed with the possibility of suicide. But the cloud lifted: "These fears disappeared as soon as we were reconciled, because I loved him almost like a father and because I had an essential need to hope, which constitutes the mainspring of life and especially of youth."[10]

---

10. Poniatowski, *Mémoires*, vol. I, p. 155.

The portrait of the Germanic Venus drawn by the Sarmatian Adonis, recalling the day of their first and perilous pleasures, would have enchanted Mme Hanska's lover, had Balzac been able to penetrate the State Archives of Nicholas I where Stanisław's *Mémoires* remained in secret during the entire nineteenth century:

> She was twenty-five. She had scarcely emerged from her first childbed, and was at that moment of beauty that is ordinarily at its peak for any woman to whom such a thing is granted at all. With her black tresses, her skin of a dazzling whiteness, the brilliance of her great blue eyes set shallowly but expressively between extremely long black lashes, the short, sharp nose, a mouth that seemed to crave kisses, perfect hands and arms, a svelte waist, rather tall than short in stature, her gait altogether light and lively, yet of a distinct nobility, the sound of her voice very pleasant and her laughter as gay as the moods that made her pass with equal ease from the most whimsical, even childish games to a message at the decoding table, which physical labor daunted her no more than the text, however important or even dangerous its substance. The discomfort in which she had lived since her unfortunate marriage, the privation of any company analogous to her own mind and spirit, had made reading her great resource. She knew a great deal. With a caressing turn of mind, capable of grasping each man's weakness, she made her way henceforth, by the love of her people, to that throne which she has subsequently occupied with such glory.... I cannot resist the pleasure of indicating here the very costume in which I discovered her that day: it was a little gown of white satin, a light scarf of lace interwoven with pink ribbons her only ornament. She did not realize, it would seem, how I came to be in her private apartments, and the truth is that I have often asked myself the same question, when on days when the court was receiving company I had passed amid so many guards and watchmen of all kinds, how it could be that I had already penetrated so frequently, as

though wrapped in a mantle of invisibility, into the regions that I dared not even envisage in public?[11]

To their terror, their youth, and the ambition that possessed them both was added, kindling their desire to a white heat, the abstinence they had so eagerly left behind. She had just given birth to the child of her first lover. As for Stanisław, "by a remarkable singularity," as he explained with disarming roguishness, "I could offer her, though at the age of twenty-two, what no one had yet taken from me."[12]

Far from London, far from Vienna, far from Warsaw, at the court of St. Petersburg one was in ancient Thebes, in the Scotland of Macbeth, or in the seraglio of Roxane and Bajazet, unimaginable in Paris, that capital of the Enlightenment. Stanisław knew the watchword Peter the Great had left upon his death: "*Il faut espionner.*" And indeed spy one did in St. Petersburg "upon great things and small." The Medusa countenance of the head of the secret chancellery, Aleksandr Shuvalov, a cousin of "Monsieur Pompadour," Empress Elizabeth's official lover, was well known to the young Pole. "As if to augment the terror that the mere name of his position inspired, nature had given him certain nervous tics that horribly disfigured his countenance, hideous moreover, on each occasion he was seriously occupied."[13] Sir Charles had fathomed the strong and also the weak points of this police system whose equivalent France was not to know until after 1792, thanks then to the Jacobin genius of Fouché. In this sense, Russia was politically ahead. But every precaution was taken by Sir Charles's cunning and cash to keep the lovers from being discovered.

In the course of her pillow talk with Stanisław, the grand duchess, turning the pages of her lover like a book, studied the Paris that he knew well and whose favor she knew, from Frederick II's example, to be of such importance to modern potentates. Above all

---

11. Poniatowski, *Mémoires*, vol. I, p. 158.

12. Poniatowski, *Mémoires*, vol. I, p. 157.

13. Poniatowski, *Mémoires*, vol. I, pp. 325–326.

she was fascinated by the chief French trumpet of fame, Voltaire. Together the two candidates for enlightened despotism reveled in reading his blasphemous *Pucelle d'Orléans*, long kept from ordinary consumption, but a copy of which Count Poniatowski, enchanted by Stanisław's grand ducal amours, had obtained from the Maréchal de Richelieu and passed on to his son. And while the grand duchess perfected her French style and glimpsed what she must say and do to captivate Voltaire, her lover learned from her those state secrets that he eagerly transmitted to Sir Charles, spinning the web of an improbable Anglo-Russian alliance.

UNDER THE PROTECTORATE OF CATHERINE THE GREAT

Twice Stanisław returned to Poland, and after the second time, in December 1756, he reappeared in St. Petersburg with the title of ambassador from the court of Saxony, hard-pressed since Frederick II, having now turned against France and supported by England, had invaded the electorate, bombarded and pillaged Dresden, and brought Augustus III to his knees. Fearing to be taken for an English double agent, the new ambassador from Saxony was obliged to break officially with Sir Charles Williams, who nonetheless continued to supervise Stanisław's amours with Catherine. But the Englishman, whose diplomatic situation became untenable under pressure from the French ambassador, the Marquis de l'Hôpital, was obliged to leave St. Petersburg during the summer of 1757, his mind deeply troubled. He was to commit suicide two years later. He left behind him two lovers at a loss. With good reason, for Shuvalov and the empress had ultimately managed to discover the plot, and Stanisław, too exposed, had to decamp quite suddenly in his turn, on August 14, 1758. He would not see his grand duchess again for thirty years. During all this time, having become king by her good graces, the ex-lover would never cease to feel the claws of the Russian bear, whose fur and ferocity Catherine II had meanwhile assumed.

On January 4, 1762, Tsarina Elizabeth died. Her nephew Peter III assumed the crown. He overturned alliances and rallied Russia to Frederick. Catherine was threatened with repudiation. Stanisław longed to fly to her rescue, but she discouraged him curtly. Her new lover, the giant Gregory Orlov, and his brother Alexis took charge of the coup d'état indispensable to her safety and her ambitions: it succeeded on the night of July 9. The tsar was imprisoned. He was soon to be assassinated. The new empress of all the Russias immediately sent a message to her ex-lover: "I am now sending Count Keyserling as my ambassador to Poland to see you crowned king after the present tsar's death, and should he not succeed in your case, my choice falls on Prince Adam Czartoryski."[14] Whatever the outcome, "the Family" would triumph. But Stanisław, already dreaming of marriage, had not yet taken the measure of the steely will that had appeared in St. Petersburg in place of his voluptuous mistress. Catherine II no longer regarded her passing fancy as anything but far away and far beneath her, a passive pawn in her grand scheme.

On October 5, 1763, it was Augustus III's turn to die. The struggle for the Polish succession became frantic, "the Family" having candidates other than Stanisław, the Radziwill clan promoting its own, and the foreign ambassadors working for one faction or the other. Catherine and the proconsul whom she dispatched to Poland, Prince Nikolay Vasilyevich Repnin, settled the matter. Repnin obtained the support of the English ambassador, Thomas Wroughton, the favorite of Frederick II who then needed the Russian alliance, and ignored the opinion of Louis XV's and Choiseul's ambassador, Marquis de Paulmy, weakened by the disastrous outcome for France of the Seven Years' War and opposed on the spot by a rival dispatched by the King's Secret, General Monet, bearing quite different instructions! Versailles could afford the luxury of two rival foreign policies and two *corps diplomatiques*.

Russian troops moved toward Warsaw. On August 27, 1764, the elective Diet convened and unanimously elected Stanisław, who was

---

14. Fabre, *Stanislas-Auguste Poniatowski et l'Europe des Lumières*, p. 223.

crowned before an enormous crowd in St. John's Cathedral on November 25, Saint Catherine's Day. He took the name of Stanisław II Augustus. He was thirty-three years old and to his own mind represented not Russia, despite the decisive support he had received from that empire, but hope and renewal. Among his first concerns were to invite Voltaire to Warsaw; to address his friendliest greetings to Grimm and Diderot, the powerful editors of the elite handwritten journal *Correspondance littéraire*; and to furnish adequate information to the journalists of the *Leiden Gazette* and the *Courrier du Bas-Rhin*. All for nought: to interest the French-language press, in other words, the press itself, other arguments were then required than the simple goodwill toward philosophy expressed by the wretched Stanisław.

Internally, the weakness of the new king's position, though he was determined to serve Polish independence and enlightenment, soon saw the revival of old clan jealousies. His reform activities with regard to the state, education, and the tax base, which tended to be favored by public opinion, excessively conflicted with old habits and vested interests, and did not fail to pass for anti-Polish cosmopolitanism. The religious question—Catholicism being the state religion in Poland—also offered an excellent pretext for foreign powers, Protestant in the case of Prussia, Orthodox in the case of Russia, to contest the gradualist policy of Stanisław, who was reluctant to appear precipitate and counted on the long-term effect of Enlightenment influences to convert the Poles to denominational equality. Proconsul Repnin, on Catherine II's orders, used this argument to humiliate the king publicly in the presence of the Diet. The Russian troops moved once again. The Diet, under this pressure, voted for the return to the *liberum veto* that paralyzed it, but before disbanding confirmed "in perpetuity" the civic incapacity of Polish non-Catholics. The Russians, with good reason, and for the time being, did not insist.

The "republican" grandees, regrouped by the Radziwills in the Radom Confederation and approved by the majority of bishops, then defied the king, accused of being servile toward Russia, while themselves appealing in secret to the support of Proconsul Repnin, all too happy to possess a new instrument of pressure against Stanisław. Catherine's representative realized that his hands were free for a strong move: Russian grenadiers rushed into the Diet in full session in order to arrest and carry off the prelates who shouted in favor of the realm's unity of faith.

Despite this rebellion, which favored the Russia enterprise, Stanisław nevertheless managed to save the essentials of the administrative reforms he had already caused to be adopted. The Radom Confederation, reaffirmed in February 1767 in the town of Bar, crossed the line, took up arms, and set off a civil war against the king. Stanisław had to watch impotently as the Russian repression took its course against the rebels whose patriotism he approved, though they had not hesitated to flatter Russia to prevail against him. He was caught between several lines of fire. A tragedy was imminent. The England of George III, David Hume, and Edmund Burke was the only country where Stanisław's good faith was recognized and the crime brewing against the the Polish nation denounced. But England did not intervene.

Maria Theresa was the first to advance her troops into Poland. Frederick II, who gleefully published lampoons deriding the ex-friend of Sir Charles Williams, imitated the Austrian empress. Stanisław had yet another brief respite when, victim of a kidnapping by the Confederation of Bar, he managed to escape his probable assassins and triumphantly regain the royal palace in Warsaw on November 3, 1771. Two months later, on January 4, 1772, Austria and Russia signed an agreement for the partition of Poland, and on February 17, a Russo-Prussian convention delimited the slice of the pie that fell to the "philosopher-king" of Sans, Souci. The entire Parisian philosophical party, and Voltaire from Ferney, greeted these treaties with a sort of *Te Deam Catharinam*, as if they were marking the triumph of the Russian goddess of Tolerance!

Stanisław, under a masked Russian occupation, and with an internal rebellion on his hands, over which, unfortunately for him, the Russian troops had won a fierce and definitive victory in August

1772, lacked the means to unite his nation against Russia and the nobiliary *fronde*, as Gustav III of Sweden managed to do in September 1772. Nor did he possess, like the king of Sweden, the support of Versailles. He had to be content to flood with eloquent protests a Europe waiting until the crime was committed.

To give that crime an appearance of legality, Catherine II sent to Warsaw a new proconsul, Baron Otto Magnus von Stackelberg, whose manners were perfect but whose ultimatum brooked no kind of answer: "Submit or abdicate." To quell both king and Diet, Stackelberg found numerous "collaborators" among the grandees who hated the reformer king. Under the direct pressure of the Russian soldiers, the Diet swallowed the treaties ratifying the amputation of a third of the realm's territory and of two thirds of its population; it further imposed on Poland a constitution even more paralyzing than its traditional one had ever been.

The king too was obliged to bend, but did not break. He continued to embellish Warsaw, where the Venetian painter Bernardo Bellotto was put in charge of representing a panorama from every angle; he also sought a reconciliation with the survivors of the Confederation of Bar and, calling on the economic expertise of a Du Pont de Nemours or the pedagogic skill of a Condillac, pursued his program of economic and judiciary reforms and construction of a national education. His model was no longer Louis XIV but Henri IV. As his most recent biographer has elegantly written, he "cultivated his garden" with perseverance. But it was an autumn garden after the storm, smelling of decomposition. The France of Louis XVI and Vergennes had of course become favorable toward him, but offered no real aid. Plotters and adventurers of both sexes pullulated around the king, who sought in pleasures and the hope of some sort of miracle a compensation for his anguish. He could neither bring himself to collaborate frankly with the Russian protectorate nor to deny his sympathy with the decimated opposition that sought to be "republican" and "national." For his part, the Proconsul Stackelberg, who did everything to diminish a vassal he mistrusted, did not even support him against repeated Prussian aggressions.

In 1785, Stanisław tried to reconnect with Catherine II, and to exchange the stifling protectorate for an anti-Turkish military alliance. He went to meet her at Kanew. After thirty years, he found himself in a tête-à-tête with his former mistress on the imperial galley that was carrying the tsarina down the Dnieper to the Crimea. He repeated his offer of an alliance. He was also able to meet with Emperor Joseph II, who had joined Catherine incognito. The Prince de Ligne was with the party. All to no avail. Abiding by the treaties of 1775, the tsarina wanted nothing to do with an alliance that would have permitted the remilitarization and the very existence of a Polish state.

The young generation of Poles, formed in Stanisław's schools, were enthralled in 1789–1790 by the news of the French Revolution. Rousseau was their *maître à penser*. The king preferred the views of Edmund Burke, whose *Reflections* he read in 1790. In any case, the hour had struck for a great constitutional debate between the English model and the new French one. The threats of England and Pitt weighing on Russia had seemed to offset certain dangers, but Pitt gave up pursuing his advantage. Nonetheless, on May 4, 1791, amid general enthusiasm the king swore an oath to abide by the new liberal constitution voted by the Diet: it made Poland a hereditary monarchy.

On May 14, 1792, 9,700 Russian armed "liberators" crossed Poland's borders, "summoned" by a confederation of grandees hostile to the new constitution. The young state's newly levied army offered a courageous resistance. On July 23 Stanisław signed a letter of capitulation addressed to the tsarina. The Russian protectorate became a military dictatorship. A second treaty of partition, reducing Polish territory to insignificance, was signed on January 23, 1793, between Russia, Prussia, and Austria. And this was only a beginning.

Stanisław, whom the Confederates of 1792 made responsible for the new partition, was now a king in name only. When on March 23, 1794, a revolution led by Kosciuszko exploded in Kraków, then in Warsaw, massacring the Russian occupiers and their most evident collaborators, Stanisław unhesitatingly sided with them.

The response was overwhelming. In June 25,000 Prussians joining with 15,000 Russians under Suvarov's command laid siege to Warsaw, where a Jacobin Terror commenced. Once the city was taken, Catherine erased the little Poland of 1793 from the map, declared it to be occupied territory, and sent Stanisław to house arrest in Grodno. The third treaty of partition, this time confirming the suppression of Poland, was signed on October 24, 1795. Stanisław was forced to abdicate. He had never ceased writing devotedly to Catherine, hoping against hope for a change in her policies.

"MAMAN GEOFFRIN" AND THE DUPLICITY OF PARISIAN CONSCIENCES

The character of Stanisław as a philosopher-king had a good many flaws in its metal: they would suffice to attest to the Enlightenment's contradictions. The policy of Versailles toward Stanisław's Poland would suffice for its part to belie the reputation for cleverness that French diplomacy had acquired since the treaties of Wesphalia, Ryswick, and Utrecht. But what could now be said of the attitude of the Parisian philosophers and their leader Voltaire toward a king who, by their own admission, was their pupil and toward a country that he had labored against time and tide to "enlighten" according to their own views? If the French court showed itself to be stupid, the capital of the Enlightenment revealed itself as odious.

It all began with Mme Geoffrin's journey to Warsaw in 1766, concerning which Voltaire had managed to write that "in France this must be a great period for all thinking people." The Patronne of the philosophic salon of 372, rue Saint-Honoré, until the coronation of 1764, had regarded Stanisław Poniatowski as no more than a "little boy" whom she was obliged to instruct in the elements of good behavior. For fear that he might connect with the best art connoisseur and adviser of the period, the Comte de Caylus, she had banned her Polish protégé from her "Mondays," her day for artists and amateurs, and henceforth reserved for herself the role of intermediary for his purchases of pictures and statues. The new king was to acquire for his collections, to his great despair, many mediocre works and many fakes.

Once Stanisław had become king, he regarded Mme Geoffrin as what she appeared, a precious intermediary between foreign princes such as himself and the philosophic pundits who frequented her salon. He therefore addressed to her, during her visit, the same promotional circulars he sent to his Western correspondents. In exchange he received, from the woman he called, outside her reach, "la Geoffrin," torrents of tenderness to which he was not accustomed and that he certainly did not desire. Yet this eternal "son" could not long resist grasping the hand one more *maman* held out to him.

The Patronne of the philosophes, unlike Proust's Mme Verdurin, had not even an ounce of wickedness in her character. But she was intoxicated with snobbery, and put her remarkable practical sense and her psychological flair in the service of this violent passion. "Her" philosophers' ideas interested her only as politically correct notions that had to be endorsed if she was to keep them attached to her, for they were, after all, men of letters famous enough to attract to the house of a bourgeoise like herself any number of people in high society and many members of foreign nobility as well. In all fairness, she had no illusions about Frederick II or the tsarina, and she was one of the rare French people, male or female, who sincerely sympathized with Stanisław. Devout, prudish, charitable though tightfisted, and conservative through and through, like her daughter whom she had "made" Marquise de La Ferté-Imbault, her entire life as a hostess, indeed as an "ambassadress" of the Enlightenment philosophers, was based on a profound misunderstanding that she herself as well as her habitués understood well enough to conceal with great care.

This hidden misunderstanding grafted Mme Geoffrin's power onto that which her philosophers had acquired to dictate French and indeed European public opinion. And it was the obscure desire to verify to its fullest extent this power, a mere reflection of that of her habitués, that led her to conceive—she who at seventy had, like Boileau, never set foot outside Paris—a journey to the remote capital of her enthroned "son." She went so far as to allow herself, understanding nothing of politics or diplomacy, to write to Choiseul on March 11, 1765, suggesting that he proceed to recognize her "child" too much ignored by Versailles: a suggestion that indefinitely ruined Stanisław's project to warm in his regard the sentiments of the king, Choiseul, and the Comte de Broglie, head of the King's Secret.

Stanisław resisted for some time, but was obliged to resign himself to approving this journey. On May 21, 1766, Mme Geoffrin's comfortable coach set out on the cobblestones of the rue Saint-Honoré. For the entire length of the extensive journey she was received from capital to capital as the queen of the Enlightenment, notably in Vienna where she received honors of the court she would never have dreamed of expecting from Versailles. Europe had its eyes fixed on this messenger of the philosophes, duly accredited as she was by Voltaire.

The stay in Warsaw did not last, however, beyond ten weeks. Posing as the Mme de Maintenon of the realm, meddling with the political decisions of a country she knew nothing about, save that it was "Gothic" and that it would be vital, with the help of the good Russian regiments, unequivocally to impose the enlightenment desired by her Parisian habitués, interfering in family quarrels she managed only to embitter further, intervening with all her prudery in Stanisław's private life and with all her parsimony in his court's financial affairs, this pretentious interloper, initially welcomed so effusively, was soon reduced to quarreling by correspondence with a king too preoccupied to see her too long and too often. If Stanisław had ever supposed that the presence at his court of "la Geoffrin" might install at Warsaw a bucket brigade of philosophers and convince the world of his European prestige, he soon realized his mistake. Of course one revered in "la Geoffrin" the shades of Grimm, d'Alembert, Marmontel, and Voltaire, but in her unaccompanied presence, the royal reader of French classics had plenty of occasions to realize that she was ultimately no better than Mme Pernelle in *Tartuffe*. Moreover, neither Voltaire nor d'Alembert ever dreamed of going to Warsaw, and Grimm made only the briefest of disdainful stopovers there; Diderot en route to St. Petersburg actually managed to detour around the Polish obstacle!

Furious, La Patronne retraced her journey on September 13, and though she managed to receive from the king certain letters of reconciliation, she answered them by a curt "Everything has been said." Even so, the correspondence straggled on, so anxious was Stanisław not to sever any ties with Paris. Exasperated as he was by her advice to abdicate or else submit to Russian power, it was nonetheless to Mme Geoffrin that he confided, at the height of the Confederation of Bar rebellion, the secret of his wavering and persevering royal policy: "Whenever the Russians tell me, 'You speak for those who seek to dethrone you,' I answer, 'As I see it, they sin out of ignorance, but their motives, at least as regards the majority, have patriotism and national independence as their objective; they are Poles, hence I must try to aid them as well as I can.'"[15]

A mere reflection of philosophical clichés, poor Mme Geoffrin was in spite of everything an angel of good faith in comparison with Voltaire, who by midcentury had reached the peak of his European fame and authority, in Poland as elsewhere. The lord of Ferney saw Catholic Poland against the dark background of Gothic ages in which, according to him, France itself had wallowed until the greatness of the century of Louis XIV and the progress of the century of Voltaire. In his eyes, this cave of fanaticism stained an Eastern Europe where the Enlightenment of two Louis XIVs shone in all its glory and well deserved the entire favor of the Republic of Letters. It is difficult to imagine an optical inversion more obtuse. One of these beacons was Frederick the Great, from whom no quarrel would permanently detach Voltaire, and all of whose defects provoked him to no more than an indulgent irony. The other was Cath-

---

15. Fabre, *Stanislas-Auguste Poniatowski et l'Europe des Lumières*, p. 310.

erine, she too labeled "the Great" by him and his parrots, having won all his philosophical sympathy during the "liquidation" of Peter III and again during the assassination, on August 16, 1764, of another nuisance, Prince Ivan. Sure of matching Voltaire's sentiment—though only the year before Voltaire had published *Traité sur la tolérance*—d'Alembert, Voltaire's local Parisian agent, had sent him this commentary at the time:

> According to the proverb, "Better kill the devil than let the devil kill you." If princes adopted mottoes, as was once the custom, this would be the tsarina's. Yet it is really too bad to have to get rid of so many people and then to remark in print how sorry one is about it all, but that is hardly your fault. One ought not make this sort of excuse in public too frequently. I agree with you, philosophy shouldn't be overly proud of such pupils. But what can you do? We must love our friends, faults and all.[16]

Evidently philosophers can tell the difference between powerful friends and helpless friends. Catherine was generous with her rubles; her orders of political promotion were paid to the last sou; she purchased the horological production of Ferney, as well as Diderot's library while leaving him the usufruct thereof; she agreed to purchase several French works of art of which Diderot hastened to play the honest broker; and finally she distributed pensions as generously as Louis XIV. Another point in common with the Great King: she had an army. In one and the same person she summed up for her friends and French propagandists the entire Enlightenment by which she claimed to illuminate Russia. It was quite natural that its progressive rays should extend to the reactionary shadows of Poland. Stanisław, always short of money and battalions, would have to be satisfied with being the moon of this Petersburg sun, and if possible at the same time, of the Potsdam sun as well.

"I don't know," Voltaire wrote to d'Alembert in November 1764,

---

16. Fabre, *Stanislas-Auguste Poniatowski et l'Europe des Lumières*, p. 317.

just when Catherine's lover had been elected king of Poland, "who is the greater philosopher: Stanisław, or the king of Prussia, or the Tsarina. One is amazed by the progress reason is making in the north."[17]

During his campaign in favor of Calas, the Sirvens, and tolerance, Voltaire had obtained from Stanisław two hundred ducats for the Sirvens. Having received the text of the speech the king of Poland had made in 1766 before the Diet, in which he encouraged civic equality for non-Catholics, Voltaire took him at his word and regarded the matter as settled: "But, Sire, the benefit you bestow upon all humanity by establishing a wise tolerance in Poland emboldens me somewhat. It is a concern of the human race, to which you belong. *I shall die in peace, since I have seen the days of salvation.* True salvation is the benefactor. Sire, you will pardon the aged Simeon for exclaiming: Benefaction!"[18]

By a wonderful semantic rearrangement, the splendid pretext the tsarina would invoke to justify in 1767 the entry of Russian troops into Poland and the repression of the Confederation of Bar rebellion enabled her advocate Voltaire to offer Europe this violation of peoples' rights as a brilliant victory of his own campaign in favor of tolerance: "Not only is this princess tolerant," he wrote, "but she desires her neighbors to be so as well. ... She has sworn that she does not covet an inch of land, and that everything she does is only for the glory of tolerance."[19] A pseudonymous pamphlet, which circulated throughout Europe, brought Voltaire sumptuous gifts and bribes from St. Petersburg. *Les Dissensions des églises en Pologne* describes the tsarina and her armies as the secular arm of philosophy performing what Stanisław had been pleased to encourage: the defeat of a bloody fanaticism dishonoring Poland and humanity. The pseudonymous author went so far as to write:

17. Voltaire, *Correspondance*, edited by Theodore Besterman (Oxford: Voltaire Foundation), letter D12185.

18. Fabre, *Stanislas-Auguste Poniatowski et l'Europe des Lumières*, p. 321.

19. Fabre, *Stanislas-Auguste Poniatowski et l'Europe des Lumières*, p. 319

It was astonishing to see a Russian army living in the heart of Poland with much better discipline than was ever shown by Polish troops. There has not been the slightest disorder. The countryside has been enriched instead of being devastated: the army was there only to protect tolerance....One might have taken this army for nothing but a Diet convoked for the sake of Liberty.[20]

"Humanitarian war," preventive protection of minorities, the right to intervene—the moral masks of realpolitik had already been invented. Even so, Voltairean initial enthusiasm for the civilized and civilizing Russian troops was somewhat confounded by the news, in 1772, of the brutal partition of Poland by which the two Louis XIVs of the North had dealt themselves such winning hands. This time the philosopher, who at first was reluctant to believe in this crime of philosophers, refrained from mentioning it in public, even under the veil of anonymity. In private, in his correspondence, he confined himself to quoting La Fontaine—*My friends, the Solitary said, things of this world are of no concern to me*—or to sadly disowning his habitual declamations against the "Welches" and his hymns to the glory of the Reason of the North: "I still prefer being French to Danish, Swedish, Polish, Russian, Prussian, or Turk; yet I would be a Frenchman *solitaire*, far from Paris, a Frenchman Swiss and free."[21]

In his correspondence with Frederick, he limited himself at first to an ironic remark on the motto of a medal the king of Prussia had struck in imitation of Louis XIV in order to celebrate his part in the Polish banquet, *Regno redintegrato* ("the realm restored to its frontiers"), to which Voltaire would have rightly preferred *Regno novo* ("one realm more"). Not one word of condolence to Stanisław, to whom he was never to write again. Mme du Deffand, though, had not failed, with a certain secret pique, to invite the sage to make for

20. Fabre, *Stanislas-Auguste Poniatowski et l'Europe des Lumières*, p. 322.
21. Fabre, *Stanislas-Auguste Poniatowski et l'Europe des Lumières*.

once a generous gesture. "I should so much like you," she had written him, "to make some sort of *factum* for the poor king of Poland. Only a voice such as yours could make itself heard."[22] Of course she knew perfectly well that Voltaire had mentally adopted in this painful affair the motto paraphrased from Corneille's Prusias: "Ah, don't make quarrels for me with my philosopher-kings!" Lindsay's brilliant English pamphlet did not fail to ridicule Voltaire's shameful silence, following so much hollow propaganda that retrospectively gave him the unfortunate figure of no more than a dupe.

In defense of the great man "outstripped by history," it must be acknowledged that he did not dupe himself. To Frederick, to whom he sent the severe English pamphlet as a proof of sacrificial loyalty, he went as far as he could go without directly colliding with his old accomplice:

> I was trapped like an idiot when I foolishly supposed, before the Turkish war, that the empress of Russia was in league with the king of Poland to do justice to the [Protestant and Orthodox] dissidents and solely to establish freedom of conscience. You kings, you're like Homer's gods who make mortal men carry out their plans without the poor devils suspecting a thing.[23]

Despite this jilt, and Stanisław's awareness of how much Voltaire's moral smoke rings had encouraged the tsarina's appetite, the king of Poland persisted no less obstinately in regarding the king of the Enlightenment as "the honor of his age." Three busts and a full-length statue of the great man continue to this day to embellish his castles and parks. Up to the final triumph of the author of *Candide* at the Comédie-Française, he kept himself abreast of his every gesture and remark. He gleefully leafed through his personal file of the great writer's letters and manuscripts, and continued to regard

22. Fabre, *Stanislas-Auguste Poniatowski et l'Europe des Lumières*.
23. Fabre, *Stanislas-Auguste Poniatowski et l'Europe des Lumières*, p. 328.

himself as the Sage of Ferney's disciple, faithful to the ideal of progress gleaned from his writings, if not to his person and his passing fancies. He admired Rousseau as well, all the more perhaps since the latter had written in 1772 of his project of a constitution for Poland at the request of the Confederation of Bar, crushed, in spite of Stanisław's impotent objurgations, by General Apraksin's Russian troops. His reign had nonetheless permitted the Poles, if not Poland, to participate in the general movement of minds in Europe. One could hardly say as much for the Russia of Catherine II.

STANISŁAW II AUGUSTUS, FRENCH MEMORIALIST

Stanisław Poniatowski, ending his days in the Marble Palace of St. Petersburg to which Tsar Paul I had summoned him upon Catherine II's death, would have been surprised to learn that his earthly fame might one day become that of a French writer. He left *Mémoires*, but that was in his eyes his political justification for the Poland to come, and not a French literary monument. Even today, it is true, the French themselves are unaware of the centrality of the genre of *mémoires* in their own literary tradition, and only a forgotten book, though one that merits rediscovery, has hitherto done justice to the distinction of the king of Poland's *Mémoires* in this ultra-French tradition.

The superiority of *mémoires* over the best historiography is that they show instead of trying to explain. And they show in that secondary state of a witness who knows he is going to die, leafing through his still-searing memories of what he has seen, what he has done, what he has heard, what he has felt, illuminated one last time in the gathering darkness by the light of a sun that will not rise again. If the genre of *mémoires* is of aristocratic origin, if it was so brilliant during the ancien régime, this is no doubt primarily because the sinewy art of dialogue and narrative, the talent of portraiture and anecdote, were necessary elements of the spirit of conversation that extended quite naturally into written correspondence, and that was, so to speak, concentrated in *mémoires* when their hour had come. In writing his *mémoires*, a court aristocrat was sustained by the sentiment of having been a part of historical events and associated with the group of men and women who epitomized the period in which he had lived, all of them included in the milieu of power in which he had grown up. The extraordinary interior film postulated by the final projection of *mémoires* had initially been recorded and, so to speak, shot during a previous existence on the lookout, in the dangerous, breathless, sometimes intoxicating suspense of the court and the "companies" gravitating around one. One does not forget what has made one tremble with fear or pleasure.

But why should this aristocratic genre have been a French genre, born in France with Joinville, and accompanying the successive reigns of our kings, the successive states of our language, with an abundance, a variety, a vitality culminating in the seventeenth century with the various *mémoires* of the Fronde? Perhaps because the French aristocracy was at once very attached to its kings and in a perpetual *fronde*, an open or intimate rebellion against their yoke.

The fact is that in the eighteenth century, the great foreigners who wrote *mémoires*—Frederick II and his sister the Margravine of Bayreuth, Baron de Besenval, the Prince de Ligne, Giacomo Casanova—regarding the genre as a product of French soil, have written them in our language. If Stanisław Poniatowski also wrote his *Mémoires*, with even more talent, in French, it is because he knew better than anyone the French tradition of the genre, to the point of inhaling at Versailles and at Paris, when he discovered them in 1753, a fragrance from the Baudelairean flacon, a savor of déjà vu and déjà lu, of names and characters who had already "become familiar" to him.[24] If Stanisław's *Mémoires* (especially in their early volumes, from which I have already quoted a good deal) have a brilliance and a suspense exceptional among the eighteenth-century *mémoires* by foreigners written in French, it is not only a question of language and of style: it is because he began them and continued to write

---

24. Poniatowski, *Mémoires*, vol. I, p. 93.

them in the archetypical situation of the classics of the genre, under the threat not only of death but of *damnatio memoriae*. The genre has been made illustrious in France by great lords and ladies, conquered and in disgrace—Retz, the Grande Mademoiselle, Saint-Simon—who confide to their family, even to a remote posterity, the desire to rescue the precious bottle from the sea into which they secretly flung it to them. Stanisław knew his great authors virtually by heart. The day came when he found himself confined by the same life drama and he resorted to the same literary release.

Dictated in French to his secretary Christian-Wilhelm Friese between 1771 and 1798, reread, and corrected in his own hand, the *Mémoires* of King Stanisław have all the characteristic features of this singular genre. They reflect the living speech of a man of action who is not a professional writer, but who is a past master in the virtuoso usage of the French language. The *Mémoires* of Stanisław Poniatowski are exceptional for their freshness, their freedom of tone, the felicity and abundance of their oral improvisation, but an improvisation that follows its own impulse and has no need to rehearse its effects to carry off its *vocalises*. Against a background of classical prose, in the Voltairean sense of the term, something of Rousseauan *Sehnsucht* can be heard as well.

He began to write in 1771, when the first partition of Poland was already being conceived, when the imprudent Confederation of Bar had drawn the Russian army onto national territory, and when Stanisław realized that his reign, hanging by no more than a thread, would never be a source of glory to him. What the state of Richelieu and of Louis XIV had been for Retz, for the Grande Mademoiselle, for Saint-Simon—a figure of *Fatum*—was what Catherine, who had trampled it underfoot, what Frederick, who had violated it, what Louis XV, who in 1753 had not deigned to speak a word to him, and what Voltaire, who after 1772 had once and for all ceased writing to him, summed up for this eternal pupil of the Enlightenment.

The fate his *Mémoires* met with is also archetypical of a genre by definition posthumous and threatened by long disappearances. Written in clandestinity, *mémoires* sometimes surface long after their author's death. This delay is frequently a matter of state. The *mémoires* of the Fronde saw the light of day only after Louis XIV's death. Louis XV, upon Saint-Simon's death, had sequestered the little duke's *Mémoires*, which it was known in high places might well damage the glory of Louis XIV and the honor of numerous great families of the court. What had happened in France was repeated on an entirely different scale in tsarist Russia, where *mémoires à la française*, an exotic genre, were not, to say the least, protected by a literary tradition, and where nonetheless the ex-king of Poland was obliged to end his days, forswearing his own people in the Marble Palace where he died in 1798.

The eight morocco-bound volumes, a state secret at high risk, were immediately transported and deposited under seal in the Archives of Foreign Affairs, then, for greater security, in 1832, on the orders of Nicholas I, in the State Archives. They emerged only briefly in 1891, when Tsar Alexander III was curious enough to glance through them. Aside from their entirely personal content, they contained a collection of diplomatic and political documents (all in French) essential for the Russo-Polish history of an unfortunate reign. It was only in 1907 that Serge Gouaïnov obtained Nicholas II's authorization to publish them on the press of the Academy of Sciences, more than a century after Stanisław's death.

To this day only one Frenchman, Jean Fabre, in the magnificent book he published in 1952, *Stanislas-Auguste Poniatowski et l'Europe des Lumières*, has fully accounted for this masterpiece of our language. Few copies of this biography are to be found in French libraries. Stanisław's *Mémoires* are one of the best panoramas of Enlightenment Europe that can be read, a gallery of striking portraits, and it also the archive of an Enlightenment sovereign who reigned in an Eastern Europe to which such illumination came from far off, from high places, but was nowhere better received than in Poland where it suffered, long before 1793, the same series of tragic denials and disappointments suffered, in our own days, in Warsaw, Budapest, and Prague, by "socialism with a human face."

INDEX

OTHER NEW YORK REVIEW CLASSICS*

TITLES IN SERIES

* *For a complete list of titles, visit www.nyrb.com or write to:*
Catalog Requests, NYRB, 435 Hudson Street, New York, NY 10014